REID BUCKLEY

AN
AMERICAN
FAMILY

THE BUCKLEYS

THRESHOLD
EDITIONS

New York London Toronto Sydney

Note to Readers: This work is a memoir. It reflects the author's present recollections of his experiences over a period of years. Some dialogue and events have been re-created from memory and, in some cases, have been compressed to convey the substance of what was said or what occurred.

THRESHOLD EDITIONS
A Division of Simon & Schuster, Inc.
1230 Avenue of the Americas
New York, NY 10020

First Threshold Editions hardcover edition May 2008

THRESHOLD EDITIONS and colophon are trademarks of Simon & Schuster, Inc.

For information about special discounts for bulk purchases, please contact Simon & Schuster Special Sales at 1-800-456-6798 or business@simonandschuster.com.

Designed by Jan Pisciotta

Manufactured in the United States of America

10 9 8 7 6 5 4 3 2 1

ISBN-13: 978-1-4165-7241-1
ISBN-10:   1-4165-7241-4

DEDICATION

To my siblings, living and dead;
to my wife, Tasa;
to my mother and father

ACKNOWLEDGMENTS

I am indebted to Pamela Schreiner for invaluable aid in batting out the manuscript and to May deLoach for assembling the photos; invaluably am I indebted to Alex Hoyt for his initial reading, his sagacious editing, and his unflagging good humor, as well as his marketing skills, and I am no less indebted to Ed Schlesinger for his patience, tact, and encouragement.

This book could not have been written without the aid of my cousins Joan Perrier of New Orleans and Edmund Buckley of Houston.

Contents

FOREWORD

IN ONE OF THE MANY DELICIOUS FOOTNOTES THAT HE INCLUDES HERE, my uncle Reid notes that he has already had his tombstone carved and that it says, "Shut Up At Last." After reading this book, with which, he notes toward the end, "I have finished my oeuvre," I'm grateful that he wasn't silenced before he was able to finish it. While I can't predict whether the general reader will be as mesmerized as I was by Reid's account of our Buckley family, I can truthfully and flatly aver that it strikes me as some kind of masterpiece of the genre.

What genre exactly is harder to say, and this brings me back to the wonderful footnotes. Inevitably, after he has told some riveting story, generally about his father, my grandfather, William F. Buckley Sr. (note the "Sr."), there will be a footnote stating, "My sister Priscilla adamantly rejects this version of Father talking Pancho Villa out of shooting the train conductor." If I found these clarifications, such as they are, deflating at first, I soon began to look forward to the next one.

Reid does nothing conventionally—which is why he is so beloved of his nine siblings (five of whom survive) and forty-five nieces and nephews. So why would any of us expect that he would produce a conventional family history? It was said of Edward Gibbon that he lived out his sex life in his footnotes. *Mutatis mutandis*—as William F. Buckley *Jr.* might put it—there is something of that in Reid's luxuriant footnotes.

Take this one, for instance, about the great elm tree in Sharon, Connecticut, which lent its name to the house my grandfather raised his family in:

> It fell to the Dutch elm disease in the late 1950s; the four sugar maples planted in the gaping hole it left are now half a century old, and large, and serve in my eyes only to remind me of the grandeur of the old elm,

one of whose gigantic branches, sprouting off the main trunk about twelve feet from the roots, three feet or more broad and almost horizontal until it swept upward, I could lie upon in perfect security on my back, as though on a garden bench—gazing up at the sky through the elm's corona of bright green leaves, its canopy falling all about me and hiding me from view. It required seven adults holding hands to circle its base. In my mind, as a young man, I associated the Great Elm with my father—and when it was stricken, I remember looking anxiously at him, whose absence would leave a corresponding hole in my existence; who was felled by the first stroke at just about the same time that Great Elm was diagnosed with the disease.

This book is substantially about the world that man, my grandfather, created for his children and other descendants. However qualifying some of the footnotes are, he was by any measure remarkable, and though I knew a great deal about him before picking up Reid's book, I didn't know the half of it.

He was born poor in Texas in 1881, the same year as the shootout at the OK Corral and Garfield's assassination, and died a wealthy man in New York City in 1958. *His* grandfather had been an Irish Protestant who married a Catholic girl from Limerick and, as a consequence, had to leave the country. A good thing, too, as he and my great-great-grandmother beat the Irish potato famine by just a few years. They debarked in Quebec and moved to Ontario, where their son, a future Texas sheriff, was born. The reason I am American—this I learned from Reid—is that he had asthma, which forced the family to get into a Conestoga wagon and trek south in search of drier climes. They ended up in the very dry clime of San Diego, Texas, a hardscrabble place northeast of Corpus Christi. Now I know why asthma has been such a part of my life. This may not be riveting to you, but I assure you it is to me. More interesting to you might be the detail that one of Sheriff John C. Buckley's closest friends was Pat Garrett, the lawman who shot Billy the Kid. He—that is, Garrett, not The Kid—was a frequent guest at my great-grandfather's home.

The story gets more interesting when Reid's father—William F. Sr., the sheriff's son—goes to Mexico after getting out of law school and sets up shop as a lawyer and wildcat oilman. He lived in Mexico between 1908 and 1921, which would be like living in Paris, say, between 1789 and 1802. And he was in the thick of it; he knew everyone. It was to his house that U.S. Marines went after bombarding Veracruz in 1914, asking him to be governor civil. He indignantly refused. He detested Woodrow Wilson's interventionism—as did another American of the time, Mark Twain— and became a minor hero to Mexicans. The Huerta government paid him the great compliment of asking him to represent Mexico as its legal counsel at the ABC Conference in Niagara Falls. Later he was expelled from Mexico by the then-government-of-the-month. *I'm out of here. Gracias for the memories.*

You'll find my grandfather in the midst of great adventures. On one page, he's talking Pancho Villa out of shooting the conductor; on another page, he's escaping execution by bandits who have taken him and a colleague out into the desert to be killed. His fellow captive, a close friend, presented them with a laundry slip and told the illiterate would-be murderers that it was a note from the local chief granting permission for their prisoners to "stretch their legs." He and his colleague stretched their legs energetically that rain-swept night, through a jungle and across a swollen river. He later named his oil company Pantepec after that river. I never knew that until now.

He had guts, my grandfather, but my favorite Mexican anecdote— again rendered in a footnote—isn't about heroics but involves a nifty bit of one-upmanship on a train that will have you laughing out loud. I won't give it away.

I never knew him. I was only six when he died, but Reid has given him back to me and my forty-nine cousins and their umpteen children and grandchildren, and I'm humbled, not just by the man he was but also by his son's ability as a writer and a historian to re-create him.

He's only half the story. The other half is his wife, my universally adored grandmother, Aloïse Steiner Buckley. We grandchildren called her Mimi. Here I'll confess to being frustrated at a secret hope I've long nurtured.

Mimi's maiden name was Steiner. Her mother was a Wassem. Looking at some old family photos one Thanksgiving, one of my cousins grinned and said, "Tell me we're not Jewish." When I mentioned this suspicion to my friend, the distinguished author and editor Walter Isaacson—like my grandmother a native New Orleanian—he laughed and said, "Most of the old German Catholic families I knew from New Orleans were Jewish." Alas, no such luck. Mimi's maternal grandfather, George Henry Wassem, fought (quite valiantly) for the Confederacy at Shiloh and other engagements. *His* father fought with—oh, dear—the Hessians, alongside the British in the Revolution. (We can only hope less valiantly than his son fought in his war.) George Wassem hung up his battlefield decorations and became a New Orleans barber.

As for Mimi's paternal side, the Steiners, they were Swiss, from the canton of Saint-Gallen and the city of Bergt—as my uncle Jimmy relates here, "the only Swiss municipality I have ever seen that seemed totally devoid of charm." No wonder our forebear left there in 1845 and set up shop in New Orleans as a boot and shoemaker. So we descend from a barber, a shoemaker, and a sheriff. How *did* we end up Republican?

As I write, I have this creeping feeling that I'm sounding like that person on the bar stool next to you, droning on about matters of absolutely no interest to you. If I do, then I have truly failed and can only promise you that this book is far more interesting than I am making it out to be. So let me tell you now just a little bit about its author, my uncle Reid.

We Buckleys are a scribbly lot. My father has written fifty-five books and is now, at age eighty-two, at work on his fifty-sixth. (Never mind his other writings, which are voluminous enough to choke the Yale archives, where they reside in one thousand boxes.) Of the ten Buckley children of W.F.B. Sr. and A.S.B. seven wrote books, most of them more than one. *Seven.*

Reid is . . . how do I describe to you my uncle Reid? I, a professional writer, grope for words. Reid was the fun uncle. He'd turn up to visit his son and me at boarding school, ginger-bearded, dressed in plus-fours and Inverness cape (I'm not making this up) and smoking a calabash pipe. The monks didn't quite know what to make of him. He was a dashing expatriate who lived in Spain and wrote about bullfighting and knew all the great matadors and was close friends with Ava Gardner. He returned from Spain after fifteen years remarried to a glamorous, beautiful Spanish widow with five children of her own. He's spent the last thirty-five years in Camden, employing half the town at the Buckley School of Public Speaking and Written Expression. So Reid is . . . I revert to my prior statement, as we Washingtonians say: Reid is Reid.

But the Reid who concerns you is Reid the writer. His 1973 novel *Servants and Their Masters*, a family saga set in late-Franco Spain, is a considerable work of art. I was a Yale English major, and I know literature when I see it. It's the only eight hundred-page novel that I've read a half-dozen times and hope to read another half-dozen times before I die. It's a masterpiece. I was reminded of that book as I read this very different one. I don't quite know, as I mentioned earlier, how to classify this one. *Life with Father* meets *Treasure of the Sierra Madre?*

It is not a feel-good book. Of tragedy my family has deeply supped. Though you may not personally know the players, I doubt that you won't be moved by the image of my eighty-nine-year-old grandmother Mimi, herself less than months away from death, weeping alone in a limousine at the graveside of her eldest son; or of Reid, walking alongside the train platform as his father's train pulls away, tears streaming down Grandfather's face, knowing that this is their final parting. There are so many deaths told in this book, and so many left to come.

But there's happiness here, too, in abundance. My family's profound Catholic faith has allowed us, in the midst of these and other, worse griefs—two of Reid's sisters were taken cruelly young, one leaving five children, the other ten—if not a triumphalist note, at least an echo of Saint Paul's "Death, where is thy sting?"

And good times. Heavens, what great times, especially in the chapters about growing up in those teeming households in Sharon, Connecticut, and Camden, South Carolina. They tell of worlds gone now, perhaps all the sweeter for having vanished. Gone, as it were, with the wind, to quote another Southern writer.

Children will never again sled down almost two steep miles of ice-and-snow-crusted road, hitching their Flexible Flyers to milk wagons pulled by plow horses to get back up to the top of the hill. Nothing will ever replace or restore the elms of Sharon Green. Nothing will ever replace or restore the Sterling elm, our Great Elm. Nothing will ever restore or replace the America of the first years of her bursting upon history. Nothing will ever replace or restore our parents, Aloïse Steiner Buckley and Will Buckley, individually and bonded together one flesh, one body, one will, one devotion.

My grandfather and grandmother left behind ten children, fifty grandchildren, and Lord knows how many great- and great-great-grandchildren—enough, anyway, to swing a presidential election in Florida. Among those they left behind was a son, my uncle Reid, to tell their story. This is an elegy, but amidst its melancholy strains you'll catch the bagpipe notes of joy.

CHRISTOPHER BUCKLEY

Prefatory Remarks

It occurred to me the other day that, over the years, I had put down quite a lot about my parents and the upbringing that we, their children, had of them—scattered in articles, books, and unfinished projects all through my files.

I have lost some of those fragments.* They may be dug up by my heirs and literary executor (my nephew Christopher Buckley, who has consented to the thankless task). Meanwhile, I thought I would dump what I remember and could find between these covers . . . adding to those documents as I feel impelled to do.

This will not be a programmatic (i.e., scholarly, well-organized) biography of my parents, both because I am (1) temperamentally incapable of being (a) scholarly or (b) organized and because I am (2) in search of something else, something that to me is deeply mysterious. Father often said to our mother, "Aloïse, our bloodlines clicked." He was referring favorably to us, his children, with whom he was (on occasion) well pleased. It is this tantalizing dimension that I seek: the interior psychology of Aloïse and William F. Buckley, their immense (no lesser adjective will do) moral stature, which I extrapolate from myriad sources, including that ever fickle and mischievously deceiving trove we call memory, and the essence of their remarkable impact on their children.

My parents were both born . . . two whole centuries ago now, he in 1881, she in 1895. They were unusual human beings; their upbringings (especially my father's) evoke the nostalgia of pioneer and immediate postpioneer America. The family ambience they provided for their children was in many ways unique and was instrumental in developing un-

---

*My files may be described as places of deposit where all documents are secure, especially from recovery by me.

usual, and in cases remarkable, human beings. The Irish literary heritage has been prodigious. Of the ten of us, for example, three (Priscilla, Bill, Patricia) have edited magazines professionally, nine (by my count) have published articles or essays; five (Jimmy, Priscilla, Bill, Patricia, your servant, and Carol) have published books; two have edited books (Bill, Patricia, and YS—Trisha for publishing houses, with unparalleled expertise); two have had their tales collected and posthumously published (Aloïse, John), gaining high acclaim from professional as well as lay readers; and one (Maureen, such a striking personality) was the subject (after she was struck down by cerebral hemorrhage) of an appreciation that delights anyone who chances on a copy of it.*

The writing bug is a curious phenomenon. I suppose there are as many Americans of Irish descent who are free of it as there are Americans of Irish descent notable for the absence in them of humor. A sense of humor is high among our values, quite possibly too high. We all treasured Ronald Reagan partly for his wonderful grace, which consisted in his hilarious insights into the dissonance between pretensions and reality. I forgave John Kennedy much for his sense of humor, and I continue to forgive Bill Clinton (without quite granting him a plenary indulgence) for his droll perception of the ridiculous (who else in our lifetimes has had the wit, nay, the cockaninny genius, to question the validity of the present tense of the verb *to be*?). In both men, dead and alive, their humor was rapid and spontaneous and spanned ideological chasms on a bridge of mirth. We Buckleys are suckers for a sense of humor, as was our father.

The writing bug is different. Not all of us are bitten by it with the same itching intensity. Nobody (in my memory) has written more marvelously about this peculiar temperamental affliction than Richard Holmes, the incomparable British literary biographer (*Coleridge: Early Visions, 1772–1804* and *Coleridge: Darker Reflections, 1804–1834,* among others). He tells us about his introduction to London in 1967, when his pen was unproven:

---

* Two nephews (Christopher, son of Bill and Patricia Taylor, of Vancouver, and John, son of John and Ann Harding, of Omaha) have published fiction; another (Brent Bozell III, son of Patricia and the unforgettable Brent Bozell II, also of Omaha) has published a sizzling book on the media called *Weapons of Mass Distortion* (2004) and has another on the way (*Whitewash,* a study of the indulgence Hillary Clinton has enjoyed from the press).

[W]ork was easy to find in those days, and I had a good circle of friends. Yet the truth was that I felt suicidally lonely and depressed for much of the time. This was not particularly unusual for a young man coming to the big city. But I was mad to write, I felt I was nothing unless I could write. The inky demon drove me night and day, and I simply could not see how he (or she) could be appeased. I am not sure that this feeling has ever left me. I think all writers, of whatever kind, must have such a demon. I believe the demon follows them in the street and ends up sitting on their graves.*

This well expresses my condition, though I have tried to anticipate it by having my stone engraved in advance of my demise, with a message designed to spook the demon muse into leaving my ashes in peace.[†]

Mr. Holmes speaks, I think, for all writers. Coleridge famously divided human beings between Aristotelians and Platonists—that is, between inductive and deductive thinkers, between those who move easily into abstractions and those who prefer dealing in particulars. Genius spans the divide. Our mother was, I think, an Aristotelian by impulse, hence her dazzling non sequiturs, in which genius is latent also.[‡] Father, a practical man, extolled the platonic virtues while suffering lifelong from a romantic nature. Novelists are Aristotelians by wont, essayists Platonists. Essayists break down the compound statement, "unpack" it, as Coleridge was fond of saying, "differentiate," as Eric Voegelin put it. Novelists concoct a private universe in the swirling neurons of their imagination, with its own laws.

The creative verbal imagination—most of us agree—is torn between polarities: the polemical and the Dionysian.[§] My brother Bill tends to the first, I (and his son Christopher and our nephew John Buckley) tend to the second. There is that eximious infatuation with language, the sheer,

---

* *SIDETRACKS:* Explorations of a Romantic Biographer, p.3, New York: Pantheon Books, 2000.

† The message, which is covered by a cement slab to prevent nosy humanity from viewing it prematurely, runs: "Shut Up At Last."

‡ Only mystical religious genius can make sense of this proposition: Mankind has sinned; therefore will I send my only beloved Son to suffer, be crucified, and redeem the world.

§ This distinction was suggested to me seven or eight years ago by my nephew Christopher. I was at first dubious, but now I accept it.

lush love of the sound *for* the sound of it, sense be bothered—those harsh, plosive warrior consonants herding between their vertical disdain the soft, sensuous, infinitely plangent (and oh so fingent) vowels—in which every writer born, even the most vulgar Madison Avenue publicist or the sleaziest political spinmeister, partakes. The danger here is, of course, excess: the melon so sweet it is rotten at the rind, the luscious sonorities we associate with Swinburne.

At the other pole is the intellectual joy in sublime logical impulsions pounding irresistibly to their resolution, at their best dispositive, set forth with the polyphonic exuberance and majesty of Bach. The danger here is cerebral aridity and intellectual licentiousness. By licentiousness I mean savoring the argument for its sole sake, instead of for the right reason that it should advance. (Against which vice Plato warned when he opposed teaching young men the art of dialectics, for fear that they, like the sophists, would revel in "eristic" pleasure from the exercise, spurning virtue.)

This book will indulge in no such highfalutin' musings, though its matter is the creative imagination deriving from two extraordinary people, Aloïse Steiner and Will Buckley. On the whole, the literary output of their children is less exalted than the first rate. It has been as diverse as the authors, comprising entertainments and novels in fiction, a play, short stories, a children's tale, fishing and hunting stories, yarns of the sea and high adventure, articles on skiing and bullfighting, personal reminiscences, autobiography and travel (Priscilla), two memoirs (James, Carol), polemics (Bill, obviously), social criticism and political science (Jim, Bill, and YS), reflective essays . . . Not surprisingly, brother Bill has published in all these categories, with exasperating aplomb, prolixity, and indefatigable élan. But the literary output of the clan, such as it has been (it is doubtful that any of us has written a book that will surpass antiquarian interest), is a very little measure of what makes our parents and the upbringings they got unusual. Did I mention that two of my sisters, like their dam, had ten children, and another had six? (I contrived to have ten children, five of whom I borrowed.)* Did I mention that we are all imbued with a high, sly sense of fun (when Allie died, one of her children said, "Nothing will ever be fun again"), which we got, I think, equally from both our parents, who loved fun? Oh, and that we were (are) all different?

---

*I married a Spanish widow with five children, I had four, we had one.

Allie, the eldest—an introvert who lived in her imagination and in the children who were the concrete projections of her deepest soul—had a shattering eye for pretentiousness and pomposity and skewered these human failings with wicked barbs. John differed from his siblings in his sociability (next to Priscilla, he was the most popular of us) and devotion to that most contemplative of pastimes, fly fishing, and also shooting *pelo y pluma*,* not to mention a withering wit to match his elder sister's (which he used sparingly). Priscilla differed in her gregarious charity, her sparkling good humor, her quiet competence and unsentimental affection; Jimmy in his soft-spoken manner, his prudence, his realism, his very private inner life (rooted in a shyness that was sometimes misinterpreted as social diffidence), and his devotion to natural history; Jane in her unsparing realism, in her battlecock love of children and family, and in her profound faith and heroic long suffering, which her siblings were to discover about their sister when a concatenation of wasting illnesses besieged her in her old age; Bill in his prodigious intellectual curiosity, the astounding fertility and audacity of his imagination, his loyalty to family and friends, compassion toward ideological enemies (I'd boil 'em in oil), and vast personal charity; Patricia in her bottomless love for her late husband, Brent Bozell, her brood of ten redheads, and her siblings, for all of whom she would shed her blood gladly, and for the Holy Roman Catholic Church, to which she has devoted her deepest being; Maureen in her fearless perception of reality (sharing this trait with Aloïse, Priscilla, Jim, Jane, and Carol), her warmth, humor, practicality, and intelligence; Carol in her militancy and tenderness and compassion, which is boundless (the proper symbol of our sister Carol is the pelican of the Holy Spirit, which warms the world by tearing the feathers off its breast).

All of us are generous, some of us to reckless excess. All of us, even Priscilla, are subject to occasional black moods, which can fasten on us for hours (even days), bringing us down and making us unpleasant company. We are at these times acutely aware of our failings and suffer from dissatisfaction with ourselves. We never euphemize wrongdoing by calling our failings "mistakes," which is the language of moral cowards. We confront our sins, by which we are tormented, withdrawing even from siblings and spouses. These times we are best left alone, because we are volatile and can

---

*Furred and feathered.

be savage. We are thus not always easy to get along with, and some of us—humanly speaking—are more likable than others.

None of us is false. Ever. We may hold fire out of tact or respect for another's sensibilities (which is not the same thing as respecting his or her opinion); we never, in my experience, deceive, though out of affection we often do our best to dissemble our disagreement. We have, every one of us, in our personal and professional lives scraped (and ground) our keels on reefs. Three of us have divorced. We have prospered in material terms variously.

Some of us have struggled with faith. But now, in the fast deepening twilight of our lives, four of the ten of us and three in-laws, including Pat Taylor, Bill's wife, gone to their rest as I write these lines,* two of the surviving six stricken with ailments (stroke, emphysema, diabetes, cancer) that will harvest us in short order, we can, I think, all say truly, without braggadocio, that we have fought the good fight, we have kept the faith our parents bequeathed to us, and we have not shamed our heritage or the expectations that our good fortune laid upon us.

We have all been shaped by a part real, part mythic inheritance. Mother was a natural storyteller, who, as she knitted woolen scarves that got longer and longer and never seemed to be finished, would pace up and down the library of "Great Elm" in the evenings, after supper, before the eight-thirty bedtime for the youngest of us, kicking the ball of bright yarn behind her while regaling her children with tales of Nancy, a Revolutionary War twelve-year-old heroine; Rastus, Nancy's brave, lovable, ingenious, and devoted Negro body servant; and wicked, wicked—oh, detestable!—General Howe . . .

The burning wood in the fireplace would sometimes shoot showers of sparks, which ignited in our retinas as we listened, our dreams that night phosphorescent. Mother's tales were incandescent with creative imagination; episodes were never repeated, though we clamored for them. "Tell about Nancy and the Great Dismal Swamp!" "Tell about when Rastus fooled the whole British army!" She invented a fresh one every performance. Father's tales were all based on events that had actually happened and in which he took part, one way or another.

From this rich humus, fictional and real, creative and moral, we drew

---

*In July 2007.

sustenance. That which was myth is—for being morally true, right, and just—as important as whatever the underlying factual reality may have been. (Facts do get in the way, I've discovered while plugging along with this book. Can anyone believe how hard it has been to establish our paternal grandfather's exact date of birth?) We were inspired by our parents. And we have been steadfast in the moral principles in which we were inculcated, even though—in the depths of emotional crises—we may have temporarily abandoned and even dishonored them. But as far as I know, we have all been ultimately true. We have never been treacherous; we have been honest about our failings, to ourselves and to our siblings, who, after the Lord, are the high court before whom we pray to scrape by. We have done our best to keep our parents proud.

This speaks enormously well of them. The long shadow of Father and Mother (none of us—in the stupor of drink, in the rhapsody of the oxygen-starved stratosphere, in our lowest despond or basest moment—would *ever* say—ugh!—*Dad* and *Mom*)* gives the lip to dour Marcus Aurelius. Their moral estate has endured many, many years beyond their graves, down to this and that grandchild (not all of them) and remarkably in these our hostile times, which my brother Bill once, in the mid-'60s (turning to me as we were driving to his home in Stanford—perilously, because to be a passenger in a vehicle driven by my brother Bill is to court quick release from this vale of tears—I fresh in from Spain, both of us recounting problems with our teenage sons; I had asked him, "Bill, does Christopher *read*?" to which he replied, "I've *written* more books than Christo has read!"),† presciently defined with the deep philosophical sorrowfulness that few have perceived in his public persona, "Reid, this is the Age of Dislocation."

I'm not sure how I got out of that sentence, but I'm glad, as must you, the reader, be, that I managed. In this, the postmodern age of dislocation, the ugly poststructural age of shattered faith, sloppy sentimentalism, solipsism, hedonism, animality, hermaphroditic self-righteousness, and neo-

---

* Symptomatic of the low-class sentimentalism that, alas, disfigures the character of George Bush II.

† Bill had written just eight books at the time; Christopher, of course, has gone on to write one book in prose, a play, and nine (as of 2005) funny, highly regarded novels, the latest of which is *Florence of Arabia* (which is studied by the Department of State), another of which, *Thank You for Smoking*, has been made into a hilarious movie (September 2005).

pagan despair, the children of Aloïse Steiner and William Buckley have devoted their careers, publicly and privately, to expostulating and defending those religious and human truths to which their parents were devoted, and which defined their lives. This is out of the ordinary. We were ten, remember. We are so diverse, yet when the line is drawn in the sand, we close ranks with our heritage. Our brother John became, alas, an alcoholic* and died horrifyingly of that affliction; but though he and I were ten years apart in age, we knit close as his disease progressed and he sought company (he became a round-the-clock drinker, the consequent physical and psychological debilities compounding); yet to the end—to his last, his faults and derelictions apart, which were plenty—he was, I know, true to the faith we had inherited. He was born with a ferocious redhead's temper and deep gentleness and sweetness also; as alcohol rotted him, the ugly temper subsided, the gentleness and sweetness won through. He could be dead drunk and true. I am witness to this, and say this with total conviction: he was a gentle man and a humble, fervent Christian to the end.

So what's in this compilation? There's a full chapter from what likely may be the last book I will put together, a ruminative essay (*Credo*); there's the preface to *Speaking in Public*, the first book I wrote on the topic, of which I have been puffed by publishers to the status of guru, which is too funny, and which does cause me to howl with laughter (how delicious it is to deceive the willfully self-deceiving, especially if they are from New York), but to which scam I have passively acquiesced in the interest of my very good—what the hell, my fabulous—school.†‡ Some of the material is repetitive; if I have not blue-lined it, that's because it is necessary to the context in which it appears. There are excerpts and borrowings from

---

* This is a family disease: two of our father's uncles were alcoholics, I gather, and two of my sisters are "recovered" (they don't touch liquor) alcoholics.

† The Buckley School of Thought, Reflection, and Communications, whose three divisions teach disciplined thinking, written expression, and public speaking, in the first of which any of my siblings with tell you that I am personally deficient.

‡ In the other two of which I can ascend to sublime heights, which rise often out of a cheekiness that is tongue-in-cheek and subversive, because I am only then truly myself and truly serious about the absurdity of my pretensions, which have me laughing at myself ten times a day.

everywhere. My memory is often at variance with that of my siblings respecting family lore; where I do not defer to them, I supply their versions, when I am aware of them. (When I am unaware of them, *tant pis.*) The impression made by our parents on me is reflected in almost anything I have written, but principally in my fiction, which my brother John was wont to describe, accurately, though not kindly, as "widely unread."

In much of it, the experiences of my family reverberate. The characters of my father and my grandfather John C. Buckley, in this or that respect, moral and physical, are, I now realize (to my surprise), strikingly evident in the principal male protagonists of my novels, all of whom aspire to integrity; to which my siblings and I have always aspired; which my wife, Tasa, exemplifies; and to which we trust, hope, pray—are *confident* (we will not settle for less, though we will get what we deserve)—our sons and daughters all aspire.

An acknowledgment. Back in 1971, I was asked to do this book, or something like it, by Walter Minton, then president of Putnam. Things came in the way, among them my worry that I might wound certain people who were still alive. I asked myself also, was I mature enough to do justice to the project? Now, however, since, in a long and goodly life, I have not yet (alas, alas) attained the maturity that is acceptable in decent bourgeois liberal society (and very much fear that I am doomed to perish before attaining it), here goes.

Mother's and Father's imprint on their children, and our memories of it and, through it, of them, reveal their personalities more comprehensively than is possible in a straightforward biography, which (a straightforward anything) I am incapable of writing. Existence is carving into the future one's past, in one's idiosyncratic fashion. What we think, feel, do lasts for all time, is genetically and experientially continued in our children, even though our children may have no knowledge of us. We children of Aloïse Steiner and William Buckley have reflected our parents. There is in every one of us a facet here, a trait there, a development in that other place—in physical resemblance, personality, character, striving, choice, and in cases accomplishment—of our parents, whom some of us have surpassed in certain dimensions, as they would have wished, but whom none of us, alas, as complete human beings, has equaled. The uniqueness of being brought up by them attests to the uniqueness of their beings, which, in my opinion, is unrivaled.

The sobering irony is this: we, the second generation, have not been able to pass down the special quality of this inheritance to our children, the third generation; and it will not be repeated, ever.

"Casa Santa"
Comillas, Cantabria, Spain
August 2007

PART ONE

---❧---

The
Buckley Mystique

———— ⌁ ————

CHAPTER ONE

The Conservative Movement Elects Its U.S. Senator

THE DAY JIM BUCKLEY WON HIS SEAT AS JUNIOR SENATOR FOR NEW YORK, my family became camp.

The next day—November 7, 1970—the *New York Times* called my brother Bill and asked him to write a piece entitled "The Buckley Mystique," which made him acutely uncomfortable. He tracked me down to the Midwestern college where I was lecturing, proposing that I discharge the commission. As I recall, it was eleven o'clock in the morning. The piece had to be completed within the hour and telexed* to the *National Review* offices, whence it would be relayed to 229 West 43rd Street.

The assigned topic made my flesh crawl also. We were not Roosevelts. We were not Kennedys. There was no "mystique" about us at all. We were an ordinary, though large and rambunctious, American family. We had extraordinary parents, principled as no Kennedy going back to old Joe (and from him back to old Nick) ever was, inclining us to a radical dissent when it came to popular culture and to political opinions that were at the time unpopular and that are now once again in eclipse. I'd never have used *mystique* in connection with my family. *Difficult*, yes. *Talented*, yes. *Pugna-*

---

*No e-mail then . . .

cious, yes. *Argumentative,* yes. *Principled,* yes. We were brought up to be fastidious about the English tongue. The term *charisma* was loosely flung about in those days, particularly in connection with John F. Kennedy, but if that rogue was filled with the grace of God, I'll eat my broccoli. The *Times's* use of *mystique* descended from a hero-worshiping inflation of language that we Buckleys as a tribe detested and that was to me and my brethren disgusting. As br'er Bill pointed out, however, the *Times* was willing to pay one thousand bucks.

The prospect of earning such a fat sum from the cathedral of Northeastern liberalism was too tempting to resist. I secured a classroom where I could seclude myself, placed my battered Smith-Corona on the desk, and batted out the eight hundred words. What I did was to deny that there was any "mystique" about us. The whole point of our politics was what our parents drilled into their children: that "God, family, and country," *in that order,* demanded our unswerving loyalty, that we as individuals—we Americans—had to have "character," that we individually had to develop integrity, and that the people of a republic (and a proud country like the United States) had to be self-reliant. We were not serfs, beholden to crown or state.

Our upbringing was peculiar. Though Father was a man of almost painful personal shyness, respecting his children, he abandoned modesty for a pride that could be ludicrous. Privately he fretted over our moral and intellectual failings. At dinner parties, on the other hand, he was complacent that his poor guests were hugely entertained by hearing us howl through Mexican ballads or by listening to me, age seven, Charge Through the Light Brigade. We like to died.

At the age of eight, I finally put a stop to calls for my recitation by whipping out a toy but lethal-looking metal sword* and, with wild histrionic thrusts, brandishing it at Cossack to-the-right-of-me and Cossack to-the-left-of-me, nearly slicing the choker chain off one venerable lady and all but decapitating her husband.

I was the rebellious child, among nine others of similar deplorable nonconformity. Checked, but never daunted, Father persisted in embarrassing us right down to the toenails, even when we were adolescents,

---

*Bought for me—to my huge delight—in London, in 1938, when I had just seen the movie version of *The Prisoner of Zenda.*

grasping our upper arms in his freckled rancher's grip and propelling us into the breast or bosom of startled visitors, proclaiming our most recent accomplishments, say a B in math. He would beam on us those round, pale blue eyes, magnified by his pince-nez into exophthalmic infractions of a delight perfect in its assumption that we were wonderful.

Yes, we revered our Texan sire; and reciprocated his with our love; and were painfully conscious that our accomplishments did not approximate our father's boundless fantasies. We have all been moderately possessed by the compulsion to make good on his (and Mother's) enormous (and undeserved) pride. This has stung us into working harder than some people, if not as hard as a good many others. And it has caused us to shrink—with the same childhood embarrassment—from the limelight, something frequently observed about my brother Jim during his political campaigns, less often about Bill, except by those who know him well. Sister Priscilla, who became the formative managing editor of *National Review* (arguably the most influential political journal in the second half of the twentieth century), once flew all the way to France in order to escape an (otherwise unavoidable) speaking engagement. Aloise—Allie—could not bring herself to stand up and ask a question at a public meeting. Patricia, managing editor of *Triumph,* an ideologically embattled Catholic magazine, had to disguise herself in a red beret* before summoning the courage to demonstrate against the abortion laws.

I doubt any of us enjoys public attention, which is why so many of us have hidden behind the metal arras of the typewriter. Professionally, Bill has been soaked in klieg light since he wrote *God and Man at Yale* back in 1952, when he was just 27. There survived in him, nevertheless, the self-deprecatory spirit that, often by sleight of wit, objectified the public personality—he doesn't allow himself to be confused with those who sell themselves into believing in their own myths. The status of celebrity, as distinguished from the obligations thereof, Bill treated always as frolic, hoping you wouldn't be so undiscriminating as to take it too solemnly, either. And so with Jim, different as he is: temperamental humility that made campaigning an agony, until the cause began to carry him.

As a tribe, we find it difficult to blow our own trumpet, to pose as charismatic leaders, to feel the self-assurance that permits others to be-

---

*In honor of the Carlist *requetés* of Navarre (Spain).

lieve in their indispensability to the world at large. We are, therefore, happier as advocates of someone else (a sibling will do); of, by preference, an intellectual or moral idea.

THE STRENGTH OF PERSONALITY OF FATHER AND MOTHER AND THEIR rigorous systems of belief nourished in us, their children, a similarity of perceptions that has characterized us our whole lives long. Our bonding as a family of individuals has expressed itself in the social, spiritual, and intellectual dimensions in astonishing degree. Though we differ widely among ourselves, and almost always, when coming together, argue fiercely, it's often as though the ten of us were extruded from the same toothpaste tube.

And that's so. I don't know how to reduce this in abstract fashion, and I can only hope that what I venture to hypothesize is not nonsense; but the strong unity of consciousness that we siblings have always exhibited is directly received from our parents. Take things mechanical. Mother famously spent half an hour in the kitchen attempting to open a can of tamales with a pencil sharpener.* Father understood intellectually what consequence a hammer had on a nail, but he was deprived of motor intelligence. If ever he had tried to bang a nail into a wall, it would have entered at an inauspicious angle, he would have smashed his thumb, or the wall would have collapsed. Bill is fatally fascinated by mechanical wonders, possibly because, though their dialectic is at least in design autotelically dispositive, conceptually evoking a theorem in Euclid or the perfection of a Bach fugue, in practice they defy him. Reading his books on sailing the high seas, one concludes that Bill is cursed either by a native ineptitude or by an inherited ill fate. His sonar and other expensive systems of navigation are forever breaking down.† This puts him out of sorts, as I have suggested, because mechanics demonstrably are based on the elementary logic of cause and effect, and it is unjust that he, a master of such relationships in statecraft and prose—if one says A, one must say B;

---

* The type whose base is screwed into a wall and resembles a revolver's cylinder, with different-sized holes for different-sized pencils. It has a long handle.
† See his son Christopher's hilarious address before the Bohemian Grove in early June 2007 for an account of Bill's vicissitudes as skipper. See Priscilla's account in her *Living It Up with National Review* (2005) of a Christmas vacation in the Bahamas spent on a boat hired by Bill.

if the adverb accomplishes no purpose, strike it; if a wing nut is attached to a bolt *here,* there is a discernible explanation for the connection *there*—is more often the victim of disorder than the agent of effect. Once sailing into Stratford-on-Avon (Connecticut), as we were setting forth for a bit of the bard and supper in town, he switched the bilge pumps on, and when we got back, only the tippety-top of the mainmast was visible, its burgee bravely fluttering. The pumps had reversed, flooding the hold, and the boat had sunk at its mooring. That was spectacular.

Jim, I am told by his wife, Ann, used to assume a bemused expression when she handed him a screwdriver, directing him to a cupboard door that was hanging from its hinges, at which he would stare and then retire to his study for some reading. Our sister Aloise was fascinated by gadgets and novelties, but they almost never performed for her as advertised; the funky birthday candle that could not be blown out set the tablecloth on fire. Priscilla uses word processors and such with aplomb but is wisely content to inquire nothing about the zillion little gremlins inside who do her bidding at the touch of a key. Our sister Maureen was given the fouled-up subscription department of the fledgling *National Review* magazine to put in order. Subscriptions conceptually are a simple mechanism, but not at *National Review.* To one frustrated gentleman who, alternately, received either no copy of the magazine or two copies, and for whom there was nothing that could be done, no matter how often he complained, she wrote, "Dear Sir: Having reviewed the record, my advice to you is that you cancel your subscription and then resubscribe under an assumed name." As for me, there is nothing mechanical with which I am not at odds. The history of my tractors, my bush hogs, my balers, my disk harrows, my irrigation systems, my ice makers, my laptops, my ink-jet printers (which jet ink profusely but do not print), has been of one calamity after another. 1964: As I reached to open the front door of my shiny-new Spanish SEAT 1400 station wagon, the handle came off in my hand. 1986: As I eased my brand-new Jeep Cherokee from first gear to second, the stick shift came off in my hand. (There is little so stupefying, or such an instant's reduction to impotence, as to be holding a detached gearshift lever in the air. When I asked the laconic chief mechanic at the American Motors agency had that happened often, he replied, "Not hardly.") 2007: The *Check Engine Oil* dashboard warning on my four-month-old Ford Explorer flashed on when I had just recently changed the oil, and there was no coming to an understanding with it. Only our brother John had a *don* for the workings of complicated instruments, such as state-of-the-art cameras and high-powered rifles and scopes, but he never could get the heaters of the Jaguars he persisted in buying to function, so that he drove through Connecticut winters cocooned in wool overcoats, his neck wrapped in a wool scarf, lips blue.*

There is a metaphor here. Our incompatibility with the twentieth and twenty-first centuries is expressed in our failure to come to terms with ordinary expectations. This has placed us at odds lifelong with contemporary American culture and political expression. It has inclined many of us to tilt at windmills, which creak. There is no excuse for a national Mother's Day, an invention by shopkeepers inspired by avarice and playing to the most awful sentimentality in the human soul, as though written by Hallmark, produced by Disney, and pronounced by Eleanor Roosevelt, but we are stuck with it. Sentimentality is a moral evil.

We were taught that early.† In our society, sentimental worship of power and glitz is a plague. Just try stomaching another Oscars celebration on television. And why, for example, has George Washington's birthday vanished from our national calendar, to be replaced by Presidents' Day? Who is responsible for this abomination? (I suspect Lyndon Baines Johnson, who exposed his gall-bladder scar to the public.) It's like fascist architecture. It belongs to *1984*. This is rank royalism. I have scant personal regard for the majority of our presidents. Most of them were either forgettable mediocrities or sorry mistakes. George Washington was the father of our country. By honoring his birthday, we were paying tribute to a great man, not to the office. We sons and daughters of the Revolution do not do homage to the office; we are not a subject people. How sneakily has that distinction been erased, and with it critical discrimination in the public. The vulgarity of the conforming egalitarianism is revolting to us. This was, I think, material to our father's contempt for Roosevelt and the New Deal, in which (as in its successor, the Great Society) vulgarity of

---

*Our sister Carol, who is sensible, does not attempt to do battle with practical necessities; she hires professionals.

† See Jacques Barzun's excoriation of sentimentality in his *500 Years of Western Cultural Life*, HarperCollins, 2000.

perception, of aspirations, and of ideals are rampant. We inherited his fastidiousness.

All of which makes us Buckleys prickly. Our parents possessed quick, sharp, analytical minds, moral balance, and an indissoluble integrity: their intellect and their emotions were symbiotic as well as congenial and produced an uncanny similarity of mind and feeling in their offspring. One dreary early February in 1972, I was booked into Scottsdale, Arizona, for an address before a meeting of that state's GOP. The prospect made me morose, first because I am not comfortable in political company, where the meanest human venalities are on display, from obsequiousness to naked ambition, and second because Richard Nixon had in my opinion betrayed conservative tenets wholesale—flamboyantly during the high summer of that year, when he slapped wage and price controls on the country. Little could have been economically more ignorant, and as far as pandering to his left-wing critics, more abject. In a press conference that fall, he had similarly made hash of the intellectual justification for our gruesome war in Vietnam, reducing it to the most trivial dimensions. Asked at a press conference why we were fighting in that godforsaken land, he answered that it was to afford the South Vietnamese the right of self-determination. Was that it, Mr. President? Yes; we have no other ambition, territorial or otherwise. "Do you mean, sir," pressed one dumbfounded reporter, "that once North Vietnamese aggression has been contained and the people of South Vietnam are secure in their freedom, should they nevertheless vote 51 percent to 49 percent to elect a communist regime, this would be okay by you? You'd be satisfied . . . our sacrifice in blood and treasure would be justified?" Nixon answered yes.

The frivolousness of that reply was so appalling that, reading of it in the Spanish newspapers, I was stupefied. I thought he had been misquoted or that the translation had been bungled. (Not, alas.) And now, as I prepared for the evening, our president was in Beijing courting the favor of Mao Tse-tung, the most monstrous of all twentieth-century tyrants, who publicly boasted of slaughtering millions of his countrymen. My disgust was the more keen because I was performing in the hometown of Barry Goldwater, to whom such betrayals of conscience as these would have been unthinkable. I had cochaired the Goldwater effort in Europe. A few months after his defeat (we won in my territory, by the way), I had gotten to know the senator well. He visited me several days at the four-hundred-year-old mill I rented in the enchanting valley of the Tajuña, outside Alcalá de Henares, recovering from the brutality of the campaign, which had wounded him to the quick. All through the overlong preliminaries of the GOP banquet, I brooded. Had Barry Goldwater suffered slurs, slanders, and defamations of a viciousness not equaled since the Quincy Adams–Andrew Jackson brouhaha, to prepare the way for Richard Nixon? When I was at last called to the lectern, I tossed away my prepared remarks, instead delivering a eulogy to the integrity of the senator from Arizona coupled with a diatribe against the skunk in the White House. For thirty minutes, I tore into Richard Milhous Nixon. It was a bitter, savage, and merciless rant . . . and it was received with shocked disfavor by the local Republican nabobs. (Never again was I to be invited to address the faithful.)

Getting back late that evening to my hotel room on the outskirts of Phoenix—bitterly aware that I had expelled myself from lucrative bookings—I flicked on the late night's news . . . to behold the image of my brother Jim, junior senator of New York, announcing his break with the president on matters of conservative principle. God bless Jim! The next morning, I read Bill's column, posted from Beijing, in which he roasted Nixon for his ignominious opening to Red China. God bless Bill also.

Of note here is this: there had been no prior consultation among us. We three brothers had not been in personal contact for weeks, and in my case months, past. We were not telephone chatterers; we shrank from airing our private thoughts even to one another, the paternal taciturnity we had inherited cringing from emotional excess. On occasion, we wrote one another letters, which placed a decent distance between our interior lives and the sibling to whom we might be confiding something intimate. I lived in Spain, furthermore. I had been on lecture tour since early January. To my knowledge, I had never mentioned to Bill or Jim my growing disenchantment with Nixon. I don't know whether they had voiced similar discontent to each other—they were brought professionally close in those days. But dismay at the man in the White House who was masquerading as a conservative gestated in us at roughly the same time, and though we were thousands of miles apart—Reid, the least of the brothers, in Arizona;

Jim, maverick Republican senator, in Washington, D.C.; and Bill, the founder of the conservative renaissance, in faraway China—we went public at roughly the same time.

This took place, I should add, months before the scandal of Watergate hit the airwaves. Our disaffection with the president was philosophical, and we were unable to live with it. Our actions emphasize the seriousness in which we hold the moral and intellectual underpinnings of the conservative case, which are to us more precious than reasons of state, than politics, than political opportunism. Despised by the liberal left for mostly the wrong reasons, Richard Nixon was (as far as we Buckleys were concerned) indeed despicable. Why? Because he was not *sérieux*. He had revealed himself as shallow in his convictions, whatever they were other than desire for power. The happy consequence of this episode was that I telephoned Tasa Leguina in Madrid and persuaded her to fly to Los Angeles the next day, so that we could elope and be married. Richard Nixon is responsible for thirty-seven years of bliss.

WE WERE UNCANNILY CLOSE YET VERY DIFFERENT. IT HAD REQUIRED THE flush of triumph and the euphoria of election night two years earlier than the episode I have just related for Jim to pronounce that "there is a new conservative politics, and I am the voice of that politics." (Bill quipped: "Who in hell does Jim think he is? *La politique nouvelle, c'est* goddam well *moi!*")* I am confident that Jim was flushing with mortal embarrassment the next morning, even though the proposition may have been, at that time, in a way, true.

My elder brothers stood out. When Bill had run for mayor of New York five years earlier (1965), the freshness of his views tossed conventional thinking into a twit. One morning at the 60 Sutton Place South apartment on 54th Street that Jim, Priscilla, and our mother shared, Jim and I were having coffee for breakfast. He was reading the news section of the *New York Times;* I was buried in the sports pages. He said to me, "See this?" He had the *Times* opened to a full-page photo of Bill (it was an ad

---

* This sentence was inserted by Bill when he transcribed my piece by telex to the *New York Times.*

for a charitable function of some kind). Shaking his head, half smiling in disbelief, Jim said, "I'm afraid we have to get used to this, Reid. Our brother is a celebrity." As in a few short years he himself was to become.

Jim's instant rapport with the people he met during the 1970 senatorial campaign was quite wonderful. Here was a second paladin of conservative thought, a brother of William, and in his stammering, wholly unpretentious manner, as hard to stereotype.* His simplicity has been evident always. Compared with Bill, Jim can seem stodgy. (This first impression is wildly wrong: Jim, like our sire, is an adventurer to the quick.) Bill having sliced a path through the left-wing hegemony with his wit, Jim didn't need to conceal the sweetness of nature that is his special gift. (From our mother.) There's charm when he evokes even the "eternal verities," and in just those words, without a stylistic shudder—plainly because he believes so wholeheartedly in them.

Bill and Jim *are* as different as brothers can be in their expression of a shared philosophical context, and in whom that essential is evident. If there is a "Buckley mystique," it is embedded in the abiding recognition of our moral and intellectual deficiencies measured against the goal of perfection that our parents held out to us. We learned from them to prefer the good man to the brilliant man. It is a sacred humanity in people that we respect. Our compassion is engaged in the equality of the human condition. People are surprised to discover that we, princelings of Dame Fortune (as we have been judged to be), tread the same hard interior landscape.

And it may be this that comes through, that attracted public attention, that prompted the *New York Times* to commission such an embarrassing op-ed . . . because we do not presume, "Come, let us lead you," instead petition, "Come, our philosophy is your true way, the human way, and it is you who will and must lead yourselves." We have never been, God help us, messianic, though reflecting upon these past sixty years, I have now come to wonder whether our role has not been that of Cassandra. We remind people that self-reliance in all spiritual and intellectual dimensions is everyone's sweet burden, the dread price of our dignity as human beings who are endowed with a free will. And we are forever letting people know

---

*If I were to compare Jim's political appeal to that of any other politician, it would be Barack Obama, assuming profundity lurks somewhere in the man.

that we *believe* in their God-given capacity for shouldering that burden. We therefore reflect the higher estimation for the self that every man may aspire to: his fulfillment as a moral being.

I wrote way back then for the *Times,* "And this is an ennobling philosophy, to which everyone can be attracted: that we are all aristocrats in the private domains of the soul." The ebullience of this statement is historically tracked in the following chapters.

———— ⚭ ————

CHAPTER TWO

William Frank Buckley of Texas (I)

THIS CHAPTER WAS ORIGINALLY WRITTEN FOR THE DECEMBER 16, 1970, edition of *Life*. I signed the contract (which was fat) in New York the Friday afternoon after Thanksgiving. My deadline was the following Tuesday. That night, my eleven-year-old son Claude and I boarded a TWA 707 for Madrid. As soon as we reached cruising altitude, I unlimbered my portable Smith-Corona and began typing, to the extreme mortification of Claude,* who begged the stewardess to find another seat for him, preferably in the tail of the jet—as far as possible in distance from the demented man it would have appalled him to acknowledge as his father. The piece was finished as, with the first rays of dawn, the 707 hove in over the gigantic and gloriously gold-and-rose-tinted cross of the Valle de los Caidos, in its approach to Barajas airport—an approach, alas, that is no longer used, reflecting the new paganism that has afflicted Spain. The story was telexed to New York that Monday.

MY GOD, HOW THAT MAN COULD LAUGH!

How he enjoyed laughing. It was an irruption from the seat of his

---

*Who would grow up to become a distinguished painter of portraits, landscapes, and murals, his work in the collections of (discerning) people in the United States, South America, and Europe.

being. That great rib cage would swell. The whole upper torso would jerk in its seat. His shining dome of a skull would be flung back, the lower jaw would drop like an unbolted bear trap, and out of the cavity of his mouth gusted laughter: explosive, wholly surrendered to, porcelain eyes swimming and pince-nez fogging.

He possessed joy. Zest brimmed in whatever he flung himself into, whether a corporate battle or Christmas at Great Elm. I remember the ten of us gathering by the fountain of Great Elm's patio on Christmas Day. The twenty-foot fir we'd trimmed was a dazzle of ornaments. From its base, expectation tumbled in crimson and blue wrappings, silver and gold. Father had disappeared since Mass, gone to fetch Santa in some mysterious meeting place. We pressed our knees together against the moment.

It came suddenly—the chimes of harness. Through steaming panes of glass we saw the sled rounding into view, Father at the reins and Santa Claus beside him, Father beaming as Santa began spelunking for gifts in a bottomless red sack. We children shouted, we lobbed exclamations back and forth in a jumble of French, Spanish, and English. Father's eyes clouded momentarily. "Aloïse," to our mother, "has it occurred to you it's been years since we understood a word our children say? We ought to think about . . ."

Speech instructors. So they were added to what was already an international menagerie of tutors in math, history, grammar, poetry, music, and the languages. A Texan, Father also saw to it that we had a riding instructor, but he began to fear that we were becoming effete in our Eastern environment, so he imported a whole boxcar of broncos from the West, homophobic mustangs, as it turned out, that nobody but a rodeo hand could have ridden, and so wild that they leaped every fence on the farm and had to be rounded up across the length of White Hollow Valley and shipped back to wherever they came from (Hades).*

Father's Western heritage abided in his love of livestock. He squandered minor fortunes on everything from merino sheep to Irish hogs. On moonlit winter evenings, with the crust of snow sparkling underfoot and

---

*Brave brother Jim, not a lover of horseflesh but sixteen years old, was elected the first of his siblings to mount one of the broncs, which, after promptly bucking him off, did its ornery best to kill him.

the lace of gigantic elms frostbitten against the sky, our romantic sire would swoop Mother outdoors—to admire the conformation of a recently acquired Jersey heifer. "Aloïse, isn't she the . . . most . . . bee-u-tiful thing!"

He could be severe. "Reid, I'd like to see you in the Empire room after lunch." We trembled when we heard those words. He was thirty-six when he married, forty-nine years old when I was born, old enough to be the grandfather of half of us and as much a figure of awe as of fun. We did not realize until we were older how Father himself suffered—agonized—over those meetings, first consulting with Mother in their upstairs suite and then girding himself for them. It hurt him to recognize some delinquency of character in us. It hurt him to be obliged to point that delinquency out to us.

He began always in an embarrassed manner, asking us how we were and how we were doing. Abruptly, he might break into our replies. "Reid, I've called you in for this talk because . . . because I was very sorry to hear that you lost your temper again last week and hit Maureen over the head with a golf club. Did you?" "It . . . it was a croquet mallet, Father." His cheeks flushed. "I am not going to put up with this sort of behavior. You are old enough to learn . . ." He became heated now, his index finger wagging admonitorily, his jaw set, and his expression stern. Tears would sting high up in our nasal passages; a sob might choke in out throats. It was an awful thing to invoke the wrath of our father, especially when we ourselves burned with the disappointment we had caused him. Before the interview was over, we might dissolve in tears, and then bewilderment would enter his expression. Good heavens, had he been too harsh on us? What should he do? He had to impress us with . . . "Aloïse! Oh, say, Aloïse!" Mother, who had awaited apprehensively in the library, would come dashing in. "Will! Ohhh, *Will*, I told you not to lose your temper. There, Reid, there . . ."

At supper, the chastened child would be silent. There was general (and unusual) silence at the table. Mother would gaze reproachfully at Father, who was so miserable by this time that efforts to rouse him into one of his tales were useless. "Another time, John."

Then he would leave on the Sunday afternoon train for the week's work in New York. And before that week was out, the chastised sister or brother would receive through the mails an absolutely stupendous gift.

I remember him at age seventy observing us play one-a-catch and, upon our encouragement, stepping up to the batter's box, where he proceeded to slam home runs across the swimming pool and into the tennis court or beyond, until we tired of chasing after them. And I remember him when he was an aging, ailing man, undertaking the wearisome drive after a full day's work in the New York office, to Princeton, only because he had heard that a friend and I were representing Yale in the triangular debate championships.* He listened keenly, congratulated us, and then drove the solitary road back to the city.†

He was born in 1881 in the Texas-Mexico border town of Washington de los Brazos.‡ He studied law at the University of Texas, then opened practice in Mexico, where he was joined first by his brother Claude and later by his youngest brother, Edmund. ("My, you should have seen your uncle Edmund, children, when the three of us rode a flatcar to Mexico City that first time! There was, of course, a revolution going on. Corpses were strung from every telephone pole for miles along the way. Your uncle Edmund's eyes popped out. 'Will,' he said, 'this is a wonderful country!'" And that laughter would boom.)

Buckley, Buckley & Buckley prospered,§ becoming counsel for the major oil companies and then, as individuals, being themselves drawn into the search for black gold. Along the way, Father backed down Pancho Villa and others. He had inherited the nickel-plated Colt .45 Peacemaker his father, the sheriff of Duval County, had owned but never once wore. Physically, Grandfather John was a bull of a man, but it was something else in him that persuaded volatile, gun-slinging cowpokes to submit in saloons when Grandfather extended a palm for their revolvers. Father also relied on that something else in the lawless Mexico of his time, when every man down to the pharmacist's assistant packed a pistol. He walked his imperturbable way unarmed, even when he was hunted.

The major oil monopolies then vying for Mexico's treasure discouraged upstarts, but Father was an especially nettlesome one. Somehow he

---

* Harvard, Princeton, Yale.

† We won, that year and the next. My teammate was Jeremy Butler, who became a judge in Phoenix; our substitute was Edwin Meese, attorney general under Ronald Reagan.

‡ The geography is off here: Washington (which no longer exists) was not close by the Mexican border. It was in Grimes County, on the southern coast of Texas, and, my brother James recalls, "teeming with malaria."

§ In Tampico, near Mexico's Gulf coast.

signed up the best leases. Father used to tell of the time someone decided to remove the nettle by hiring Monty Michael, gunman and robber of banks.[1] Monty took to shadowing Father wherever he went. After about a week of this, Father wheeled suddenly from the door of a restaurant, striding directly to the outlaw. "Monty, I'm having lunch in there with some friends. Why don't you and your boys pick up something to eat in the meantime?" Monty was scandalized. "Mr. Buckley, don't you realize that I've been hired to scare you out of Mexico, and if that doesn't work, to kill you?" Father said, "Well, never mind about that, Monty. Meanwhile you have about an hour before I leave here."

Father made a habit of advising Monty wherever his schedule took him. Often he worked late into the evenings. It can get cold in Mexico, and Father conceived pity for his putative assassins, who spent their vigils in the unheated vestibule of the building. He sent them sandwiches and coffee. It became too much for the outlaws. One very late night, Monty and his companions crashed through the door of Father's office, lurching inside. Their faces were flushed. Tequila fumed out from between their teeth. Each carried a Colt at the hip, a cartridge-studded bandolero slung over a shoulder, and a sawed-off shotgun [I suspect now more likely a Winchester 73 .35-caliber carbine].

Father was taken by surprise. The Peacemaker rested in a desk drawer, out of reach, the barrel probably stuffed with paper clips. "What is it, Monty?"

The man stumbled two steps closer. "We've been talking it over, Mr. Buckley. Look, the people who hired us to kill you are in the casino. They're drunk. Now, if it's all right by you, my friends and I'll amble on down there and blast them to kingdom come. How's that, Mr. Buckley?" Monty was grinning now. "We'd rather work for you."*

Against General Álvaro Obregón, revolutionary president of Mexico, Father mounted a hopeless insurrection. Losing, he lost everything he had earned and built in his adult life. Father was ejected from Mexico under perpetual condemnation of death should he return. That happened in [1921]. Will Buckley from Texas, [40] years old and something

---

*Father persuaded Monty not to carry out his massacre . . . and declined Monty's offer to work for him.

of a public scandal, established himself in Connecticut and New York City.

A press agent approached him. "Mr. Buckley, for a fee of three hundred dollars a month I'll guarantee that you and your wife and children will appear once a week in society columns and at least monthly in social magazines."

I pity that man. I pity his having exposed himself to the ice-blue fullness of contempt in eyes of uncompromising candor. "I'll pay you the same amount to keep me and my family out of the papers."

Father was next to broke. It was going to take him 18 years to come back. But hunger for personal publicity, Father felt, showed that a person was unable to approve of himself on his own terms, lacking in the strength and certitude of his own worth.* That's poverty. Where he was reared, plain survival tended to prove a person and tended to translate into prosperity. Economic class distinctions were rare. Success was like a fine quarter-horse stallion: to be admired or envied, not, should one happen to possess it, to be ashamed of. Money was good to have; it was for building beautiful houses and raising packs of children and giving them the best education. But the worth of a man as a person was what counted. As children, we were taught neither to fear material poverty nor to despise riches.

Father was as at ease in crass New York as he had been in violent Mexico, where he had shrugged when a general swore with Latin flourish, "If I don't live to kill Will Buckley and his sons, my sons will live to do it." In New York, he was something of a cougar to Wall Street wolves, whom he startled by his catawampus eye for their pretensions, by his irreverence for some of their institutions, and by his total indifference to the values that seemed to consume so many of them. If, to them, he was an outlander, to him they were (with several distinguished exceptions) a sad bunch.† He was amazed by what seemed to be a fundamental insecurity in them.

I grew up without need for stories of adventure. The legends about

---

*In this and in so much else (including integrity), he was the diametric opposite of old Joe Kennedy, determining the very different stars that his children chased.

† He found them culturally narrow, ignorant, and provincial, and his taste of their ilk in Tampico bred a scorn that he maybe found difficult to dissemble.

Father's early years in Mexico sufficed. They were kept alive by visits from usually short, swarthy, corpulent men, one of whom [at least] had risen from banditry to governorship, which is just about the same thing.

Their reminiscences could be confusing to a child. Often we were told how Father had disliked the president of Mexico. But we were also told that when President Wilson had sent Marines to invade Veracruz (on April 2, 1914), Father was bitterly opposed. It roiled his Southwestern Republicanism, and, as the premier American expert on Mexico at the time, he testified against the invasion before the Senate of the United States. Father told the senators that the U.S. envoy who persuaded President Wilson to send in the Marines "is typical of the provincial American, who in need of civilization himself, seeks to civilize the rest of the world."

Father's testimony before the Senate was perhaps the one time he accepted the glare of public attention. So shy a person was my father that he preferred the garrote or even (even!) an inappropriate wine to giving any sort of speech. But he knew the time can come when a person has to give witness to his beliefs. He preferred [brother] Bill's way: persuasion through intellectual channels. But now [brother] Jim—dragged—had entered the political arena. This has incurred a pile of publicity that makes every one of us [siblings] nervous. What would have been Father's reaction? He had the habit of writing us memoranda, dealing with everything from minutiae of personal appearance to delinquent bank accounts.

I remember a "Memorandum to William F. Buckley Jr." he wrote concerning my activities at Yale: "Jane tells me that Reid has quite extensive side-burns. When he started growing them I mentioned them to him very casually and he said that that was required of the Glee Club—which sounds rather extraordinary. If you could gently suggest to him that he remove them, it would be a great relief to the family. I would rather he not belong to the Glee Club. Father."

Our promiscuous use of the automobile, sister Maureen's difficulty with diction (despite the instructors), Jimmy's punctiliousness about a ten-dollar debt (held up as an example to us all), the heinous American habit of never listening to someone else, the importance of keeping one's promises—his concern for us was all-encompassing.

It isn't hard for a son of such a sire to imagine the memorandum we would all of us receive before this week were out, were he still alive.

To: Ben, John, Priscilla, Jimmy, Jane, Billie, Patricia,
Reid, Gerry, and Carol.
From: W.F.B.

Children:

There has been a great deal of unfortunate but unavoidable
public attention as a result of Jimmy's election to the Senate. To a
degree, one has to put up with it. But I suggest that you keep your
children from the newsstands for the next month or two. Should
they happen on a *Life* magazine themselves, you might tell them that
their uncle's new position makes not the slightest difference as far
as they are concerned. They have not (yet) accomplished a great deal
(although your mother and I were thrilled to hear that Bruce is
captain of his soccer team at Hotchkiss and that little Aloise has
made such a hit in New Orleans). As for you children, I know that
you are all too intelligent and too well balanced to have your heads
turned. Keep in mind, however, that your brother is no more than a
freshman senator, and in standing, ninety-ninth out of one hundred
at that. (I know it is unnecessary to remind Jimmy of this, whose
personal modesty some of you might emulate.) You should keep in
mind also that the only one of you to have established any genuine
call on public interest is Billie, whose interest to the public will
steadily diminish if he continues slurring his words, as he has taken
to of late. As far as your mother and I are concerned, we are made
very proud by Jimmy's success. But I suggest that the next time
Life magazine is invited to share Thanksgiving with us, a strand
or so be cut from the hair of Reid's elder sons, which will not,
I dare say, weaken them unduly, but which may benefit their
postures.

Your mother and I are now settled in Camden, which I must say
strikes me as lovelier every year. We would be delighted to have any
and all of you for Christmas, and for as long as you and your children
care to stay.

Affectionately, Father.

To which memo Mother would have rushed to append: "Good heavens, fifty-nine of you all at once! Your father is out of his senses! But do come, dears, and as many of you as are able."

PHOTOGRAPHER ALFRED EISENSTAEDT, WHO WAS COMMISSIONED THAT Thanksgiving of 1970 by *Life* to photograph the newly elected U.S. junior senator for New York in the bosom of his family, was an aged (seventy-plus), spry, fussy, and magical professional, who, with his assistants, attended all our traditional holiday activities click-clicking, flash-flashing, and snap-snapping away.

He must have consumed ten cans of film, which amazed us but did not concern him in the least. He photographed several of us socializing in the capacious patio of Great Elm (which, when it was built in the late 1920s, scandalized the WASP community of Sharon, Connecticut; whoever *heard* of building a *patio* in New *England,* moreover embedding it in an antebellum* farmhouse!). He recorded us playing touch football on the lawn;† playing the grand piano in the Empire room (Mother and Bill) and singing along (Mother and I), in a remarkable triple image of almost identical profiles; painting (Bill, the artistic atrociousness of whose works never dimmed his enthusiasm);‡ during the Thanksgiving banquet that evening, featuring sister-in-law Ann Coolley toasting her husband, Jim, visible to her right—in order—darkly handsome Ben Heath, widower of sister Allie, yours truly, sister Jane, Bill, Mother (to Jim's left, her normal place at the head of the table having been usurped by the new-minted senator at Mr. Eisenstaedt's insistence), and to Jim's right, coming forward in the picture, darling María Elena, Ben's second wife,§ sister Priscilla, sister Carol's second husband, Raymond Learsy (where was Carol?), a com-

---

* Ante-Revolutionary war, that is: 1756.
† Mirror, mirror, on the Kennedy wall, except that our game, though spirited and fun, was less ferocious than the Hyannisport version.
‡ Pitts and Jane were the true painters (inheriting their talent from aunts Priscilla and Eleanor), and some of their work is astonishingly good.
§ Who used to work for me in Madrid at my ill-fated Bique export house. See my pamphlet, *Good Taste Doesn't Sell: Bad Taste Sells Loads,* P.E.N. Press, 2005.

modities trader and art collector (and now an author),* my first wife, Betsy (looking spectacularly beautiful), Bill's wife Pat, and Br'er John . . . and that midafternoon, not to miss out on a single Buckley family Thanksgiving custom, grouse hunting at White Hollow Farm.

This was the most marvelous event. Participating were crackshot John, ever game Pitts, and a somewhat bemused Jim, who almost never swung a barrel at anything. Jim's tall, handsome, and beguiling ten-year-old son Billy brought up the rear, alongside dear old Uncle Reid, then not so old (though every bit as dear), being just forty.

Tramping after New England's ruffed grouse is an arduous avocation, rarely rewarding in terms of game flushed and bagged. The ruffed grouse is sparse, courageous, erratic, and cunning, and to bring it down requires the highest shooting skill along with a good dose of luck. The New England variety is not to be confused with the "fool hen" of the upper Michigan peninsula or elsewhere. Centuries of avid pursuit in the hills of Connecticut, Massachusetts, New Hampshire, Vermont, and Maine have made the ruffed grouse the wariest, wiliest, and most explosive of game birds. It rockets out of deep coverts at the least expectation. It may explode up from one's very feet or come hurtling out of thick, high hemlock crowns (aiming at the gunner's face, compelling him to duck while it whooshes by), or as silent as a ghost break covert one hundred yards beyond gunshot, soaring majestically across wooded ravines, rays from a setting sun burnishing the chestnut plumage of its chest and isolating unforgettably the blurred vision of its short wings whirring as it alternately powers itself and then glides breathtakingly to safe haven half a mile away.[2]

It was this supreme quarry (there is no game bird in the world to compare) that Mr. Eisenstaedt and two assistants wished us to flush, shoot, and down for his cameras. Brother John said quietly, *"Il est fou."* Which was not quite the case. My revered elder brother, while suffering from the same malady—he was engaged in the bipolar-making business of drilling for oil where almost nobody else except his similarly deranged father might dream it existed—should have understood that though enthusiasm

---

* *Over a Barrel: Breaking the Middle East Oil Cartel,* Raymond J. Learsy, New York: Nelson Current, 2005.

is always half intoxicated with hope, it is yet sometimes inspired. John and Pitts and Jim explained to Mr. Eisenstaedt and his assistants how dangerous it could be for them to back down the old game trail twenty feet in front of the guns, they having not the least idea that if (most doubtfully) a grouse flushed between them and us, there would hang tremulously in the balance a moment of tension during which we would each of us, Priscilla, John, and I, separately engage in struggle with our competitive natures as we debated whether to risk peppering Eisenstaedt and company with bird shot in the act of downing the prize or grimly permit it to sail by unscathed; and moreover how unlikely it would be that we would as much as glimpse any game at all while marching in a small posse along the westernmost flank of White Hollow Farm—old fields abandoned to hemlocks, cedars, ancient apple trees, hoary oaks and sugar maples, hickories, and here and there a white birch, all draped almost impassably with bittersweet and grapevines, barberries tearing at one's knees . . . the grouse would be in that thick stuff, not exposed on the open path.

Never mind, Mr. Eisenstaedt would have his way. Besides, for the convenience of his cameras, we must walk bunched close together along the path running across the top of the farm to its boundary line and then dipping steeply down an even narrower trail, at the bottom of which we would make a ninety-degree turn north, moving alongside a strip of hardwoods and the sterile sedge of a beaver swamp.[3] None of us was to be allowed to penetrate the seductive cover we were passing in order to flush out any silly grouse that might improbably be lingering long enough to observe us approach. "Iss there not one *auerhuhn* on this entire property?" Mr. Eisenstaedt complained after he had backtracked half a mile or so, colliding with shrubs and trees and twice nearly falling when his heels stubbed a root—his assistants rushing forward to help him back up to his feet, for which he was not grateful. We explained patiently a second time that the ruckus we were making was simply contrary to a successful stalk of *Bonasa umbellus umbellus* ("thunderbird"); and that if by miracle a grouse did show itself, the flush would be so greasedlightningfast he'd never get his cameras on the bird before John shot it (while Jim looked on bemusedly, Pitts fired and missed, and I, bringing up the rear, swung my barrels futilely at a target that was already mortally stricken or on its merry way to safety).

But he was adamant. He was German-bred and an inhabitant of New

York City, and this may have been his very first venture into the back-country of the United States, of which he knew not the first thing but the prospect of which wildly excited him. Alfred Eisenstaedt (a sweet man, by the way, and a genius at his art) desired to photograph us shooting grouse, and nature would cooperate.

We shrugged our shoulders. "This is a monumental waste of time, and none of us will get a shot," Br'er John predicted dourly, to which pessimism sister Pitts assented—Br'er Jim gazing distractedly and uncomfortably away (he wished not to be blamed for all this fuss; he was senator thanks solely to a split vote, which was hardly his fault; he passed that entire Thanksgiving weekend keenly embarrassed and uncomfortable). I, ever the optimist, formally agreed . . . meantime peering hard at coverts we marched by, glancing behind me at likely-looking spruce tops from which a skulking bird might yet spring. The improbable is the nature of the hunt, I told myself.

But I am *au fond* also sensible, though my siblings may not agree, and that I was infected with John's pessimism can be inferred clearly from the farcical group photo that Mr. Eisenstaedt took shortly after we had descended to the road running along the beaver swamp. There strides John, grim-visaged and solemnly faux-alert, as though walking up a bird. Crowding ridiculously close behind him comes Priscilla, the barrels of her gun slung down across her knees, to the right and away from John, her expression under the corona of silvery hair, with its a-touch-vacant half-smile, conveying that she knows this is preposterous but is grittily contributing to the charade. Slightly behind her stands Br'er Jim, disgustingly handsome as usual, peering with apparent intentness ahead and slightly to John's left (he may have spotted a late prothonotary warbler—who knows?—or more likely a nuthatch). Jim's son Bill, avid neophyte hunter (he would make photographing game and gunners his life's vocation), is barely visible close on his father's heels, while I, in dark sunglasses, have my shotgun propped vertically against my left shoulder, standing with no pretense of stalking anything other than my chilled toes, staring down at and blowing on the cupped fingers of my raised right hand.

I was cold. I'd come over from Spain in September to discharge my lecture bookings and to help out with Jim's campaign, carting along little Claude. I was appointed to rallies throughout upper New York State that Jim, because of scheduling conflicts, could not attend. My companions were Jim's drop-dead-gorgeous daughter Priscilla (future freelance writer) and her equally wonderful-looking mother, Ann. Both were articulate champions. So utterly charming were they, and unaffected besides, and so plainly enamored of their candidate, it was plain to me that any of the faithful who met them would work their hides off securing Br'er Jim's election.

I was not prepared, however, for a late-fall northwestern Connecticut grouse-hunting expedition. I had on Levis, a black cotton turtleneck, an unlined Levis jacket, and a thin camouflaged hunting vest. As for the gun, I had borrowed it that noontime from Br'er John's vast collection, a dandy little Browning over-and-under .20 gauge. While my siblings were busily feigning that they were hot on the fleet heels of a grouse, I was trying to warm my stiffened fingers. The frame was snapped, and on the instant, a grouse burst with that heart-stopping brr*rooom!* from a copse of mixed hardwoods and firs high on the slope, radically to my left.

I pivoted instinctively—catching sight of the bird for a split second as, framed by the chill gray sky, it hurtled high, wide, and handsome across the road behind us. Flinging my barrels ahead of it, I fired. Ba-hooom went the gun . . . and the grouse thumped plumply to the ground, fifty or sixty yards to our left, just short of the stream.

There was a moment of startled stillness. As John had predicted, everything happened much too fast for Mr. Eisenstaedt and his assistants to do more than blink. Then the grumble of my eldest brother's voice broke the silence. "Cut it out, Reid," he said.

NOTES

———

1. My sister Priscilla remembers the Monty Michael stories in radically different form, which she wrote down in *W.F.B. An Appreciation.* Pitts (our nickname for Priscilla) is of the eldest four of our clan, who, as children, were closest to our parents. Further, when Allie, John, Pitts, and Jim were young, Mother and Father were much younger; Father was in his late forties when Priscilla was eight or nine years old, and since she was just thirty-five when she wrote her recollections (not yet in her dotage!), I give her version more credence than my own.

2. One of the most sorrowful adjustments I have had to reconcile myself to since a stroke and emphysema assailed me four seasons ago is that I am no longer able to spend a

few days in late October or early November in my beloved Connecticut hills hunting the ruffed grouse. I fancy that I could be parachuted into the woods at midnight in a snowstorm all the way from Mudge Pond up into Sharon Mountain and across to White Hollow Farm, and almost immediately orient myself, because I have known every inch of that ground and retain its feel in the soles of my feet, and in my nostrils its different intimate whiffs of scent. I dream still of my favorite coverts: the sweet smell of hickory and sodden mashed leaves on the ground, the scarlet pippins of barberry bushes, the distant metallic calls of blue jays and crows, the silver birches with their bright yellow leaves, the upland marshes bordered by abandoned apple orchards, fat hemlocks, and tall, gloomy spruces. I remember almost every kill and almost every miss I made on grouse, and most of these memories stand out vividly in my mind. I doubt that the most promiscuous Casanova can make such a boast about his favorite quarry, which places grouse hunting on a plane superior to sex.

3.   Ordinarily, upon reaching the corner of our property, we would have fanned out half a gunshot from one another, Pitts to the right, descending the open path along the fence that bordered on Margaret Scherr-Thos Church's farm, John in the choice center cover, while I, the youngest, flanked out to the left, bulling my way down and up a ravine and through the thickest grapevines, briars, and cornellberry patches as well as I was able, hoping that maybe maybe maybe (never never never—not once—did this happen!) a woodcock would whistle up out of the alders near the bottom of the slope.

PART TWO

Origins

CHAPTER THREE

William Frank Buckley
of Texas (II): Claude Buckley

THE FOLLOWING LETTER WAS SENT BY OUR UNCLE CLAUDE TO HIS nephew Edmund (son of our uncle Edmund). It describes the raw frontier violence of San Diego as well as the city's extraordinary cosmopolitanism.

Uncle Claude, born in 1884, was close to my father. He was the more severe of the two brothers, I deduce. Tall, spare, and fit, I remember him mowing the lawn of his house in San Antonio in the blazing sun with an old-fashioned muscle-powered mower. He was in his mid-eighties. He scorned a self-propelled or a rider mower, which was for wimps. He and Aunt Dora greeted me always with fond kindness,* the memory of which kindles warm affection. I listened intently to his vivid memories of Mexico, and I recall my surprise when he told me that he much preferred Mexico's Napoleonic system of justice to ours, because, he said—for a lawyer, freed of *stare decisis*—it was more creative and thus more challenging. I look back happily on his and Aunt Dora's after-Mass ritual, driving with their grown children to a breakfast place for pancakes. It was Uncle Claude's treat. He and Aunt Dora enjoyed a marvelous relation with their

---

*When Bill was in the infantry in 1944–45 and stationed nearby, Aunt Dora and Uncle Edmund were second parents to him; he remembers them always with great tenderness.

brood, of whom I was very fond also and who, this branch and generation of my cousins, are now, every last one of them, dead also!

My mother and father were natives of Canada.

They were born and raised in a rural community somewhere near Hamilton, Ontario. My sister Priscilla and my brother John (who died in San Diego at the age of 18)* were born in that community. . . . Shortly after Priscilla's birth, my Father contracted a bad case of asthma, which became chronic and serious. He and his family left this cold country and migrated to Texas and settled in the old town of Washington in Grimes County, a town which was the first capital of the Republic of Texas.

As this country was a low coastal one, wet and teeming with malaria, his ailment worsened. He just had to find a new place to live. . . . A friend got him to move down to the San Diego country, a somewhat desert land on which thrived only the stunted mesquite and cactus. This happened in the later eighteen seventies [actually, the early 1880s, as my father was born in 1881—JLB]. He became engaged in the mercantile business . . . Then he was elected Sheriff of Duval County and served in that office all through the eighteen nineties.[1]

My Father was an unusual man. He was honest, fearless, unassuming, and uncommunicative.† At that time San Diego . . . had about 200 Americans and 2000 Mexicans. The American Colony, if I may call it that, was most cosmopolitan. The six main merchants of the town were from France, Canada, Germany, England, Poland, and Spain. The town carpenter was directly from Scotland. The one and only hotel, the Marinet, was French owned. Two of the town's prominent stockmen were from Ireland. The chairman of the School

---

* The first and only reference of our uncle John that I know of on record by a sibling. What may he have been like? Cantankerous, quick-tempered, a firebrand? A habitué of saloons, with a loose tongue? Or had something been said about his father, the sheriff, that he was unable to let by? His existence is a mere name, a shadow.

†This is a Buckley character trait, male and female, present in my generation. It surprises people who know of us—or assume chiefly through Bill's public life that they know of us—as a voluble clan. We are also taciturn, private, brooding, morose, and at rare times savagely immersed.

John C. Buckley, Texan sheriff,
c. 1888.

Board was from Ohio and the principal from Colorado.* With one or
two exceptions, all schoolteachers were Mexicans. The town's wool
and cotton buyers were Frenchmen. San Diego's richest citizen
Norman G. Collins was from Minnesota. At the time of his death
he owned 27 ranches in Southwest Texas. . . . Among the Mexican
citizens were some very high class folks from Camargo and Monterey
Mexico. The town doctors were a Frenchman and a Spaniard.

　　The town itself and the county and the whole southwest was wild
and woolly. They abounded in law breakers of all types and kinds.
The worst of these were the cow thieves and the smugglers, the latter
were a mean bunch† who made a living by smuggling tequila from
Mexico to San Antonio and other points in Texas. Their direct route
from Rio Grande City to San Antonio came right through San
Diego. They carried the tequila in goat skins which they tied to their
saddles. At times as many as twenty smugglers traveled together.

---

*Note that for the Texan Claude Buckley, the states of Ohio and Colorado are lumped in
with other foreign countries.
†A euphemism for a murderous bunch.

Will Buckley, c. 1910–1915. First row: Will Buckley, Edmund Buckley (on stool), Aunt Beryl. Second Row: Uncle Claude, unknown, Mother B (Mary Ann) Buckley, Edmund Buckley, Dora Buckley. Back Row: Tía Eleanor Ann Buckley, Tía Priscilla Buckley.

Then there were the gunmen among the Americans and Mexicans of the town. My Father had to deal with all the elements.[2] He rarely toted a pistol. He carried one only when traveling in the country. And he never used a holster. He stuck the pistol inside his trousers at the waist and on the left side. He didn't smoke and he rarely indulged in liquors. Several attempts were made to assassinate him but each one was foiled. He had bitter enemies,* particularly among the low white trash of the town. They even went to the extreme of having him indicted by a Federal Grand Jury in San Antonio for aiding and abetting a revolution against Garza of Palatio Blanco, a little community some twenty miles south of San Diego, [on the border between] the United States and Mexico.† This revolution was initiated by one Caterinogo. And the revolution was intended solely to oust Porfirio

---

*Among them (we have always supposed, but this is now in doubt) the famously corrupt Archie Parr machine.

† His son, our father, Uncle Claude's brother, was "indicted" in Mexico for plotting a Christian insurrection against the incumbent revolutionary regime, for good reason.

Díaz from the Presidency of Mexico.* As Garza was a close friend
and political follower of my Father, the latter's enemies had him
indicted for aiding and abetting this revolution. The indictment was
later dismissed and quashed. Garza was able to enlist some three
hundred Mexicans throughout the counties of Duval, Starr, and
Zapata. The U.S. had to send in soldiers to put down the revolution. I
saw Garza only once and that was when he made a political speech in
favor of my Father at a torchlight gathering one night in the main
plaza of San Diego. I remember that he had two pistols on him and
that he was heckled from time to time during his speech. It looked for
a while that shooting might start.

My Father was defeated in 1900 for Sheriff.† After that and until
his death he became a sheep buyer and annually shipped thousands
and thousands of sheep to Kansas City. He died in Rockport in 1904
from a cerebral hemorrhage.

UNCLE CLAUDE WAS THE FIRST BROTHER THAT OUR FATHER BROUGHT
to Mexico and enrolled in his law firm.

Temperamentally quite different, they were nevertheless close, from
every account we have and from what we can deduce. Uncle Claude was
just three years younger than Father, and he was imbued with the same
seriousness, though I wonder whether he was as fun-loving (a happy trait
that Father shared with his youngest brother, the scapegrace, Uncle Edmund).

Father and Uncle Claude took a summer jaunt to Mexico, which Father often described in moods of fond recollection. It's difficult to pin
down when this occurred. Surely our grandparents would not have allowed their son Claude to expose himself to the evident dangers of Mexico (though the country was still under the firm rule of Porfirio Díaz)
until he was, say, eighteen. This places the trip in the year 1902.

There's a difficulty here nonetheless. We surmise that our father en-

---

*Grandfather John's son Will, Uncle Claude's brother, was memorably to be introduced to
Porfirio Díaz years later, in Mexico City. See Chapter Eleven.
†Court records tell that he was *elected* in 1890, defeated in 1896.

tered the university at Austin when he was nineteen (if not earlier). That would be the year 1899. Aunt Priscilla, the eldest child after the violent death of their brother John, had arrived in Austin maybe one year earlier, using her earnings as a researcher in the Land Office to help pay for her brother Willie's college; and he, Father, did part-time work at the Land Office and also taught Spanish part-time in order to help defray the costs. So when and how was he able to get off for several weeks' vacation in Mexico?

We just don't know. But say the jaunt took place during a summer in the first two years of the new century. As brother Jim reminds us in his memoirs,* the John Buckleys were among the poor in a poor (though unusual) frontier town (San Diego). Father and Uncle Claude couldn't simply indulge themselves in several weeks of traveling without earning money as they went. So what they did was cart along with them several hundred pounds of soap.† This was a new soap with wonderful cleansing properties. It made white cotton clothing gleam like snow, and this was what the Indians and *peones* of Mexico mostly wore in those days (and still do, in remote places), what we call pyjama suits. The brothers would stop at a village and ask people in the plaza to let them have a dirty piece of clothing to wash in the town's basin in order to display the marvelous powers of their soap. All were amazed; the soiled garments emerged dazzling white. The two young Texans sold dozens and dozens of bars as they ventured from village to village (on foot, I imagine; horses were expensive, though they must have brought along a pack animal for the soap).

Alas, as they doubled back on their journey, they were greeted at the last village they had visited with yells and curses and fist waving and cries of *"Bandidos!"* And thrust before them were garments that had been washed in their soap, filled with holes. There was too much carbolic acid (or whatever) in the mix. It not only wiped stains away magically, it ate into the cotton fibers. The brothers were shaken, appalled . . .

"What did you do?" we children would ask our father at this point.

"Why, we paid them back with what we had."

"You gave them back all their money?"

---

* *Gleanings from an Unplanned Life*

† According to sister Aloïse's recollection, the boys *made* the soap. Her account of this episode differs from my recollection. See the chapter, "Supper at Great Elm."

I don't know which of us asked that. And I am not sure whether, inasmuch as the brothers presumably must have used part of their profits to subsidize their travels, they returned to Texas and then made their way back to Mexico with sufficient funds, which they raised somehow, to make good. I have a suspicion that this is what they did, prompting the question "You gave them back *all* their money?" but I cannot be sure.

What is vivid in my memory is Father turning his sky-blue eyes on us and saying quietly, "They trusted us."*

NOTES

1. He served just one term, 1890–96, losing his bid for reelection to a fellow Irishman called Michael Corrigan. Walter Meeks told me about fifty cowhands being voted at gunpoint against John Buckley just as the polls were closing, and I had consequently assumed it was the Parr machine that got Grandfather John ousted; but Mr. García, town clerk of San Diego/Duval County (2006), tells me that Archie Parr did not move into the county's politics until Corrigan was defeated in 1902. Grandfather was defeated by some other Anglo interest, apparently.

2. A detail that Uncle Claude omitted in this account was Grandfather John's close acquaintance with Sheriff Pat Garrett, who killed the Brooklyn-born badman named Billy the Kid. This connection may have been of little importance to Uncle Claude, but it was of supreme interest to me as a boy, and he affirmed the acquaintanceship to me many years later when I visited him in San Antonio. (We boys who grew up in the 1930s were filled with the lore of the West, and Pat Garrett, like Sheriff Wyatt Earp— ("I never met a rich man who didn't have a guilty conscience")—was a legendary figure to us: "Our grandfather knew Pat Garrett, wow!") Garrett was the sheriff of Lincoln County and had captured the Kid and other men in a gang of rustlers at a place called Stinking Springs, a name I find supremely perfect for a Western saga. The Kid, a cold-blooded killer, had escaped jail and swore that he would one day come back and settle accounts with Garrett. Garrett thought that the Kid was in Mexico or elsewhere, but then he got word that Billy was in Fort Sumner, in San Miguel County, which put him outside Garrett's jurisdiction. Garrett had once been appointed a deputy U.S. marshal, however, and he had besides personal reasons for tracking down and doing away with Billy for good.

   This was the summer of 1881, the year my father was born. Billy was aware that

---

*My sister Aloïse recalled a different version of this incident in her *Supper at Great Elm*, for which see Part Two.

Garrett was coming for him, but he stayed the night in Fort Sumner anyhow, visiting a Mexican girlfriend. It was well past midnight when Garrett pushed open the bunkhouse door where he had been informed *"el Niño"* was sleeping. He was so terribly frightened of the killer that on hearing him respond to his question "Billy?" with a sibilated *"Quién es?"* he fanned three shots out of the drum of his drawn revolver, the first hitting the floorboards, the second killing Billy, the third slamming into the rafters.

There are several versions of this event, a couple of them more dramatic, but this is the way I remember it from a history I read many years ago that was published, I recall, by the University of Texas Press. Garrett, a fellow Irishman and lawman, was apparently well liked by our grandparents, because he stayed several times at their house in San Diego. He had a sad end, alcoholism reducing him to mule skinning for a living. On one trail he became irritated by the slow pace of the mule train ahead of him, shouting peremptorily, "Move out of my way." The young driver shouted back, "Why should I, old man?" To which the enraged former hero of the frontier replied, "Because I am Pat Garrett." Unimpressed, the fellow shot him dead.

CHAPTER FOUR

———— ✧ ————

William Frank Buckley of Texas (III): The Great Gift of Being Poor

THIS CHAPTER IS LIFTED FROM *CREDO: REFLECTIONS ON THE REPUBLIC 2000–2004,** under the title "Quintessential Americans—I: William F. Buckley, Sr."

MY FATHER WAS THE MOST COURAGEOUS MAN I EVER KNEW.

I did not know him well enough. He was forty-nine when I, his youngest son and eighth child, was born. Two generations separated us: I could as well have been his grandson.

His birth took place in Washington-on-the-Brazos (de Cristo), Texas, on July 12, 1881. Once the capital of Texas, Washington is now no longer even a town, just a graveyard. As I understand the story, his parents were trekking in a Conestoga wagon down from Canada, when they were compelled to stop for the event.

They continued to San Diego, just northeast of Corpus Christi, close by the Mexican border. San Diego was supposed to have a salubrious climate for people suffering from asthma, which was my grandfather John's

———————

*Peor Es Nada Press, 2005.

affliction.* The town boasted as well assorted *pistoleros* of Anglo and Mexican antecedence, wild but mostly harmless cowboys who hurrahed the place on Saturday nights, political caciques (the villainous Archie Parr machine, "Duke of Duval County"), and several well-educated residents (from Mexico, Spain, France, elsewhere) who came to the desolate town for the same reason that drew my grandfather. The few old houses still standing are built like forts. Comanches last raided in 1876, four years prior to my grandparents' arrival. (A posse was assembled that quickly and fruitlessly set out after those superhorsemen, dragging back to San Diego the next day, having accomplished nothing.) Gun play was frequent. An old gentleman[1] one afternoon pointed out to me the cavities in the paving stones of the sidewalks near the courthouse into which the blood of slain duelists puddled, a deadly fracas he had witnessed in his early boyhood.

Grandfather John raised sheep in cow country. An Irishman and a Catholic, he championed the oppressed Mexican laborer against the Protestant Anglo overlord, clashing with the politically tainted Texas rangers,† and in a short-lived blow for independence against the corrupt Parr machine was elected sheriff,[2] where he displayed unbecoming integrity and foolhardy courage, pacifying cowboys on their Saturday night sprees by inviting them to sober up in jail (he owned a nickel-plated Colt .45 Peacemaker‡ but almost never wore it). He was ousted from office after one term when—just as the polls were closing—thugs of the Parr machine voted some fifty Mexican *vaqueros* against John Buckley at gunpoint.§ After he died suddenly at the age of fifty-four, in Rockport, the train bearing his body to Austin for burial was followed by hundreds of mourners on horseback, most of them Mexican.

He left a straitened widow and a two-fifths-grown brood of five children.[3] Grandmother B removed to Austin, where her daughter Priscilla, the eldest child, getting a job in the Land Office, helped put her younger

---

*Inherited by children and grandchildren.

† One riot, one ranger: of whom, when I asked my aged Uncle Claude in San Antonio about them, he—rising up from his seat to stand tall above me, shaking with ire—declared, "They were the lice of the frontier!" So much for Hollywood.

‡ Passed down from my father to his eldest son, John, who passed it down to his son of the same name.

§ According to Mr. Meeks.

brother "Willie" through the university. He studied law and, to help pay his tuition, taught Spanish, in which he and his siblings were letter perfect. They were maybe not quite dirt poor, but poverty was their material condition. In everything else, they were rich.

They had their religion, they had family, they were reared in the great state of Texas and in the greatest country the world had ever known. "God, Family, Country" was my father's creed, which he repeated often to his children, adding always, acidly, "And in that order." He was a son of the frontier, and family unity was the axis of his life. When he graduated from *the* university* in 1903, he scented opportunity in Mexico City and set up his practice there, in the Zócalo, the old part of town—in turn helping to pay for the education of his younger brothers Claude and Edmund and his sister Eleanor. Claude joined him first. Their apartment was open to any young Texan down on his luck. Then, in 1907, in Tampico, the first of the oil booms gushed,† and Father and my uncle Claude moved there, bringing young Edmund along as soon as he had graduated. The brothers set up Buckley, Buckley & Buckley catty-corner from the imposing Greek Revival customs house, on the second floor above a saloon, reaching their offices every morning by stepping over the bodies of soused clients sleeping it off on the rickety outdoors staircase.‡

They prospered outrageously, clearing two hundred thousand dollars their second year, my father told me.§ Inasmuch as they were the only American lawyers in town who spoke Spanish faultlessly and were familiar with the Napoleonic Code that governs Mexican law (when the ubiquitous *mordida* does not subvert it),¶ the oil companies all wanted the Buckley boys to represent them. The brothers would flip coins to determine who pleaded for Companie Française, who for Standard Oil, who

---

*Oxford, Cambridge, Harvard, and Yale did not rate in his parlance. There was only one "the" university, and that was in Austin.

†The city was commonly referred to as First Oil Port. The wells were mostly short-lived gushers; the more permanent boom extended south, toward Veracruz.

‡This description came to me directly from Uncle Claude. (Their mother would have been scandalized.)

§ An enormous amount of money at that time.

¶ Known in France (in typical Gallic fashion) not as the "bite" but as the *douceur,* the "sweetness."

for British Petroleum, when these companies disputed a lease. What is relevant here is something he said to me, of a sudden, half a century after those early days in Mexico.

It was the summer of 1958. He was in Bad Gastein,[4] an Alpine village in Bavaria, crippled by several strokes, seeking refuge from his terrible asthmatic and bronchial allergies. His thoughts were concentrated on the welfare of his children, in witness a letter that he dictated to sister Priscilla at this time. God granted me the boon of visiting him for two weeks in late August and then for three days more, in Paris, prior to his departure on the boat train to Cherbourg. We had finished lunch at an outdoor garden restaurant, and my mother, my wife Betsy, our two little boys,* and Cuban acquaintances had departed, leaving father and son alone.

This was unusual for us. Through much of my childhood and adolescence, my father had been for me a distant, severe, formidable, though loving figure. I noticed early on that when he entered a room crowded with adults, attention immediately swung to him. Longtime business associates, all save one,[†] addressed him as Mr. or Señor Buckley, never as Will. They held him in a respect that bordered on nothing less than, as it seemed to us, reverence, impressing his children. The many exotic guests from Mexico who spent weekends at Great Elm, our house in Connecticut, including mustachioed onetime generals and governors of Mexican states, told stories about those early days that awed us. Behind his pince-nez and unassuming manner, our father had led a life of high adventure. He had been captured by bandits commissioned to murder him and had escaped thanks to his great friend and accountant, Cecilio Velasco (the bravest man, my father always said, *he* had ever known). He had faced ferocious Pancho Villa down twice, the last time when Villa was drunk[‡] and banqueting in Mexico City, in the gardens of Xochimilco, with Zapata, surrounded by his and Zapata's armed bandit-soldiers, the first time in a railroad coach of a train that Villa and his men had boarded

---

*Sons Hunt (William Huntting Buckley) and Jobie (Fergus Reid Buckley Jr.); Elizabeth was a very little girl, tended by her Scottish nurse, Anne Roonie.

†Tall and himself imposing, George Montgomery, a Coudert Brothers lawyer and a World War I ace who lost a leg in a crash following a dogfight.

‡This is wrong: Villa did not drink; it was his "Dorados" who were drunk.

and robbed, talking Villa—homicidal maniac as well as a patriot—into sparing the life of a conductor he was about to shoot.

No one awed our father. He had "indignantly" cold-shouldered President Woodrow Wilson when he was asked to accept the post of civil governor upon the American invasion of Veracruz ("We had no business meddling into Mexico's internal affairs"). He was booted from his own invention, the Petroleum Club, when he publicly inveighed against the corrupt habit the big oil companies of sweetening their positions through bribes.* He acted always according to his principles, which were deeply American, deeply independent, isolationist, self-reliant, distrustful of all government, and profoundly Catholic.

While scorning Wilson for his provincial Anglo arrogance, he himself plotted a counterrevolution in favor of the Cristeros, who were rising up against the atheist revolutionary government; if *that* wasn't meddling in Mexico's internal affairs, what was? In his eyes, however, a horse of a different color. All over Mexico, churches were being burned, nuns raped, and priest murdered or gunned down by firing squads.† His duty to God was plain. He procured grisly snapshots of the execution of the beloved and saintly Padre Pro Juárez, making hundreds of copies (I have a pack of them still), taking them to Washington, and showing them to influential congressmen. Using his personal funds, he bought guns and munitions and attempted to run them into Mexico from Brownsville. The shipment was intercepted, and he had the honor of having Article 33 of the new revolutionary constitution applied against him, its first victim. He was ex-

---

*Father was a many-barbed thorn in the association's side. His close friend, accountant, and business partner, Cecilio Velasco, wrote of him at this time: "At every meeting that took place in the petroleum club, W.F.B. found himself conducting a heated battle in an attempt to make his fellow Americans understand that they were in Mexico, a free and sovereign nation that demanded and deserved respect. But these gentlemen, who were ignorant of the Castilian tongue, were also ignorant of the English tongue when it was a question of advice that thwarted their ambitions and restricted their profits, and they reached the conclusion that W.F.B. was a poor, ignorant man, sick with a case of Latinism, contracted on the border, a baby in diapers with respect to the material, almost divine power of the unlimited money available to their companies. And at last, W.F.B. was expelled from said association as a pernicious and quarrelsome individual." *W.F.B.: An Appreciation.*

† Father's experience with militantly anti-Christian Mexican governments inclined him to be sympathetic to Franco, in Spain, fifteen years later.

pelled as an undesirable foreigner (we children were indignant over this injustice: our father was doing the right thing!), and all his valuable real estate and oil leases were confiscated.

He had at the time a wife fourteen years younger than he, two children, with another on the way. In an argument that, strictly speaking, was not his but that impinged on his faith, he had risked two decades of hard work and lost it all. The next eighteen years were to be for him a desperate struggle for survival. He had lost none of his nerve, none of his imagination. He proposed for example, that oil was to be found under Venezuela's Lake Maracaibo.* What an outrageous notion. This was the Depression. If anybody had money in the bank, who wanted to risk it with "Dry Hole Bill," as Wall Street mockingly dubbed him? He persevered. He went to Europe for financing, which is why my sister Maureen and I were born in Paris. And in 1939, he was at last vindicated.

Only in the high summer of 1958, when I was twenty-eight and he in the fast-closing days of his life, was I invited into his confidence as an adult. He told me wonderful stories about his parents and boyhood that I treasure.[4] But this afternoon he uttered the most important words I had from him ever. He said, "There's one gift, Reid, that I have not been able to give you children. You weren't born poor."†

Nor on the southwestern Texas frontier, where Washington was hard weeks of riding by horseback to the railhead at Kansas City and then another two days by train away; where egalitarianism was determined by the moral credentials of the individual, not his antecedence or wealth. He had told me how he and his friends were unable to afford the ten-cents admission to *the* university baseball games (they loved baseball; in his old age, he was still able to whack a softball one hundred fifty yards over the lawn and swimming pool of Great Elm). He and his friends would walk 'round and 'round the fenced ballpark, listening to the crowd, trying to deduce the score, meantime engaging in the earnest conversation of young men, confirming everlasting friendships.

Otherwise, all entertainment was in the bosom of the family, at the

---

*He may well have proposed this, as our childhood memory instructs us, but his concessions at that time were in the jungles of eastern Venezuela.

†To which my witty and irreverent eldest brother, John, retorted, when I first told him this story, "Thank God!" But brother James makes this point clear in his memoirs.

two-story Victorian house on a corner of Lavaca Street. There was no money to spend outside the home, and there was no place to go except to a saloon or dance hall, which, under the strict eye of Grandmother B, these young people shunned. Conversation with siblings and close friends made up their social life. The girls sang, and some young person played piano. They loved to dance. The gramophone was a boon. Waltzes, polkas, Virginia reels. I remember vividly my spinster aunts Priscilla and Eleanor, in their late seventies (Aunt Eleanor had been a beauty and had aged with beauty yet tracing her faded features), raising their skirts to dainty ankles, singing and dancing in tandem, "Put your little foot, put your little foot, put your little foot right down!"[5] They loved Mexican ballads, accompanied (if at all) by piano, the guitar, the mandolin, and banjo. Father, who played no instrument to our knowledge, raised his children after this manner.

I stray. "You were not born poor," he repeated. That great boon he could not bequeath to us. Born to poverty, he and his siblings had learned to cultivate the human bonds that made their poverty light. Material rewards were in the hands of God, who would provide what was best for what mattered, which was the souls of His creatures. Father translated this general concept, or worldview, into a single word: character. Character was the most important attribute that any of his children should cultivate (along with modesty). Character gave sand, spine, grit, fortitude, daring. Character enabled a young person to shoulder responsibilities that might founder other young people. To God everything was owed. Family was otherwise the foremost and unbreachable responsibility. To country went everything that was not owed to God and family. Character was what saw a body through the hard times and, when fortune smiled, prevented him from losing his humility of spirit. Character was what turned the lonely young man's steps in a strange city firmly from the saloons and the bawdy houses (these were unmentionable) and prevented him from "wasting his substance" in cards. Character was the self-discipline that in old age had him at Mass every Sunday and holy day (even when there was medical excuse for letting the worship slip by), and that, until the succession of strokes disabled him, brought him to his knees every single night beside his bed, to pray to our Lord God for forgiveness, faith, hope, and strength. Character was what enabled him to face down Pancho Villa, President Wilson, and General Álvaro Obregón of Mexico.

"Because we were poor, Reid," he explained simply, his round, china-blue eyes resting on his maverick son (we had clashed several times in my difficult adolescence), "I was able to . . . I was inclined . . . I wasn't [he searched for the right word] *prevented* from—risking. Everything. You see, when you are born poor, you can never be worse off than you were."

It was poverty that endowed my father with character and the compassion to do countless anonymous charitable works. I saw Father and Mother off on the boat train to Cherbourg. As the train began moving and gathering speed, I caught his face gazing out the window at Betsy and me on the platform, staring hard at us, tears flowing down his cheeks. When the news of his death reached me ten days later, in Marbella, Spain (he was stricken on the high seas), I called my Chesapeake Bay retriever to my side and walked up through a young forest of umbrella pines high on the sere slope of the Sierra Bermeja, where I sat on a stone and looked out upon the sea far below, gusts of grief shaking me and tears blinding me as I gazed at the wedge of Gibraltar in the opalescent distance, watching the sun set and the sky turn violet and pink and yellow before night billowed in from the west, lapping the straits up. I have never felt so bereft.

NOTES

———

1. Walter Meeks by name, longtime town clerk, railroad engineer, childhood playmate of Aunt Eleanor and Uncle Edmund—an extraordinary man whom Tasa and I visited and lodged with in 1974. He is the source of my knowledge of San Diego in the times of my father and grandfather.
2. This may be family myth, according to Mr. García, county clerk of Duval County; but Grandfather John's stand against the corrupt Parr machine is such a vividly recalled family tradition that I think it safe to suppose that the Corrigan who defeated our grandfather was a Parr man.
3. The eldest son, named John also, was killed when he was not yet twenty-one (he was, we think, eighteen) in a knife fight, in a saloon, with a Mexican. (My sister Patricia recalls that it was a shooting.) His name was never in my memory mentioned by my father or uncles.
4. Mother at once invented a tale about twin brothers, Bad and Good Gadstein, with which she entertained my two little boys. Had something to do with a witch and why there was a roaring river creating a chasm between the two parts of the town.
5. Among his accounts of family life, he explained how it came about that we Buckleys

emigrated to the new world. Our great-grandfather John (1805–1880) was an Irish Protestant, and a member of the Orange Society to boot. But he married a Catholic girl, Ellenor Doran (1821–1899), from the south of Ireland (Limerick).* This led to complications. The Orangemen used to have an annual celebration on July 12, and there was always a parade. Part of the parade route cut across the bottom piece of our ancestor's farm. He went to the chiefs of the Orangemen, asking them to alter the route, since he had recently married and did not wish to offend his bride. He said, to the effect, "I respect her religion just as she respects mine."

But they told him they had always cut across his farm, and no Catholic, even if she were the wife of a good Orangeman, was going to stop them. He tried to reason with them, my father related, but these things weren't to be reasoned over. So he went home.

Early in the morning of July 12, Great-grandfather John went out and stood guard by the sty the Orangemen would have to cross to step on his farm. He waited there until the leaders of the parade came up to it, warning them, "Don't put a foot on my land." They paid no attention to him—and one of the leaders, a young man, began climbing across. John took up a plowshare† and brought it down on his head. Unsurprisingly, he was seized and thrown into the clinker and was kept locked up several days while everyone waited to see whether the fellow was going to die. He didn't. But upon Great-grandfather's release, it was thought wise for him to depart from Ireland.

This incident took place in the 1840s. The family went to Quebec first and then on to Ontario. The first John Buckley of which we have any notion didn't change his faith, but the children were raised as Catholics. Which gives us some idea about our great-grandmother Ellenor Doran. She must have been pretty enough to motivate her farmer husband into an act of violence against his coreligionists, or attractive enough to displace, in her passionate husband (if that is what we can judge him to have been from the one definite thing we know about him), one passion for another. It was their asthmatic son John C. Buckley who moved south to Texas.

He was a large and lovable man by Father's account, uncommunicative by Uncle Claude's account, and like his father (and also like his son Willie, our father), he was prone to unpopular attitudes. Grandfather was a sheepraiser in cattle country, and he never used a gun in his life in a culture in which gun play was frequent. Physically, he was bull strong, challenging Terrible Turks in the ring—yet he died of a stroke in Rockport, Texas, at just fifty-two, when our father was a very young man.

Father remembered distinctly when he got the news of his Orangeman grandfather's death. He was just a boy, he told me, and as he was coming back home with a load of firewood (mesquite and cottonwood branches, I think we can guess), his father

---

*He was sixteen years older than his bride, establishing a male Buckley custom; our father was fourteen years older than our mother.
†This word was used in describing the incident to me. Our great-grandfather John must have been an immensely strong man, as we know was his son John, our grandfather.

met him at the doorway and said to him, "Come in, Willie. There's something serious your mother wants to tell you."

My father put down his wood. Grandmother B, born Mary Ann Langford, in 1848, in what is now Burlington, Canada, died the year I was born, 1930. Our father never-failingly referred to her as "a saint," but she has survived in the memories of my older siblings as a formidable personality. We celebrated Father's birthday on July 13. Actually, he had been born a day earlier, on the 12th—Orangeman's Day! Grandmother would not have that, so she concealed the birth of the infant for twenty-four hours.

Her pictures show a little woman with evident moral authority. I think we can assume that Father wiped his hands on his britches and scraped his shoes on the mat of the veranda before walking into the parlor. There sat Grandmother B, he related to me, red-eyed and weeping, the letter that brought the news on a little table in front of her. (The table was round, he recalled, covered with a velvet red cloth from which tassels hung.) She drew my father to her, and she said, "Willie, a sad thing has happened—your grandfather died last week." She went on: "But we have a great consolation. Just before he died, he accepted the Last Sacraments." Grandfather John leaned toward his son Willie at this point, whispering behind his hand, "He must have been unconscious."

These are probably the only words in the history of our family that have come down over the three generations exactly as they were spoken. How my father laughed when he recounted the story to me!*

6. They were a droll pair, Aunts Priscilla and Eleanor, with lively, acerbic wit, Eleanor's the more gentle but every bit as cutting as Priscilla's when it touched on family, religion, or Texas, on which topics they became instantly serious. They dressed commonly in lavender or black with white lace choke collars (Priscilla) or deep V-necks (Eleanor) and maybe a lavender or red shawl. Aunt Eleanor possessed one of the softest voices and most beautiful Texas accents I have ever heard. She had been "crossed" in love. We children were never given to know the how or the why, but for many, many years, until the very last, she never went to Mass. This in no way affected her loyalty to the Church, which could be fierce.

---

* There's a historical problem here that I'll mention further on.

CHAPTER FIVE

———— ᐅᐣ ————

Aloïse Steiner of New Orleans (I): George Henry Watson, Shiloh, the Lee Connection

THEN THERE WAS THE LEE CONNECTION.

Robert E. Lee, *the* Lee. My siblings and I grew up under the impression that we were collaterally related to the hero of the Confederacy, which was all right with us, because he is surely the noblest man of historical stature to have been produced by our American nation, surpassing in his Christian character George Washington.

Alas, there is nothing on record to suggest kinship between Mary Ann Lee of St. Louis and the Virginia Lees. My Perrier cousins* have searched municipal records in New Orleans and have discovered *rien*. (Of everything, too). No matter, cousin Claude Perrier's dear wife, Alice, is convinced of the story. My cousin Joan, Claude's sister, on the other hand, a very practical woman not given to fond fancies, deems it bunkum. In one of the census pages studied by Joan Perrier, Mary Ann Lee responded (more than a century ago) that her parents had been born in Ireland, which makes it highly improbable that she was related to the Virginia line. Mary Ann was born in St. Louis in 1857. She was traveling on a

---

*Mother's sister Inez married Claude Perrier, a doctor who was born and brought up in the Vieux Carré of New Orleans.

boat, presumably a paddlewheeler and down the Mississippi, presumably on the way to New Orleans, when her mother died (we have no knowledge of the fate of her father or of the year and date), which is when she was befriended by a French family, Debeaux or Devaux—the memory of our source for this information (Joan's mother, Inez, my aunt) is not certain here.

We know almost nothing about Mary Ann Lee or about her guardians (except their last name). The suggestion has passed down that she had a little money and that it was stolen by the French couple. This may be a canard. (Which is worse than canned humor and ketchup, as Andy Warhol would tell you.) I have heard nothing to verify it. To the contrary, I recollect hearing from I-cannot-pin-down-what-source that they were affectionate guardians, so I prefer to believe that if they took any money from Great-grandmother Mary Ann, this was necessary for their (and consequently her) survival.

Cousin Joan, however, the realist, writes me flatly: "They took what money she had. Similar to the story of Lady Jane." Joan found a Mary Ann Lee in the New Orleans census, "a maid servant of a large family. . . . I next find Mary Ann in a marriage certificate to Henry Wassem in 1869." I *know* that Mary Ann was stunningly pretty redhead. (I extrapolate back from her daughters and granddaughters.)

George Henry Wassem was a giant for his times, six feet four inches tall. It is from him (if we ignore Mary Ann) we have the red hair that ran through my aunt Inez and to her children and surfaced in my brother John, my sister Patricia, and me.* (The hot temper comes with it.) It is from him also that we have the six-footers in my generation (Jim and Bill).† His daughter Marie Louise (our grandmother) measured an imposing five foot eight (or ten, depending on the recollection), but she married Grandfather Aloysius Steiner, who measured five foot four (or five, depending on the recollection), hence our mother (five foot one), our wee sister Carol (five feet flat), my other sisters (five-three to five-five), my brother John (five-eight), and I (five-nine plus).

---

* And my grandson Aiden, by my artist son Claude.
† Irish peasants are not tall. On the paternal side, our family was Anglo-Irish. Our father measured five foot eleven, which was tall in his times. He was so slim into his early middle age that he seemed taller.

Aloïse Steiner,
c. 1910.

George Henry Wassem sprang from a military tradition. His father, John Henry, born in 1804, had served in the Hessian army (he was a sergeant)* before moving to New Orleans, when and for what reasons unknown.† His son, born in 1843—our maternal great-grandfather—fought in Shiloh and other battles, was wounded, and returned to his regiment for more fighting.

We have a eulogy delivered at Great-grandfather Wassem's funeral by

---

*And a Lutheran. (Thanks to Philip the Magnanimous, Hesse's greatest prince, who introduced Lutheranism into Hesse in 1526.)

†The meager details of his hegira became the basis, I now realize, for the villainous Dr. Horace Forsthoefel in my novel *Saving DeSaussure Swamp: A Love Story.*

Martial Gosselin, former sergeant in Company F of the Crescent Regiment.* It paints a poignant picture of the war from the point of view of a humble participant who obeyed orders unquestioningly and who did his duty with unflinching resolve.

According to Sergeant Gosselin, it was in the latter part of February 1862 that Henry Wassem enlisted. He was nineteen years old and a volunteer, as were they all. Son of an immigrant of modest means, he owned no slaves, but Louisiana was the state into which he had been born and for which he would fight.

The Crescent was mustered early in March and one month later, on April 4—with almost no training—was ordered to "the seat of war" at Shiloh, Tennessee.

The young men arrived "drenched to the skin." It continued raining all that night, Sergeant Gosselin reports. The following morning, "the regiment was ordered to advance, which we did." Please keep in mind that these were city boys in the main, who, having never in their lives shot a rifle or musket at as much as a squirrel, now, with just one month of training, were being ordered into battle, where they would shoot at blue-clad boys their age. The action began lightheartedly, Gosselin reports:

> In going to the position assigned to us in the line of battle, we came up to General Beauregard, who was mounted on a stump near the enemy. He called out to us: "Boys, fire low and make every shot count." We gave him three rousing cheers and were very shortly after engaged in the great battle. After driving the enemy from our front, we were ordered to *double quick* [emphasis in the original] to the left. After running about two miles, we were halted to catch our breath, and soon after that the regiment was ordered to charge Gen. Prentiss, which it did in gallant style.

Notice the absence of introverted morbidity in this relation, so unlike a contemporary news agency battlefield account. There is no mention here of the dead and wounded, of the screaming shells and the rattling musketry and the cries and shouts and yells and shrieks of pain. No, the charge

---

*The accompanying letter is dated July 24, 1907, five years after the event; someone in the family back when must have asked for a copy.

was made "in gallant style," which was the important matter to record, even half a century later.

> The result of the charge was that Prentiss and his brigade were cap-
> tured. We took 3,500 prisoners with a force of about 1000 men. [What
> does one do with captives three and a half times one's number?] The
> fight was continued in another part of the field late in the evening.
> After the firing ceased, we threw ourselves down on the field of battle
> and secured what little sleep we could, as the enemy's gunboats shelled
> us all night.

Note also the clear moral position: the men they were fighting were the enemy. These were young men, too, giving battle for what they believed, but they were the enemy. The enemy gave no quarter during that long night, and none was expected the next day.

> Very early the next morning, the battle was renewed with great vigor
> on our side, but Gen. Grant was reinforced [that] night with 15,000
> men, and we were compelled to fight him with our rank[s] very much
> depleted and worn out by the long march. We were then fighting an
> army more than double our own. The fight raged all day, which was
> then the 7th of April, until late in the evening.

Here Sergeant Gosselin does reflect on the cost of battle, in terse, economical, and manly terms.

> It was a terrible slaughter, the ground being covered with dead and
> wounded. We were ordered to fall back, which we did, in line of battle.
> It was a beautiful sight to see our retreating lines facing the enemy.

There is awesome beauty and heart-wrenching humanity in this simple statement. They had been defeated by superior numbers; they were not licked (and never would be—it was the generals who surrendered, beginning with Robert E. Lee, not the cripples and the young boys and the aging men who, toward the end, filled the ranks). The Battle of Shiloh, which our great-grandfather fought, was in retrospect the crucial contest of the Civil War. It was during that first day of battle that William Tecumseh Sherman redeemed a sunken military reputation—by his courage, three horses shot out from under him, twice wounded, balls riddling his uniform jacket yet miraculously missing his chest.[1] (On the other side, in the course of proving himself a charismatic cavalry officer, Nathan Bedford Forrest also narrowly escaped death.) Shiloh determined the long-term destinies of victors and vanquished, giving rise to the self-exculpating myth that fastened on the South after Appomattox, severely disfiguring the moral character of my mother and her coevals, and breeding one hundred years of wrong (for an explanation of which, see Chapter Six).

Back to our narrative:

Grant was so badly used up in these two days fighting that he did not pursue us. We kept falling back until we reached Corinth. The army rested at the battle place for about three weeks, when we were ordered to the front again, and we met the enemy in force at Farmington, Tenn. We engaged the enemy on the 12th of May, and a spirited fight took place, but we were forced to retreat on account of overwhelming numbers.

Young men were wounded, disfigured, mutilated, killed at Farmington, which was no small matter to them; but Sergeant Gosselin reflects that what happened here

was a small affair compared to Shiloh, and very little mention is made of it. The regiment went back to Corinth where it was engaged in several skirmishes. Henry Wassem was in all these engagements and was conspicuous for his bravery.

The Crescent Regiment at last went into bivouac, "resting and recruiting our depleted ranks," which was followed by a series of maneuvers up and down the regiment's sector of the war, where feasible boarding steamboats but mostly getting where they had to go on foot and fighting almost all the time.

[T]he little army marched down Bayou Lafourche, where we nearly froze to death. We reached Labadeville in the middle of October, where we [once again] met the enemy, and here we fought a bloody battle, the Crescent Regiment losing more than half its number, many were wounded and some taken prisoner. We retreated down the Bayou to Thibodeaux, and took [railway] cars from Morgan City.

The wearying forced marches continued until the regiment crossed Berwick Bay and pushed up Bayou Teche "as far as Brisland, where we halted and entrenched ourselves."

The sergeant is speaking now of veterans of one very great battle and several succeeding actions, and in parentheses, he takes stock: "The punishment inflicted on the enemy was very great, as we killed and wounded more of them than we had in the engagement." Once more, note the clarity of purpose and the absence of self-pity: they were not girly men during the Civil War.[2]

But the Crescent Regiment was taking losses in every engagement that it could not afford, and the pursuit was relentless.

On the 9th of April, 1863, the enemy being about 15,000 strong, attacked our little force of 5,000 men, and we drove them back every time they charged us. After fighting . . . for two days, we were compelled to retreat, as the enemy was cutting us off at Franklin, and we only escaped by taking a back road, which the enemy, fortunately for us, knew nothing about. The first day of the retreat, we marched 35 miles . . . we had to do it to keep from being taken prisoners. We kept on retreating until we reached Natchitoches, where we camped for some time to rest.

The respite was brief, however; within three short weeks, they were called back into action, in the process of which a homely side of Great-grandfather Wassem is revealed.

[A]fter resting . . . we were ordered back to the Teche country. [They crossed Berwick Bay north of the city] by taking skiffs and all kinds of water crafts . . . after we had formed our line, we charged Morgan City and captured all the troops quartered there, also a large quantity of [commissary] stores, among the lot was a barrel of wine, which the writer of this article confiscated, Comrade Wassem and a good many of the boys helped me drink it up.

The fighting and the marching do not let up for the Crescent Regiment, inflicting losses on the enemy, taking losses. They are in action all over south Louisiana, once, near Hog Point, engaging the enemy's gunboats on the Mississippi River for two days (this was "infantry and light infantry fighting gunboats," Gosselin writes, emphasizing the disparity) and slogging "many weary miles through rain and the most sticking mud that I ever saw—the mud was so sticky that it pulled off all of our worn out shoes, and we were compelled . . . to march barefoot."

Here is the last installment of Sergeant Gosselin's report, which describes in spare but excruciating detail the dirty, frustrating, and exhausting war that my great-grandfather's regiment was called upon to endure:

We crossed the Red River over to Pineville and started for Monroe. After marching many miles through roads almost impassable with mud, we finally reached the Ouachita River and crossed it on the 1st day of January, 1864, under a blinding rain. After we got to camp, it was impossible to sleep, on account of the wet grounds. It began snowing during the night, and a freeze set in. On our march to Monticello, Ark., it was nothing but "ice" "ice" "ice," every man in the regiment being nearly frozen to death. Comrade Wassem was with us all the time, and helped to keep our spirits up. After reaching Ark., we were ordered back to below Alexandria to [stop] Gen. Banks, who was marching up Red River with a very large army, also a fleet of gunboats. Our little army was sent to hold him in check, but we had to fall back before superior numbers.

Gosselin does not mention the psychological exhaustion that must have preyed on the Crescent Regiment, which in almost every action over three long years of war was ordered to attack or to defend against forces heavily outnumbering them. Great-grandfather's role in keeping "our spirits up" must have been invaluable and testifies to his strength of character (we don't know what he actually did, or said, or made manifest by example). In this age, when people scarcely exercise at all, and drive or ride everywhere in a controlled environment, it may be difficult for readers to imagine for themselves what it must have been like to slog barefoot through mud, to endure sweltering heat and bitter cold, and to fight mortal actions again and again against prohibitive odds.

Concluding:

> Our force at that time comprised 5,000 troops, and all we could do was to harass the enemy as much as possible. We continued retreating until we arrived at Mansfield. Here we received reinforcements of 4,000 men, making a total of 9,000. Gen. Taylor decided to give battle to Banks, and on the 8th of April we advanced and formed our line of battle. We waited for several hours for the enemy to open the engagement, as they were three times more numerous than we were. Mouton's brigade composed of the 18th, 28th, Crescent Regiments and Polignac Brigade of Texans were ordered to charge the enemy who was [sic] concealed in the woods and behind rail fences. We charge[d] through an open field right up to the enemy, where we met such a hot fire that we had to halt. We made another charge and captured 28 pieces of artillery [which had been firing at them], over 250 wagons loaded with commissary stores and over two thousand prisoners. It was a dearly . . .

And there the fragment ends, leaving this reader in a fit of frustration. That begun sentence must have said something on the order that it was a dearly bought victory, costing one can only guess how many casualties, dead and wounded.

Heaven knows what happened to the rest of the story; but the covering letter by Sergeant Gosselin is headed "Sheet #4," and it reads:

> Every Captain in the Crescent Regiment [he must be referring to the charge described above] was either killed or wounded, with the exception of Captain Claiborne. It was in this battle that Comrade Wassem was wounded. After recovering . . . he rejoined the regiment and participated in the Battle of Mansura. A few days after that he was again in the Battle of Yellow Bayou, where we drove the remnants of Banks' army to the cover of his gunboats. The last fight of the regiment was at Simsport, on the Atchafalaya River, with a fleet of gunboats, which we finally drove off. From there we were ordered to Natchitoches,

where we camped until our surrender on the 6th of June, 1865 [two months after Appomattox].

The sergeant's parting words about our great-grandfather are these:

Comrade Wassem was with us all through the war and participated in all the battles of the regiment, with the exception of Pleasant Hill and Monetts Ferry. He would also have been in this battle had it not been for his wounds. I can only add that he was a brave and gallant soldier, and performed his duty like a man, throughout the war. His life, after reaching his native city, until his death, was a most beautiful and honorable one.

After Appomattox, our maternal great-grandfather plied the barber's trade on Royal Street in New Orleans. The equipment for Henry Wassem's shop, according to Aunt Inez, was designed by John Henry, his father, who was reputedly an engineer.

Truly? Or a plumber? (The Steiner girls had a tendency to romanticize.) Some time around 1870 or 1872, the young couple moved to Port Gibson, where George Henry continued cutting hair and shaving beards and popping facial pustules for a living, which could not have been handsome, because, according to the records cousin Joan diligently researched, he owned no property. For those who don't know the place, Port Gibson is a beautiful Mississippi town, set on a curve of Bayou Pierre. Not far from the great river, it is filled with fine houses that survived the war thanks (surprisingly) to Ulysses S. Grant, who, in May 1863, having defeated the Confederates (Great-grandfather Wassem among them) in a sharp clash and marching through the town on his way to Vicksburg (twenty-eight miles to the north), pronounced that it was too beautiful to burn.*

Mary Ann Lee and George Henry Wassem had three children: Marie Louise (my grandmother, who married Aloysius Steiner), Josephine Edvidge ("Aunty" to everybody; she married Émile Berthier), and George, who died in 1878 of yellow fever. Old John Henry Wassem died in Port Gibson in 1890; his son, George Henry, barber and Confederate war hero,

---

*Is there in the sanguinary annals of war a statement from a general more endearing?

died in New Orleans on December 26, 1902, fifty-nine years old, while visiting his daughter Marie Louise for Christmas.

The event must have been sudden and shocking, though Great-grandfather Wassem had to have been suffering for a long time. It took place in the Steiner home of that time on 3634 Magazine Street. The certificate states that George Henry Wassem, resident of Port Gibson, died (miserably) of Bright's disease (to people who are gifted with split tongues, commonly known as glomerulonephritis), which is an infection of the kidneys producing inflammation and severe back pains before shriveling them up until they are little more than scar tissue.

Descended from a Confederate hero we are; excepting fond tradition and admiration of the man, however (I, for one, venerated him), there is no evidence linking us to Robert E. Lee. That tradition, nonetheless, ran strong in my mother. For her, it was formative. In turn, it was formative for her children.

NOTES

1. It was his experience in Shiloh that determined Sherman never again, if ever he could help it, to indulge in the formalized massacre of conventional battle, which implanted in him the strategy of marching through the South's infrastructure and destroying it as ultimately more merciful than killing thousands upon thousands of young men in ferocious combat.

2. The point I am making here in no way disparages our volunteer forces fighting in Iraq and elsewhere, who are worthy of all respect. The entire American population was involved, was committed, and gave battle. That moral character is absent in the American people today; in substantiation of which, see my prose books *USA Today, Credo,* several pamphlets, and the novels in the trilogy *Canticle of the Thrush.*

CHAPTER SIX

——— ⌘ ———

Aloïse Steiner of New Orleans (II): The Education of a Southern Belle, the Lost Cause, and Racism

ON JANUARY 18, 1907, GENERAL STEPHEN D. LEE VISITED NEW ORleans.

This was a major event to which the *Daily Picayune* devoted a major article. Charleston-born (1833), distantly related to the Robert E. Lees, Stephen Lee was a distinguished gentleman. A West Pointer and an artillery officer, he commanded cavalry as well as cannon during the Civil War. He rose to be the youngest lieutenant general in the Confederate Army (he was just thirty years old), seeing action in First and Second Manassas (Bull Run) and Antietam, where he demonstrated that he was personally valiant and a reliable captain under fire. Ho-hum.

We tend to trivialize the past. We tend to summon to our minds potbellied American Legion veterans in tasseled blue garrison caps and foolish uniforms that never fit, sweating as they march down Main Street under a broiling fourth of July sun; the image we have of Confederate veterans is of goateed, white-haired, red-faced blusterers unable to let go of the past or forgive it.

To my generation, Pearl Harbor is a fading trauma. Not six years gone by, as I write, the shock of September 11, 2001, is fast diminishing. Most Americans in this androgynous and self-indulgent generation cannot begin to conceive the horror of the slaughter of the Civil War. During the fifteen years of the Vietnam agony, which had us tearing at the entrails of our republic, we lost a net 55,000 men killed. At that time, the population of the United States was around 250 million.

Back in the 1860s, the population of our country ran at around 30 million, North and South. Yet in a single engagement—the three days of Gettysburg—casualties on both sides exceeded 51,000, a very high percentage of whom died (there was no penicillin). Repeat, back then, when our country's population, North and South, was one-eighth the population of the Vietnam years, the casualties of *a single battle* almost matched those suffered a century later over a time span of fifteen years. In Iraq, as I write, we have lost 3,500-plus dead in four-plus years, we are 300 million Americans strong, and we are weary.

The comparisons instruct. During the two days of Shiloh, in which our mother's grandfather fought as a recruit,* 20,000 young men fell. The Civil War was a horror that is almost unimaginable, only to be compared in the New World to the War of the Triple Alliance (1865–1870) that pitted Paraguay against Brazil, Argentina, and a puppet government in Uruguay; to World War I's ten-month Battle of Verdun, which killed 800,000 Frenchmen, Germans, and Englishmen, or the 1.4 million French soldiers killed during that awful holocaust, destroying the French nation; to the Spanish Civil War (1936–1939) with its eerie similarities to our own (the Spanish population was 30 million during their terrible ordeal; they sustained losses of 600,000 dead);† and to such horrendous ideological massacres as those of the *kulaks* under Stalin, the peasants under Mao, the entire Cambodian people under Pol Pot, and, recently, the genocide in Rwanda‡ and Darfur. It is little wonder that feelings ran high in the South until the veterans of the Civil War died off.

We are hard put indeed to conceive in our imaginations the terrible struggle that the Civil War was and the enduring effect it had on Northerners and Southerners alike, but mostly on Southerners, the defeated; and young people in this country today, including my children, my nieces

---

*It was not at Shiloh that he was wounded, but later.

†The number of dead is popularly recalled as one million, that figure is an estimate of the casualties (of which many, many died also).

‡The appalling human tragedy of which is reduced to a Gilbert and Sullivan libretto because of the names of the victims (Tutsis) and their persecutors (Hutus).

and nephews, and my grandchildren, cannot imagine what it requires in terms of moral grit to command men in battle—to send them to die. Only 11 percent of living Americans have been under arms. We are now almost a generation removed from the last time when we, *as a people,* united in our determination and righteousness, fought a war. The fate of America in the War on Terrorism rests on the valor and resolve of a volunteer army. The experience of personally engaging in combat and leading other men to their deaths is beyond the ken of most Americans, spoiled by the freedom and security others have earned for us.

Young Stephen Lee, for example, not yet thirty, was ordered to take command of the defenses of the strategically crucial city of Vicksburg. This was an enormous responsibility, which, it is written, he discharged with "great credit" until the surrender of the city on July 4, 1863, to Ulysses S. Grant (who, you will remember, had marched up from Port Gibson). Stephen Lee was taken prisoner. He was later exchanged, getting right back into the fray under the fiery and impetuous General Hood of Texas in the hell-for-leather attack on Nashville.* Stephen Lee fought commendably in that engagement, too. He was credited with keeping his troops "closed up and well in hand" for three consecutive days while the rest of the army disintegrated around him, and though he was wounded, he formed a fighting rear guard in what was otherwise a rout. The man was heroic.

After the war, he settled in Mississippi, which had been his principal territorial command. He was out of a job, as were all regular army officers who served under the Confederacy. How he supported himself I don't know, though his wife hailed from Mississippi, which may have helped. (Nepotism is a time-honored Southern tradition, bred of the need for survival.) In 1878, he became president of what was then the Agricultural and Mechanical College (now Mississippi University) and served also as commander-in-chief of the United Confederate Veterans. He helped promote women's rights, wrote on historical subjects, and strove to preserve the Vicksburg battle sites, where he died in 1908 at the ripe old age of seventy-five—one year after his visit to New Orleans. (Google has nothing more to say of the man, so I shan't, either.)

He was in New Orleans for the celebration of the one-hundredth an-

---

*He played hell in Tennessee, as "The Yellow Rose of Texas" reminds us.

niversary of the birth of his distant cousin, who was commonly alluded to in those days, in the South, as the "immortal" Robert E. Lee. Were it not for the racism that was so often attached to the awe, regard, and affection for Lee, his near worship by the South would be commendable. He is, of course, not to blame for the sins of his contemporaries. He opposed secession. He freed his slaves in his lifetime (catch liberal icon Thomas Jefferson doing that!) and advocated emancipation during the war. When, at a meeting of I forget what Episcopal church, in what town, shortly after Appomattox, a tall black man in the otherwise lily-white congregation stood up and presented himself first at the communion rail (just dwell a moment on the courage this must have required), Robert E. Lee rose from his pew and knelt beside the man. Lee died of war-related exhaustion in 1870, having served dutifully and with surprising success as president of Washington College (the students revered him), now Washington and Lee.

New Orleans went all out for General Stephen D. Lee's visit. The city was just then emerging from Reconstruction, and people were (at last) making a little money. This General Lee was met at the railroad station by committees of various Confederate associations. In its report (after the smug practice of the day), the *Daily Picayune* editorialized that the people of the city "are very glad that he [Stephen Lee] had consented to be present." We don't truly know how the unwashed masses felt about it, of course, not to mention ex-slaves, but among those giving the general welcome at the station were W. O. Hart, Mrs. D. A. S. Vaught, Miss Katie Childress, Mrs. J. Pinckney Smith (may we assume of the Charleston Pinckneys?), Miss Belle Van Horn, Mrs. Paul Israel, Miss Lelia Lee Riddell, Miss Shaw (who she?), Mrs. H. Riddell, Colonel E. M. Hudson, Gen. John Glynn, General W. J. Behan, T. W. Castleman, "and others."

Names. These were all living persons, and one presumes *personages* in the city, in their day. (There is no Steiner mentioned here, nor a Mr. Moriarity, successful new-rich constructor that he may have been.)[1] The bosoms of the ladies were aflutter, we may suppose that the men were no less impressed with the solemnity of the occasion. The program for the Lee celebration at Gibson Hall, Tulane University, promised "some very interesting features," the newspaper continued. Ceremonies were to open properly with a prayer by Rev. Dr. Rice, "followed by the singing of General Lee's favorite hymn, 'How Firm in Foundation, Ye Saints of the Lord,' by the Tulane choir." President Craighead of Tulane was then to deliver an address, and "Miss Josie Handy, of Newcomb [College] was to recite [the thrilling] 'Lee At the Wilderness.'" A. Giffen Levy, otherwise unidentified, presumably known to the readers of the *Daily Picayune* and New Orleans society, was then to read General Lee's farewell address to the Army—mercifully brief, yet one of the noblest messages in the annals of this country—and Miss Emily Miller "will recite 'The Sword of Lee.'" This was just for starters. Only then followed an oration by a gentleman called Theodore Wilkinson.

One may assume Mr. Wilkinson's address ran not less than an hour, recalling the nobility of Robert E. Lee and the great victories at Second Manassas, at Fredericksburg, at Chancellorsville with its tragic aftermath, and, possibly, the strange, disastrous, dilatory delay of General James Longstreet in opening up his artillery until *too late* on that desperate third morn of Gettysburg—had Jackson been alive, there would have been no bullheaded disagreement with the great Lee's orders—thus dooming George E. Picket's glorious and unforgettable charge and, with it, the Confederacy.

This merely commenced the ordeal of General Stephen Lee. Sundry more events were scheduled for his two-day visit. The social endurance of human beings in the nineteenth century does not fail to amaze. Responsible committees and the names of everyone serving on them are duly recorded in the *Daily Picayune* account. The Howard Memorial Library had arranged for an exhibition of "a complete collection of books bearing on the life and work of General Lee and will exhibit [the next day] on the 19th a large collection of his portraits." Massa Robert was an industry. A Mr. J. B. Rosser Jr., of Camp Beauregard, was "assigned to deliver an address on General Lee at the Beauregard School today," which doubtless dwelled on the nobility of Robert E. Lee and the great routs of Union troops at Second Manassas, at Fredericksburg, at Chancellorsville, and, quite possibly also, the inexplicable dilatoriness of General James Longstreet (Lee's "bulldog") in opening up his artillery until *too late* on that tragic third morn of Gettysburg, which doomed George E. Picket's glorious charge and the Confederacy.

The exercises of the Robert E. Lee School concern us. "The building has been beautifully decorated with Confederate and American flags," reports the *Daily Picayune,* switching, for some reason, to the past tense, "and on the platform was a representative gathering consisting of delegates from each of the Confederate organizations of the city: Mrs. D. N. S. Vaught, President of the United Daughters of the Confederacy . . ." There follows a lengthy list of notables, after which comes a description and biographical sketch of General Stephen D. Lee, who, at last—at long last—rose to speak.

What he said was wholly satisfactory to his audience, in heavy proportion female. He was proud to see the centenary of his distinguished namesake celebrated with so much "éclat," not only here in the South but also in other states of the Union, thanks to the Daughters of the Confederacy and the Confederate Memorial Association. He paid "splendid tribute to the women of the South" and stressed that it "was not only during the war . . . that the noble characteristics of the Southern women asserted themselves, but in the dark days following that terrible struggle and in the trying days of reconstruction, did their noble bravery shine [how else?] forth."*

He continued to gratify his audience, which included at least two nervous young ladies. "The Southern people . . . had so maintained their self-respect at all times that they were universally respected [oh, sweet to the ears!], and Northern publishers were requesting that the Southern people write the history of the Civil War, confident that a fair statement of both sides would thus be given." The speaker spoke "very tenderly to the little girls [hearts pitter-pattering!], who, he said, looked very much like the little girls of long ago. He told the children [thrilling!] of the many battles he was in under General Lee, and gave details of the Battle of Bull Run, Sharpsburg, Gettysburg, Parker Creek and others." In reviewing some of the awful scenes of those times "the speaker was overcome with emotion" (he was an old man; he would die within the year) and said, "God forbid that any of the little ones present would ever have any associations with scenes like these." (They were to live through WWI, WWII, Korea, and, some of them, Vietnam.)

And now, and now, and now . . . came the moment! "At the conclusion

---

* There are ritualistic locutions that can drive the fastidious soul batty. Following the phrase "we will go" at the ends of the sentences, for example, no politician can restrain himself from appending "forward," which not sufficing, he will further append "together," as though the plural pronoun "we" never was.

of General Lee's address," reported the *Daily Picayune,* "little Aloïse Steiner pinned on his breast long streamers of the Confederate colors."

The Lee connection. What we children have to remember is that our mother was not only Southern born and bred, she was Southern to the roots of her being. From their lips, she heard the war stories of heroes of the Confederacy. These were vivid in her memory lifelong. Her mother and father had lived through the war and survived the terrible times of Reconstruction; her grandfather on her maternal side had shed his blood in that war and had married Mary Ann Lee. The visit of General Stephen D. Lee was not only an important event in the city of New Orleans; it was the most exciting thing ever to have happened in the young life of an ardent eleven-year-old. Mother (and, in her recollection, I am almost sure her younger sister Vivian) was appointed by her school to pin the colors on the breast of General Lee. There could be no greater honor. The reason for it—the reason she (and her sister) had been selected—was that the little Steiner girls were generally reputed to be Lees (true) connected to the Robert E. Lee family (false conjecture), or maybe, says cousin Joan, simply because they attended the Robert E. Lee School, or maybe, says I, because they were about the prettiest little girls in New Orleans.

MY MOTHER WAS IN HER EARLY SEVENTIES WHEN SHE DESCRIBED THE occasion to me (I have her on tape), her green eyes sparkling, recalling every last stitch and tuck and lace and ribbon and the hue of her (and her sister Vivian's) frock. The importance of the family legend to my siblings and me is that we were brought up admiring Lee second only to Washington. Admiration of Lee has had, I think, in the historical dimension, a discernible influence on our values. We have fought lost causes aplenty, and we experienced our Chancellorsville in the election of Ronald Reagan and the triumph over the Soviet Union, which high watermarks of the conservative (now lost) cause have been followed by defeat on all, or most, critical fronts, and by shame in the 1994–2006 Republican-controlled Congress, which betrayed almost every principle in the support of which our brother Bill first, our siblings Jim and Pitts and Trish next, and the rest of us in our lesser ways fought so valiantly and, in Bill's case, brilliantly. Conservatives are in the Wilderness now, waging a doomed campaign of attrition. Little matter. In what resides the greatness of George

Washington and Robert E. Lee? Why, in what our father extolled as the fundamental human virtue: character. Indomitable character. What fairly describes the United States today? Almost total loss of character.

Our mother was thus filled with the dreams of the Lost Cause, which Victor Davis Hanson, among others, has eviscerated.* The mortal wound sustained by General Albert Sidney Johnston at Shiloh while leading a last-ditch (futile and unwise) Confederate charge late in the afternoon of that first day was the romantic foundation of the Lost Cause myth that sustained post-Civil War Southern pride with pernicious consequences but that was nevertheless as bright as a polished silver newel post in the minds of Mother's generation, which happily sat through much florid oratory and endless posthumous commemorations. To Mother, the Civil War was not fought about, or for, the perpetuation of (she would shudder at this ugly fact) slavery; it was fought for the constitutional right of the Southern states to secede from the Union they had created as equal partners and had pledged loyalty to so long as the Union did not betray its charter. Contemporaries ride over this *casus belli* as tendentious, but we have to recall that Virginia was Virginia, Louisiana Louisiana, many generations longer than the United States had been a political entity (the Union was just seventy-four years old at the outbreak of the war). Loyalty to *la patria chica* went deep and deeper. The federal republic was a construct that few scholars of the time (the 1840s, '50s, '60s) gave a nickel's chance of surviving.

The Union was an experiment. As Jay Winick points out in his brilliant *April 1865: The Month That Saved America,*† the United States were plural until after the war; the concept of the American *nation* was primarily a mystical peculiarity of Abe Lincoln.‡

To Aloïse Steiner and so many men and women of her generation, the South had been conquered. The North had imposed its view of an indissoluble Union on the dissenting South by brutal force of arms—burning cities, laying waste the countryside, waging an unprecedented, despicable,

---

* In his fascinating book, *Ripples of Battle: How Wars of the Past Still Determine How We Fight, How We Live, and How We Think.* Doubleday, 2004.
† Perennial, 2003.
‡ "When it came to articulating America as one nation the men in Philadelphia flinched. This was the one nut they couldn't crack. The word 'nation' or 'national' appears nowhere in the Constitution" (p. 14).

unchivalrous, *un-Christian* war against civilians (had there been a Geneva Convention on warfare at the time, the Union would have been charged with breaking most of the rules), and forcing on the Southern people (read white Southern people) an alien culture, which, *newly,* included abolition.

The rebel in Mother ran deep. She imbued her children with the desire, the courage, and the duty to oppose unjust compulsion, whether in childhood (at school) or as adults (in government).[2] It was not just our father's Southwest republicanism that branded our consciousness and formed our temperaments; it was our mother's Southern romanticism. The federal government in Washington was an object of suspicion when it was not outright an agent of repression. Its intrusions on states' rights were to be resisted with all one's might and power, short of (since Appomattox) armed rebellion.

Notwithstanding, within this postbellum Southern frame of mind, this Southern consciousness and psychology, our mother was a patriot. She told us stories about Nancy and Rastus outwitting evil General Howe in the Revolution. Not once did she spin a yarn about brave Southern lads and fair Southern ladies resisting the crude and vulgar manufacturing power of the North, or the gallant Klu Klux Klan fighting back under Reconstruction. Not one word ever did we children hear from her in this vein, though once she did tell me that Grandfather Steiner (or was it—more likely—Great-grandfather Wassem?) had been a charter member of the KKK in Louisiana, which, she hastily observed, was (in its first founding) not the same criminal organization that it became. Her heart melted and her eyes grew teary when Old Glory was strung up on the mast of the town green in Sharon during Fourth of July celebrations and the high school band played "My country 'tis of thee, sweet land of liberty." America the beautiful. God *bless* America. She was proud of (though she feared desperately for) the three sons who joined the colors (that would have been her Southern idiom) after the Japanese struck at Pearl Harbor. Before that attack, she and Father had been isolationists. After that attack, the issue was settled: America was at war.

She was a patriot, an American through and through, and raised us in a love of country that has been for many of us, I know for myself, the principal loyalty after God and family our whole life long. I love America. I weep for America because I love this country so much. My eyes fill with tears also and my chest heaves with blubbering emotion (age!) when I watch Fourth of July celebrations on television and see the Washington and Lincoln monuments and the White House and the Capitol all lit up, dazzling white, and hundreds of thousands of fellow Americans on the Mall wading in the reflecting pools hand-in-hand with their children and cheering the speeches and bellowing "My country 'tis of thee, sweet land of liberty." These are my people, black, brown, yellow, and white, whom I love, wonderful—magical—in their diversity, magnificent in the loyalties that bond us, one nation under God. I have been at any time prepared to give my life for this country, which is not bombast.

And what about that diversity? What about the Lost Cause and the loathsome institution of slavery that it implied? What was Mother's attitude about that, and what did we imbibe from her?

Mother was a racist, if that term is to be applied in today's usage, with no discrimination—as a compact statement permitting no "differentiation," no "unpacking." Aloïse Josephine Steiner assumed that white people were intellectually superior to black people. She had been raised surrounded by Uncle Toms and Auntie Belles—by former slaves. She was by no means a racist if by the term one suggests fear and hatred of, and disdain for, the Negro. She truly loved black people and felt securely comfortable with them from the assumption of her superiority in intellect, character, *and station*. They were dear, kind, simple people. Their goodness was a reproach to many white people. But they had their place, and she and her kind had their place. The duty of her kind was to care for black people, to extend affection and loyalty to them, from whom she and Southerners of her day and class expected loyalty and affection in return. I recall Aunt Inez telling me that her longtime black cleaning woman said to her, responding with head-shaking disapproval to a civil rights march, "Miz Inez, dey is plenty of fishes in de sea, and dey all swim according to their kind." There was nothing false about these assumptions, which were shared by many blacks of that generation. (One of the sad fundamental truths about human beings is that we become accustomed to injustice.) There was nothing forced about these assumptions, either; the affection and loyalty were real and came naturally as well. These virtues were a Christian duty incumbent upon both blacks and whites, but they rose also spontaneously from mutual regard.

Right through her long widowhood (twenty-three years) and to the end, Mother was surrounded by servants who had been in her employ twenty, thirty, forty years. They were loyal, their affection was great, and only decrepitude retired them. She caused her children to cringe with embarrassment when she referred to them as "my people." ("Oh, my God," we'd exclaim, "*Newsday* is coming to interview Mother—pray she doesn't talk about 'her' people!") But in Mother's mind and imagination, that is what they were: *her* people, just as she was *their* benefactor and protector. After Father died, and when Mother became old and senile, we kept getting letters from black people expressing their gratitude and also their affection.* I don't know how many mortgages my parents paid up for straitened "colored" servants and their kin or how many children of those servants, and others, they financed through college and law school. (Mother was godmother to a son of our unforgettable yardman,† who was indicted in New Jersey for manslaughter, which startled her when she heard about the offense but did not change anything. She sent him sweets and socks and I don't remember what else.) I repeat: the concern of my parents for the black servants who worked for them was not simply Christian charity. It was not just "doing the right thing," expected of them. It was, of course, expected by them of themselves. It was *noblesse oblige,* which was part of the deal. But the basis of it was mutual affection and respect that arose out of human interaction. It was essentially a feudal relationship, which existed among whites long before it came into being between Southern whites and the emancipated servant-class black race.

The unpardonable aspect of that relationship, and in this peculiar to white-black relations, was Jim Crow. Jim Crow was a social fact of life that my parents did not question. Its quotidian cruelty and humiliation did not occur to them. I find this almost impossible to understand . . . except that it did not occur to me, either, until the early 1960s. I grew up at a time when there were two water fountains, one shiny and enameled, for whites, the other a rusty spigot, for blacks. I grew up when—of all imbecilic things—there were two sets of gas pumps, one for lily-white hands, the other for the black hands that swabbed your bottom when you were an infant, washed your clothes, cared for you when you were sick, cooked and

---

*One such letter, written by a black man, praising her, appeared in the *Camden Chronicle-Independent* this past August, 2006—17 years after Mother's death.
†I have written about him elsewhere, in my book *USA Today.*

served your food, but which—my, no!—were not to touch the same gas pumps.

Jim Crow was cruel, was ugly, was crazy. But it went unnoticed by me and my siblings. Moral obtuseness is another fact of life with which I am continually impressed and have written novels about. Things were as they were when I grew up, as they had been for my parents when they grew up. All people belonged to social stations. Poor people rode coach, wealthy people rode Pullman. Father knew poverty firsthand. Anyone Southern-bred of my parents' time knew it historically. For decades after the Civil War, the South was poor, poor, poor. The servant, black or white, did not ride up front in the buggy or the carriage or the bus. Though miscegenation was unthinkable to them both,[3] Mother (and I am sure Father also) detested redneck racism. That was the attitude, and those were the acts, of white trash. White trash were morally leagues beneath black people. (Because they should know better?) They were not to be compared to black people. They were beneath contempt. Not all black people were good and kind and gentle, of course, and there were "uppity" Negroes who did not accept their station, but these rebellious exceptions aside, the Negro people we knew were family.

Such sentiments are almost impossible to comprehend now, even by us, Mother's children. The story of this republic is, I have come to believe also, one of a continuing moral revelation, directed by the Holy Spirit. I was not granted this insight, if such it be, until twenty or so years ago. As a nation, we were slow to comprehend the implications of the Declaration of Independence. This took us until the Civil War, seventy-three years. Lincoln did not come fully to understand what his war was about until his second inaugural address. Liberty was not solely for white folk—metaphysically an unsustainable proposition. Liberty was a moral condition of mankind, black or white, brown or yellow, or it was false. It took us another sixty years before we passed the Nineteenth Amendment, extending the rights and liberties of free Americans to women. It required a whole century after the Civil War (I date the revelation to Martin Luther King Jr.'s great speech in 1963 before the Lincoln Memorial) for us to rid our hearts of the injustices and contradictions of racism. Our history as a people has been a continuing moral revelation. (Alas, the moral temper of the people has been simultaneously declining.)

We children were raised in the attitude that we received from our parents. Father spoke little about the matter (for that matter, Mother spoke little about it, either), but the intellectual superiority and also moral superiority of the white race, incumbent in which was a duty to black people, was an unspoken assumption. Mother struggled, I know, with the idea of black men being ordained priests. This came about in conjunction with the second Vatican Council, in the early 1960s, and it taxed Mother's faith: "Reid, I have asked the Lord, can I, will I be able to bring myself to, receive communion from the hands of a black priest? Will I be able to go to confession to a black man?" She agonized over the hypothetical situation.* The class distinctions, the given of a right and moral paternalistic relationship between white and black peoples, ran so deep that the idea of an ordained black man serving as her spiritual arbiter became an obstacle she had to compel herself to overcome by strength of faith. (Hence the necessity of the *Magisterium*.) The Church demanded that she topple lifelong attitudes. Slavery was an accepted social institution in the South, as it had been in the time of Jesus. The Lord Jesus demanded that masters be just to their servants (often, in the context, slaves) but did not stipulate their manumission. (He spoke, remember, of the "wicked servant" being put to the torturers, in just retribution—for His times—of evildoing.) It was not a moral issue (though some Protestant Southern evangelists preached that slavery had been ordained by heaven).†

Mother did not think that way at all. She assumed (I know not on what grounds) that within a generation of having gained their independence, the Southern states would have renounced the institution of slavery. (She assumed also that the Southern states would seek readmittance to the Union.) She often told me this when I was a boy. Father believed that it was an economic inevitability: slavery was archaic in the industrial age. That it was *morally wrong*, however, I don't think that Mother (I am not so certain about Father) ever came to acknowledge (Father was of Irish extraction, and he knew about the Great Famine and Anglo society's suppression of and disdain for the Irish going well into the twentieth century, when he grew up; his firstborn son, John, was the first Irish Catholic

---

*She never encountered a black priest in her lifetime, but I am confident that had she, she would have made a point of going to confession to him . . . as Lee made a point of taking communion alongside a black man.

†On this whole question, there is no authority that I know of more gifted than Eugene Genovese. See his *Roll, Jordan, Roll* and his *The Mind of the Master*.

admitted to a secret society at Yale, way up in the 1930s). The abuses associated with slavery (harsh treatment, whippings, sexual exploitation, the heartless breaking up of families) disgusted them both, as they did all decent people of Southern descent. They were disapproving of and disgusted by the Klu Klux Klan of the 1920s (which, recall, as well as being anti-black and anti-Semite, was anti-Catholic; the KKK included the lowest of the Scots-Irish Protestant redneck population, white trash). Extremes of what is now bundled up in the epithet *racism* revolted them; lynchings were shocking, horrifying, savage, revolting, lawless, and to be condemned.

But they were born into their times and stamped indelibly, lifelong, by the attitudes of their times.* The Negro race was on the whole inferior. The average Negro was, they thought, incapable of competing with white people in a modern industrial economy. Father disapproved of the idea of white athletes playing in the same sporting events with black athletes. Blacks would, of course, win. They were physically more gifted, which was a fact. But this would give them a false sense of security. They would assume an equality (if not superiority) that was competitively unreal and therefore pernicious, giving them the idea that since they were able to lick whites on the track or compete successfully with them in the ballpark, they were able to succeed in areas demanding a background in the liberal arts or technological proficiency. The false supposition would inevitably produce tragic consequences: they would be deceived and suffer cruelly from the deception.

We children were raised in these attitudes, which were paternalistic. We worked our way out of that, each in our separate manner.†

NOTES

———

1. At the funeral and burial of darling Aunt Inez, her daughters, my cousins, said to me as we drove to the cemetery, "Do you see that tall pillar standing near our [Steiner]

———

* The position of southern Americans of goodwill born in the late nineteenth century and brought up in the first decade of the twentieth century with respect to racism is cognate to the position of moderate Muslims today with respect to their terrorist brethren.
† For more about my personal moral revelation on this matter (if anyone cares), see my other writings.

family crypt?" Craning my neck about in the front passenger seat, I did see it, barely: a very tall marble column, surmounted by statues of human figures that I could not make out. "That's the vault of a man called Moriarity," I was told by Joan or Karen or little Inez, "who made a lot of money in New Orleans in construction at the turn of the [twentieth] century. He planned an elaborate pantheon, and he imported Italian marble and an Italian architect and Italian sculptors and workmen to build it. The marble blocks were so heavy that Moriarity had to lay railroad tracks from the harbor to the cemetery to transport it. That must have cost a pretty penny! Well, one day, the Italian architect called Mr. Moriarity and asked him to come look at what they were doing. They were raising the column—the pedestal—at the time. On three plinths at the top were the allegorical figures of Faith, Hope, and Charity, just as Mr. Moriarity had ordered. But that left a fourth plinth unembellished. 'What do you want us to put there, sir?' he was asked, to which he replied, 'Why, Mrs. Moriarity.' "

At which my cousins burst out laughing, because that is what the workmen and sculptor did—as I saw when we drove into the cemetery and got out of the car. High up on three plinths one sees Faith, Hope, and Charity, heroic female figures draped in flowing robes. On the fourth plinth stands dumpy Mrs. Moriarity, dressed in the fashion of her time, with long black hoop skirts and a hooded bonnet. Queen Victoria and the Three Graces.

2. It is the impression of this native dislike of conformity that has made our (principally Bill's and mine) ambivalence about the rebellion of the 1960s hippie generation, of whose ideals and politics we are critical and more often than not contemptuous but whose attitude of defiance we admire.

3. Sex, *qua* sex, was unthinkable to them. I well remember my father becoming mightily embarrassed when I ventured to speak at lunch (I was nineteen) about my wonderful mare Ventura growing old and the desirability of breeding her soon, to which he said curtly, "Reid, this is not a subject to talk about at the table . . . see me after lunch, in the Empire room." In putting together this book, I discovered that none of us has the remotest idea where our parents honeymooned. (Jim thinks maybe New York; I vote for San Francisco.) Their honeymoon, with its plain sexual implications, simply was not mentioned by either of them.

4. Its apogee in due process was achieved in 1965 by the (unconstitutional in some provisions) Civil Rights Act. Since that triumph, the movement has been tarnished by post-King and Abernathy black demagogues and black and white affirmative-action absolutists. I observed sadly in the mid-1960s and 1970s on lecture tour how black students began to resegregate themselves in college dining halls. It was cool for a black student to date a white girl but *verboten* for a white dude to date a black girl. Hostility steamed from the black student body; and my children, supporters of civil rights, bitterly resented preferences granted to their fellow black students when they held these to be unmerited. Thomas Sowell has written copiously and eloquently about this degeneration in a glorious crusade.

CHAPTER SEVEN

———— ⌒◦⌒ ————

Aloïse Steiner of New Orleans (III): Steiners, Scraps

ÇA SUFFIT.

Getting back to my maternal ancestry, it is a myth propagated by the charming and lovable James (Jimmy) Steiner, our mother's kid brother—everybody's favorite uncle; every family should have a favorite uncle to whom children can confide what they can't to their parents—that Steiners do not make money and that anyone fated to carry Steiner genes is fated to have no money sense (what our mother never failingly disparaged as "monkey brains").*

Uncle Jimmy may have been extrapolating from his uninspiring business career, which was doomed to modest returns. He set himself up as a money lender, of all unsuitable choices, for which his happy temperament and kind heart singularly disqualified him. (He was forever fishing into a lean wallet for loose bills to give to deadbeats who had previously de-

_____

* This is important, the ambivalent—the insouciant—attitude about money in which we children were brought up. Put simply, though we enjoy having plenty of it, money does not dazzle us. This stood me in good stead during my long sojourn in Spain, where I was surrounded socially by inherited fortunes of astonishing size and in cases also antiquity, to which fact I was indifferent. My siblings share this attitude. We are most of us extravagantly generous, few of us have ever had a surplus of funds, but getting rich ranks not high in our values.

faulted on their debts—carefully annotating bad money after good in a little notebook, which served only to remind him of his folly. It was such a farce!) Uncle Jimmy notwithstanding, I carry early childhood memories of the big old frame house, a handsome and imposing structure at 1738 South Carrollton Street. Built by Grandfather Aloysius Steiner, it stands still,* the initials of his name incised on the glass of the entrance door.†

Number 1738 is the residence and address of well-off people—not rich but securely middle-class. We know that Grandfather Steiner had married and fathered children before meeting the twenty-three-year-old Marie Louise Wassem (at a card game). Br'er Jim says charmingly in his memoirs, *Gleanings from an Unplanned Life: An Annotated Oral History,*‡ "How a quiet 39-year-old 5'5" widower§ managed to woo and capture the heart of a lively 23-year-old 5'8" woman remains an enigma." He was a pillar of his church; we know that, too. His name is engraved "in marble," Jim tells us, "as a member of the . . . building committee of Mater Dolorosa Church, on Carrollton Avenue," where our parents were married. Marrying into the Steiner clan, I should add, was an economic legup for our Wassem forebears.

The Steiners hailed from Switzerland's German-speaking canton, Sankt Gallen, city of Bergt. They were Catholics in a society that registered Protestants as well. Joseph Alois Steiner, our maternal great-grandfather, was born in 1806 in Benken, Bezirk Gaster, Sankt Gallen. Brother James recalls visiting Sankt Gallen and the city of Bergt, whose phone book, he reports, is rife with Steiners, at least two of them Alois's. "When we entered the town [of Bergt] itself, on a cold and rainy Saturday afternoon, it became immediately apparent why our branch of the family might have chosen to leave. Bergt proved to be the only Swiss municipality I have ever seen that seemed totally devoid of charm."

The whole of which, speaking of charm and extrapolating from descendants, decamped with Joseph Steiner, who emigrated to New Orleans in 1845, when he was thirty-nine years old. Why? We don't know. The

---

* Or it did before Katrina. I have not checked with my cousins.

† Present owners will not part with that door (I can't blame them), though my cousins have offered to buy it.

‡ Intercollegiate Studies Institute, 2006.

§ Grandfather Steiner's former wife and their surviving children (two were stillborn) dying of the yellow fever (we may, I think, safely assume).

Aloysius Steiner home,
Carollton Avenue, New Orleans.

Swiss have a sweet tooth. Maybe he liked sugar cane. Or maybe he found his fellow Swiss dull. We know nothing about our maternal great-grandfather except that we may assume he was short and dumpy and had gumption (to emigrate). This ignorance grieves the storyteller in me. Joseph Alois Steiner is like those names tediously listed in the *Times Picayune* article covering the visit of General Stephen Lee. Once they were living, breathing human beings, of consequence even though maybe only to their descendants. They felt, they thought, they shook, they moved. Now they are wraiths. Had old Joe Steiner had enough of the dank and dreary, and was it the subtropical climate of Louisiana that lured him? (How was he able to tolerate *the flatness* of Louisiana?) Did he dislike fresh milk? (My mother did.) Did he suffer from eczema? (My mother did.) Was he able to collapse from laughter, as my mother was, and did he have a fiery temper, though, like my mother, forbearing from loosing it on his children? He is no more than a datum in the shadowy chain of existence linking us to the primeval ooze, though I am indebted to him for one-eighth of the genes in my body. I owe my existence to him and seven other human beings who have been dissolved into the stream of being. (Without them, someone else, not I, would be writing this.) Maybe my fascination with tropical fish came from the old fellow, or my abhorrence of bullies, or my gluttony for chocolate ice cream, or my passion for the second movement of Brahms's Third Symphony and my rational, aesthetic, and ontological disdain for joggers.

I tell you what! I bet Great-grandfather Joseph Alois Steiner was as little able to tolerate the smugness of Jeffersonian liberals of his day as I am able to tolerate that same smugness today. That dreary Calvinist Swiss climate! I bet he would have detested WASP society, preferring Latins, as do I.*

The Steiners, unlike our Buckley forebears, were not of farming stock. They were petite bourgeoisie in origin. The New Orleans directory of the time labels Great-grandfather Joseph Steiner, immigrant, as a boot- and shoemaker. His son Aloysius was born in New Orleans in 1855. Grandfather worked for Eustice & Company (cotton distributors) until the panic of 1894. He then "served" (as they say) as secretary-treasurer for A. Baldwin & Company until his death, which took place on April 19, 1919, when he was sixty-four, my brother James reports (he got this information from our uncle Jimmy).

I accept this prosaic account only so far as it goes. As brer Jim points out, the embarrassing disparity in height between Grandmother Wassem (she so tall) and Grandfather Steiner (he so short) explains why one never sees them standing or seated at the same time in the rare photographs that survive. One, almost invariably Grandmother, is standing. Grandfather sits in a chair—fortifying the notion that he was ailing after his midforties, suffering, as my mother once mentioned, from heart disease. Uncle Jimmy recounted that, in fact—when he, Jimmy, was a little boy—his father had had his chest stove in by the shaft of a runaway milk cart, which plunged through the side of a cable car Grandfather happened to be riding. Uncle Jimmy indicated that Grandfather was never the same man

---

*Perhaps I should make this clearer. Of the people I have met, I prefer to do business with Anglo-Saxons but to socialize with Spaniards, Italians and Italian-Americans, Irish and Irish-Americans, American Jews, black Americans, Austrians, French, gays of all provenances, swindlers, con men, and Britons, in that order. I do not prefer to socialize with Germans, in that order.

MARY LOUISE WASSEM STEINER
1871   1950

JOSEPHINE WASSEM
BERTHIER

EMILE
BERTHIER JR.

JAMES EMILE WASSEM
STEINER   1910

DETTE BERTHIER

INEZ STEINER
PERRIER
9/15/1899 N.O.
M. 4/14/26
D. 198? N.O

ALOISE STEINER BUCKLEY
B.3/11/1895 M. 1917 N.O.
D.3/10/85 Sharon.Conn.

EMILE BERTHIER

MARY ANN LEE
WASSEM

ALOYSIUS STEINER
7/9/1855 M 4/9/94
D. 5/19/1919

MARY VIVIAN
STEINER
LOMBARD
8/23/1896
M.10/25/191
6/24/73

Home of Aloysius and Mary Louise Steiner
Carollton Ave. New Orleans, La. 1910

Family picture, Steiner branch, taken at their home
on Carollton Avenue, New Orleans.

thereafter. If he was indeed partly disabled yet kept his job with A. Baldwin & Company (at the time this country's largest wholesaler of sugar-refining equipment), this suggests (a) to his worth as a businessman, despite Uncle Jimmy's remark that making money is not in the Steiner blood,* and (b) his character, his will and fortitude.

What else may we infer of Grandfather Steiner from the sparse facts we have? That he was droll, for one thing; that he was gentle and loving, for another. He was of a scholarly bent, I gather also, a voracious reader (Mother said), who kept a dictionary always by his side, and a strict grammarian. He would have his daughters write short pieces (essays? book reviews? travel accounts?—Mother published poetry in the *Times Picayune* when she was a young woman), which he would painstakingly review for solecisms or awkward syntax. In this respect for right order, or structure, he was not unlike my father; speaking of whom, when he was in deep coma—while Mother was reading aloud from the Psalms—he suddenly

---

*My first cousin, Uncle Jimmy's nephew, Aloysius Steiner's grandson, Claude Perrier, has recently retired after a brilliant and remunerative business career.

spoke out, saying, "Boy, how those Jews could write!" and then slipped right back into coma. For her part, Mother corrected her children's grammar with absentminded fidelity: "You may be right, Reid, dear Maureen had no business to tell your friend Peter Coley that you are afraid of the dark, but it is 'Maureen and I' who stumbled over Jocko [her big old English setter] when the lights went out during the storm last week, not 'Maureen and me.' Which reminds me, have you tried on those trousers [*never* "pants"] I bought you at Rogers Peet? Henning must stop sneaking you candy bars, and I must say it's time your father bought himself some clothes. The suit he put on this morning was a disgrace, not that he would notice."

THE TRANSLATION OF THIS WAS THAT I HAD PUT ON WEIGHT THANKS TO the kindness of Henning, our butler, who knew of my sweet tooth, and that our father was utterly indifferent to clothes, a trait his son Bill inherited (brother John, on the other hand, was a dandy).

Mother told us that when she was first married to our father, she was distressed and then irritated by his carelessness about what he put on. Her father always dressed carefully, I gathered, which befit his station. But of her husband she would declare, "Your father is capable of walking into an important business meeting wearing the pants of one suit, the jacket of another," probably exaggerating. (We trust.)

One evening when he changed for supper (the custom, through my childhood), she watched him fling his jacket over the back of a chair in their bedroom, as was his habit, unlace and step out his shoes (wiggling his cramped toes), abandon one shoe in the middle of the floor, the other beside the chair he sat upon, peel off his socks, and then drop them one after the other to the carpet while walking to the bathroom, from which an arm protruded as he tossed his trousers to the floor also. She said nothing, though she squirmed with indignation. She decided, "I will not pick up after him!" When, later that evening, as they were going to bed, he kissed her and said, "Good night, Aloïse," she scarcely answered, whipping about on the mattress and wrapping herself securely in the sheets.

Early the next morning (he was a Texan; he rose always early, often before dawn), she was wide awake when he got up—yawned, went to the bathroom, brushed his teeth, and then came back into the bedroom, looking for his clothes. He expected to find a fresh suit folded over the back of an armchair, a fresh white shirt over that, a fresh tie, a pair of black shoes neatly placed on the floor, fresh black silk socks balled on the armchair's seat. But no, his bride had not only refrained from picking up after him, she hadn't provided him with a change of clothes from the wardrobe. She said his eyes widened at that realization; but then, bemusedly, he went to where he had discarded his socks the night before on the floor, retrieving them, tugging them on. She watched covertly as he went to his shirt, in a rumpled pile on the floor also, and put *that* on (he would have had to fish one of his stiff starched attachable collars from the chest of drawers); she watched unbelievingly as he retrieved his trousers from the floor and pulled them on, and then as he picked his jacket off the back of the chair and donned that.

When he had sat down on the armchair to lace up his shoes, she could stand it no longer, jumping out of bed and crying furiously, "Will, you are impossible! You *know* I won't permit you to go to the office like that." She said he regarded her, amazed at her show of temper, failing utterly to understand her.*

Father's indifference to clothes abided famously with him into his late years. (It went with his personal modesty and distaste for show.) He was a very clean person, showering once or twice a day, and sternly advising his sons never to wear the same pair of shoes on consecutive days. But he was frugal. We were therefore astonished at one famous supper at Great Elm, during the early 1950s, when he announced that he intended to go shopping in town that next week, for clothes. "Oh, Will," exclaimed Mother, "I am so glad. Not one of your suits isn't threadbare, and I am so tired of them; they must be twenty years old." His children chorused her reaction. He blinked at us all. "I must say, I never realized that I was embarrassing all of you by my appearance," he mumbled defensively, huffily, and seemed genuinely taken aback by our answering roar of laughter.

It was Father's custom to telephone Mother once or twice a day every day that he was away in New York, and the conversation this magi-

---

*Bill's wife, Pat, used to tell me despairingly that my brother is very much like our sire in this respect. Bill pays no attention to what he takes with him on trips (she packs his bag), and when Bill would return from one of his lecture tours, she was forever telephoning motels to reclaim a shoe, or a shirt, or a pair of pants.

cal week ended always with his telling her that he had visited this or that haberdasher—and ordered himself a new suit. "Oh, Will, and you must buy yourself some new ties also!" He favored bow ties; his four-in-hands tended to be floral, Southwestern in taste, and we his (snob Northeastern-raised) sons (in our regimental uniformity) thought gaudy-awful. But he agreed: "I'll buy one or two." "Six, Will, you must have six new ties at least!"

When he returned that Friday evening, he announced at suppertime, with a touch of smugness, that he had splurged. "I'm ashamed of myself," he added quickly, grinning bashfully at us all, mostly at Mother. "I did not buy myself one new suit, or two. I bought *seven new suits,* if you can believe it! I declare, I've never spent so much money on myself in all my days."*

Which was probably so. He was abashed by his extravagance, he who would not hesitate at purchasing a new three thousand dollar jumping horse for his children. "Oh, Will!" cried Mother. "I'm glad!" "Father," we all shouted, "how wonderful! When will they get here?" "Yes, Will, when can we expect them? I'm thrilled. I can't wait." "Oh," he answered, losing interest, "next week sometime, I suppose."

Wednesday that week, a box arrived in the post from Brooks Brothers. Later that afternoon, there was a delivery from Saks. Next morning, Thursday, came another box from Brooks Brothers . . . and one also from Sulka! And on Friday morning, *two* more boxes arrived, addressed to Mr. William F. Buckley. We children could not stand the suspense. "Let's open them, Mother!" She itched to see the contents as much as we. But she shook her head. "No, children, we mustn't. We can't deprive your father of that pleasure."

He was weary from the week's work that Friday evening, however, not in the mood for a grand opening. Early that Saturday morning, right after breakfast, we children gathered in our parents' suite on the second floor of Great Elm. There Mother, in her peignoir, kneeling on the carpet beside

---

* As far as personal valuables are concerned, he owned one gold Gübelin pocket watch, which Mother gave me and I wore many years, passing it on to my eldest son, Hunt (the eldest of the Buckley-named grandsons), a set of inexpensive amethyst cufflinks (he wore shirts with French cuffs always), which sister Priscilla gave to me (and which I treasured, only to have them stolen from me in a motel near Buffalo), and a set of inexpensive mother-of-pearl dress studs and cufflinks, which I have.

her mahogany sleigh bed, armed with a pair of garden shears, began slitting open the boxes and tearing the tissue paper off the clothes they contained. Father, standing at the door of the connecting bathroom in cotton pyjamas and a striped cotton bathrobe that Mother had given him for Christmas, watched with a silly grin on his face. I remember how excited we all were. The first article of clothing to emerge was the jacket of a handsome double-breasted midnight-blue wool suit with thin pinstripes. We admired it. The next to emerge was the jacket of a handsome double-breasted dark gray wool suit with thin pinstripes. We admired that one also. The third box contained another suit, midnight blue again, and the same as the first two—wool, double-breasted, thin pinstriping. The fourth item was a dark gray suit, and the same. The fifth, sixth, and seventh were suits also, the same!

They were identical, in cut and style and texture, except in almost indistinguishable shading of dark and darker blue, dark and darker gray, or black. Not a single-breasted jacket. Not a tweed sport coat, or a flannel, or anything of casual cut. He forgot to purchase himself a single tie.

"Father!" we children all moaned in our dismay. Mother looked up at him reproachfully . . . and burst into tears. He gazed at us, bewildered, muttering, "Well, I declare," and retired to his bedroom. He was testy the whole weekend, I remember—long after we, his wife and children, had recovered and begun to laugh. Mother's Galahad who rode out of the West. Mother's swain from Texas . . .

I skip ahead, which, in a professional biographer is impermissible. But I have already begged the reader's indulgence on that score.

Father's indifference to sartorial matters led to a wonderful episode in London, when I was maybe five years old.* That winter of 1934, he was away all week in France, desperately seeking financing to sustain his explorations for oil in Venezuela. We—the youngest ones, Maureen and I—were parked in an apartment in London with Mother (or maybe in a house he rented in Edward's Square, though that may have been earlier), while our older brothers and sisters attended English boarding schools.

---

*I am told that I asked my Mexican nurse, *"Nana, quién es el señor que viene cada fin de semana para pasar unos días con Mamá?"* (Nana, who's the man who comes every weekend to spend a few days with Mama?) To which I received the scandalized reply, *"Cállate, niño, es tu papá!"* (Hush, child, it's your daddy!)

Father said incautiously to Mother one evening, "Aloïse, you always accuse me of being careless about my clothes."

"Darling Will, I accuse you of being careless about your clothes only because I love you. Otherwise I would accuse you of being slovenly."

"I declare. I never suspected you felt that way about it."

"Never mind. What were you thinking about?"

"Well, I do admit that I am always forgetting whether I have packed the slippers for my tuxedo . . ."

"You have never forgot your dress shoes because I remember always to pack them for you."

"But I forget my collars, socks, change of ties . . . you know what I am talking about, Aloïse!"

"Yes, I do . . ."

"Well, I have the most marvelous idea. The British have the reputation of being the best suitcase makers in the world."

"Like British winters and British plumbing."

"What does . . . ? "

"The long, dreary, cold London winter. You're in Paris all week . . ."

"I know it's hard."

"I miss you so, Will!"

"And I miss you. Maybe this will be our last separation, if we close the deal with Companie Française. Pray, Aloïse, pray hard!"

"You know I do. Oh, Will, I hate to complain. But this morning the hot water suddenly turned cold as I was filling my bath. Twice. With me in it. Yesterday the ice box leaked water all over the kitchen floor. The other day the heat went off in the whole building, and we nearly froze to death."

"That's not the plumbing, Aloïse."

"Then what is it?"

"The central heating."

"Central nothing of the sort."

"May I ask, what's this got to do with . . . ? "

"Everything, if you are so frigid your fillings ache."

"I'll speak to the superintendent . . ."

"Fat lot. Did you like the gumbo soup James cooked for you tonight?"

"Very much!"

"Be sure to tell him. He misses New Orleans, for which I can't blame him."

"And we must send fruit to the children away at school. I will bet you, Aloïse, they get no fruit in their, in their . . . what are those terrible boxes?"

"Tuck boxes."

"Yes, filled with the chocolates and sweets that ruin British teeth. We must send them fresh oranges if they have any, Aloïse, I'll go down to Fortnum & Mason's tomorrow and order what they have. Now, I've been thinking of designing my own bag. Yes, I'll do just that, too. I'll design my own suitcase. Each item of clothing will have its special compartment. There will be a place for the patent-leather shoes, another for a change of street shoes, a place for my collars, a special little compartment for studs and things, and one for ties, and fresh changes of underwear, and . . ."

The more he thought about it, the more entranced he became. "Aloïse, all I will have to do before I shut my suitcase is see whether any one of the special compartments are . . ."

"You mean is."

"Of course. Is empty. *If* it's empty, I've forgot something."

Mother pondered a moment. Then said in her happy, enthusiastic way, "Will, I think that's a wonderful idea. It's ingenious!"

"Isn't it! I'll go directly to [was it Breeg, the Mark Cross of London of that time?] with a few drawings and have them make me a bag. Of the finest English leather, mind. Yes, I think I'll do just that."

We can suppose there were several excited evenings devoted to drawing the interior compartments that were to accomplish a transformation in his lifetime habits. The suitcase was ordered. Weeks of suspense slipped by. Then one Friday afternoon, before Father had got back from France, we heard a heavy thudding on the building's service staircase well; and into the apartment trudged two burly British delivery men, hefting Father's dream suitcase, which was so fantastically equipped with special compartments that, empty, it required both men to lift it from the ground.

CHAPTER EIGHT

———— ✺ ————

Aloïse Steiner of New Orleans and William Frank Buckley of Texas (I): Courtship

ONE CAN'T SAY MOTHER AND FATHER KNEW EACH OTHER WELL WHEN they were married.

It was a whirlwind courtship, four months from first meeting to wedding, by brother Jimmy's count. I count a critical four days.

Mother was nearing twenty-two years of age; in her Creole society, looming over her was the dread status of spinsterhood. Her younger sister, Vivian, had already married. She, Mother, had had beaus aplenty, of course. The pretty, vivacious Steiner girls were sought after. But she had then suffered what used to be called a cross: she had fallen in love with a handsome, older fellow, who, she learned to her dismay, was divorced.

We know neither his name nor what he looked like. I presume he was good-looking, and older. I firmly believe that he was a cad, not confessing his divorced state until Mother had given her heart to him. We can suppose also that he was Southern and well off. He could not have been New Orleans born and bred, because his personal circumstance would have been known by her before she fell for him. I do suppose that he was a fitting beau in every respect except for the divorce, which rendered marriage impossible.[1]

She "gave him up." It was hard, hard; she loved him, she thought. She fell into a worrisome depression for several months, staying in her bed-room, weeping there in seclusion, thinking her young life done. She even fell into a dry period as far as her faith was concerned, which must have upset her parents to no end, because they were both devout. Mother had a history of temperamental instability; she had quit Sophie Newcomb after just one year because of a "nervous breakdown," which is, I suspect, a medical euphemism covering all sorts of undiagnosable indispositions of the heart. At last, under Grandmother's urging, she went to confession—to a priest who had known her since she was a toddler.

She poured out her story to him, and then she said, a bit grandly, proud of herself, that she had decided to become a nun.

At this, the confessional unaccountably rocked with laughter. With uproarious, gasping, choking . . . indecent laughter. "You . . . Aloïse, a nun? Oh, my! Oh, my! I've known you since . . . Aloïse Steiner, a nun?" And the rude, awful man, with whom she was furious, burst into that shocking and indecorous laughter again, guffawing. She accepted what-ever light penance he meted her with clamped lips and an angry heart, humiliated. (Forty, fifty, sixty years later—how she laughed at herself when telling this story. The dear priest knew her well. Aloïse Steiner was not born to be a nun, dear no!)*

Shortly afterward, one late morning in April, a gentleman calling him-self Will Buckley, of Texas and Mexico, presented himself at the door of 1738 South Carrollton Street, Stetson fedora in hand, asking to speak with Mr. or Mrs. Steiner.

He was admitted into the parlor, where he spoke with Grandfather and Grandmother—their daughters Aloïse and little Inez maybe eaves-dropping on the conversation from the hall, hushing their baby brother Jimmy, but not, I think, invited into the parlor to meet the unexpected visitor.

Not yet. This Will Buckley had met Mrs. Marian Lombard (née Viv-ian Steiner, mother's younger sister) in Mexico City, where she was visiting with her uncle Émile Berthier (actually, her second cousin, once removed).[2] He had an introductory letter from Vivian, the contents of which I do not know but which must have said nice things about the bearer.

---

* This scene in the confessional, in one rendition or another, I have repeated in four of my five novels.

I try to imagine his appearance: tall, spare, austere, dressed in a dark suit, with a beak of a nose and nerdish pince-nez, from behind which sparkled brilliant round china-blue eyes. He had a broad brow, high, wide cheekbones, a firm, round jaw, full lips. I assumed until recently that he wore a gray or black fedora, in which I was accustomed to seeing him when I was growing up, perched squarely, uncompromisingly, on the crown of his skull, by which I mean to convey with not the least effort of tilting in a more becoming or rakish angle; but since seeing a snapshot of him a few years earlier than his visit to New Orleans, sitting at the beam of a punt on the murky waters of Xochimilco, with three ladies in the boat, I now wonder whether he may not have been wearing a bowler, which in fact suited his features.* His handshake was firm, the fist well muscled, the fingers short and strong, immaculate nails clipped square. His light brown hair (with chestnut glints) was thinning, already graying at the sides. He was a gentleman in early middle age.

What impression he made on Aloysius and Marie Louise Steiner I can only guess. This was plainly a serious person. He was straightforward, polite, but direct. He explained that was on his way from Mexico to attend the wedding of a friend that was to take place in New York City on Saturday (this was a Wednesday). He was best man. But Mrs. Lombard (people were strictly formal in those days) had spoken so highly of her sister, Miss Aloïse Steiner, that he, Will Buckley, wondered whether Mr. and Mrs. Steiner would permit him to take their daughter out for lunch.

This request was not exactly froward—he arrived well introduced—but it was precipitous, according to the conventions of the times. "Well," Grandmother or Grandfather said, "Aloïse must agree to that." Their daughter had moped for months, so they may have been very well unsure what her reaction might be to this fellow who was so much older (at thirty-six) than she (just twenty-two).[3]

They called in their daughter, who entered closely followed by curious seventeen-year-old Inez and eleven-year-old Jimmy.

"Aloïse, this gentleman is Mr. William Buckley of . . . ?"

"Tampico, Mexico."

"Yes, and of . . . was it Austin?"

"Yes, Texas."

---

* Or is that hat a trilby?

"He is visiting New Orleans for a short while, on his way to New York. He has met your sister Vivian, and he would like to take you to lunch. Your mother and I have approved; but it is, of course, up to you."

I can't be sure what Mother's first reaction was to Father, though the brilliance of his blue eyes and the directness of his gaze must have impressed her. As for him, he had to have been struck by her brunet loveliness, the sea-green eyes in their immaculate whites and almond-shaped casings, her fair complexion (Southern girls did not expose themselves to the sun in those days), bright rosy (or rouged) cheeks, perfect nose, petite figure, and lively manner. (Mother always told us that Aunt Vivian was the beauty, but she had a better figure.) She was well bred; he might well have inferred that from her delicate hands, slim feet, and long, slim legs.*

He would not have known of the grandmother who had been a maid and of the grandfather who was a barber, nor would this have mattered to him, the Southwesterner. Breeding to Will Buckley carried a different sense than the purely social. He was Irish. He meant by good breeding good stock, a good upbringing, and firm principles. He must have been freshly struck by how very young she was, though he had had to have been prepared for that. And by the differences in their backgrounds, hers genteel in the grand old city of New Orleans, his rough and straitened in the frontier town of San Diego, and further tested in the revolutionary climate of Mexico.

He had started from scratch less than ten years ago, and he had amassed a small fortune in real estate—working himself into serious illness, at one juncture—while earning the respect of Mexicans and anyone else who met him and who was able to withstand his frank, scrupulous, unflinching gaze.† He was a man who had made his way in the most turbulent era of the most alien (in terms of culture) of countries, dealing with unscrupulous American speculators,‡ unscrupulous and thieving Mexican government authorities, and gunmen, both native and Texan.

They could not have been more different in person, background, or

---

*Both stated to their children long years later that it had been "love at first sight."
† In this respect the model for my characters Jonathan Wright in *Eye of the Hurricane* and Simeon St. James the Younger in *Marbella!*
‡ Scallywags, he was to call them. A scallywag was a white Southerner who supported Reconstruction policies after the Civil War. For our father, that translated into an unsavory character, not to be trusted.

blood, could Will Buckley and Aloïse Steiner. But he fell in love with her, if not at first sight, within hours.

They had lunch. Where I can't guess—but someplace proper, maybe at the Café du Monde, which was open and airy and even in those days filled with visitors from out of town. I am certain that Mother fell for Will Buckley almost immediately. We can have no idea what their conversation was. It likely began with Aunt Vivian, and their uncle Émile Berthier, the coffee planter and mining engineer who had discovered the fabulous Dos Estrellas silver mine in Taxco;[4] which must have led to Will Buckley's activities as a lawyer, real estate developer, and oilman in Tampico; and maybe he told her that luncheon, for the first time, a few of his wonderful stories. She must have admired the deep bass of his voice and the lively intelligence of the brain behind the high and remarkably broad forehead.

What he saw in her is more difficult to imagine, apart from her physical charms. In keeping with her proper upbringing, she was almost devoid of worldly experience. But the art of conversation came naturally to this Southern girl, and though she had had only one year of formal college training, she had read. This would be important to him, who was himself a reader. She had been encouraged by her father from childhood to curl up with a book. She may have impressed Will Buckley by references to the poetry and novels of their time, of which he was unlikely to have read much. His reading was more serious: histories and biographies, largely. Maybe he mentioned William Prescott's *The Conquest of Mexico*, which she might very possibly have read and admired also. My nephew Christopher Buckley has introduced me to a lovely Gaelic word: *anamcara*. It means soul mate. Aloïse Steiner and Will Buckley.

In any case, when he returned her to South Carrollton, he immediately asked her parents' permission to take her out to supper. Now, this *was* froward (how fond I am of the word!—evoking an entire era). Grandfather and Grandmother must have hesitated. Mother herself, she told me, was astonished by Father's impetuosity. (They were bourgeois, all right: what would neighbors say?) But he had already made up his mind in one respect, of which she was mercifully ignorant: he wanted to test his determination by a second meeting with her, and promptly. He did not have much time. (There never seemed to be sufficient time.) The elder Steiners consented. Father would return for their daughter at seven o'clock.

Where they went to supper I do not know, either, but I strongly suspect Antoine. (It had to have been a splendid restaurant.) I know from Mother that their conversation was brisk. They seemed to have so much to say to each other, this mismatched couple. The differences in age, in upbringing, vanished. Mother must have impressed Father by her fund of sprightly stories, because, until her final illness, she was an acute (witty and amusing) observer of humankind all the blessed years that we, her children, knew her. They must have laughed a lot and discovered in each other delicious senses of humor, which he probably attributed entirely to her one-fourth-Irish descent. (Humor was important to them both, perhaps third only to religion and character.) Maybe they talked about their Catholic faith; yes, I think they must have lapsed into serious conversation at one juncture or other and talked about that, because it was of such importance to them both. (It was historically of first importance to him: it was a dispute to do with religion that prompted his grandfather to emigrate from Ireland and that would shortly impel him to challenge Mexico's revolutionary governments.) Whatever the case, Father turned to Mother as the meal was ending, saying, "Miss Steiner, will you marry me?"

Mother was shocked, truly, profoundly. "Why, Mr. Buckley," she answered, "you have no right to ask me such a question!"

She was not putting on. She was furious with him, she assured me years later. As soon as he had paid the check, she gathered her purse to leave. It was unthinkable that this, this stranger, this, this . . . Texan should have had the gall—the impertinence—to advance such an indecent proposal. Marry him? Was he out of his mind? She was scarcely acquainted with him!

When he escorted her into the front garden of 1738 South Carrollton Street, he asked her whether he might take her out for lunch the next day.

"Absolutely not!" she answered coldly.

He reminded her, saying, "Miss Steiner, I leave for New York tomorrow evening. I don't know when I will be able to get back to New Orleans. Lunch tomorrow is the last opportunity I will have of seeing you."

She resisted still. Matters of such importance—the delicate matters of the human heart—simply were not handled in this manner. She said, not cordially, "You will have to ask my parents."

He walked right in after her and did just that. The elder Steiners were, of course, sitting up waiting for their daughter.

Both were astounded by William Buckley's request. He explained patiently once again that he had little time left in New Orleans. (He did not mention that he had proposed to their daughter.) There was something about the man that appealed to Grandfather Steiner, who nodded, who (I am imagining this) gave his assent before Grandmother acquiesced. (There was the very real scandal of the matter to consider.) But Marie Louise Steiner answered yes at last. Will Buckley may have smiled, bowing (or nodding) to them both, then to Miss Steiner, and—saying he would call for her sharply at noon—departing.

During that lunch, he asked her once more to marry him. She refused indignantly, she told me. "I was mad, Reid!" But when he left her at the door of her home, she felt a terrific pang in her heart.

She tried to put him out of her mind in the two months following. She heard not a word from him. But now she had plenty of beaus who came calling for her. She found them insipid. There was something about the austere-looking Will Buckley that stormed her resisting heart. One of his winning attributes, she explained, was his charm. She had never met such a charming human being. (We hear this from other sources, Mexican and American.) The explosive and on occasion startling boom of his laughter—his wholehearted surrender to mirth—may have astonished and pleased her, did she hear it. Another attraction may have been his passionate nature, evidenced physically in his wide and full lips, though neither of our parents, to their dying day, would have mentioned such a coarse dimension. She put Will Buckley out of her mind.

As was his custom every year, wealthy uncle Émile Berthier invited the Steiners, mother and daughters and little Jimmy, to spend July and August with him in Mexico City—to escape the heat and humidity of New Orleans, as well as the very imminent menace of yellow fever. (Mother never mentioned her father joining them, I conclude either because he could not get off from work or because he was too infirm to travel.)

It was a long, tedious, hot, dusty, and tiring trip. They stopped as usual at Austin, for a change of trains bearing them south into Mexico. Mother may have been thinking of Father when the train left the bayous of Louisiana behind and chugged across the endless Texan plains. But she could not have expected that Will Buckley would be there, at the railroad station in Austin, to hand her mother and little sister Inez and herself off the first-class coach!

Mother professed to me that she was totally astonished. How he found out on what date they would arrive in Austin he never revealed.* She did not dream she might be meeting him again, she swore—certainly not in this fashion, which was more than froward: it was importunate, a serious breach of decorum. Before God, she had not given Will Buckley the slightest reason to hope that she might accede to his outrageous proposal. But he compounded the breach, escorting the Steiner family into waiting cabs and driving them directly to his mother's house on the corner of Lavaca Street, to freshen up and lunch. Arranging for *her* mother to meet *his* mother permitted only one interpretation, and that was impermissible.

I don't know directly how Grandmother Steiner reacted, but I imagine that she was as shocked as her daughter. I presume she was scrupulously polite. I have no knowledge at all of how Marie Louise Steiner's meeting went with the severe little woman dressed in coal black, Mary Ann Langford Buckley, this Will Buckley's mother, or whether she formed a favorable impression of the plainly dressed woman. Grandmother B may have been surprised by her son's impetuosity also, though I doubt it. She may have disapproved of the fashionable clothing of the tall, not yet stout, younger woman from New Orleans† and that of her two daughters.

The scene and the undercurrents are difficult to re-create. That Mrs. Buckley was evidently a Catholic must have been some recommendation to Mrs. Steiner, who surely noted the framed engraving of the Sacred Heart that (as surely) greeted her eyes in the vestibule, and the pictures of Our Lady and the Infant Jesus in the parlor. There were crucifixes in all the rooms, we can guess. How the conversation went among them all we can have no idea (I imagine Grandmother B was kind to little Inez and Jimmy Steiner, if not so kindly intentioned to their sister Aloïse); but at one juncture, privately (were they in the hall, on their way to the dining room, were they just leaving?), Will Buckley asked Aloïse Steiner once

---

*Had he somehow been in communication with Grandfather Aloysius and discovered from him the exact date that Grandmother and her two daughters left New Orleans for Austin?
†Mother never failed to boast to her children that when her mother was married, Grandfather could circle her waist in both his small hands; and that she was a stylish "equestrian" well known throughout the city for her horsemanship (sidesaddle, of course). But when I knew her, Grandmother was perfectly what a grandmother was supposed to be, stout and warm and sweet-smelling, and with one of the kindest Southern contraltos my ears have ever heard.

more to marry him, to which she replied, "Mr. Buckley, if you were the last man on earth, I would not marry you." And—we learned later—almost immediately bit her lip and felt tears of regret threaten her eyes.

He was apparently abashed, turning very pale, falling silent. It was as though he hadn't for one moment imagined that she wasn't of the same mind.

I don't know how that short interlude in Austin ended. (We never, to my knowledge, heard one word about their courtship from our father, who was awkward about all personal and intimate matters.) Mother did not see Will Buckley for another two months; but in Mexico City, she found herself thinking of him often. His name came up in the conversations of the many prominent people she met, and he was spoken of with high regard always. Will Buckley was a go-getter. He was imaginative—dredging the river that ran by Tampico to build himself a private island, who would have thought of that? He took chances few people were inclined to accept, and he possessed the single-minded determination to make them work for him.

Such conversation could not have sat well with Mother's second cousin, once removed, "Uncle" Émile Berthier, who held a not-so-secret ambition for his son and Aloïse to marry—which was uncomfortable for Mother, consanguinity aside. Though she liked young Émile well enough, and adored his sister, the glamorously beautiful and tempestuous Odette,[5] and was very fond of his mother (her aunt, Josephine Edvidge Wassem), whom she called "Aunty" and who was referred to always by the family in that way, and was greatly fond of "Uncle" Émile, she simply had no intention of marrying the son and heir. She kept thinking about Will Buckley, she told me, and regretting her harshness to him; and she cried a little sometimes at night thinking of him and how she had dashed any prospect of becoming engaged to him. One has to comprehend the passivity to which her upbringing condemned her. She had blown it, for good. He had been rejected by her three times; his dignity must have been mortally affronted. Oh, what a mess she had made of her life! *Aloïse, Aloïse, did you have to be so cutting!*

One fine morning late that August, unannounced, he appeared at the Berthier home in Mexico City and invited the whole family, Berthiers and Steiners, to lunch at the country club.

Mother's emotions were thrown into a turmoil. She did not know what to think. He was courteous to her, though, she thought, distant. He spoke mostly to the Berthiers, with whom he was well acquainted. At one moment in the proceedings, he turned to her and said quietly, "Will you marry me, Aloïse? . . . I'm asking you for the last time."

"Oh, Will, Will, of course I will marry you!"

They were wed shortly thereafter (December 29, 1917) in New Orleans, in the cathedral, and lived fearfully, frantically, desperately, blissfully together forty-one years, until his death in 1958. She conceived twelve times by him, one a miscarriage, another, my immediate older sister, Mary Ann (named after her Buckley grandmother and maybe also after her Lee great-grandmother), who died within a week of birth. Then there were the ten of us . . . [6]

FOR THE RECORD, THE CAST OF CHARACTERS, SECOND GENERATION:

Aloise (Allie), b. 1918 d. 1968; husband Ben Heath
John, b. 1920 d. 1984; wife Ann Harding
Priscilla (Pitts), b. 1921
James (Jim, Jimmy), b. 1922, wife Ann Cooley
Jane (Janie), b. 1923 d. 2007, husband Bill Smith
William (Bill, Billy), b. 1925, wife Pat Taylor
Patricia (Trish, Trisha, Tricia), b. 1927, husband Brent Bozell
(Mary Ann b. 1929 d. 1929)
Reid (Reidy), b. 1930, wives Betsy Howell & Rosario (Tasa) Leguina
Maureen, b. 1933 d. 1964, husband Gerald A. O'Reilly
Carol (Carolita), b. 1938, husbands Tom Charlton & Ray Learsy

NOTES

———

1. The impermissibility of the divorced state in those days was not peculiarly a Catholic objection, as it is now. Divorce was not countenanced by society; it was held to be a moral fault and a dereliction. Promiscuity was implicit. This attitude prevailed right up into the 1930s and was only softened with the advent of World War II. We children are aware of an earnest discussion our parents had in the privacy of their bed-

room suite about whether to invite a very dear friend to visit Great Elm for the weekend because of her divorced and remarried state. They were seriously concerned about the example and precedent for us children. This was not personal intolerance; it was a reasoned and heart-wrenching dilemma. (At the last, they did invite her, as Mother told us long afterward; but their doubts and the deliberation serve to remind us how much social tolerance has expanded in the past one hundred years, and also how human compassion has been twisted so that it challenges both religious belief and the instinctive protections against wrongdoing that society commonly relied upon.)

2. Émile Berthier's father had refused to accept the Union victory over the South and had left New Orleans to make his way in Mexico City.

3. On the other hand, the divorced man she had unfortunately fallen in love with was also in his early thirties, we deduce, and Grandfather Steiner was himself sixteen years older than our grandmother. The disparity in age was not unusual in times when a gentleman was not considered fit to ask the hand of a lady unless he was able to maintain her in the comfort to which she was accustomed. (My Spanish sons have ruled themselves by this convention, though the two youngest were raised in the States from their sixth and seventh years.) The prospective son-in-law of a solid bourgeois family had either to possess a substantial inherited fortune or to be a proved breadwinner, which generally meant that he would be older by some years than the bride. This may account for the greater stability of marriages in former times: sexual infatuation played a lesser rôle, there was love, we may suppose, but there was also practicality.

4. Which, eighty-six years later, on a nostalgic trip I took with my wife, Tasa, nobody in Taxco whom we encountered remembered or had ever heard of: though I recall distinctly as a child being taken by my mother to a small church in that village (I could not find this, either) that Uncle Berthier had sworn he would cover in gold and silver if ever he struck it rich, a pledge he fulfilled. Awfully—I remember my reaction to the sight of it. It was as though he had poured gold and silver all over the altar and elsewhere.

5. My future godmother, a formidable personality, of whom my father said always that she scared young gentleman suitors off not only by her uncommon beauty but by the superiority of her intelligence, which she scorned to conceal; who unaccountably announced a vocation in her late twenties or early thirties, becoming a deeply devout nun of the Visitation Convent in Mobile, Alabama. She took the name of Sister St. Francis de Sales. I treasured her letters, which are safely stored in my files, where they are safe from recovery by anyone, including myself.

6. Brother Jim's version of our parents' courtship differs widely from mine and may be more accurate historically. He allows several more days for the courtship but agrees that it was nevertheless "precipitous."

PART THREE

The Mexican Experience

---⌘---

CHAPTER NINE

William Frank Buckley
of Texas (IV): Tampico, Banditry—
Mexican and American

THOSE WERE THE HALCYON YEARS FOR OUR FATHER AND HIS BRIDE.

Everything must have been new for them both, she gently bred in New Orleans, he in the rush of his mid-thirties and succeeding beyond his dreams.

He wrote his lifelong friend Pope boastfully at this happy time (which began for him three years before he met and married Mother):

The New Willard*
May 17, 1914

My dear Pope:
Of the many letters I received in Vera Cruz, none was appreciated as was yours. I had thought of you so very often, and have started a great many times to write. Writing, however, to me, is a very poor means of communication, and I seldom indulge in it.

---

*Replacing the famed Willard Hotel to whose bar such luminaries as Ulysses S. Grant and Mark Twain bellied up; that bar now constitutes the principal decor of Lucy's Restaurant in Camden, South Carolina.

I often think of our old friendship, and of what it has meant to me. You were very kind to me at a crucial period in my life when it counted. [1] I have often hoped I might see you in Mexico.

Well, I presume you saw it in the papers that I declined the appointment [to be U.S. civil governor] at Vera Cruz. I was one of the four appointees who did decline, and, consequently, the only one who was not embarrassed a few days [later] by being decapitated by Washington. I was in Mexico City when Vera Cruz was taken [April 21, 1914], and went on down with the intention of returning to the city with General Funston, to whom I had no doubt I could be helpful.* Things were pretty exciting. I hung around Vera Cruz for a couple of weeks waiting for something to happen. Then the Peace Commission came along, and Mr. Rabasa, the President of the Commission, who is my consulting attorney in the City,† asked me to come to Washington to deliver to the President a message that the Commissioners could not very well with dignity deliver themselves.‡ I did this, and then went to New York, where I spent last week, and I am now back to stay, maybe until the Conference adjourns, or perhaps a few days. [2]

You must be a very happy man with your sweet wife and your fine boys. I envy you very much. My mother always speaks of you when I come home, and appreciates your always coming to see her.[3]§

Pope, I think I have had as much experience in the past six years (since going to Mexico) as the average man sixty years of age. Mexico

---

*Frederick Funston (1865–1917). Winner of a Congressional Medal of Honor, he measured only five feet four inches, but he was every inch a fighting man. He had a distinguished career in Cuba during the Spanish-American War as a brigadier general and then later in the Philippines, where he performed a number of heroics, for which he earned the respect of his men and his commanders but a slashing attack from Mark Twain, who opposed American intervention. In 1914, he led 5,000 U.S. troops into Veracruz on the orders of President Woodrow Wilson and, promoted to major general, was appointed military governor of the city. Father was bitterly opposed to the invasion, but he was apparently on reasonably friendly terms with the general, whose personal gallantry he must have admired.

†In his testimony before the Senate's Fall Committee on Mexican Affairs, Father stated: "they at once selected the three ablest Mexicans in Mexico, Lic. Emilio Rabasa, Lic. Luis Elguero, and Lic. Agustín Rodríguez, all lawyers of note."

‡We have no idea what this message could have been!

§ I bet this was the kindness that Father valued so deeply, and would not forget. He loved his mother profoundly, as we, his sons, love the memory of our mother.

is a most interesting country, and business there is so different, everything is done on a large scale, even though the foundation be no more substantial than wind. I have been up against every imaginable kind of game.[4]

I had a terrible time for the first two years. For eight months I worked for a powerful attorney (a crook) and then quit him, with no money, and no friends. He has been a very bitter enemy ever since. For a year, I didn't make a living.

Two years ago [1911? 1912?] I opened a law office in Tampico also and took Claude and Edmund in. Times were getting hard in the interim and I thought I saw a big opening in the oil fields. It was a big step, and another firm, when I told of the opportunity, rushed in and opened their office a few days before mine. I had only about 1,000 (Mex) in cash, and realized that either we or the other people were going to get the big business and the other firm the small business.

I borrowed money and fitted up a magnificent office costing 7,000 (Mex); I got the District Judge to resign and work for me, and high priced translators, and turned down all small business. The payroll the first month was 2,000. Well, we got the big business, and took in in cash the first year 70,000 Mex. [5] I worked myself down to a nervous wreck and spent all last summer in the North under medical treatment. I then quit the practice and turned the law business over to Claude and Edmund. [6]

To me, the practice of law is the most trying thing in the world. I have some good property in Mexico, worth at least $100,000 American money. From a pecuniary standpoint, I have done all right. [7] All the above, of course, and especially as to my mission in Washington,* is confidential.

> As ever your friend,
> W. F. Buckley

[1] *"You were very kind to me at a crucial period in my life when it counted."*

Referring to what act of charity by Walter Pope is lost, but Father never would have forgot it.

---

*What that mysterious (and fascinating) mission could have been we children have no idea.

[2] *"I did this, and then went to New York, where I spent last week, and I am now back to stay, maybe until the Conference adjourns, or perhaps a few days."*

It must have been a heady sensation for the thirty-three-year-old Texan of humble antecedence and upbringing to find himself playing an intimate part in relations between Mexico and the United States.

In 1913, General Victoriano Huerta (1854–1916) overthrew the fumbling government of Francisco Madero (1873–1913, murdered). He dissolved the legislature, establishing a military dictatorship, whose rule (like Madero's rule before him) was both inefficient and repressive.

Madero, an idealist, had toppled longtime dictator Porfirio Díaz (1830–1915, died at his desk).

Woodrow Wilson refused to recognize Huerta's government, claiming that he had seized power "by objectionable means" (Huerta arrested Madero, who was then mysteriously done away with in prison) and did not represent "the submerged 85 percent of the people of that republic who are now struggling for liberty."

This statement expresses the righteous moralism that drove Father up the wall. (What in the world did Thomas Woodrow Wilson, son of a Presbyterian minister, raised in Georgia and North Carolina, who taught as a young man at the Columbia Theological Seminary of South Carolina before becoming a Princeton professor, dropping his first name—he was known as Tommy to his coevals—because he thought that plain Woodrow Wilson sounded more "dignified"—*what did he know* about 85 percent of the Mexican people, whose religion he despised and whose history he scorned, whose language he was ignorant of, and whose territory he had never once touched foot on?)

Wilson supported the anti-Huerta revolution led by Venustiano Carranza (1859–1920, assassinated), Carranza's ally General Álvaro Obregón (1880–1928, assassinated),* the outlaw Pancho Villa (1878–1923, ambushed and assassinated), and Emiliano Zapata (1879–1919, ambushed and assassinated). Wilson proposed an armistice between the warring parties, to be followed by free elections in which Huerta was not a candidate.

---

*Obregón, a capable general, was a rabid anticlericalist; when he defeated and replaced Huerta, he established the 1917 constitution, with which Father took exception as a Catholic and as an American businessman.

Huerta not unexpectedly declined to go along. Wilson retaliated by placing an embargo on arms entering Mexico—declaring a period of "watchful waiting" as riots, revolution, disorder, and death bedeviled the country. Wilson's embargo was "lifted" in 1914 . . . to the effect that, while arms were permitted to reach Carranza and Villa, U.S. Navy vessels stationed in the Gulf continued to prevent any from reaching Huerta.

It was in this tense context that an unarmed party of American sailors from the USS *Dolphin* came ashore on Huerta-controlled Mexican territory for supplies and, in doing so, trespassed on a restricted area.

They were arrested by a Huerta officer for violation of Mexican martial law and marched through the streets of Tampico. (That was a mistake: in those days, humiliating Americans was viscerally resented by the American people.) A superior officer quickly ordered their release, offering an oral apology for the unauthorized action of "an overzealous subordinate." That wasn't enough for Admiral Henry T. Mayo. He demanded that the Huerta general in charge (1) apologize formally, (2) promise to punish the "overzealous" officer, (3) raise the American flag on Mexican soil, and (4) give it a twenty-one-gun salute.

The Huerta general made a formal written apology, and Huerta himself expressed his regrets for the incident . . . but he refused to raise and salute the American flag on his turf. (Given the circumstances— Woodrow Wilson's open hostility—I would have refused, too, wouldn't you?) Vital American interests were hardly threatened, but Mr. Wilson's vast dignity had been affronted. On April 20, he asked Congress for authority to intervene in Mexico by force of arms, citing the Tampico incident "as only the latest" in a long list of grievances.

Congress granted his request two days later. Meantime, however, on April 21, 1914, while Congress was debating, news reached the White House that a German ship was approaching Veracruz, loaded with a large cargo of arms for Huerta. At Wilson's orders, eight-hundred Marines and sailors from the battleship USS *Texas* landed at Veracruz, seizing the city on the pretext of protecting U.S. citizens from harm and danger and securing them in their rights. Mexican defenders against the invasion suffered one hundred casualties.

Anti-American sentiments boiled through the country. Carranza, Obregón, and most of Mexico with them united behind Huerta, insisting upon the removal of U.S. troops. Huerta broke diplomatic relations with the United States and prepared for war.

It was this crisis that prompted the convening of the so-called ABC Conference, named for Argentina, Brazil, and Chile—the "peace conference" to which Father alludes in his letter. Ambassadors of these friendly neutral powers got together in May and June of 1914 on the Canadian side of Niagara Falls. Father attended as the Huerta-appointed counsel to the Mexican delegation. (I wonder what he felt and thought upon first viewing that thundering cascade, coming as he did from the drought-ridden Southwestern desert.) It was known that Father had "indignantly" turned down Wilson's invitation to accept the post of civil governor of Veracruz. His appointment as Mexico's counsel at the ABC Conference is an astonishing testament to his reputation for independence, probity, and sympathy for Mexico, of which he was justifiably proud.

An agreement was reached by the neutral powers. Under its terms, (1) Huerta was to step down, (2) a reform government was to be established in Mexico, (3) the United States was to receive no indemnity for the cost of occupying Veracruz.

Mexico (read Huerta) unsurprisingly rejected the plan, but after defeat in battle by Obregón, Huerta fled the country, dying a couple of years later peacefully—the only major figure of that revolutionary decade to escape assassination or murder of which I am aware. On November 14, seven months after the invasion, U.S. forces departed Veracruz, and Wilson at last had the pleasure of recognizing Carranza as president of Mexico. Five years later (1919), Father would be testifying before the Albert B. Fall Senate Subcommittee on Mexican Affairs (under Henry Cabot Lodge's Committee on Foreign Relations), delivering a scathing denunciation of Wilsonian interference in the business of other nations,* of Wilsonian ignorance, provincialism, bias, and self-righteousness. Appalled by the bungling of Washington, he would be an isolationist thereafter, until Pearl Harbor.

Again: What is notable is the trust that so many Mexicans, such as the mentioned Señor Rabasa, placed in Will Buckley, the young gringo from

---

*Wilson had a propensity for sticking his nose into the affairs of other peoples: he sent Marines into Haiti to set up a government to his liking, liberal and democratic; but he also sent American troops into Santo Domingo, there to prop up a dictator.

Will Buckley at Xochimilco, c. 1915. Pictured: Emily Maverick Miller (brunette, second from left and next to WFB), her aunt Georgie Maverick Harris (far left), and her grandmother and chaperone, Mrs. Sam Maverick.

Texas. He was not only sympathetic to them, he was incorruptible. The influence here of his Irish ancestry and Catholicism (in gut opposition to Anglo Protestant imperialism) can't be underestimated, though I doubt he would have ever framed it in these terms; as I doubt that he was given to such introversion ("Writing, however, to me, is a very poor means of communication, and I seldom indulge in it") except as a weakness that he would have dismissed wryly from his mind.

Which is curious on several counts. He was a man of action, yet he was also very much a reader who lived a rich internal life. (It was the philistine boorishness of Wall Street that alienated him.) I don't think I have known anyone with a such a respect for books—for the bound volume of prose or poetry or even novels (historical, in the main; I remember him praising *Los Cipreses Creen en Dios,* by José María Gironella, who was little known at the time). He detested dog-earing. He considered this a desecration, even when he might disapprove of the author or the work. He established the strict rule in our house that nobody who was reading was ever to be interrupted or disturbed, by anyone, no matter the circumstances.

All of us—I *often*—took conspicuous cover behind the open leaves of a book when he was irked with us for some (good) reason. Father would search through the sprawling rooms of Great Elm. There he would come upon us in the library, legs flung over the arm of an upholstered armchair, engrossed in a book. He would find us in the playroom that doubled as a schoolroom and occupied the entire ground floor of the capacious eastern wing of the patio, lounging or propped up in one of the deep window benches, engrossed. He would find us in our bedroom, sprawled on one of the beds, engrossed. And he would stop short at each sighting, begin to utter our name, then contain himself, withdrawing, his irritation on each occasion mounting, but he was hoist on the petard of his stringing, and he never once broke his rule! (And by next morning, the cause of his annoyance with us forgotten, we were safe to come out from behind our books.)*

[3] *"You must be a very happy man with your sweet wife and your fine boys. I envy you very much. My mother always speaks of you when I come home . . ."*

I can bet grandmother B was saying to her bachelor son on his visits from Mexico, "Willie, look at your good friend Walter Pope. Don't you think it's time you found a good, sweet Irish Catholic girl to marry?"

Mother was a good, sweet (maybe a trifle too young and spunky, for Grandmother B's taste) Swiss-German girl with a dose of redeeming Irish blood, but she was Catholic from her crown to her tiny high-heeled soles, and that would have won over Grandmother B, who had a beautiful cedar chest made for her, one I will mention elsewhere.

[4] *". . . everything is done on a large scale, even though the foundation be no more substantial than wind. I have been up against every imaginable kind of game."*

Here his love of gambling—characteristically a Western trait—breaks through, in prose of youthful exuberance. Business was a game with him; it was never his life, never engaged his depths or in itself satisfied more than the fun of it, the joy he took in doing business, the competitive pit-

---

* The origin, I conjecture, of his oft-repeated remark about me ("You never see that boy without a good book in his hands"). I was most often guilty of some infraction and had taken protective cover.

ting of his intelligence and foresight and determination against these same three attributes in others, and, of course, the money he made from it—when he was lucky!

[5] *"Well, we got the big business, and took in in cash the first year 70,000 Mex."*

I make the guess that 70,000 pesos amounted to some $14,000; further, that one may multiply that dollar amount by fifteen to arrive at an approximation of contemporary spending power. Resonating in my eardrums is Uncle Claude telling me that they made an astounding $200,000 that first year Buckley and Buckley was in business, but if I did hear that, I now assume he meant the contemporary spending power.

Will Buckley's opportunism and audacity were characteristic . . . and these are traits he passed down to several of his children. He spent wildly extravagant sums decorating his law offices in Tampico. One did not stint on appearances when it came to business; that was pound foolish. Somehow one scraped up the money. (Hence the handsome Catawba office building in New York many years later and the lavish establishment of Great Elm, to which he frequently invited business associates for weekends. And hence, in my modest case, the palace I hired on the Paseo de la Castellana in Madrid for my Bique* showrooms and the simple yet pleasing Federal-American Gothic frame building in Camden, listed in the National Register of Historic Homes, which houses my school.) Uncle Claude spoke dismissively of the law offices in Tampico above a saloon and reached by a "rickety" (his word) outdoor staircase, but Señor Velasco wrote† that Father "had set himself up in a spacious and magnificent office with a nameplate that read: Buckley and Buckley, Attorneys at Law. William F. Buckley and Claude H. Buckley." (That was in 1911. Young Edmund had yet to be dragooned into joining his elder brothers.)‡

---

*Acronym for Buckley-Irujo Quality Enterprise, a Madrid-based export-import firm, famous for its impeccable taste, even more famous for its red ink, of which I have written elsewhere. See *Good Taste Doesn't Sell, Bad Taste Sells Loads,* P.E.N. Press.

† See *W.F.B.—An Appreciation.* Did Father have two offices, the splendid one referred to by Señor Velasco in Mexico City, the humbler establishment in Tampico?

‡ The Benson Library in the University of Texas is surely mistaken when, in supplying a chronology for our father, it lists Edmund as his partner in Tampico; it was Claude.

[6] *"I then quit the practice and turned the law business over to Claude and Edmund."*

My uncle Claude, who loved the law and practiced it in Mexico for forty years, told me several stories in this connection when I visited him (which I did as frequently as I was able) in San Antonio, in his retirement. Those $200,000 (spending power) were split equally among the brothers, including young Edmund, who promptly went out and bought himself a Cadillac.

Scandalizing his elder brothers. It was "showy" in the opprobrious sense, serving no purpose other than vanity. Why, Edmund had never had two silver dollars to jingle in his pockets before this! It was boastful and extravagant . . . but it was also very Edmund, whom they loved. He was the frolicsome son and much younger brother. He gambled in the casino, and he drank—which would have killed his mother, had she known (she must have suspected it). Our brother John told the story that when Father and Uncle Edmund were visiting Grandmother B at the Lavaca Street house in Austin, she would upbraid her youngest son, saying, "Edmund, aren't you ashamed of yourself? Your brother Willie is up every morning promptly at six. He has breakfast with me and then goes out on business until noon, when he comes home. Then after a short nap he goes out again on business and sometimes doesn't get back until six o'clock in the evening, having worked the whole day. But you, Edmund, I never see you for breakfast. You loll in bed until nine or ten o'clock mornings and then go out and don't tell anyone where you are going and don't get back for lunch and sometimes don't come in until after ten o'clock at night— wasting your time all day doing goodness knows what. It's disgraceful. When you think of your brother Willie, aren't you ashamed?" To which Uncle Edmund replied brightly, "Mother, the difference is that Willie likes to work, I don't."

Uncle Edmund led an adventurous career of boom and bust. It was legendary in my family that around Christmastime he might send us an invitation to cruise the Gulf next April on his newly acquired yacht; then in March we would receive a telegram announcing, "Broke. Sold boat. Sorry." Then in May or June we would get another telegram with the jubilant news, "Sank my last dollar on a wildcat well, hit oil. Bought new boat. Come join us in July.[1]

He was the lovable brother, a term that would, I think, never be used of Uncle Claude and Father, whose reticence, except under special, intimate, and familial circumstances, they inherited from their sire, John C. Buckley.[?] When I visited Tampico in 1970, on research for a book I never wrote, I was advised to order a "Petroleo" at a certain bar, which was an undrinkable draught (taken neat), dark as castor oil, half tequila, half Mexican *magay* sauce, with a strong squirt of lime and salt. In my experience, only Fermet Branca, the evil-tasting Italian liqueur fermented from hearts of artichoke, and a surefire cure for queasy stomachs (if it doesn't cause you to retch out your entrails at first gulp), is as awful.

And potent. This was the invention of Uncle Edmund, who led a happy life in Tampico, marrying an uncommonly beautiful woman in Aunt Beryl and buying himself a 100,00-acre ranch by the River Santa Clara, about eighty miles from Tampico, on which game of every description abounded. He'd instruct, say, his stunningly beautiful daughter Beryl and handsome son Edmund, both of whom (unsurprisingly) grew up crack shots, "Your mother and I have thirty or forty people coming for supper next Saturday. I think you ought to shoot several dozen doves for a pie . . . say, oh, seventy quail, forty or maybe fifty ducks—teals, please—and a young buck or two." It was like filling a shopping list.

That was the popular patriarch of his immediate family; but as a young man, he was the despair of his stern older brothers, Claude and Will, visiting casinos and once, according to Uncle Claude, gambling away the payroll. He nevertheless listened to their admonitions about the Cadillac (whose glistening steel skin was in any event encased in, and hidden beneath, leather chaps, necessary to protect it from the thorny bush country of Mexico's *tierra caliente*), announcing one afternoon that he had sold the Caddy and bought himself a Ford sedan, greatly to his brothers' relief. "But then," said Uncle Claude to me (chuckling), "Edmund also announced that he had taken the balance of his share of the profits and sunk it all in the purchase of an oil lease . . .

"Your father and I were appalled," he went on. "Our brother was incorrigible. Four hectares in some woebegone locality south of Vera Cruz. There was an American sucker born every minute who bought, and a sharpie of a local Mexican *cacique* who sold, worthless leases, most of them entailed or of doubtful ownership, *we* knew that as lawyers who dealt in the business every day!

"*Edmund* should have known better. There were times when your father and I wondered whether it had not been a mistake to bring him to Mexico, which was a wild country that tempted him in every bad way. Well, you know," he went on, "Edmund drilled those four hectares, and he struck oil with his first well—a gusher, seventy-four thousand barrels a day until it ran out, which was soon, which is the habit of gushers. But it was at this news that your father turned his gaze on me in the office and said, 'Claude, there's something in this world besides lawyering.' Yes, it was Edmund's folly, and Edmund's astounding luck, that made your father quit the law."

[7] *"I have some good property in Mexico, worth at least $100,000 American money. From a pecuniary standpoint, I have done all right."*

If my previous reckoning is a fair approximation, that $100,000 amounts to $1.5 million in contemporary terms. The hint of boastfulness to an old friend is excusable. Father had been a poor boy. Now, in 1914, at age thirty-three, on his own in a turbulent land, he had made it—he was a man of means. We children tend to forget that real estate was his first love and the foundation of his first fortune.*

IN 1917, AFTER THE WHIRLWIND COURTSHIP, HE MARRIED ALOÏSE Steiner of New Orleans and brought her to Tampico, where he built a two-story house for her, with a capacious basement and garage.

It was the first or one of the first proper structures on the silt and clay that he had dredged out of the river and piled up behind the little city, creating an elevation that became (and is still) Tampico's prime residential quarter. Señor Velasco wrote in 1958 that "Tampico owes to W.F.B. no less than 80 percent of its development and important works, all [moreover] developed with foreign capital."

Tampico was a sultry, mosquito-infested, and malarial backwater on the Panuco River, six miles from the Gulf of Mexico, conditions that would not have disconcerted Father's New Orleans-bred bride but that he

---

*In modest fashion, real estate became my big paycheck. Almost all of Father's children have an eye for land.

determined to relieve for her. The house stands still, and it is today surrounded by many other and more opulent residential structures. It is nevertheless well built,[3] with pleasing lines, the street running alongside
dipping down sharply to expose the foundations of the basement as it descends toward the city. Mother told me that she had to be careful to keep
the downstairs windows (French doors) shut, despite the heat, because
loafers would walk along the steeply descending sidewalk, hidden from
the view of anyone in the living room, using a fishing rod with a big gang
hook to poke through open windows with the object of hooking a lamp
by its shade or some other object (what other object? I have wondered
often), which they would reel in and run off with. It seems improbable,
but Mother spoke of this matter-of-factly. When she moved in, she and
Father were alone on the hill, for which he had ambitious plans.

One version of the story is recounted marvelously by my sister Priscilla
in *W.F.B.—An Appreciation,* and I quote from her until my version of it
diverges from hers. It concerns, she writes, "La Isleta, Buckley Island," the
tale "told the first of many times during a walk when we were living at I
Avenue Ingres, in Paris, Father with hat high on his high forehead and
cane swinging, Mother on one arm. The three oldest of us [Aloïse, John,
and Pitts] on the other, and knock-kneed six-year-old Jimmy, in his absorption, walking half backwards, always underfoot, totally impervious to
the running commentary, 'Jimmy, get out of the way. . . . Mother, tell
Jimmy to get out of the way. . . . Honestly, if you're not big enough to walk
right . . .' And through it all a tale traced of delightful skullduggery and
counter-skullduggery.

"This may not be exactly the way it happened," she continues, "but this
is the way I think Father once said it happened and if it is not so, I for one,
don't want to know it. . . .

"Tampico, as you know . . . is terribly hot. On the river was a sandbar,
visible only at low tide. Father thought the sandbar would make a cool
breeze-swept residential area, so he persuaded some dredgers already on
the job clearing the river channel, to dump their loads of silt on the sandbar. The land which emerged was known as Buckley Island. Well, he developed it, put in streets and sewers and lights, and was ready to sell lots
when ('. . . that crook, what was the name of that fellow, Aloïse, my lawyer . . .') his lawyer, in collusion with the local judge, forged a set of deeds
and titles to land which had never existed before. The lawyer forged the

deeds, the judge declared them valid and Father, with several hundred thousand dollars sunk in Buckley Island was ordered to get out. . . . 'I called in Rox Beaumont (a Texas badman but a good badman because he sometimes worked for Father)* and told him to get a dozen of the toughest fellows he knew and go out to La Isleta. They each had a shotgun and I paid them t-w-e-n-t-y-f-i-v-e American dollars a day.

"'Well, the crook was trying to sell lots on the island, but when the customers wanted to see the lots, he couldn't show [the property] to them, not without running into Rox Beaumont. That went on for some time and one day, the judge came to see me. "Mr. Buckley," he said, "no one is making money this way. That lawyer of yours is a fool." So we fixed it up. . . .'

"Father took the case back to court and the judge declared that the titles and deeds he had previously honored were rank and amateurish forgeries. And Buckley Island was saved."

The story I have to tell either concerns another piece of land (one that I have myself walked, in the upper reaches of residential Tampico), or it is a development from, an evolution or mutation of, sister Priscilla's story. What I know certainly about this land was Father's intention to build houses for his brothers on it and then to offer parcels to Tampico merchants and the oil-company executives. But one morning, as he peered out of his second-floor bathroom window, he saw workmen by the base of the hill, by the riverbank. Opening the window wide, he heard hammering and cheery shouts.

He finished dressing hurriedly, walking out for a better view. There were about a dozen men, who had ferried themselves across the river in boats, and who were putting up ramshackle houses, built with any opportunistic material, crates, sheets of zinc, bricks, old doors, planks of wood—whatever was at hand. Within a day or two, he was going to have a half-dozen squatters on his costly and valuable property, which he had created out of the river; and within a few weeks of those initial settlements, dozens more squatters would come creeping up the hill to the summit.

There was no telephone. He drove to town and went straight to the

---

*I believe his name was Rox Underwood. And if this is the man, he was a gambler by profession, a gunman sometimes by necessity. I interviewed his charming widow in 1969.

police station, where he registered a complaint with the chief, who listened to him airily. "How will a few neighbors affect you, Señor Buckley?" "A few neighbors will become several dozen and more in three months, as you very well know, and they will ruin the value of the property that I built." The chief was nonetheless unsympathetic. "I very much doubt that the good people of Tampico would break the law by trespassing on your property, Señor Buckley." "Well, then, why don't you come see for yourself?"

The chief was reluctant to bestir himself, but he grudgingly agreed to pay a visit that evening. When he arrived, at just about six o'clock, Father took him out and pointed to all the construction that was taking place at the base of the hill, by the riverbank. Four or five of the dwellings were almost completed. But the chief of police stared and stared and, turning his broad face to my father, said blandly, "I see nothing, Señor Buckley. Nothing at all. Your complaint is groundless." With that, he walked back to his car and drove off.

Father had a caretaker (my sister Priscilla remembers him as Ramón) whom he summoned after supper. "Ramón," he said, "I want you to go into town this evening, and to the poorer barrios, and I want you to spread the word that anyone can have anything he can carry off my property for free, but that it must all be taken away by dawn." He explained his psychology to us children in terms that today jar, because we know of no more industrious and diligent workers than our Mexican immigrants, refugees of want. Until well after World War II, however, the operative stereotype was represented by those alabaster bookends (once so popular, originating in Puebla) of the Mexican *peón* sitting with knees drawn up, covered by his *zarape* and sombrero, fast asleep. "I knew," he said, "that any Mexican would work eight hours to steal what he could earn in one hour legitimately." And early next morning, lo and behold, when Father looked out over his property, there was no sign of construction whatever. The ramshackle, half-completed dwellings had been razed. They had been obliterated. There wasn't a board or a brick or a nail to be seen. But presently, plying their way across the river in boats, came the workmen, who began shouting as they approached the landing—waving their fists and cursing.

Before another hour was up, a vehicle toiled up the sharp hill from the city, and out huffed the chief of police, purple with indignation. "What is this I hear, Señor Buckley? What have you done with all those houses that were being built down there?"

"What houses?" asked my father in the same bland tone of voice used by the chief the day before, when denying the existence of any construction. "I don't see any houses, do you? As you said, what honest citizen of Tampico would trespass on private property?"

Oh, how we relished this story as children (the middle three, Jane, Bill, and Patricia, and the bottom two, Maureen and I—Carol had not yet been born): our ingenious father outfoxing the corrupt policeman. When we heard it and its cousins, it was always, in my memory, summertime, and a Friday or Saturday evening, when Father had got back from New York for the weekend, supper nearly done. We would be at the long mahogany dining-room table, sitting in the high-backed Chippendale chairs that I loved so much, giggling and laughing and begging for more stories. "Tell about what happened afterward," Mother prompted. "What's that, Aloïse?" "The bandits, Will, and Ramón—that brave man!" "And terrible shot," said our father, grinning caustically in recollection. "But the children all know the story, Aloïse, they don't need to hear it again." "But we do, we do—tell it, please!"

Oh, how we enjoyed those long, long July evenings with the sun setting at well past nine o'clock, crimson and purple over the blue haze of the distant Catskills, on which those lucky of us to be sitting along the eastern side of the table were able to gaze our eyesful through the multipaned dining-room windows; when, after the mellowing and relaxation of two glasses of red wine, our father became teasing—bantering with the wife he adored and the children he alternately doted on and was concerned by (were they building up character?); and the tales about his Mexican days began to flow.

"Well," he said, after a very little more urging, "Ramón was just as your mother said of him, a very brave man. But he was also just what I said about him, a very poor shot. One evening after that business with the police chief, Ramón came into the dining room as we were just finishing—you, Aloise [directing himself to our oldest sister], were just two, I believe, and you, John, you hadn't been born . . ."

"Why, Will—John was six months old!"

"Well, he wasn't at the dinner table."

"No, and neither was Aloïse. They were too young."

"Well, Ramón apologized for interrupting our supper, but he had seen a boat approaching from the river by where all the construction had taken place, and he said that two armed bandits were in the boat and disembarking."

"Oh, I was frightened, children," put in our mother, her green eyes registering the memory. "Except for Ramón and the house servants, we were alone on that hill."

"Yes," said our father. "I had my father's pistol, of course, but otherwise there wasn't a weapon in the house, no rifle of any sort.[4] Calling the police station would be no help; the bandits would have climbed the hill long before the police arrived, and in any case, it might very well be the chief himself who had sent them, or his cousin, who I suspected was the money behind the squatters. So I asked Ramón, 'What do you suggest we do?' He said to me, 'Finish your supper in peace, Señor Buckley. I will stop them.'

"I looked at him curiously, asking him, 'With what, Ramón?' Well, sir,[*] he pulled the biggest pistol you ever saw out of his trousers, with the longest barrel you ever saw. I don't know what make it was—Spanish, probably. 'With this, Señor,' he said with great dignity, and then he rushed out.

"Well, I decided I wasn't going to miss this, and I followed him outside; and there he was, standing on the top of the hill, with the bandits halfway up it. They were short and paunchy and bandy-legged—used to riding horseback, not walking. Regular outlaws one saw just about everywhere in those days: huge sombreros and bandoleers slung over their shoulders, studded with cartridges. And when they spotted Ramón above them, they broke into a run, pulling out their pistols and shooting at him. *Bang, bang, bang, bang*, they went," Father said, poking the nearest of us to him in the tummy with a blunt index finger. "*Bang, bang, bang*—running up that hill. Ramón stood there like a statue, bullets whizzing all about him. Then, as the bandits neared the hilltop, they run out of ammunition—and Ramón went running at them down the hill, pulling out *his* enormous pistol and shooting, *bang, bang, bang*.

"The bandits wheeled about and ran back where they came from, lickety-split. They *flew!* But by the time they got to the bottom of the hill, they had reloaded, Ramón's pistol was empty, so they turned around and

---

[*] Pronounced as though it were one word: "Wellsir."

began chasing him back up the hill, *bang, bang, bang.* Well, Ramón ran as fast as he was able to go, reloading as he went. The bandits had twice as many bullets as he did, mind you, but they didn't hit him, they were terrible shots also, and before Ramón reached the summit, they were out of ammunition again, and out of breath.

"Ramón spun about and began chasing them back down that hill, shooting at them as he went. *Bang, bang, bang; bang, bang, bang.* The bandits fled to the bottom, reloading as they ran, turning and running a third time uphill after Ramón, but more slowly now, they were exhausted— shooting at Ramón as he ran back up the hill, also more slowly. They never hit him, and this time when Ramón turned on them and began shooting more deliberately—*bang,* he went, running a few steps, then stopping and taking aim. *Bang,* he went again—why, the bandits gave up, they ran as fast as their short legs would take them, jumping into the boat that was tied to the landing and rowing for all they were worth into the river, with a last shot from Ramón spurting the water behind them. Oh, they were terrible marksmen," he concluded, his eyes swimming with tears of laughter at the memory.

"And thank goodness for that," said our mother, her green eyes merry—yet also, I sometimes thought, reflective.

Oh, how we children loved that story. "And they never came back?" we asked.

"No," said our father. "That was the end of it. I don't think they were a bit scared of Ramón, but they did not want to run up that hill again." And he laughed explosively.*

When these events took place, our parents could not have been so lighthearted about them. We children reflected on that, after our laughter had subsided. Had the bandits wounded or killed the valiant Ramón, they would have turned their pistols on Father and probably Mother as well. When he was in town conducting his business, she was alone on that hill (I am unclear about whether Uncle Claude had yet built his house), with the two-year-old Aloise and the infant John and Priscilla on the way.

On one of my visits to San Antonio in the 1960s, Uncle Claude explained the change that took place in Mexico after 1910, when the decade of revolution began. "Your father and I were still in Mexico City," he said

---

* My sister Priscilla tells another version of this story.

to me, "and the oil boom on the coast was just beginning. I had to verify leases for clients, so I would take a horse and ride down to the *tierra caliente* for as long as two months at a time. I carried provisions and a pen knife. I never carried a pistol.

"Reid," he said, "I can't begin to describe how sweet and gentle Mexicans were in those days. I am talking about the poor, both the Indians and the mestizo population. It never occurred to me to carry a weapon! They were dirt poor, those good people, but they were the soul of generosity and as honest as the day. I would pull into a tiny farm during a rainstorm and ask to be admitted to their *chabola* until the storm passed. Often I spent the night. They welcomed me. They fed me beans from the stew pot. They made me a rush bed by the stove or fireplace. They would take nothing from me in return, though I was able to get around their resistance."

"Why did the revolution change them?"

"I am not sure, but it released a lawlessness that has plagued Mexico ever since. Now, you won't find much of that in the humble people, they are still—many of them, most of them, I believe—as simple and as kind and generous and honest as their parents were before them, but they have been terribly exploited. I blame a lot of unprincipled Americans who came to Mexico during the revolutionary period to make it rich. But what I blame more is the politics, which are totally corrupt. The worst of them are the *caciques*. Every village in Mexico had a *cacique*, a head man who made decisions for everybody and who fattened his wallet by that means.

"When your father and I set up the offices in Tampico," Uncle Claude went on, reminiscing, "we did a lot of business buying leases from the peasants. A poor Indian couple would come up the outdoor staircase that admitted to our offices, following their *cacique*. He might even be literate. I'd be behind the cashier's desk—a wooden table—on which gold coins were piled. The *caciques* would accept nothing but gold, and I understood that. Paper currency was worth nothing. Whoever the general was who ruled the province printed his own paper money at ridiculous arbitrary par value against the dollar, and used that to steal whatever he wanted. As well as bullion, we had American eagles and Austrian coins and even some Spanish pieces of eight. We were paying enormous sums for those leases at one point—the bidding between the big companies became hysterical. Sixty thousand, seventy thousand, eighty thousand dollars in gold—more!

You may not believe this, but the piles of gold on that desk sometimes reached so high that I had to stand on a chair to look over them.

"The *cacique* weighed the gold, and then, when he was satisfied, he directed the Indian couple, man and wife—who never said a word all this time—to put their mark on the lease. Then he would take a sack— sometimes two or three sacks—and sweep all that gold into them. Generally it was the *cacique* who dragged the bulging sacks out—they were too heavy to carry—followed humbly by the owners of the property."

"How long did this go on?"

"Beginning in 1912 and lasting until 1920-something. Years."

"And the owners of the property, the Indians—did they prosper?"

Uncle Claude's lean, flat cheeks reddened and then went white when I asked this question, his voice quavering with indignation. "I knew some of those poor people. A year or two later, I might drive by their little clearing in the bush and see them hoeing their one or two *milpas* of corn, just as they had before the oil boom. It was shameful! They profited very little from the leases, if at all. The *cacique* took most, or all, of the gold. It made me so mad I would punch the palm of one of my hands with the fist of the other."

"There was nothing you could do?"

"There was no legal recourse at all. The *caciques* were in league with the politicians and the police."

Murder ended disputes in those days. Cecilio Velasco writes diffidently about the lawlessness of those times, but one long weekend visit to Great Elm—I can't remember the occasion, was it at the time when Father lay half crippled in his bed upstairs, slowly dying?—Señor Velasco explained how it was.

Swifter and more certain than pursuing one's end through the courts was the expedient of hiring roaming bands of outlaws to kidnap one's op- ponent, take him into the jungle of the *tierra caliente,* and there eliminate him. The trick was to remove the victim far from his locale, and to leave the corpse where only wolves and coyotes and panthers and vultures would ever find it. One fine day, Señor D. José María González or Mr. Harold Smith simply vanished, and were never heard of again.

There were plenty of unscrupulous people, among them Americans (including J. D. Rockefeller's Standard Oil), who opted for this recourse. Señor Velasco spoke from personal experience. He and my father had been abducted by bandits and taken into the mountainous wilderness near Huastecas Veracruzana, a distance from Tampico.* I am not sure of the year when this occurred, but if this version of the story has any validity, I am fairly certain that my mother was in Tampico at the time; so the abduction, given these allowances, probably took place in 1919 or 1921. Neither Señor Velasco nor my father ever mentioned who was responsible, which of their sundry enemies (maybe someone from the Petroleum Club whom Father had accused of corrupt practices, or some Mexican official about whom Señor Velasco had made the same charge), but one early morning as they were approaching the Buckley, Buckley & Buckley offices (Uncle Edmund had joined the firm by this time), they were taken at gunpoint, mounted on horses, and ridden out of the city. When neither man showed up for supper, the young wives could assume what had happened, and knew that it was a death sentence.

The bandits rode hard all day up into the hills and through heavy rains. At around seven in the evening, at a clearing in the forest, their chief called a halt. I am not sure whether he had his prisoners bound (no mention of bindings was made by either Cecilio Velasco or my father that I recall; the bandit chief may have reasoned, where could they go, in pitch dark of night and in that jungle?), but one of the outlaws was appointed to guard them while the others gathered around the crackling flames of a campfire, pulling out flasks of tequila, and, laughing and joking, proceeded to drink and feast on the goat they roasted.

The rain had slackened. The young outlaw appointed to guard Señor Velasco and Father gazed longingly and resentfully toward the festive circle. Señor Velasco whispered in English to my father, "When they finish eating and are drunk, they will finish with us. If not tonight, tomorrow morning. We must do something now."

Father agreed, but what they could do about the situation was not clear to him. Señor Velasco was meantime fishing in one of his pockets. He pulled out a slip of paper, gazed down at it meditatively, and then glanced up quickly at Father, giving a thin smile. "This may help us," he said.

Father raised his eyebrows, failing to comprehend.

---

*Huastecas is a district that lies primarily in the state of Hidalgo, which is some eighty miles north of Mexico City. Some churches of the Huastecas district sprawl into the states of San Luis Potosí and Tiaxcala.

"It is the receipt for the laundry I dropped off just before we were taken," Señor Velasco said cryptically.

He went to the guard, brandishing the slip of paper. "This is a permit signed by your chief, saying that you may let us stretch our legs. It has been a long and wearisome ride."

"So?" said the guard. "I don't believe you."

"Read it for yourself," said Señor Velasco aggressively, pushing the receipt into the guard's face. "Read it, or . . ." He paused, and then he continued mockingly, "Or is it that you are illiterate and cannot read!" He spat with contempt. "If that's the case, you ignorant fellow, go to your chief yourself and ask him."

"Of course I can read! What do you take me for?"

Cecilio Velasco played his entire hand on the bandit's pride. Literacy was a major desire, a major hope, a major attainment in those days. Universal literacy was a goal of the revolution in all its permutations. When I was in Mexico as a thirteen-year-old some twenty years later, literacy was still a fetish, and it was billed at my school (Cristobal Colón) as a major social responsibility of the Mexican citizen: to teach someone else to read.

Señor Velasco wagered his life on the man's pride. Of course he could read . . . and he stalked off, saying gruffly, "Don't go far."

Father and Señor Velasco strolled to the edge of the clearing. The rain had intensified again, bursting in a deafening tropical downpour. They slipped into the forest and began to run as fast and as hard as they were able.

I don't know in what direction they went or what track, path, or lane they followed—maybe none. They ran several hours through the rains, it is my impression, sloshing across fast-flowing streams, each harder to ford than the last. Señor Velasco was in his late twenties or early thirties, Father in his mid-thirties. They led sedentary existences, the one as an accountant, the other as a lawyer; but the stake they were running for was their lives. I have no idea when they heard the hallooing or hoofbeats of the bandits in pursuit, but they kept running until they half swam across yet another torrent that roared down the mountainside, dragging themselves up on the opposite bank and falling to the ground, wind-broken, unable to move another inch.

They lay there panting and panting, the blood pounding in their eardrums. It never ceased pouring rain, and presently—within minutes—

before they had had a chance to recover, the sound of the bandits approaching the other bank of the stream came to them. Father and Señor Velasco scarcely had the energy to conceal themselves under shrubbery. They could hear the bandits arguing sharply among themselves, the bandit chief cursing. He was urging his men to cross over, but none of them dared kick his horse into that angry torrent. The waters had swollen providentially for my father and Señor Velasco; probably unable to swim, the bandits feared drowning. After more angry palaver, they turned back from where they had come.

Later, Father identified the river that had saved him. It was the Pántepec, which was the name he gave to the company that many years later, in Venezuela, struck black gold at last.*

ONE AFTERNOON AT KAMSCHATKA, AFTER LUNCH—WHEN I WAS IN MY early forties—Mother added this to the story.

"I had had no word of your father in four days. Everybody was sure that he and dear Cecilio Velasco had been murdered. I wouldn't let myself admit that. I kept praying to Our Lord and to the Blessed Virgin—telling her how much I needed your father with the two little children and a third child coming on. The evening of the fifth day, as I was finishing supper— the dear cook [was her name Clemencia?] had fixed floating island† for me, which she knew was the only dessert I liked; I could scarcely touch it, I had been weeping off and on all that day and all that evening. . . . That evening there came a loud knocking at the front door. I must have sent [Pepita?] our maid to find out who it was. Ramón wasn't in—either in his *chabola*, with his wife and children, or in town, asking after your father—he was a dear, loyal man. But I wished that moment he was with us on the hill, because those days one never knew who might come knocking, robbers or the police, and there was little difference between them. Pepita asked, *'Quién es?'*—at another loud rapping on the door. She unlocked it, pulling the door back a crack on its brass chain. A man burst through—

---

* The Pántepec (along with the Vinazco) flows into the Tuxpan River, which is named as such some thirty-six miles from the Gulf of Mexico. The Tuxpan is navigable and is used in the transportation of oil.

† A custard.

rupturing the chain, knocking poor Pepita out of the way, stumbling. And then she went, '*O! O! No me lo creo!*'

"I didn't properly hear her, I was so buried in my grief. I was aware only of that stranger coming through the door into our house. I could glimpse him from the dining room across a corridor—in the vestibule. He was filthy, his clothes sodden and mud-stained and tattered. He wore heavy whiskers, and his forehead and cheeks were scratched and had been bleeding. 'Will!' I had risen from the chair. 'Will! Will! Will! Will!' "

THERE ARE PROBLEMS WITH THIS STORY.

My brother James remembers it not at all. It was his impression that Father had at one time camped by the River Pántepec and was impressed by the beauty of the stream.[5] But Father's longtime and devoted partner, George S. Montgomery, the WWI ace and Coudert Brothers lawyer, who was close to Father and knew him intimately well, places a footnote in his posthumous tribute (see *W.F.B.—An Appreciation*): "W.F.B. chose the name 'Pantepec' for his operating companies in Venezuela after a little river in Mexico of the same name, in whose hospitable banks he once took shelter against revolutionists who were after him."

Pantepec was father's Mexican oil company, founded in 1914,* not in 1919–21, the time frame for the story I have just spun. If it is so (and I firmly believe that it is so)—that Pantepec oil company was named for the river whose providentially swollen waters saved Father and Señor Velasco—then this abduction took place sometime early in 1914, before the company was incorporated. (Pantepec was later reincorporated in Venezuela.) Mother wasn't on the scene. She and Father were not married until 1917.

But she absolutely remembered her shock at beholding Father with a heavy beard, unrecognizable to her as her husband. And I remember absolutely her telling me this. I am almost certain Father had grown the beard because he was abducted. Why else? I have reconstructed the scene of his arrival at their home in Tampico—the dialogue, for example—but

---

* Texas University's Benson Library in its chronology of our father places the date of the incorporation of Pantepec in 1913.

it is essentially what I remember from Mother. Was there a second abduction? Were two abductions conflated into one?

It matters, I suppose, historically, but not in the context of this recollection. The story I told is the story that is graven in my imagination and the imaginations of my siblings from childhood. It is the rich mulch of fact and mythic renditions of fact that has nurtured and formed us, for the better.

NOTES

———

1. Life was not a perpetual hayride for Edmund Buckley. Can one be "a touch" manic-depressive? The ups and downs of his business career corresponded to highs and lows in his spirits. He was subject to Buckley black moods. He was the youngest of his siblings to be born, and the first to go, when he was fifty-four, as I recollect. I interviewed his widow, Aunt Beryl, in 1971, in San Antonio. She must have been in her late seventies. She had not been a favorite aunt or a favorite sister-in-law. She was a small woman, and her legendary beauty was still evident in deep, dark eyes and soft, unwithered cheeks. She surprised me by the warmth of her invitation over the telephone. "Reid, Reid Buckley? Are you in town?" She had a deep, thrilling contralto voice with a soft Texan accent. "Oh, do come visit me, there's nothing I would enjoy more. Eleven o'clock, for cocktails."

This was a startling invitation, not for the lateness of the hour but because (as I had been warned by her daughter Beryl) she indicated eleven o'clock in the morning. She rose at two or two-thirty A.M., breakfasted at three or three-thirty, lunched at eight o'clock in the morning, had her cocktail at eleven, dined at noon, and was in bed by one o'clock.

A Mexican butler answered the door of her apartment, which was luxurious and beautifully appointed. Uncle Edmund had evidently left his widow well fixed. She greeted me with an affection I had no reason to expect, and I now think of her always fondly. She had a no-nonsense bourbon on the rocks, a couple of them, as I remember; I had a V-8 juice. She told me about Uncle Edmund's black moods. Once it became so unbearable that she left him. Theirs was a lifelong love affair, but she decided that she could no longer stand living with him. She went to San Francisco, leaving no traces. He was desperate, searching for her everywhere. Somehow he tracked her down at last. It took several months. They both wept when they saw each other, clasping each other in their arms and kissing. "But I told him, 'Edmund,' I said to him, 'I'll come back to you and to Tampico, but if ever you allow yourself to fall into one of those moods again, I'll leave you forever.' And he never did, Reid—the poor, darling man. He was the most darling, loving, fun man, your uncle."

2. This family reticence about personal matters runs in all my siblings, with the notable exception of our sister Carol, who wrote a (marvelous) book about her intimate life (*At the Still Point,* Simon & Schuster). Neither Bill nor Jim will write his autobiography, as such. This private trait of character does not exclude sociability. Father was reputedly charming. We have this from several contemporary sources. I was impressed by that trait at the last great New Year's Eve Ball at Kamschatka, which occurred three months before his operation for a stomach cancer in Charlotte (the agent of the stroke that ultimately killed him), where I saw our father jovial, rubicund, funny—utterly charming—probably having had one too many of our butler Jeff Boykin's delicious bourbon old-fashioneds. But my guess is that his convivial nature was generally engaged in the company of intimate friends and family. It would not be a contradiction to assume that Father dreaded "social occasions" as much as I, and several of my siblings, dread them. Receptions, banquets, cocktail parties. Yet all of us, like our father, have made lifelong friends. Our brother James is particularly noted for that, despite his self-professed shyness. During the 1950s, the irritating refrain with his siblings in reference to him went, "No, Jimmy can't make it, he's best man at somebody's wedding—as usual."

3. I visited it in 1968 at the invitation of its then owner, Señor Moreno, who operated a stationery shop in Tampico's principal plaza, opposite the palatial Customs, and who, with his charming wife, graciously invited me for tea at the house my father and mother had once called home. It was large, comfortable, and conventionally laid out. Toward the end of my visit, Señora Moreno said to me, "I have something to show you"; and she took me down a back stairway to the basement garage. At the far rear of the garage, to the left, there was an ell, a sort of alcove, half obscured, to which she led me, her husband following close behind. In that ell, among other objects, there was a large chest, five feet wide, two and a half feet deep, three and a half feet high, whitened with many years of fallen plaster. She brushed the dust off the center of the lid, revealing not only beautiful (I am guessing the source) Dominican mahogany but also a raised, carved, and garlanded inscription: "Aloise."

"This must be your mother's," Señora Moreno said simply. "It has rested here all these years—since she left so suddenly in 1921, when your father was expelled from Mexico. We had no idea where to reach her, of course."

I called Mother that night from my hotel. She remembered the chest as though it were yesterday. "Grandmother B had a linen chest made for her three daughters-in-law, for Dora, Beryl, and me. By wonderful Mexican artisans in Austin—mahogany on the outside, cedar lining on the inside. Oh, Reid, forty-five years! I can't believe it has survived! We left in such a hurry, with just our clothes and personal belongings—there was no way to arrange for its shipment, everything we owned was confiscated. But I'm happy to know that it belongs now to those nice people."

Who, when they heard the story the next day, would not hear of remaining in possession of the chest. Nor would they accept payment for it. Two months later, it arrived in Camden, South Carolina, and stood on the ground floor of Kamschatka until Mother became ill and the house was sold. For the past nearly thirty years (since 1982), it has been in my farmhouse northeast of Camden.

4.   Father used that pistol once. In the late 1920s or early 1930s, an intruder entered Great Elm. I recall no details—how Mother and Father heard the man, what it was that roused them from their sleep. But Father got up and, with Mother close behind, went downstairs, holding the loaded pistol high in his right hand. It was wintertime. The house was filled with sleeping children, the Mexican nurses Nana and Pupa, Mademoiselle Bouchex, our governess, and, of course, in their separate quarter, the three or four servants.

Mother and Father had called the police. There was a full moon. Flipping on no light switches, they searched Great Elm room by room—the dining room with the gleaming mahogany sideboard holding the silver, the little music room at the foot of the stairs, the long, wide hall that traverses Great Elm from east to west, the "dark" room that was a passageway leading into the large "Empire" room and the library, which they searched first and second; and then, from the library, into the small pine-paneled downstairs "office" that he sometimes used to work in when he was home; across a narrow hall and down that to the very large playroom/schoolroom, across the patio from the Empire room. There they found the intruder. He had hidden under a very large couch (our favorite couch to stretch out and read in, as children), but he was an uncommonly tall man, and his feet protruded from one end, betraying him in the light of the moon. Father told the robber (which he was; he had a record) to get out from under the couch, clicking the hammer back on his .45 Colt and holding the fellow prisoner until the (one) town policeman arrived.

5.   The beauty and sonority of the name stood Father in good business stead, during those long years when he was looking for investors. In 1958, my wife Betsy and I and our three children and a Scottish nanny, Miss Rooney, shipped over from New York to Gibraltar on the Italian Line's *Cristoforo Colombo*, on which we met Otto Bemberg, a distinguished patriarch of the famous Argentine family. We were introduced by his son, Teddy, a friend who was living at the time in Salisbury, near Sharon. "Buckley!" the elder Bemberg exclaimed upon our introduction. "Son of William Buckley?" "Yes." "Well, I must tell you this. When I heard about an oil company whose shares were going to be floated on the market called Pantepec, I was charmed by the name, what a wonderful name it was, I thought, and anybody who would call an oil company by that name had to be an unusual person. And so I bought Pantepec stock. Yes. Quite a lot of it, in fact. I held the stock for years and finally sold it and made a very handsome profit. Pantepec! What a beautiful and *audacious* name!"

CHAPTER TEN

William Frank Buckley of Texas (V): Tampico, Cecilio Velasco

WHEN THEY WERE INTRODUCED, CECILIO VELASCO FELT THAT HE HAD met a kindred spirit.

Father must have responded in the same way about the diminutive, blade-faced Mexican dressed in a brown suit, with the razor-thin mustache, dark eyes, and serious manner, a few years his junior.

Velasco, from Mexico City, was looking for work out of the humdrum, which he thought he might find in booming Tampico. He was an accountant by trade, had business experience. He relates* that Father "had been graduated in Mexico City . . . after having completed his studies and having passed the examinations pertaining thereto"—whatever that meant, maybe that Father took courses in Mexico's Napoleonic code of law and passed his bars in that country.†

They conversed frequently after that first meeting, and at one point Father asked Señor Velasco whether he would like to work for him. Señor

---

*Almost all of what follows is derived from Señor Velasco's contribution to *W.F.B.—An Appreciation;* my brothers John and James knew him far better than I.
†There is no mention of this in the Benson Library chronology, which states simply that Father earned an LL.B. and his license to practice law in Texas in 1906.

Velasco hesitated, having no notion, as he writes in his modest manner, how he could be useful. But "the first piece of advice he gave me was that in a law office there is no such word as 'can't,' and that I should never say 'No,' no matter what proposal might arise."

Which precipitated Señor Velasco into his first crisis as an employee of the Buckley firm. He writes:

> It happened that on a certain occasion when his secretary did not turn up for work because of a hangover [W.F.B.] asked me whether I could take down in shorthand a contract which he proposed to dictate to me. . . . Although it was true that I knew no shorthand, it is equally true that I had studied it, and remembering the advice given to me on the first day of my new job, I said to him right away, "Of course."

Father apparently dictated a spate, and when he was through, Señor Velasco (making use "of the few facts which I had succeeded in catching") drew up his own contract. "Luckily," he writes, "it was short and not complicated," and when he presented it to Father, "and he read it, realizing that it contained nothing of what he had dictated to me, said . . . very amiably, as was his custom: 'Not so bad. Next time you can dictate it to yourself.'"

I can imagine the wry, amused manner in which Father delivered those words. What attracted him to Cecilio Velasco was his evident intelligence, to which virtues Father soon added energy, loyalty, and an intrepid character. Señor Velasco was meanwhile discovering the peculiar way Father conducted lawyering, which often had his accountant's soul in despair. "The business progressed," he writes, "the profits rose, but because of I know not what good or evil arts, expenses absorbed and exceeded the profits." As a matter of course.

My father told me not once but several times, "If they named me president of General Motors, I'd bankrupt the company within a year." Señor Velasco moans:

> Financial aid to colleagues in the Capital, loans to friends in need, new business projects, etc., etc., kept my cash box empty, and the accounts . . . with debit balances. To begin with, there was the problem of Buckley's generosity.

He gives an example from the early days of the office. Father had "a friend who was also a lawyer, a one hundred percent Mexican.* This friend came to the office one morning with a very familiar and very urgent need: he had to have five thousand pesos, the good pesos of long ago." That was heavy money. Father apparently asked his cashier how much there was in the box. He was told $250, which included loose change. So Father hied himself to a bank and signed a note for five thousand pesos that he did not have, payable in fifteen days. His Mexican friend, Señor Velasco relates, left Father's offices mightily impressed by how many thousands of pesos W.F.B. must have at his disposal.

This tale amuses his son. All my life, wherever I have sojourned, acquaintances have assumed I am ten times better off than is the case. Señor Velasco concludes this topic:

> He had, and still has, many friends in Tampico and Mexico City, some of them Americans and others Mexicans, to whom he never shut the doors of his safe which was sometimes empty of money, but was always filled with optimism with respect to future business. Let those many widows of W.F.B.'s friends, who both in Mexico and the U.S. have lived or continue to live on the contents of that safe, speak for themselves.

Velasco's personal gratitude to Father was lifelong. On his deathbed he gathered his large family around and said to them sternly, to the effect, "Don't ever forget that everything we have we owe to William Buckley."

He spoke of two other sides of my father's personality: (1) his charm, of which we, his children, exposed as we were on occasion to his paternal severity, were not, I think, adequately aware (we used to joke that the photographs taken of him in the Tampico days made him look like a dyspeptic Baptist preacher),[1] and (2) his entrepreneurial spirit, of which we were well aware:

---

*It is curious to me that Señor Velasco thought it necessary to underscore this point. Though his eyes were open as the eyes of few others to native weaknesses, he was nevertheless a fervent Mexican patriot and must have been first attracted to the gringo from Texas because of his un-Anglo respect for the Mexican people.

W.F.B. soon knew almost everybody in Tampico and had many friends. He possessed great personal charm, he was persuasive, he inspired confidence, and all who knew him loved him.* He was a man of extraordinary vision . . . he foresaw a boom in Tampico, with a derivative growth in population, and he constantly talked to me about buying land to be subdivided. He founded a bank [!] . . . he acquired undeveloped parcels of land in the suburbs of the City; money came from the United States in appreciable quantities, and he interested his friends in the deal. The underdeveloped properties were improved and offered for sale.

My sister Carol divides people into givers and takers. Father was among the former. Wherever he went, he felt driven to improve matters, sometimes to his convenience, or to satisfy his aesthetic sense, or to his eventual profit; often simply discharging what he felt was the right thing—the obligatory thing—for a person of any vision and decency to do. I attribute this generosity† not only to his strict Christian upbringing but to the influence of the Southwestern frontier. If a friend needed a hand, you extended yours. If your town or community was in need, it was a personal obligation for you to help.

Cecilio Velasco sums up Father's career in Mexico by saying, "he entered the battle with the rank of soldier, and rose on his own merits; and the fight itself was his greatest pleasure." This last trait I know has been expressed in the careers of brothers John, James, and Bill, and also in several of my sisters' public and personal lives. We don't seek out contention, but neither do we shun it‡ and when we have been obliged to struggle for this or that reason, even when our personal well-being or our livelihoods are in the balance, we are imbued with excitement. In a word, our natures

---

* This is a rare exaggeration in Señor Velasco's testimony: not everybody loved our father or fell for his charm, which so impressed those who were favorably disposed toward him. There were many people who hated him, who became serious enemies. One of the most loyal (though clear-sighted) friends Mexico ever had, he is still listed in official circles as an enemy.

† Which is so notable in sister Carol and our brother Bill.

‡ I, however, have a deep aversion for controversy. I find myself in the midst of it frequently, but I detest it.

are combative. Señor Velasco discusses at length the appalling corruption of those days in Mexico, distributing blame on gringos and fellow countrymen alike. Father was intimately aware of the crooked methods "by some of the old companies in order to acquire lands."

> He had to stand up to the power of those great enterprises whose moral standards in their dealings were deplorable. They were highly organized [down to] secret bands of spies, guards, and gunmen in the towns and on the road of Huastecas, and to compete with them it was necessary to bring into play great energy and intelligence, as well as faith; and to that risk W.F.B. devoted all his skills.

Black gold was oil. People killed for it. He mentions some of the legendary wells: the Juan Casiano, with a "*per diem* production of 50,000 barrels," the Portrero del Llano gushing 115,000 daily, and the Dos Bocas with "an initial production" of as much as "260,000 barrels a day, which could not be controlled, and ran out, with the loss of all the oil it had produced."* Cecilio Velasco and the Buckley brothers were disgusted by the swindling that dispossessed humble people of their property and their rights; and Velasco speaks contemptuously of the "big leaders" of the oil companies who met "every week or two" at the Petroleum Club.† What disturbed them, he alleges, were rumors circulating in Mexico City that the government was going to take action against the highway robbery that was preventing more of the profits from "those enormous torrents of black gold flowing from the oil fields of Vera Cruz and Tamaulipas" from entering into the national treasury, whence, I interpose, it was the more easily filched by whoever was the reigning general dictator at the time (and his cronies). This pillaging continues in Mexico, by Mexicans who are the traitors of their country.

It is nonetheless hard for us to place ourselves back in the first years of

---

*When musing philosophically on his and Jim's sometimes frantic explorations for the elusive stuff, our brother John often quipped, "I can hear it now! I am on my deathbed, someone rushes into the room shouting, 'Oil! Oil! John, we've found oil!'"

†This term is used consistently in describing what may be the American Association of Mexico, whose founding by William F. Buckley the Benson Library places in 1919. I think Velasco was talking about the same entity.

the twentieth century and fully appreciate how arrogant and how stupid we Americans can be. Señor Velasco slams the provincial chauvinism of the managers of the leading oil companies of that time, who, he charged, were for the most part nepotistically appointed to their posts, and who (like Woodrow Wilson and his envoy) understood neither a lick of the Spanish language nor Latin ways and culture and who were "tactless in their relationship and their official dealings with ... government representatives and scorned the Mexican people. They knew little or nothing about the industries placed in their hands, but their conduct and their manners compared with those of any emperor, they knew it all, but were aware of nothing."

This could have been my father speaking; he was scornful of these same provincials, his fellow Americans. I ran into this sort forty years later, when I was doing business in Spain.* I am sure my brothers John and James had similar experiences in their far-flung dealings, though the oil business had become relatively civilized over the intervening years. In our upbringing and in his stories, Father taught his children to be sensitive to other cultures and to despise, as he put it memorably in his testimony on Mexico before the Senate, those provincial Americans who, in need of civilization themselves, seek to civilize the rest of the world.

As Cecilio Velasco puts it:

[I]t was that W.F.B. at every meeting ... in the Petroleum Club found himself conducting a heated battle in an attempt to make his fellow Americans understand that they were in Mexico, a free and sovereign nation that demanded and deserved respect; that good faith and good deeds were absolutely necessary in the diplomatic field; that justice, fairness, and ethics could not be dispensed with in their dealings with the landowner; that they must respect the latter's reasonable rights, granting them appropriate profits and just prices; and that they must treat them with greater generosity and less avarice, if they would avoid lamentable consequences, killing off, all by themselves, the goose that laid the golden egg.

---

* To wit (and it *is* witty), see my pamphlet, *Good Taste Doesn't Sell, Bad Taste Sells Loads*, P.E.N. Press.

Father's advice went down poorly, and he was ultimately expelled from the club he founded "as a pernicious and quarrelsome individual." Cecilio Velasco describes in wry terms his own part in this struggle against corruption:

> [S]ince I could not fight with judges and tribunals [which the Buckley brothers were doing] because I had no knowledge of law, I was struggling with governors and mayors [municipal presidents], fortunately with a fair amount of luck, only twice was I invited to enter the Tampico jail because the Governor of the State of Tampico did not agree with my lively protests over the failure to fulfill promises made in connection with our urban developments; and once I was abducted, my destination being the middle of the bridge that spans the Río Grande, which point marks the boundary between Laredo, Texas, and Laredo, Mexico; not a comfortable or comforting destination for me under the circumstances, because on the one hand I did not have the papers for entry into the United States, and on the other, they forbade my return to Mexico under pain of being shot, summarily.

It was Claude Buckley who got Señor Velasco out of this fix by vouching for him in the States, so that Velasco spent fifteen or twenty days in the hotels of San Antonio and Laredo as a tourist. He accuses the Transcontinental Company, a subsidiary of Standard Oil, of orchestrating his predicament, over a lawsuit concerning rights to certain lands, "all of which corroborates what has been said" about "the methods of defense which the big companies used." (There is a revealing commentary on this story that I am placing at the end of the chapter, because it otherwise interrupts the flow.) Cecilio Velasco adds that he was rescued and returned to Mexico thanks to "the opportune orders of General Calles," which may be one of the few good deeds on that terrible man's record.

The period described was 1910 to 1921, the height of revolutionary ferment in Mexico. Velasco mentions the swift succession of "chiefs, generals, and aspirants to the Presidency of the Republic" that had been "abandoned by" Porfirio Díaz's death: Pancho Villa, Carranza, Obregón, Felix Días, Victoriano Huerta, Zapata, "and others whose names I don't remember." Everything was in turmoil, which was worsened by the printing presses that each succeeding general used to manufacture currency, "with denomination and value according to his whim, paper money that the people were forced to accept as legal tender in the region held by his troops," and which was not recognized elsewhere, "until all the money was at last declared null and void, and was withdrawn or used to paper rooms of private dwellings."

And here he admits that life "in the oil regions became dangerous. Many bands of rebel thugs, with or without a flag, sprang up there, some of them victims of the chaos that prevailed, completely at sea with no idea of which leader they were fighting for, while others were diligent opportunists devoted to plunder and pillage."

He introduces us to a Mexico most Americans never heard of. Least chaos obtained, he declares, in the oil region of Huastecas, thanks to "a self-appointed general who, backed by thousands of his countrymen, took up arms in the year 1914, with no party affiliation, but with a definite aim to maintain order and to keep out of the Huastecas bands of revolutionaries whose sole ideology was to plunder and pillage the haciendas."

This man was General Manuel Pelaez, known as the "Rebel of the Huastecas." He was given the CNN/CBS treatment (quaintly, the bum rap), according to Señor Velasco, and called the instrument of the oil companies, but Señor Velasco vigorously defends him, writing that, quite the contrary, General Pelaez opposed the "haughty conduct and inordinate thirst for profit" of the oil companies, compelling them to "respect the laws . . . without depriving them of their just dues when right was on their side."

Which was not easily determined.

LIKE ALL INDEPENDENT OIL EXPLORERS AND PRODUCERS WITH WHOM I have come into contact, Father had a low opinion of the Seven Sisters, as Big Oil used to be alluded to in his times, which included the major players and monopolies; and, in this regard, he especially despised Standard Oil. He fought Standard Oil in Mexico and then later in Venezuela, on several levels. There is besides a persistent suspicion that it was a Mexican-based official of Standard Oil who hired the bandits who abducted him and Cecilio Velasco with the intention of killing them.

But Father did not harbor grudges, and he was never foolishly inflexible, nor did the past color what might be the changed reality of the present. This pragmatical attitude was to have a hugely important impact on his fortunes. He liked to tell the story of his negotiations with Standard Oil in 1939 or '40, to which he wanted to sell the oil he had discovered in eastern Venezuela (and later under Lake Maracaibo).

He was very proud of this episode, which required of him the maximum in self-restraint and persistence. It was David negotiating against Goliath. Standard Oil arrived at the offices in New York in the person of a vice president and, I think Father said, not fewer than three lawyers. It was a battery of lawyers. Father was alone. They met, I think he indicated, on neutral ground, neither at his offices nor at Standard Oil's New York offices. Maybe at some hotel.

He had prepared a contract. SO's lawyers found it utterly unacceptable. The SO VP was disparaging about it. Father listened but bargained hard all day. "Then they went out for supper and a lot of drinking," I recall him saying. He? He went back to his hotel and had a sandwich in his room—with ice water* and a lot of coffee, I suspect. He spent most of the night weighing the objections of the other side and trying to find a way around them.

The next morning, he presented them with a brand-new contract. "Oh," he said, "they were surprised . . . and they found it just as objectionable as the first!" Again they spent all day bickering and bargaining, and in the early evening the SO crowd left to "have supper and do a lot of drinking." As before, Father had a sandwich sent up to him in his hotel room and worked on all his notes. And the next day, he had another new contract for them.

To which the SO crowd reacted with the same derision and fury of the day before and the day before that. The clear implication I got as a young man listening to this story was that the lawyers all had hangovers. The vice president lost his temper, more than once. More than once he threatened to walk out . . . but he did not, and Father shrewdly gambled on that, because he knew that Standard Oil wanted his Pantepec oil as much, or almost as much, as he wanted to sell that oil to the company. It was a third day of hard and hostile bargaining. It seemed that the differences between the two sides never would be reconciled.

On the fourth morning, Father—displaying his remarkable patience—

---

*Raised in the parched Southwest, he relished iced water all his life.

once again presented Standard Oil with a fresh contract. The SO lawyers rejected it flatly. And this day the vice president did stomp out of the consultations, leaving his lawyers alone with Father. It was the same battle all that fourth day long. I am certain Father came close to losing his composure—he was a high-tempered man and could stand neither deviousness nor pettifoggery. He nevertheless restrained his temper, his voice may have been icy, but he did not permit it to become hot.

On the fifth morning, Father had yet another contract ready, which was again totally unacceptable to the Standard Oil lawyers, who, Father had now realized for several days, were so scared of not gaining marginal advantage for their employers that they were missing the whole point of the negotiations, which was to come to a fair agreement for the merchandising of Pantepec oil. The vice president didn't show up; but in his stead there appeared the then-president of Standard Oil (or of that division of Standard Oil). I do not recall his name. He kept silent while the lawyers jabbered. I suspect he understood what was going on and what the problem was much as Father understood it, which causes me to suspect also that he was a Southwesterner. He gazed at my father, my father returning his look with that unshakable blue-eyed candor that impressed everyone. When the lawyers had ceased shouting, this man said to Father, "Mr. Buckley, I think I know what you want, and I think you know what we want. What do you say we shake on it."

At which—Father told us, grinning and mightily pleased with himself, as he had every right to be—he got up from the table and shook the man's hand. "And there has never been a contract between us," he would say proudly. "There has been no written contract between Standard Oil and Pantepec all these years, but both companies have kept their word."

My brother John on several occasions corroborated this story. This deal was an unheard-of anomaly in the oil business. There was nothing written, just a verbal understanding between gentlemen. (And with that white shark of the industry, Standard Oil.) "Yet," John would say, smiling wryly, appreciatively—John, who in his business dealings had inherited from our father this combination of acumen, gambler's daring, resoluteness, and patience—"there was never a dispute of which I am aware until Pantepec ran out of oil to sell." (I should add that many of us are largely still living off the fossil-fuel royalties that the vision and determination of these two men, father and son, made possible.)

NOTES

———

1. He looks ill humored besides in most of them—in one of which I am holding a glass
    jar of candy, and he *was* mad, because he had wanted to take it from me and empty its
    contents (bad for the teeth), but I had thrown a temper tantrum (Mother and Nana
    had aligned themselves against him) and had refused to pose for the picture unless I
    had my candy, which is clutched firmly in my hands. In startling contrast to these
    family portraits of the 1930s and 1940s, there is a marvelous photograph of him re-
    laxing with his mother, sisters, brothers, and sisters-in-law, at the house on the corner
    of Lavaca Street, Austin, in which all that vaunted charm and good humor are plain.

———— ↭ ————

CHAPTER ELEVEN

William Frank Buckley
of Texas (VI):
Tampico, Pancho Villa

ONE HOT SUMMER AFTERNOON IN THE EARLY 1930S, IN THE HIGH TIDE of Hollywood's infatuation with (and glorification of) such American outlaws as the bank-robbing Daltons, the James brothers, and Billy the Kid, Father was driving from New York to Sharon bringing, I'll dub him, Don Jorge Regino López to spend the weekend.

Señor López had been governor of the state of, say, Sonora, in northwest Mexico, bounded by the United States to the north, by Chihuahua to the east. I have no notion what business Father had with the man.

If this is the same gentleman I am thinking about, his glamorous (and much younger) wife had been expected also but was unaccountably not with her husband when Father picked him up at the Waldorf-Astoria hotel, the favorite putting-up place of South Americans, who are in the main *cursi*.[1] The drive from the city was at the time tiresome, long, and hot. There was no air conditioning in those days. At Pawling (New York), about twenty-five miles from Sharon (Connecticut), Father pulled in at a drugstore with a soda fountain.

Hanging around the entrance to the place was a bunch of what were called drugstore cowboys in those days—teenaged, pimply-faced, country louts—who gawked at the tall, thin, pince-nezed, business-suited

American with his fedora (by Stetson) planted squarely on top of his head, accompanied by the paunchy Mexican in a baggy brown suit and wide-brimmed rancher's hat, who, waving his hands about, was speaking volubly in Spanish.

Father and his guest sat themselves at the fountain and ordered Cokes, conversing the while. The drugstore cowboys, or young punks as we would call them today, pressed close behind, making derisive comments about the language they were hearing—about the tooled-leather high-heeled boots the foreigner wore, about his pockmarked brown skin (the scars of smallpox were characteristic of many Mexicans in those days). Since Señor López understood not a word of English, Father at first put up with them, thinking they'd tire and go away. But they became more aggressive in their demeanor, insulting in their remarks. So he said to Señor López, *"Jorge Regino, es verdad que usted lleva siempre encima la pistola que asesinó a Pancho Villa?"*

"Por supuesto, Guillermo."

"Me la enseña?"

"Con todo gusto!" *

Whereupon the governor reached under his jacket and pulled a huge Colt Peacemaker from the holster strapped to his chest, brandishing it high. "At this," Father would tell us, grinning widely, "those drugstore cowboys all stared, and then, thinking that their remarks had been understood, and that this Mexican was intending to shoot them, they flew! Oh, if you could have seen them run out of that drugstore—how they ran!" And he convulsed with laughter at the memory, pulling a snowy handkerchief out of his side pocket to wipe his mouth.

This may have been the first story I recollect about, or from, my father in connection with Pancho Villa. It made me laugh. But if this concerned the same guest, which I am not sure, there was a darker side to it. That evening at supper (my older siblings related to me), the telephone rang. It was for Governor López, who took the call in the hall phone closet, behind the dining room. Presently he came striding back with a satisfied

---

* "Jorge Regino, is it so that you always carry with you the pistol that assassinated Pancho Villa?"

"Why, of course, Guillermo."

"Would you show it to me?"

"With the greatest of pleasure!"

expression on his broad face. He leaned close to Father in passing—Father sat at one end of the long table, Mother at the other end—whispering something into his ear before proceeding to his place on Mother's right. My siblings tell me that Father's expression changed in the instant from that of convivial host to a severity they had rarely before seen in him. "I don't think we need any more wine, Aloïse," he said—or something like this, to hasten the end of the supper.

The adults withdrew into the Empire room, as was the custom, children trailing dutifully. Father and Governor López sat with their backs to the white marble fireplace, in handsome armchairs whose surfaces were chiseled out of Brazilian rosewood. Mother sat on a small French sofa to one side, while children arranged themselves on an upholstered Empire bench and in subordinate seats. The routine was that we lingered until coffee and ice water had been served, after which, if we were lucky, we were expected to bid our good nights. If we were unlucky, and Father was feeling expansive, which occurred often with his Mexican and Venezuelan guests, we'd be called upon (shudder!) to perform—to sing Mexican ballads that my siblings accompanied themselves with banjos, mandolins, and guitars, to the beaming approval of our (at these times) fatuous sire, who apparently never considered whether his guests might be appalled or bored. This evening, my siblings report, they escaped. Father—ordinarily an expansive host—maintained a tight-lipped minimal courtesy that frightened them to witness.

The story percolated down long afterward. Governor López (or whoever) had leaned close to Father's ear to confide that his hired gunman had been on the phone reporting that he had caught up with Señora López and her lover in San Francisco and had shot them to death, news conveyed by the governor with every evidence of satisfaction.

HE WAS A BANDIT, A COLDBLOODED MURDERER, PARTLY MAD, AND A patriot—one of the more fascinating characters in Mexican history.

There is so much legend attached to Pancho Villa's name that even the date of his birth in Durango is suppositious (1877/8/9?), but he was shot down in the town of Parral, Chihuahua, in 1923, by followers of General Álvaro Obregón, successor to Carranza.

Christened Doroteo Arango, he was born in San Juan del Río. His father died when he was twelve, leaving him at the head of his family of two younger brothers and two sisters, whom, with his mother, he supported. He killed his first man early—the son of an *hacendado* (landed squire) who had raped his younger sister.* This killing would not have been deemed a crime by many of his countrymen, by whom it would have been spun not only as just vengeance against the *gazpuchino* (derogatory term for Mexicans of pure Spanish descent) who violated his sister but also against a class of aristocrats that had abused and exploited the Indian and mestizo populations for centuries. He nevertheless became a fugitive, drifting north to the neighboring state of Chihuahua, where, in order to survive, he hunted, stole, and hid during the day, working as a cowboy and as a miner (Chihuahua is rich in zinc and silver) when opportunity offered. He was soon robbing banks on the side and rustling cattle from the vast herds of the open range, and was wanted for murder.

By the time he was twenty, he was a veteran outlaw, attaching himself to a band whose chieftain (by one account) was called Pancho Villa. When this Villa was killed, the twenty-year-old Doroteo Arango adopted the name he was to make famous, striking out on his own with several members of the old gang.

He was soon feared all along the U.S. border, where he terrorized the wealthy but where he also shared his loot with *peón* families, with whom he acquired the reputation of being a Mexican Robin Hood. Short, barrel-chested, and mustachioed, he rode rings around the hated *rurales* of dictator Porfirio Díaz, gaining the admiration of the peasantry. It was in the highlands of Chihuahua that he established his fiefdom, a perfect base for an outlaw of the early 1900s. Chihuahua is situated on Mexico's northwest central plain. Its arid landscape is familiar to anyone who has visited Arizona and New Mexico. Its deserts were at the time trackless, containing gorges larger than Arizona's Grand Canyon as well as the ramparts of the Sierra Madre, in whose heavily forested flanks and high ridges a wanted man could take refuge. This is spectacularly beautiful country—soaring hills, sheer cliffs, cascading waterfalls—the Apache territory of our Hollywood-fed imaginations; and, indeed, into the late nineteenth century, it was subject to raids by wild bands of these ferocious seminomads.

---

* To possess an *hacienda,* a ranch, was to be a member of the rural squirearchy in Mexico, a number of whom were vain, arrogant, and dissolute.

These were the days of the decline of the long, long rule of Porfirio Díaz (1876–1911), democrat turned autocrat. An almost pure-blooded Mixtec Indian from Oaxaca, Díaz assumed power after the reign of Benito Juárez (1858–1872). Juárez—a pure-blooded Zapotec Indian—was the first non-Spaniard to rule post-Cortes Mexico. He did a lot of necessary things, such as liberating his country from the baneful influence of five-time "president" Santa Ana and also from French Bonapartist ambitions, this by executing unfortunate Emperor Maximilian (in 1867), Archduke of Austria, a kindly and well-meaning fellow[2]—serving notice to European powers that Mexico was not to be trifled with. As befalls many reformers, Juárez then himself succumbed to the corruption of self-esteem.

This was the Mexico Will Buckley knew. It was not only recent history to him (he was born just four years after Díaz became president); what happened just across the Southwest frontier loomed as large as the politics of Washington, half a continent away. Mexico dyed our father's politics indelibly and bred in his children distrust of populist charmers of whatever ideological hue. Contemplating Mexico breeds despair, if not cynicism, in anyone who does not possess the fortitude, the fatalism, the inexhaustible optimism, and the irreplaceable sense of humor of Mexicans. In the history of nations, Mexico is a Greek tragedy, a statement of Promethean hubris awaiting its Sophocles. I have lived in the country as a child, heard about it all through my childhood, visited it as an adult, and read at least seven or eight long accounts of the country's tribulations. I do not apologize for the apodictical statements that follow. No exalted principle uttered by a Mexican leader since Benito Juárez was not betrayed by that selfsame leader. (Ransacking my memory, I cannot think of one glorious aspiration that wasn't dragged in the dust of betrayal, not one.) Benito Juárez, raised to be a priest, became viciously anticlerical, confiscating the *latifundias** owned by bishops and monastic orders, distributing the seized lands to poor Indians and mestizos, the *campesinos*. But as the years passed, and political pressures mounted, he began doling out former Church properties to powerful members of the social and political aristocracy, the *hacendados*, tainting his purity. This led to a curious realignment of political forces: the entrenched landed classes now supported Juárez

---

*A Chilean term for vast landholdings.

liberals, while the peasants—who have been for the most part unalterably religious in Mexican history—supported the Church-backed, anti-Juárez conservatives. If there is a constant in the story of Mexico, it is that the desultory result of all the civil strife since at least the 1850s, fought ostensibly in the cause of justice for the poor, somehow always turned out to be that the poor were further oppressed and exploited by the emerging coalitions between landed and financial gentry and the new class, largely mestizo, of political opportunists.

As Benito Juárez's "Reform War" (1858–61) dragged on, Mexico slipped into a state of near-permanent civil turmoil and lawlessness that by the end of Juárez's rule came to be associated with the country, so that foreigners assumed (then as now) that anarchy is congenial to the Mexican temperament. Dispossessed peasants and former soldiers who had fought against Juárez were driven into brigandage—giving outlaws, in some quarters, a good name. In 1868, on the outskirts of chic Guadalajara, more than a thousand outlaws were said to be raiding and pillaging, raping and killing. The regime was plagued by uprisings, some mounted by peasants, others by Indians, and still others by left-liberal military generals who had fallen out with Juárez.

The situation of Mexico waxed ever more chaotic. Apaches in the north under Cochise and Victorio were raiding across the gringo border into Chihuahua and other Mexican territories, murdering as many as fifteen thousand peasants. The Maya in the south meantime rose against civil authority, setting up an independent state in southern Yucatán that endured until 1901 (a region that continues today in tenuously suppressed rebellion under the legendary mantle of Zapata). To cap Benito Juárez's troubles, a leftist Christian movement, claiming that Jesus Christ was the first socialist, rose up against Juárez.* But though himself unalterably anticlerical and in other respects left-leaning, Juárez detested socialism; he had no qualms about sending federal troops to suppress this insurrection, further undermining his popularity.

The social unrest and the disintegration of the central government's authority in the twilight of Juárez's rule decided his onetime ally, Porfirio

---

* The first eruption of New World Christian Marxism that was to plague the Hispanic Americas during the second half of the twentieth century.

Díaz, to turn against him. In 1867, Díaz challenged Juárez unsuccessfully at the polls, then again in 1871. Díaz was the first exponent of term limitations, one might say: his battle cry was "no reelection."* In seeking yet another term as president, Juárez was plainly attempting to perpetuate himself in office (he had been in power since 1858, thirteen years). In July 1872, worn out by work, Juárez was felled at his desk by a heart attack. This flung open the gates at last for the even longer tenure of his fellow Oaxacan—thirty-five years of absolute rule that became known as the Porfiriato.

FATHER WAS INTRODUCED TO THE FORMIDABLE OLD MAN IN A PRIVATE or semiprivate audience, I don't know which or for what reason.

I am guessing the meeting took place not later than 1909, before Father removed to Tampico. Díaz had begun his rule filled with liberal egalitarian ardor, but his major concerns soon became internal stability and foreign investment. Difficult as it is for us to comprehend the political history of Mexico, so must it have been for a young American of Father's frontier background. A swift century had passed since the priest, Miguel Hidalgo de Costilla, had rung the church bell in the town of Dolores, calling for revolution under the banner of the Virgin of Guadalupe. The tragic story of Mexico since that time had been a succession of misrule, violence, corruption, broken promises, betrayals, peculations, assassinations, and defeats, with ever more radical (and anticlerical) influences sifting into the country from Europe (by way of the Enlightenment and the several French revolutions). It is safe to assume that Father was well versed in Mexican history (all his Mexican contemporaries of whom we have record attest to this) and that his sympathies were viscerally against plutocratic government and the arrogance of the upper classes (he had tasted that arrogance in the Texan Anglos of his time; his father had opposed it), but also viscerally against egalitarian leftism (which was utterly alien to the frontier optimism in which he had been raised). His sympathies were, besides, as an Irish Catholic of militant antecedence, engaged on the side of the Church; viewing with aversion the Jacobinism of so many Mexican

---

*Which was to haunt him, as similar boasts do some U.S. Republicans today.

intellectual movements, including the then-current crop, the *"científicos,"* who had gathered under the Díaz dictatorship.* I have no doubt at all in my mind that Father viewed Porfirio Díaz with a catawampus eye.[3]

For some reason—possibly because he was impressed by the modest young gringo with the studious air who spoke impeccable Mexican Spanish, possibly because the old fellow had got to the age when he seized on anyone to whom he could boast—Díaz expatiated on the many accomplishments of his long regime: Mexico's robust economy, advances in sanitation, road and railroad construction, education and the all-important concern of literacy, and so forth.

Father listened attentively to the old fellow's self-praise and then asked with his Southwestern directness, "That's marvelous, Your Excellency, but what will happen when you die?"[†]

The reception chamber—he recalled many years after—went stock still. He was hastily conducted away from the shocked Porfirio Díaz. Whispered into his ear in reproof by some beribboned plenipotentiary were the words "His Excellency will never die!"

(Father told this story on himself, shaking his head, round blue eyes bemused, amazed still by his naiveté.)

THE CENTURIES IN THEIR ANNIVERSARIES HAVE BEEN HARSH TO Mexico.

It was in 1810, with his Grito de Dolores, that the priest Hidalgo catapulted the country toward independence. It was just one hundred years later, in 1910, that revolution broke out under diminutive, idealistic Francisco I. Madero, under the Plan of San Luis Potosí (issued from San Antonio, Texas, where Madero, a political outcast, had sought refuge), bravely proclaiming the battle cry of *tierra y libertad*—land and liberty; "no ninth

---

* There is a curious contrary reflection here fifty years later, in Spain, when the Opus Dei–influenced "technocrats," Ullastres, López Bravo, Fraga Iribarne, and so forth, gathered around the aging and failing Franco regime and opened up the country to foreign investment and a viable economy, producing Spain's first middle class ever.
† Thus drawing the conversation back to the crucial and paramount political reality, which was that Porfirio Díaz was a dictator who had arranged for no peaceful and orderly democratic succession. It is this ability to draw the fine distinctions that I allude to in note 3, below.

self-elected term for Porfirio Díaz, free ballot, restoration of the stolen land to Mexico's landless millions," oh, noble—yet, in fatidically cursed Mexican wont, casting the nation into ten years of chaotic, anarchic, and murderous turmoil during which, except for the final ouster of Porfirio Díaz, every one of these principles was traduced; opening the doors to glory for such as Pancho Villa.

Villa was either twenty-eight or thirty-one years old.* He and Pascual Orozco (1882–1915, assassinated in El Paso) came down from the Chihuahuan hills bringing their ragtag armies of thousands to join the idealistic and incompetent Madero, who had called for national insurrection against Porfirio Díaz on November 20, 1910 (the Grito de Dolores). By November 1911, Madero managed to get himself elected president, but in the south, Emiliano Zapata, who had waged a bloody campaign against the *caciques,* turned against him for failing immediately to distribute lands to dispossessed Indians. If that wasn't sufficient, Madero's fumbling regime was attacked by carpers in the press and other quarters, including supporters of the deceased Porfirio Díaz, who planned a coup d'état that began February 9, 1913. Victoriano Huerta took Madero prisoner, forcing him to resign ten days later (February 19), and then ordered him assassinated; a crime that gave rise to another revolution, dubbed "constitutionalist," which was to propel the equally evil and corrupt Venustiano Carranza into power.[4]

Huerta's dictatorship was contested by Carranza, Álvaro Obregón, Zapata, and Pancho Villa, who, in command of his División del Norte, became the sensation of U.S. newspaper photographers and Hollywood producers. (It helped considerably that Woodrow Wilson had taken sides against Huerta.) They flocked to northern Mexico to record his battle exploits (several of which were staged for the benefit of the cameras), romanticizing him into a folk hero. He nevertheless led the most important military campaigns in the constitutionalist revolution, his troops victorious as far south as Zacatecas and Mexico City, as far east as Tampico, and as far west as Casas Grandes, in the northwest corner of Chihuahua.

Villa meantime ruled his home base of Chihuahua like a medieval warlord. He financed his army by rustling from endless herds of cattle, whose beeves he sold north of the border, where there was no shortage

---

*The dates of his birth vary according to the source.

of U.S. scumbags willing to sell him guns and ammunition. He issued his own currency, in the manner described by Cecilio Velasco. If merchants refused to accept it, why, they were shot. These executions were ordered by Villa on a whim. Ordinarily, but not always, he left the actual killing to his friend, Rodolfo Fierro, who was soon known as El Carnicero (the Butcher). But Villa maintained his popularity by breaking up the vast landholdings of the *hacendados* and parceling them out to the widows and orphans of his soldiers. He was bigger than life, by turns cruel and generous, vicious and magnanimous—a *zampatortas*, a swaggering, mustachioed lover, who danced all night with female camp followers and, according to one of his last surviving widows, officially married twenty-six times.

Once his armies had helped consolidate them in power, Obregón and the scheming, ambitious, most villainous Venustiano Carranza had no further use for the bandit-hero. They turned their combined forces against him. When Washington declared openly in support of the Carranza presidency, Villa retaliated by raiding U.S. border towns, infamously Columbus, New Mexico, a village of three hundred souls, all of them sleeping when the attack started at four in the morning. Eighteen Americans were murdered.[5]

Woodrow Wilson used the Columbus raid, as an excuse to send "Black Jack" John Pershing into Mexican territory on two fruitless expeditions (1916 and 1919) after Villa.[6] (American meddling in Mexican internal affairs was becoming habitual, though Villa's raids gave every provocation.) Meantime the combined forces of Obregón and Carranza were defeating Villistas in battle after battle. The free-spirited glory days of the revolution were winding down. Zapata, the only pure soul of them all, was treacherously assassinated in 1919. Carranza was murdered by his own men on May 20, 1920, at Tlaxcalantongo,* Puebla. In 1920, Villa made peace with the Obregón government, which accepted his surrender and retired him on a general's salary with fifty of his faithful Dorados ("golden ones") to a 25,000-acre ranch in Canutillo, Durango, granting total amnesty. But it was manifestly unsafe for Obregón to keep Villa alive. It was only a matter of time. On July 23, 1923, after just three years in retirement

---

*Isn't this the most marvelous name? Roll it over on your tongue a few times: *Tlax/cal/ antongo, Tlaxcal/antongo*. It's my second choice for a dream address, after Skunk's Misery Lane.

as a farmer (which time Villa spent womanizing and cockfighting), he was ambushed by a rifle-firing assassin on his way back from business in Parral, Chihuahua. His last words are reported: "Don't let it end like this. Tell them I said something."*†

That his gaudy and sanguinary life amounted to little more than a hill of frijoles? Pancho Villa's grandiloquent reputation on both sides of the border outlived him, however, which would please him to know. Though his grave was broken into in 1926, his head cut off and removed, maybe to make a drinking cup (or, as in Goya's similar case, a soccer ball), ballads have been written about him. He is folklore. To many Mexicans of those now-distant first decades of the twentieth century, and today, he was the only foreign military personage ever to have invaded continental U.S. territory, and got away with it. In the northern regions of Mexico, his name is uttered with respect, and in the United States, it has been kept alive, though not so vividly and uncritically, by Hollywood and pulp fiction. The true sad part of the Pancho Villa story is that he contributed many of the basest and most vicious attributes of his character to the Mexican political temperament.

For the November 20, 1976, annual celebration of Madero's declaration of independence, leftist president Luis Echeverría, historically one of the most shameless thieves Mexico has been unfortunate enough to suffer under to date (and that's saying something), had Pancho Villa's remains taken from the cemetery at Parral and entombed in the monument to the Mexican revolution in Mexico City, his name spelled out in gold on the rotunda. What a role model to raise one's children in emulation of.

This is a peculiarly Mexican dilemma: all the leaders and eminences of their independence and the extended revolution of 1910–1921, without exception (even Madero), were morally flawed, and most of them profoundly so: greed, treachery, betrayal of their own avowed principles, and murder. None of them—again, with the exception of Emiliano Zapata— was pure-hearted. None of them was morally admirable. And they have stained the destiny of their country with their sins.

---

*So much for the pistol that the ex-governor boasted as the weapon that killed Pancho Villa, unless it happened that a coup de grace was delivered by revolver when the bullet-ridden car in which Villa was riding came to a stop.

†Obregón, living in retirement, was in his turn shot and killed on July 17, 1928, by a fanatical Catholic, for his many crimes against the Church and against priests and nuns.

Father was clear-eyed about Mexican political faults, but neither did he fantasize about the United States. A dichotomy between political conviction and gut feelings well describes him: though he bitterly opposed Wilson's invasion of Veracruz in 1914, when he was apprised (by his friend Captain Damie?) that Mexican snipers hidden in the rooftop cisterns of the buildings were shooting down American Marines, he walked out into the middle of the street, yelling obscene insults in his perfect Spanish at the rooftops, where the snipers were skulking, so that they popped up in fury to blast away at him—thus offering targets for Marines sharpshooters. (I don't know how often he repeated this act of bravado, but I gather it was several times, until the snipers were eliminated.)* True, he held Mexican marksmanship in Texan contempt. Notwithstanding, the courage and patriotism of his actions are clear. He scorned Woodrow Wilson as an ignorant provincial, and for multiple cognate reasons he scorned Woodrow Wilson's successor, FDR, the squire of Hyde Park, who was to him a Wilson writ large, a hypocrite of the Northeastern Anglo ruling class.

The anarchy of the ten years of Mexico's revolution brought out the worst of the rapacity of American and foreign oil interests.† I return to Cecilio Velasco's tribute in *W.F.B.—An Appreciation*, beginning with his praise of the now obscure General Manuel Pelaez:

> Sole bulwark in those days capable of controlling and checking the growing indignation of the despoiled landholders and the workers who felt they were being cheated because of the meager wages they received, and were being injured by the almost inhuman treatment to which they were subjected by cruel foreigners and nationals [Mexicans] unconditionally supported by the enterprises [foreign oil companies], Pelaez served as referee in the disputes. He acted as judge and sentencer—and always left the workers satisfied, for they loved him and respected him, and the companies never refused to heed his decisions. . . .
>
> The oil companies paid tribute (something like a war tax) [we might call it protection] to General Pelaez, who, acting independently

---

*My sister Priscilla tells a different version of this anecdote.

†As the late Willi Schlamm used to say to my brother Bill, "The trouble with socialism is socialism; the trouble with capitalism is capitalists."

of the Carranza Government, had need of funds in order to pay his soldiers, who in turn provided the companies with guarantees and peaceful conditions.

The oil interests—were "always ready to hand over all they owned to armed bandits whenever they were threatened and in danger,"—but they nevertheless chafed at this tribute and conspired against Pelaez, bringing about the insurrection of his forces in the Huastecas district. It was, charges Velasco, the "treacherous, arbitrary and frightful methods practiced by the oil companies" that brought on nationalization of oil in Mexico and the expropriation of their properties.

William Buckley was different. "Of all the Americans . . . residing in Tampico, in General Pelaez's opinion, W.F.B. was perhaps the only one . . . on whom he could depend safely not to betray him." We musn't forget, Father was in fact so esteemed by Mexicans for his impartiality and knowledge of Mexican affairs that he had been chosen by them to be their counsel at the ABC Conference at Niagara. His relationship with General Pelaez did not sit well with the brotherhood of petroleum executives:

> The companies took a dim view of the friendly relationship between Mr. Buckley and General Pelaez, and they blamed Buckley for [the] increasingly severe intervention in and control of the petroleum industry on the part of the Mexican Government. They declared him their number one enemy, and they maneuvered and conspired with the Government under the presidency of General Obregón [Father and Pancho Villa shared an enemy] until in 1921 they had the satisfaction of seeing Mr. Buckley expelled from Mexico as an undesirable foreigner.

Father was stripped of everything he had not simply because of his political activities on behalf of the Cristeros, a movement of faithful Catholics that had sprung up against the priest-killing Carranza, but because he was a bone in the throat of the oilmen. Their hostility accounts in major part (along with the Depression) for the eighteen-year struggle he was to endure in reestablishing himself (Wall Street, influenced by Rockefeller's Standard Oil, shunned him). Obregón, however, apparently soon realized he had made a mistake and invited Father back to Mexico; but Father refused (there being no education in the second kick of a mule). He had moved on.

Señor Velasco ends his tribute:

William Buckley, a man of faith and goodwill, was a great friend to Mexico. He was an outstanding figure in the oil world, in Mexico and in Venezuela. [His] deportation was deeply regretted in Tampico as well as in Mexico City, for in both places he had countless friends who loved him, particularly among the families of intellectuals and professional people.

He concludes with a very personal testimony to his affection and respect for Father, which is not appropriate here. Father may have been alive to the corruption of his fellow American (and British) oilmen, and sympathetic to just Mexican complaints, as well as scornfully opposed to the Jacobinism and naked self-interest of the "generals" (some bearing the title by courtesy only) who rose up under the revolution; neither did he confuse Mexico with the United States in historical and cultural perspective, keeping in his mind a sharp critical distinction between the formation of the two nations (he scoffed, for example, at the pretentiousness of the Mexican denomination of their provinces as "states"—they were never self-governing entities). The bloviation Woodrow Wilson delivered at the funeral of American sailors killed at Veracruz was, apart from its deceptiveness, the kind of grand self-righteous moralism to which Father in his deepest entrails objected:

We have gone down to Mexico [said Wilson] to serve mankind if we can find out the way. We do not want to fight the Mexicans. We want to serve the Mexicans if we can, because we know how we would like to be free and how we would like to be served if there were friends ready to serve us.

Shades of George Bush II? Father must have been appalled by the grandiosity of this statement. His friend, the poet Nemesio García Naranjo, wrote of him that though he "understood Mexico" this did not signify that "he viewed its problems with impartiality. He was a keen observer, but there was in him—as in nearly every Irishman—more of the fighter than of the mere spectator. He took sides in every conflict probably because he felt that indifference to evil is immoral and cowardly, is to condone it, and that everyone must stand up and fight for what he believes to be right."* Blood of the plowshare-wielding first John Buckley as well as blood of sheriff John C. Buckley plainly ran in our father's veins.

Within his idealism and Irish pugnacity, he was nevertheless a pragmatist who kept a vigilant weatherwatch for the political realities. One did not (1) (Wilson-like) impose the republican standards of the United States on Mexico, which had never, not in all its long history, beginning with the Aztecs and continuing under four centuries of Spanish rule, had the remotest experience with republican government (a grasp of the realities inclining him to support Díaz against Madero, if indeed he did so—we don't know—and Generals Huerta and Pelaez against the Carranza cabal); nor did one (2) excuse the avarice and graft of American opportunists (principally oil prospectors, but there were others) who came to Mexico with the sole object of pillaging the country. One did not (3) tolerate interference by the United States in Mexico's internal affairs,† which, apart from the violence done to international law, was a mortal transgression against Father's Southwestern doctrine of isolationism.

We children were all the heirs of these attitudes, which, in his childhood and in his early upbringing, were formed in him preceptually, and which were confirmed by his experiences in young manhood. We children have accommodated ourselves to these precepts, moderating and shedding some of them, each in our separate way.‡ Father's knowledge of Mexican history and his personal involvement with Mexico from 1908 to 1921 deepened his frontier suspicion of autocratic government (and big government in general), and this attitude dyes all his children strongly. What

---

* *W.F.B.—An Appreciation.*

† Keep in mind that Wilson's intervention in Mexico's business anteceded the invasion of Veracruz; he detested Huerta and connived to replace him with Carranza by such means as providing Carranza, Pancho Villa, and Obregón with arms and munitions while blockading shipments of arms to Huerta.

‡ Pearl Harbor and the Soviet Union made us interventionists, for example; brother Bill's deep reservations about Iraq, on the other hand (winter 2006), which he has called a "failed enterprise," express the highly skeptical attitude about American interventionism that is rooted in our father's anti-Wilsonianism.

came to us primarily as tales of adventure from Father's romantic youth and young adulthood became, by and by, ruling lessons in our sifting of experience.

FATHER'S FIRST MEETING WITH PANCHO VILLA TOOK PLACE WHEN HE was riding a railroad train, I do not recall from where to where, his mission being to deliver the payroll of a big U.S. company, I do not remember which.

It was a hot day in summer. Dust, coal smoke, and cinders blew in through the open windows, stinging eyes, covering the passengers—who protected mouths and nostrils with handkerchiefs, which grew grimier with every mile of track. Pancho Villa had been regularly raiding and robbing and killing in the area, causing Father to wonder where he could hide the payroll should Villa, exalted by revolution to the status of patriot, have got wind of the loot. This was in the form of gold coins, rolled tightly in paper. After thinking hard on the problem, Father got up from his seat and, heavy satchel in hand, walked toward the back of the car, where the evil-smelling men's room was located.

Once inside, curtain drawn, he looked around him; and, satisfying himself that the chamber was empty (nobody in the toilet, nobody smoking on the leather-upholstered benches), began dropping the rolls of coins one by one into the wide, dish-shaped mouths (which were stained with spittle, phlegm, and tobacco juice, never mind) and down the hollow tubes of their stands. Should Villa's brigands board and search the train, surely they would never think of the cuspidors.

Satisfied with his stratagem, he washed his hands hard with soap, stepped out of the rest room, and took a seat up the aisle, on the right. He had fallen half asleep—head nodding with the rhythmic clackety-clacking of the railway ties—when pistol and rifle shots rang out, people shouted and screamed, and the thundering of horses' hooves burst upon his ears.

The locomotive's brakes screeched and sizzled, and with a series of jolting stops that knocked people half out of their seats, the three cars of the train ground to a halt.

In poured the bandits, Villa at their head—unmistakably Pancho Villa—shouting, cursing, pistols smoking, strutting up and down the aisle demanding wallets, gold watches, women's cameos and bracelets and wedding rings and hat pins, whatever of value anyone carried. Suitcases were torn from overhead racks and tossed to the floor, where they were broached. Father's empty satchel (it contained toiletries) was yanked down, opened, peered into, flung to the floor. "Where is it?" demanded Villa, his temper rising as gunmen who were ransacking the other cars reported that they had found nothing.

Some spy in the home office had tipped Villa off, it became plain, because he shouted, "I know the gold is here, where is it?" He turned on the terrified conductor, who was dragged toward him by two of the bandits, "You—where is the gold, tell me!" And he drew his pistol, placing its long barrel flat against the poor man's brow.

"But there is no gold!" cried the conductor, falling on his knees, wringing his hands.

"Don't lie to me!" shouted Villa, furious. "We know the gold is on this train. Do not lie to Pancho Villa. Be quick, tell me, or you are a dead man."

As the conductor continued miserably pleading ignorance, there came a shout from the back of the railway car, and two of the bandits burst out of the men's room, declaring that they had found the gold, they (or the train's hard stopping) had knocked over one of the cuspidors, and the coins, bursting their rolls, had rolled out.

At this, Villa's face darkened with anger, and he raised his pistol, cocking the hammer, pointing it at the conductor's skull. But Father had meantime got up from his seat near the back of the car and now called out in loud voice, in Spanish, "Don't hurt that man. I hid the gold. He knew nothing about it."

"Who are you?"

"My name is Guillermo Buckley. I was bringing the payroll for Company X, and I hid it without this man's knowledge."

"Oh, thank you, thank you," the conductor cried at these words, writhing on the floor in his wretchedness.

"Shut up, you disgusting worm," said Villa. "I am going to shoot you anyhow."

At this, the conductor began blubbering of his wife and multiple children, begging for pity. Father had come to within a few feet of Villa, whose face was black with disgust—saying to him, "I know you won't shoot that miserable man."

"Who are you to say that, *Ojos Azules?* You will be fortunate if I do not kill you, too."

"Because you are too great a man to shoot a wretch like this conductor. Pancho Villa has become famous in Mexico. Children all over the country are being taught to respect and revere his name. Pancho Villa stands for justice to the poor. You would never waste your reputation on such a wretch as this."

He continued shamelessly in this fashion, speaking of Pancho Villa's fair fame. At first the bandit was stony, but he liked what he heard, maybe especially from this American, and when henchmen grabbed Father to pull him away, he said no, let the gringo speak, this *ojos azules* ("blue eyes") was telling the truth. He swelled visibly with gratification as Father continued extolling his reputation, and Villa began glancing down at the conductor benevolently.

"Get up, get up!" he said at last. "Don't grovel. I have no intention of hurting you. Are we through here, *caballeros?*" he shouted at his men, who indicated that they had pried the last gold tooth out of the last mouth and were ready to go. "Good. And you, Guillermo Buckley, come see me at a better time. I respect courage. I might even have use for you."

Pancho Villa did make use of gringos, when it suited him. He recruited Americans as captains for his División del Norte, and one squadron, led by a soldier of fortune called Captain Tracey Richardson, was made up of Americans only. My brothers have told me that Father was asked by Villa, who was, of course, illiterate, to write certain letters for him. I have wondered how they went:

Dear Distinguished Sir:

I have the honor of informing you that your beautiful hacienda
has been generously apportioned to veterans of my glorious army,
which I know will meet with your approval.
    Respectfully yours,

                                        Pancho Villa

Or:

Dear Madame:

I agree with you entirely. Your house is so *linda,* and so grand, that it would be a crime against Heaven to put it to the torch.

I have therefore appropriated it for my personal use, which I trust will gratify you.

Ever your humble and devoted servant,

Pancho Villa (General)

Perhaps not quite. Those letters must have been business documents of some kind, and I languish with curiosity. But Father's relations with the bandit and the future hero of the revolution, which were few and far apart, were not all cordial. One afternoon, in the early 1950s, when Father was upstairs in his bedroom and presumably dying, Señor Velasco took me aside and described the last of them.

Pancho Villa and Emiliano Zapata, riding at the head of fifty thousand troops, took Mexico City on December 4, 1914, and met that evening to celebrate in the floating gardens of Xochimilco, which are all that is left of the ancient lake upon which Tenochtitlán, the city of the Aztecs, was built.

This was the zenith of Pancho Villa's revolutionary career. A banquet had been prepared. Pancho Villa and Zapata were heroes. Mind, neither man liked or trusted the other. They were political rivals. Pancho Villa was, besides, envious of the slim physique of this fellow from the no-account hamlet of Anenecuilco in the remote southern latitudes of Mexico, and of Zapata's fame as a horseman.

Zapata regularly performed *el paso de la muerte* ("the pass of death") at rodeos. Wild broncs were run around the circumference of a corral. Riders followed them at a hard gallop, in a tighter circumference, until they drew even. One of them (Zapata) would then leap from his saddle onto the bare back of the leading bronc and, grabbing its mane, ride it to a standstill. If in the leap he missed, or if he fell from the bronc in those critical first instants, he was trampled by the herd of horses galloping behind. Villa was too heavy even to contemplate this feat.

Señor Velasco told me that Villa and Zapata sat at the head table, side by side, their most trusted companions (in Villa's case, the Dorados, his Praetorian guard) flanking them. The head table formed the base of a square U, whose long legs—boards supported by carpenters' stools, I am guessing—were occupied on the one side by Zapata partisans, on the facing side by Villa partisans. Everybody was laughing and joking and drinking (except for Pancho Villa, who never touched a drop—I don't know about Zapata, I will bet he was abstemious, too), but every man at the table had his pistol or pistols in front of him, by his plate.

It was into this jolly gathering that Father introduced himself.

It had been quite a year for Will Buckley. He had turned thirty-three in 1914 and was in the full vigor of manhood. He had established his younger brothers in a profitable law practice, and his mother and two sisters were comfortably fixed in Austin, though neither of the girls was idle, Aunt Priscilla continuing to work in the land office, Aunt Eleanor doing I do not know what. Starting from scratch, using his lively imagination and happily accepting risk (he had little choice), he had made a name for himself and had attracted to his side lifelong friends, Mexican and American. He was incorruptible and outspoken and did not mind angering people who were neither. He had made enemies, good ones, the bad guys. He had been threatened with death and expulsion and so far had avoided both, refusing to change his ways or moderate his opinions. He had been abducted by bandits and escaped. He had founded Pantepec, the company that he would eventually ride to great riches.

But as he had written his friend Pope, he was already a landowner and developer of means and had high prospects. He had discovered oil, not yet the black gold itself but the lure and the excitement, freeing him from a profession he found tedious. He had been appointed counsel for the Mexican government in the ABC Conference, an honor indeed, considering Mexican chauvinism. He had exposed himself to the fire of Mexican snipers in order to save U.S. Marines and sailors from being shot. He had refused the civil governorship of Veracruz and watched U.S. gunboats weigh anchor after six desultory months in the harbor, bearing away General Funston and five thousand troops, who had accomplished an obnoxious mission ordered by an erratic old fuddy-duddy of a U.S. president. Mexico continued in a state of turmoil, with the Huerta dictatorship being besieged by the forces of Carranza and Obregón on the one side and now Villa and Zapata on the other, who had taken the capital city, but this was a land of opportunity for a person willing to work hard and who possessed the necessary grit, which he eminently did.

I have no idea what incident had occurred, but Father was mad, truly angry, and, I surmise, to a self-imperiling degree, out of control. Señor Velasco told me that they had apparently been having trouble with drunken Villa guerrillas, who were raiding property that Father owned—stealing, molesting women, frightening children. Had a man been murdered, a woman raped, a child abused? Something on that order must have happened. Because Father—boiling inside, disregarding his customary prudence—confronted Pancho Villa at this first opportunity.

He was alone, Señor Velasco said. (I suspect strongly, however, that Velasco was with him, because he recounted the story with such vivid immediacy.) Father walked up to the head table, where Villa was pretending to be affable to Zapata.

Villa glanced up and said to him, "Ah, Señor Ojos Azules, what brings you here? What can I do for you?"

"You can keep your men off my property," Father answered.

Villa, Señor Velasco told me, smiled—but his eyes flicked toward Zapata, on his left, whose eyebrows had cocked. What—Pancho Villa was asking himself—would Zapata be thinking of this presumptuous attitude by a gringo?

He said, "And why should I do that, Guillermo Buckley? Just what will you do if my men trespass on your property?"

Here I absolutely do not credit my memory. I shake my head at it in disbelief. Yet sticking to it like a cockleburr is that Father answered something on the order of this: "Because the next time one of your men puts his foot on my property, he will be shot."

I blush. This is (a) too melodramatic for our father to have uttered, out of character entirely; (b) too threatening, and thus foolish.

Yet he answered something—and whatever his actual words were, they were firm enough, as Cecilio Velasco recounted to me—for the Pancho Villa cronies at the head table to grow still and to place their hands on their pistols, gazing at their chief.

I remember Señor Velasco describing this scene: how the hall fell silent, how the hands of those desperados, the "Golden Ones," slid forward to cover their pistols, and how they gazed at their chief for direction, with expectancy.

There ensued moments of extreme tension; and then Pancho Villa laughed, saying something like, "My men won't be bothering you, Señor Ojos Azules, I promise you." He laughed again. "Come see me sometime."

Señor Velasco told me (I was goggle-eyed, listening to this tale) that Father turned then, and without another word began walking back between those long tables containing Villa and Zapatista *guerreros*. "He could have been shot at any moment," Velasco said to me emphatically. "Villa was always unpredictable. But we never again had trouble with his bandits."

I know from reading several accounts of him that Pancho Villa despised cowardice and admired courage. There was a level on which these two very different men understood each other.[7]

During the (for Father) nostalgic return to Mexico, the summer and fall of 1943, he took us twice to visit Xochimilco. We were Pitts, Janie, Bill (waiting to be snatched up by the infantry), Trisha, Maureen, little Carol (age five), and I. Allie was married to her movie-handsome Ben Heath (often mistaken for Larry Parks), a 1st Lieutenant in the Air Force, and living with him on his base in Sumter, South Carolina, pregnant with the first of her ten children; brother John, a second lieutenant in the 9th Cavalry Regiment at Fort Riley (he would later be attached to military intelligence), was training for the invasion of Morocco; and Jim was in Southeast Asia, then an ensign (later a lieutenant J.G.), where, on his LST, he would see action in several island invasions, including Leyte, Lingayen, and Okinawa.

Of Xochimilco I remember little other than my extreme boredom as we floated endlessly (it seemed to me) on evil-looking opaque waters in a large barge wending its way through the maze of island gardens, at which I stared dully—they were not showy and deserved their reputation little, thought I—and ate lunch (at last, hurrah!) at a mediocre restaurant. I wonder now what Father may have been reflecting upon, and whether Mother knew about his confrontation with Pancho Villa in these gardens a little more than twenty years gone by.[8]

She must have known. They confided everything to each other. But Father never said a word about his encounter to any of us, so far as I am aware. It would have embarrassed him too much. Besides, he may have thought it set a poor example for his children.

NOTES

———

1. One other—there are several—indispensable Spanish adjective for which we have no equivalent that should be incorporated into our language. *Cursi* can be associated with *nouveau riche*, but it does not refer to these exclusively. A duke with generations of station and wealth behind him can be *cursi*. The wives of wealthy Latin Americans in high proportion have a tendency to be *cursi*—all that jewelry they carry on their short, stout persons; the mink wrap when it's just seventy degrees F. *Def.* in bad taste, vulgar; pretentious; loud, showy, flashy; posh, genteel, pseudo-refined; affected.

2. For as many years as I can recollect, Mother kept the vest Maximilian wore to his execution in the drawer of one of the heavy mahogany sideboards in the Empire room—which was situated against the western wall, just south of the grand piano. It was given to her by Madame Paloma. Madame Paloma, an aged lady, was very fond of Mother and became godmother to our sister Priscilla, to whom she bequeathed that gorgeous crystal chandelier that hangs still in the central hall of Kamschatka. The vest was made of emerald-green velvet and had tiny *fleurs-de-lis* stitched into it in ruby thread. It was said that the gentle Maximilian thought it too beautiful to be pierced by the bullets that would shortly riddle him, prompting him to doff it just before he was paraded out to his death. (Curiously reminiscent of Ulysses S. Grant, who thought Port Gibson too beautiful to destroy.) I don't know what became of the garment after Great Elm was broken up and condominiumized, but I lusted for it at one time.

3. Despite the assertion by Nemesio García Naranjo (see below) that Father supported Porfirio Díaz. Here is a point I wish to stress. It was (a) out of character for Father to have fallen under the old dictator's spell, and (b) it makes no difference whether Father leaned toward him as the only answer, desirable or not, to chaos, because (c) we, his children, knew that if Porfirio Díaz (the known evil) was not to his taste, neither were Madero (a patriot but a bumbling fool), Carranza, Obregón, and Villa and the lot (murdering thieves), and this is the important thing: the ability to discriminate morally and draw the necessary practical distinction, which is what we imbibed from him.

4. Madero and his vice president, Pino Suárez, were shot "while trying to escape," the infamous *leye de fuga* that accounted for so many executions in those revolutionary times. Intellectuals such as the poet Nemesio García Naranjo, who became one of Father's close Mexican friends after the revolution, and who had been a minister in

the Huerta government, vigorously rejected the charge that Huerta had ordered Madero's assassination.

5.   This massacre turned into a humiliating defeat for Villa, thanks to the valor of the 13th Cavalry Regiment quartered in Columbus under the command of forty-eight-year-old Major Frank Tompkin, who mounted a pistol charge that riddled Pancho Villa's rear guard and drove the gang fifteen miles into Mexico, killing almost one hundred of them; yet it was sensational, feeding the Villa myth, because only Pancho had the *cojones* to take on the United States.

6.   In my sister Priscilla's folio, *The Light-hearted Years: Early Recollections, At Home & Abroad* (which is funny, priceless, and delicious), she tells a marvelous story about seeing Black Jack Pershing at a circus. He went walking around the circumference of the ring to the applause of the crowd but unexpectedly halted, reaching up to the box where Pitts and Allie and John and Jim were watching, awed, to shake the hand of onetime Rough Rider Captain Dame, who rode not only with Teddy Roosevelt but also with General Pershing on one of the latter's (fruitless) expeditions into Mexico after Pancho Villa. (Captain Dame, Father's good friend, treated my older siblings to lunch in his West Side New York City apartment two or three times, taking them to the circus after.)

7.   There is another (of several other?) meetings between Pancho Villa and Will Buckley that suggests a third reason for understanding between the two men. It's told by my sister Priscilla in her *The Light-hearted Years:* "Father knew Pancho Villa, and he told us once that he was at a banquet where lots of Mexican rebel leaders—'they were nothing but brigands,' he said in an aside to Mother—got up and made speeches. And they all said that what they wanted was land for the people. But when Villa got up, his speech was short. All he said was: 'I want land for Villa,' and gave a big laugh and sat down. 'He was the only honest brigand of the lot,' Father told us." I am tempted to believe that this was the famous meeting with Zapata at Xochimilco, which I have described.

8.   There is a photo that my sister Patricia's Vassar roommate, Elsie Dunklin of Texas (with whom I fell eternally in love when I was sixteen, she, alas, being nineteen or twenty), just sent me, showing a young Will Buckley in his shirtsleeves (!) yet dapper under a homburg hat (!!) seated in a Xochimilco punt (it looks like), in the company of two pretty young women his age. He is looking toward the stern, at a handsome older woman, Mary Maverick, matron of the famous Texas Maverick family. The Mavericks refused to brand their steers, and when one of these heads got rounded up on the range with others, cowboys would note the absence of a brand and shout, "It's a maverick." My father's whole career made that Texan point: he was never branded.

———— ∽ ————

CHAPTER TWELVE

William Frank Buckley
of Texas (VII): The Mexican
Impact and Its Legacy

HIS EXPERIENCES IN MEXICO STAMPED OUR FATHER'S CHARACTER AND beliefs ever after, in turn indelibly stamping the assumptions, attitudes, perspectives, and political inclinations of his children, though each in his and her different manner.

Father's revolutionary Mexico was a lawless mess in which the norms of society had disintegrated and the lowest human passions—greed, rapine, corruption, and murder—were rampant, half the nation living in a state of fear and exposed to the most brutal oppression. Hence:

1. Government is necessary. Its function is to prevent anarchy and to check antisocial tendencies of the human animal, which include envy, bloodlust, and savagery. Government exists to defend the society against enemies abroad, to protect liberties at home, and, when necessary, to impose order. Government's primary duty is to protect and uphold duly established law.

The arteriosclerotic Porfirio Díaz regime accomplished some of these objectives, but at the expense of liberty and democracy, and in service of an arrogant plutocracy. Mexico's subsequent revolutionary regimes accomplished almost nothing other than to deceive the people, fuel chaos, corrupt society further, and condemn the pitiable Mexican people to a decade of blood-letting, which was followed by seven decades of exploitation, peculation, embezzlement, robbery, and political impotence.

Long before his years in Mexico, my father knew that:

2. Government is always dangerous.

Every schoolchild in the Southwest had had drilled into him that government, like fire, is a wonderful servant but a fearful master. All children in those days read and pondered the Farewell Address, last counsel to his country by George Washington. In those days, even in such a remote corner of the vast reaches of the nation as San Diego, Texas, Americans were instructed in their heritage. They committed to memory the Declaration of Independence and at least the Preamble of the Constitution. They could quote you the Bill of Rights and all the Amendments (there were fewer). When they grew old enough, they studied the Federalist Papers and were familiar with the opinions and statements of all the founders.

Whose counsels they took seriously. Schoolchildren in the United States still receive instruction in the charters of their founding, but one senses with a lot less reverence—with a kind of smug academic superiority (the old story of mediocrity disdaining genius). They may be more likely to hear about raunchy Thomas Jefferson and Sally Hemmings than about his courage in Italy attempting to smuggle a better rice to his cousin, Governor Rutledge, in South Carolina, at the risk of execution, or his sage warning that the government possessing the power to do something for its citizens possesses the power to do something to its citizens.

This maxim wasn't deprecated when our father was a child. Experience confirmed it. Archie Parr in Duval County had the power to do a lot of favors for his supporters and plenty of harm to his enemies, which included our father's father.* In Mexico, every government since Juárez had proposed to do for the people what they were unable to do for themselves.

*In 1972, my wife, Tasa, and I met briefly—at supper in a San Diego restaurant—with daughters and in-laws of the Archie Parr family (we were introduced by Walter Meeks). They were charming.

The post-Díaz revolutionary regimes all promised to endow Mexico with prosperity as well as egalitarian justice, neither of which goals is within the capacity or proper to the function of government. Hence:

3. Citizens of a republic must make do without government whenever possible.

Back then, in the United States politicians of whatever partisan tint throughout the country paid homage to a "rugged individualism" that is regularly mocked by the urbanized girly men of the media today but that on the frontier, when this country was still expanding territorially, was the accepted standard. Our father called it character. He had no one to support him when he went to Mexico. His first employer (Mexican? American?) was, by his account, "crooked," and when he quit the man's firm, having earned his enmity, he did not find work for a year, which must have been a desperate twelve months for the young adventurer from San Diego with almost no social, business, or political connections.*

The West, though acknowledging the value and necessity of an honest sheriff or federal marshal—of law and order—was nonetheless natively distrustful of government. This was a political wisdom natural to Will Buckley, whose sire had contended against Anglo arrogance and the political corruption of Duval County. Our father learned from his father (and the wisdom was reinforced by his experience in Mexico) that:

4. Government, unless bound strictly by laws, unless kept humble, contains within it an ever-immanent menace of despotism, often accompanied by grandiose proclamations that disguise naked ambition.

The New Deal. The Fair Deal. The Great Society. Compassionate conservativism. In Mexico, the revolution fed fat on its promises to the poor-and-oppressed (one word, in Marxist lingo, in which no poor are unoppressed, no oppressed unpoor), to which all the revolutionary leaders,

---

*In this age of instant communications, we are fast losing comprehension of what it is to be utterly alone and dependent on one's own resources not only in a foreign country but in what was then an alien civilization.

with the exception of Zapata, and be it said to some degree with the honorable exception of Pancho Villa, were faithless. Drummed into our father by extrapolation from the Mexican experience was that:

> 5. Citizens must be vigilant always to keep government disciplined within constitutional limits, or it spills over those boundaries, threatening the freedom and security of the people it was created to protect.

From what our sire read and heard of the Juárez regime, and of the Díaz regime personally experienced, he culled easily that the tendency of government is always to expand its power, and that the tendency of strong men is always to arrogate to themselves more authority. This tendency may be benevolent, the strong man may be bursting with goodwill; it is nevertheless (a) subversive of the people's rights, (b) corrupting. Concentration of power in the center is the historical dynamic—the inertia—of all governments and all strong men in all human history, without exception; and once powers are surrendered to government or to the strong man, they are rarely, if ever, recovered by the citizens.

My father's experience impressed me strongly with the entropy that afflicts all human institutions, such as our Constitution, and consequently, such as our republic.

> 6. The natural dynamic of government is to absorb power at the expense of the citizens, usurping both the independence and the social responsibilities that must be expected of citizens if a republic is to work.

Big government is always overbearing. Big government weakens the populace by assuming responsibilities properly charged to the individual (their personal health and welfare). Big government invites corruption of all kinds—venal, moral, philosophical.

> 7. Corruption is a pathological condition of big government, not accidental. Corruption under the aegis of big government pervades society and infects every citizen with disrespect for truth and with a weakness—a desire and preference—for falsehood.

Father detested lies. I don't think any peccadillo among his children aggravated him more. And one fully understands why. Lying is moral cowardice.* A national fault of Mexicans, at least since the revolutionary period, is the incapacity to answer truly. Ask a humble Mexican, a peasant or a household servant, if it is raining outside, and he will answer not necessarily or even, though rain may be hammering on the roof and against the window panes, that it is sunny. He does not want to be held responsible. Ask him or her if it is sunny, and he or she will answer that it is raining, though not the puff of a cloud in all the vast arc of the sky casts a shadow on the day. He/she does not want to be held responsible. If the irate policeman charges you with speeding, deny it. Deny anything with which you may be charged by anyone in authority, even though you may have been going so fast that you slammed into the cop's rear bumper. If the *patrón* asks whether you took the package to the post office, as he had ordered you to do, answer is "*Sí, Señor*," though you failed to do so, which he will find out certainly when he enters the office, *as you know*. Then, when you are accused of lying through your *puta* mother's teeth, invent a thousand plainly specious and flabbergastingly fictitious reasons in justification.

The American is stupefied by the bald-faced audacity of Mexican lying. The truth Mexicans tribally know not. The truth will not set them free; it will get them into trouble. This is the inheritance of revolution coupled with increasingly despotic government. The truth could get one shot. One was asked to trust and believe palpable falsehoods pronounced by this or that politician.

This was like the funny money that generals printed; if you did not accept it, you were shot. A Mexican child is taught today to revere the revolutionary leaders who were patently crooks and murderers, who lied to the people time and again, who were venal in every respect. This is the heritage perpetrated by the PRI (the Partido Revolucionario Institucional, the Institutional Revolutionary Party) for the past seventy years.† Two full

---

* This vice has become part of the big government scene in our country. Politicians nowadays do not lie or deceive; they "misspeak." They never do anything wrong; they make "mistakes."
† The contradiction in the very title—the *Institutional* Revolutionary Party—is very Mexican and cheerfully unremarked by Mexicans. How can a revolutionary party be *institutional*? It can't, obviously, if it pleads that it is revolutionary. That the title has endured for seventy-plus years as the cover for one-party rule, or dictatorship—until the advent of ex-President Fox,

generations of Mexicans have grown up under the lies sown by big government and its minions, and they have been corrupted.

8. Government is moreover by its very nature inefficient.

Our father was able to observe this firsthand in every business activity in which he was engaged in Mexico. Nothing worked well: the police, the system of justice, the fire department, sanitation, the mails. The bureaucracy was atrocious. Our father would have blinked his round blue eyes in amazement at the astonishment of the American public at the bumbling response of local, state, and federal governments in the Hurricane Katrina disaster. A Third World response, shouted many, here and abroad; to which the answer is, just so, and the more responsibilities we saddle the federal government with, the more Third World will it get.*

Any impartial student of government knows what Peter Drucker stated as a basic fact of political biology long years ago: Government is not by nature a doer. Anybody who expects government to get things done speedily and efficiently has bats in his belfry, if not wombats in his head. Effective action is not in the nature of government. Bureaucracies are hostile to efficiency, which, if practiced, will put them out of business. (By nature, from the most elemental impulse of self-preservation, bureaucracies do not desire that the problem they were established to ameliorate or cure will go away; they subconsciously hope that it will persist until the end of time, promotions and pensions and medical benefits *amen*.) When two huge government agencies, the CIA and the FBI, failed to warn us about September 11, 2001, what did we do? We instituted a super intelligence agency on top of the other two. This is a peculiar form of American madness, which supposes that bigger in government is better, whereas all history is a lesson to the contrary. But when we anguished about national response to some future terrorist attack, what did we do? We created

---

every six years one set of PRI officeholders was replaced by another set of PRI officeholders, or, put more plainly, one set of bandits was replaced by another set of bandits—has disturbed Mexican jingoists (until recently) little.
*See my pamphlet, *An Essay on American Stupidity,* P.E.N. Press

Homeland Security to preside over (depending) FEMA and the Corps of Engineers and the Coast Guard and the National Guard . . .

Will the American people *never* learn that, as a principle, to expect swift response and efficiency from government is fatuous? Will we never heed the principle of subsidiarity (in which our fathers were bred), namely that no public agency should do what a private agency can do better, and that no higher-level public agency should attempt to do what a lower-level agency can do better—that to the degree the principle of subsidiarity is violated, first local government, then state government, and then federal government wax in inefficiency? Moreover, the more powers that are invested in government, and the more powers that are wielded by government, the less well does government discharge its primary responsibilities, which are (1) defense of the commonweal, (2) protection of the rights of citizens, and (3) support of just order.

> 9. When permitted, government encroaches on individual responsibilities and freedom, and the succeeding generations are successively less free.

My father was freer than we, his children, were, as he remarked to me a few days before he died; we siblings have been freer than our children and grandchildren are, or ever will be. I remember a wonderful Spaniard called Lolo (Manuel) who bore to his grave a passionate love for the United States. A merchant sailor, he had jumped ship in New York and had lived and worked twelve years in our country, hoboing from one state to the next. He would grab anyone within hearing to exclaim, "And all that time, nobody asked me for papers, nobody asked me whether I had a visa or a passport . . . *what* a wonderful country."

Abraham Lincoln suspended habeas corpus. We got that back . . . but will we ever again be able to stroll into an airport and board a plane without being submitted to the travail and indignities of security lines made excessively insupportable thanks to the ideological idiocy of one man, Secretary of Transportation Norman Mineta, who, in his dread of "racial profiling," insists that such as my snowy-haired, five-foot-one-inch, 105-pound, eighty-five-year-old sister Priscilla, with two hip transplants, be held under the same suspicion and subjected to the same indignities as the swarthy twenty-year-old with shifty eyes, a pilot's license, and an unpronounceable name beginning al-Fatah Something Something?* Will one day in the not distant future citizens be subjected to arbitrary stop, detention, and search on the highways by special Homeland Security cops—our (benevolent for now) Gestapo?

Oh, but the world was larger back when our father was young and active in Mexican politics. The Atlantic and Pacific Oceans were vast, protecting us from attack . . . until Pearl Harbor. Granted. But though in the twenty-first century we may not be able to resist or avoid government encroachment on the private sphere in all respects, especially concerning national security, we must never *not* resent it, and we must remember to despise it. All slave populations become accustomed to their condition, accepting it. Mexicans docilely accept the lies and deceptions and corruptions and institutional thievery of the PRI. In the United States, we have long been economic serfs of our government, beginning circa 1935 with the Social Security Act, having permitted ourselves to be reduced to wards. Will we one day in the near future become intellectual bondsmen, subjected to the political correctness *du jour,* and, under the pressure of Islamic (or other) threat, or simply because it is convenient for Washington, discover that our private sphere of action is in every dimension invigilated, regulated, and restricted?

Father, in revolutionary Mexico, lived in a society where freedom of movement, freedom of action, and freedom of conscience (the militant anticlericalism of the revolution) were severely curtailed. Education was run by the militantly secularist State. He knew how easily cherished liberties and human dignity can slip through the fingers, and how vigilant a people must be to preserve them.

10. Political rhetoric is the enemy of democratic government. It is the enemy of truth.

He learned this in Mexico, too, from the several high-flown proclamations (following on Hidalgo's Grito de Dolores) that were issued by one revolutionary brigand after another, which may have had the virtue of

---

*Mr. Mineta has at last resigned from office; one wishes him a retirement of perfected political correctness.

emotional sincerity but which were deceptions where they were not (in their militant Marxist secularism) malign. Anyone living in Mexico during those times would have agreed that wisdom and reality are not supplanted by good intentions, even assuming that these are genuine, which in politics is rare and in Mexico was nonexistent.

That wisdom tells us that:

11. Not all peoples are able to bear the burden of democracy.

This was redundantly evident to our father in Mexico. Some societies contain within them evil and destructive ideologies (to wit fascism in Germany 1923–1945, communism in Russia 1917–1982, Islamic terrorism all over the Middle East circa 1985–2____?) or, as in Mexico, a history of autocratic rule and a temperamental affinity for anarchy and banditry.

That not every nation easily takes to democracy is a historical fact the denial of which is ignorant, panglossian, or stupid (our father would have concluded). In order to fortify civil peace, avoid anarchy, preclude terror, contain theft and homicide, and secure individuals in their most basic human rights, *some* peoples under *some* circumstances require rule by a strong man. (This was the case made for Porfirio Díaz. It was the case for Franco in Spain during the 1930s.)

Authoritarian rule is not the ideal, nor is it desirable (it is in almost every instance detestable); it is always fraught with abuse of basic human dignities and tends always toward tyranny. But it is crassly self-righteous, vainglorious, and impractical to oppose it everywhere in the world that we Americans encounter it.

Weaning a society from the habit of authoritarian rule is the most dicey of political adventures. People can be bought. People accustom themselves to injustice.

12. Americans should stay clear of foreign entanglements.

Our sire would have been inclined to this attitude from Washington's Farewell Address, too, but it was in Mexico that he was confirmed in his isolationism.

Americans tend to be well-meaning democratic ideologues who wish to impose their principles of self-government on nations whose societies either are not ready for self-government or are outright hostile to it. To make matters worse, Americans are often ignorant and intolerant of the customs and history of other lands, and display themselves in foreign affairs most often as hopelessly provincial.* Further, lurking in the American character is an unfortunate universalist reformism deriving from a deep-seated Calvinist intolerance that is perilous to the country. I call it the hortatory temptation. It's a handsome paradox: the more secular we become as a nation, the more Americans desire to establish the city of God on earth.

To our father, Woodrow Wilson was an ego-inflated nincompoop—an idiot *savant*—with the Puritan self-righteousness of a self-important frog from a very little pond. But on what grounds did Will Buckley dub *other* Americans provincial? Wasn't he a hick himself? Geographically, yes, but not culturally. As we learned from Uncle Claude's letter to Cousin Edmund, San Diego, though situated deep in the cactus and mesquite scrub country of Southeast Texas, where one might least expect it, was remarkably cosmopolitan. He was brought up in the society of Germans, Frenchmen, Spaniards, Englishmen, a cultivated lot who happened to find themselves in that woebegone little town because of asthma. Besides, the Buckley children were educated by a remarkable Irish priest, Father Darcy, who was deeply cultured and who, impressed by the natural intelligence of his charges, persuaded Grandfather John and Grandmother B that they must do everything in their power to send their brood to Austin for the college education there. Directly after *the* university, young Will Buckley flung himself into finishing school in Mexico City, which, compared with any urban center in the United States of those times, was Old World worldly and sophisticated. The closest American cities to Mexico, in terms of culture, were probably New Orleans, Boston, and San Francisco, in that order.

What do we, Will Buckley's children, extrapolate from our sire? Just as Americans should have been suspicious of, and should have opposed, the utopianism of Woodrow Wilson, so should Americans be wary and skeptical of the goodhearted Christian simplicity of George Bush II, who is as provincial as Wilson before him.

---

* The shadow of George Bush II inescapably hovers over these words.

The foregoing is likely to have been our sire's opinion of George Bush's foreign policy after September 11, 2001,* a frontier skepticism that he confirmed in Mexico. His sons and daughters, however, have been exposed to other experiences in their lifetimes, largely our American confrontation with Nazi Germany and imperialistic Japan and the long forty years of Cold War against Stalin's Soviet Union, which concluded in the glorious tearing down of the Berlin Wall; and these events impinge upon, moderating, inherited parental axioms. The naive idealism of the American people grappled with evil and, at a fearful cost of lives and treasure, won.

THE WORLD HAS SHRUNK SINCE OUR FATHER'S TIME.

This is a radical change of circumstances. The world has also become interdependent in ways he could never have imagined, both economically (through globalization) and philosophically (through modern communications). The exiguous trickle of the Rio Grande separated the United States from Mexico in the 1920s as by an unbridgeable chasm. When Cecilio Velasco was forcibly suspended on the span between the two Laredos, we can begin to comprehend the cruelty of the punishment inflicted upon him by the corrupt political powers he opposed only when we understand that he was thus suspended between two civilizations. Indeed, into the last decades of the twentieth century, two wholly separate societies were divided by a skinny stream of water as though each was contained within an airtight vessel. Religion, racial origins, language, and history made Mexico and the United States as close to being absolutely alien to each other as two nations could be.

Nothing like this exists today. The jet aircraft has rendered the most distant point on the globe from anywhere a mere sixteen hours off. The Internet has rendered totalitarian control of knowledge, and hence of thought, impossible. What was once categorized as adventurism, or interventionism, may be today a pragmatic necessity or a long-term desirable.

---

*Father most likely would have opposed both the Afghanistan and the Iraq adventures unless he was convinced that they were necessary for the national defense. Bill has been skeptical of Iraq since its inception and has called it a "failed enterprise" in one of his columns (2006). I disagree with him.

Incumbent upon Americans, moreover, who have been blessed as no other people by Providence, there is—despite dangers and risks (as our sire would have been compelled to acknowledge)—a Christian moral imperative that makes acceptance of those risks and dangers morally as well as strategically unavoidable. (Since it was within reach of our power to remove the Taliban and Saddam Hussein, so was it incumbent upon us to remove the Taliban and Saddam Hussein—and it was probably also a matter of national security that we do so.)

Not everybody loves freedom. Not everybody is goodhearted. Some human beings view politics solely as the dialectic of power, which they exploit for their venal ends. Some human beings are evil. (And here enters the ontological base from which our parents judged all things.) Partly because evil is a reality, and the means to spread it have been magnified by technology, we have come into the era when, as John F. Kennedy prophesied, freedom threatened anywhere threatens freedom everywhere. We are as subject to global ideological contagion as we are to a worldwide avian flu epidemic. The world has shrunk and shrunk and shrunk since JFK's grandiloquent statement in 1961. Practically and philosophically both, we may be compelled to risk our future, risk survival, despite the evident historical perils of an action—such as the attempt to midwife democracy in Afghanistan and Iraq. Strategically there may be room for discussion and disagreement; philosophically there is less and less allowance.

We children of our father inherited many of his precepts. In their public lives, Jim and Bill reflected this. Our temperaments and our thinking on matters political are informed by our father's experiences and are colored by his native wisdom and his prejudices. But in common with all generations succeeding each other, we have adapted what was bequeathed to us to the times in which we strive, as do our children with respect to us, their parents.

The essential wisdom of Will Buckley of Texas, however, coincides with the wisdom we have inherited as a nation from the founding fathers. Which are truths we hold to be self-evident.

TWO MORE TRAITS STOOD OUT IN HIS CHARACTER, IN HIS MANNER OF being, and in his career, and these traits were notable in our aunts and uncles as well:

13. Take joy in your success, but thank God always for it as its author; take pleasure in the manner in which you contributed to your success, but remember always who was the author of that, too.

And:

14. Be generous always. Whatever wealth you may have earned belongs to God; your failures are owing to faults in your character as well as to bad luck (and are therefore instructive), and these were permitted by your Creator for reasons that are centered in His love.

I don't speak for my siblings here. We all carve out our individual destinies. Like most people, I have been up and down. I have made modest fortunes and consumed them. I have been rewarded in some of my labors, rebuked and chastised in others. My reverses have been well merited and good for me as I look back on them, though I hated them all at the time. (That good losers have plenty of practice is one of my minor epiphanies.) Nothing I have and nothing that I have achieved is truly mine; it is liened to the God who created me.

I have learned that though I am a mere spark of incandescence in the vast cosmos of existence, I am infinitely important to God. I am beloved by God (don't ask me why) and necessary to God (don't ask me why, either), who, as we all know, is sufficient unto Himself; who is indebted to no one and in need of no one. *Yet is He my father, and I, His son.* The reality of this relationship is mind-boggling. It shivers the timbers of comprehension. That He has submitted Himself to my (your) will is His will, His doing, His choice, the meaning of His passion on earth, His revelation. This is His sacrament, the original meaning of which is "mystery." I (you) cannot get along without Him, nor, it seems, can He, who needs nothing, achieve His plan, realize Himself fully, without us, because He has willingly rendered His entire object of Creation contingent on our love and obedience. This is terrifying. I am (you are) otherwise nothing—no . . . thing—a cup of chemicals, a bundle of vanities, a handful of dust, except for His commitment to our existence, which is eternal.

Meantime, speaking for myself, I hope I have been generous, good times and bad. I am haunted by the doubt that I have not been generous enough, and that I have consequently not returned to my Lord in sufficient due. (I am not just speaking of material things here, of money.) The generosity of some of my siblings rebukes me when I contemplate it; the generosity of hundreds of millions of people around the globe fills me with joy and also understanding of my inadequacy. I pray that I have never permitted self-pity to consume me. (I have come close; there have been years when it seemed that the stars in the courses conspired against Sisera and that happiness was forever to be denied me, whose bruised ego and hurt heart I elevated to the most important pulse of the universe, as, in our grief and dejection, we all—I dare say—tend to do.) Yet I hope that I have kept a healthy critical eye on myself at all times, bad and good, and neither despised nor exalted myself (the first easy, the second not). I don't like humility a lot, but I pray that I have tasted being humbled to the full and that I have learned to practice humility at all times.

Like most Roman Catholics, I was born knowing the eschatology of tragedy and its ontological significance, which is redemption. This keeps one from taking oneself too seriously. This is the necessary perspective of a sense of humor, upon which salvation may depend. Only at the expense of his faith may a Christian wallow in grief.

This is the hard thing: to know simultaneously that one is infinitely precious to the Lord God and infinitely important in His economy of salvation (oh, what comfort there is in this mystery!), yet to know also that one is nothing—nothing at all, not a speck more than a bubble in the frothing stream of existence, which will go *pop* in due, in *short*, time, never to be heard of again. But just as fear of the Lord is the beginning of wisdom, so the beginning of faith is the knowledge that it is His love that sustains the entire universe. Oh, awesome. Awe . . . some indeed.

Which comfort I, for one, owe to my parents.

Cowboys

I WAS ASHAMED OF MY FATHER ONLY ONCE.

This happened in Texas, when I was a boy—five years old? eight? I don't know how it came about. I don't recall why I was—we were—in Austin, but I remember the incident vividly.

Father had business with Robert Kleberg, owner of King Ranch. For some now inexplicable reason, I was appointed to accompany him on the long drive from Austin.

My guess is that we were in one of our big black Buick sedans, of which there always seemed to be a pair to transport the family, and that Jack, my aunts' driver, was at the wheel. Father sat beside him, and I stretched out in the back. It was April or May, and though the early morning was still cool, we rolled all the windows down. My father chatted with Jack occasionally and assayed conversation with me, which efforts flopped with the wind and dust rushing in. He was anyhow preoccupied with whatever business it was that he had with Mr. Kleberg—I could sense this—presumably to do with oil. (We younger children were blissfully ignorant of how our father made the money that fed and clothed and pampered us.) I liked Jack, who was fun when we were alone, but I liked it better when my father drove himself, because it made Maureenie and me giggle watching him stop the car, placing his right foot heavily on the brake while at the same time gripping the wheel hard with both hands and hauling back on it. He was reining in a horse, we surmised. We glee-fully predicted that one day, he would let out a "Whoa, there!"

The dreary, south central Texan landscape streamed by, sage, cactus, and mesquite, with just an occasional glimpse of cottonwoods hugging a dry creek. After several hours, each hotter than the last, we drove into a town that gave me the impression of bleak unshaded windows, rickety porches, rickety staircases, and rickety shutters. The first stiff wind off the plains, I thought, would carry the whole place off and dump it in the Gulf, or maybe somewhere in Mexico.

To my surprise, Father ordered Jack to stop at a saloon. It was the only establishment where one could order a sandwich and a glass of milk, ap-parently. (These were still Prohibition times.) Father said to me after or-dering, "Reid, I must see Mr. Kleberg now. I'll be about an hour . . ." He pulled his gold watch out of the pocket of his vest, checking the time. "It is just ten minutes to noon. If you want another sandwich or another glass of milk, just ask the waiter. Are you sure you will be all right?" He spoke these last words in Spanish, which was the language we used when we were very young and still addressed him as Papá.

Oh, yes, I would be fine . . .

He stooped to permit me to kiss his bristly cheek, and then he walked out of the premises: a tall, slim, modest man in a business suit.

Nothing happened for a very long while. I was seated at a square cor-ner table to the right of the swinging doors admitting into the saloon. The room was long and relatively narrow. Maybe it had been a feed-and-seed store, because in the back there were storage bins. There were several empty tables between me and the bar, each with its nest of wooden chairs tilted up by their backrests. A long mirror occupied most of the space above the bar, in which I could detect my forlorn image in the shadows at what seemed to be a very long distance. Above the mirror, stretched on a pine board, was the dried skin of a rattlesnake, which held my attention; it must have been a fat old snake in life, because its midsection was ten or eleven inches wide, I guessed. There was nothing else to look at except a stuffed squirrel with most of its fur missing, the head and hide of a coyote, and a fly-spotted calendar of Betty Grable in tight shirt and short shorts.

It was penumbral inside the saloon, still cool. The waiter polished glasses with the skirt of his apron, staring meditatively at nothing. It was awfully quiet, and I recall the noonday heat beginning to percolate into these recesses from the street. I ate the crusts of the untoasted white bread of my sandwich, drank the last of the milk.

Presently there came the heavy thudding of horses galloping outside, the sound of male voices shouting and of horses being reined back sharply; and in through those slatted swinging doors burst five or six cowhands, boisterous with hunger, thirst, and good cheer. They glanced briefly my way, directing their attention at once to the waiter as they ranged along the bar, one foot hoisted on the bright brass rail that ran its length, paying me no further attention. They joked, they laughed, they ordered sandwiches and coffee and Cokes.

I devoured the sight of them. These were real cowboys, the first I had seen! They were covered in white dust. They wore battered Stetsons, shirts with handkerchiefs knotted tightly at the neck, rawhide vests, tight sun-bleached Levis, tooled leather chaps, boots whose heels were rounded and unstable from wear, big, wicked-looking silver Mexican spurs. They smelled heavily of hay and horse sweat, *and they packed pistols!*

Yes! Every *one* of them. (This must have been 1936 or 1937.) I stared and stared in wonderment and joy as I drank in those cartridge-studded gun belts and the gracefully curving handles of their Colt six-guns. Forty-five caliber, of course! Oh, I was truly in Texas. There was no sight like this, no men like these, in Sharon, Connecticut—the very thought of which, of the effete East, curled my boyish lips in contempt. They drank their coffees thick and black, and the contents looked like sludge when they tipped the white mugs up to their lips and with a jerk of the hand sent the liquid into their mouths, as though they were sloshing down shots of whiskey. How they laughed and roared!

Horses now kept halting at the saloon, more cowboys pushing through the doors, letting in the harsh white light from the street, shouting their orders and greetings, so that in moments the place resounded with their Texan drawl. Some occupied tables, grabbing chairs by the tops of the backrests, twirling them in the air, and slamming them down under their seats. Most crowded the bar. I had gone to heaven—an hour swiftly slipping by. How I hoped one of those cowboys would address a word to me! None did. This was their lunch hour. They were in briefly from the range, from checking perimeters, and I knew from what my father had told me that one could ride from sunrise to sunset and until noon the next day without coming to the end of King Ranch. A few glanced my way occasionally, a couple of them smiled, but I was swiftly ignored. The waiter at one point came to my table to ask whether I wanted anything. No . . . no. How I wished I had the nerve to order a Coke, of which (for the stimulants) my father did not approve except on rare occasions. I was thirsty, but another glass of milk?

"Milk, please." How disgusted I was by my Eastern accent. The best I could manage was to pitch my voice as low as I could get it. The cowhands were now departing, in two and threes. I wished they would stay longer! As a mob of them pushed their way out, yelling so-longs to the bartender, in entered my father, walking unconcernedly right by them—turning directly toward me. There he was with that gray fedora jammed squarely down over the dome of his skull, those round, china-blue eyes magnified by the pince-nez, dressed in the starched collar from which a floral tie drooped, the pin-striped business suit, and the black shoes he habitually wore, their polish now scuffed. "Are you all right, Reid? I'm sorry it took so long." He glanced curiously at me, because my expression must have been registering (indecipherably to him) my outrage and rejection.

How drab, how *Eastern* he looked! Yet my father was a *Texan*, born and bred. *His* father had been a sheriff. True, Grandfather John had never killed anyone or even fought a duel, *but he was a friend of Pat Garrett!* I wanted to shout this intelligence to the rafters, to the few cowboys remaining in the saloon. I rose numbly instead to follow my sire out into the blinding sunlight, cheeks burning with mortification.

Conformity is a terrible vice.

PART FOUR

Great Elm, 1923–1939:
The Desperate Years

———— ⌁ ————

CHAPTER THIRTEEN

Sharon (I):
Supper at Great Elm,
from *W.F.B.—An Appreciation*

THIS CHAPTER WAS ORIGINALLY WRITTEN BY OUR OLDEST SISTER, ALLIE (Aloise* Buckley Heath) shortly after our father's death for the book *W.F.B.—An Appreciation*. It was greeted with joy by all her siblings, including those of us who were as yet "placidly unborn," because it so wonderfully captured the tenor of those suppers, which were filled with fun, mirth, wonder, and love.

WHEN FATHER DIED LAST FALL [1958], AT THE AGE OF 77, FEWER THAN A dozen of the hundreds of letters and telegrams his family received were from the people who thought of him, or who had ever thought of him as anything but "Mr. Buckley." For in the past fifty years of his life, he almost never reached the intimacy, much less the meaningless familiarity, which is implied between two people who address one another by their given names. He felt a warm affection for many of his friends and associates, a

---

* Allie styled herself plain Aloise, as did we, her children. I can't recall when, but somewhere along the line, we rewrote our mother's name as Aloïse, and then rewrote or rethought of our sister in the same way. Here I keep to the way she wrote of herself: plain Aloise.

genuine liking and admiration for many more, a fiercely enveloping and protective and, at times, possessive love for his family; but he was never completely at home, completely at ease with anyone but his wife, his brothers and sisters, his children, and any very young child. His own sons and daughters, as they entered adolescence, were taught to call him "Father." This, however, is about the days when his children were still children, when they were closest to him and he was closest to them.

The years when Father was still Papa* seem, through the haze of twenty and thirty years, to consist only and forever of family supper in the shadowed summer twilight of the big dining-room at Great Elm. Dinner must have been early on those evenings, for in memory, the sun glints strongly through the heavy elms beyond the western windows, and a curtain is always being drawn, or a blind lowered in order to present a child with a clearer and more comfortable view of his unfinished tuna fish on toast. There are no guests on these occasions, which is the reason Aloise and John and Priscilla and Jimmy and Mademoiselle are having dinner in the supper dining-room with Mama and Papa. Jane, Billy, and Patricia, too young to be so honored, are at their own table in the lowest dining-room, happily not eating their vegetables, because Mexican Nana, *their* supervisor, has her meals in the kitchen. Reid, Maureen, and Carol are placidly unborn.

One of the delicious distinctions of dining in the upper dining-room is that you have to speak English because it is not polite to speak French in front of Papa, whose other language is only Spanish, poor thing. Sometimes, though, Mademoiselle, who is absentminded, relapses into middle dining-room *mores* and says: *"Parlez français, s'il-vous-plait,"* instead of: *"Parlez anglais, s'il-vous-plait,"* which is very amusing indeed. But sometimes Jane or Billy or Patricia calls, "Papá! Papá!"—They, who speak only Spanish and a little French, aren't even *trying* to learn English!—and the big children try to wring from a reluctant Mademoiselle the admission that if it is *"pas poli"* for them to speak English in the presence of Papa, it is equally *"pas poli"* for Papa to speak Spanish in *her* presence. Mama is neutral: she speaks inaccurate French and Spanish with great fluency and nonchalance and she has told us that what Papa says about how she must

---

*Pronounced *Papá*, with either a French or a Spanish intonation.

practice her mistakes, making so many of them, is not true, they just come out naturally when she opens her mouth.*

Mama sits at the pantry, or "bell-end" of the table—("Just your mother's polite way of putting it. She's afraid if she admits it's the head of the table, you children will realize she's the head of the family," and "Oh, *Papá!*" the children giggle, thrilled by the outrageousness of his invention). Aloise sits next to Mama, because Aloise is both plain and argumentative† and Papa, often articulately, deplores these characteristics in any female of any age. Jimmy is in the chair on Mama's other side because Jimmy (a) makes smacking noises when he chews, (b) never gets the backs of his hands clean, (c) chatters incessantly in a physically unbearable penny-whistle screech, and Papa, often articulately, deplores these characteristics in any person of any age. (Another reason why Jimmy sits beside Mama is that [d] Jimmy and Mama are each other's favorite.) John and Priscilla sit in secure serenity on either side of Papa because they are by nature, clean and pretty, sweet-tempered and mellow, and can therefore only be teased about things they don't mind. Mademoiselle's place is between Priscilla and Jimmy because they are very young, still, and in more need than the others of the little murmured: *"Pas avec les mains,"* and *"Finissez vos legumes, s'il-vous-plaît,"* and *"Ne parlez pas avec la bouche pleine, Zhee-mee!* (Jimmy)" with which she punctuates all meals in the upper dining-room.

At the foot of the table sits Papa, eating, talking, laughing, teasing, dominating the table with gusto and vigor, the gaiety and the concentration on the moment at hand which, until his last illness, entered the house and left it only with him. (Only when he turns to Mademoiselle does his manner change to the grave and slightly puzzled courtesy with which he treats all plain women: "Father's 'What *can* God have been thinking of?' expression," his daughters called it, many years later.)

Papa is the biggest man in the world and the smartest. He can lasso

---

* To our chagrin, when we adult children delivered orders to a Parisian or a Mexican taxi driver in our perfectly enunciated and schooled French or Spanish, the cabby stared uncomprehendingly at us; smiling, however, in rhapsodic understanding when Mother murdered the French or Spanish language telling him to take us where we had just told him to take us—quite putting us out.

† She was to become indisputably the family beauty, with her raven hair, deep blue eyes, white (or "Irish") complexion, and smashing figure.

children by the leg while they're running. He is the strongest man in the world but also the kindest, which keeps him from beating up other children's papas. He has the bluest eyes and the pinkest cheeks in the world and he is 99 years old (Mama is 16). He is the handsomest man in the world, and aside from the King of England, the richest: he owns personally ONE HUNDRED DOLLARS. He has never told a lie in his entire life except for jokes and kneels by his bed every morning to say his prayers. God will, naturally, send him straight to Heaven when he dies, except for perhaps an hour or so of Purgatory so as not to show favoritism. He is the most modest man in the world, because he says none of these things are true; that Mama made them up to show what good taste she had when she proposed to him. He is the funniest man in the world.

Papa is George Washington and Douglas Fairbanks, Will Rogers and Robin Hood, King Arthur and Stonewall Jackson. Mama thinks so too (and thought so, to the day of his death), although as her children, growing up, began to come to her with stories of how absolutely *impossible* Father was getting to be, she used to confuse them into silence by retorting that: (a) they could count themselves lucky if they ever again, in the course of their lives, laid *eyes* on a man of their father's calibre, and (b) they were all beginning to exaggerate, just like their father.

At supper in the summertime, Papa talks to the children about the olden days when he was young, and these are the things he tells them:

—His father's name was John and John was so strong when he was only 17 years old he used to go to Country fairs without telling his parents, and win ten dollars by beating the wrestler. It was no wonder, therefore, that when he grew up he became a TEXAS SHERIFF. Unfortunately, he never shot anyone, but then, on the other hand, no one ever shot him—a circumstance from which the children are supposed to derive more comfort than they, in fact, do. He once let Papa ride all the way to Kansas City with him in a cattle car, even though Papa's mother thought he was too little.

—His mother's name was Mary Ann, not Mother B, as his children had always supposed. She was very beautiful and very good but very strict, and though Papa was born on July 12th, she celebrated his birthday on July 11th because July 12th is Orangeman's Day. (Father's 77th and last birthday was celebrated, as always, on July 11th.) When she saw Grandfather talking and laughing with a man who didn't like him, and whom he didn't like, she would say later, "John, how *can* you!" She would say, "I can forgive by an act of *my* will, but can only forget by an act of God's will." And Papa telling this, rocks back his chair, mouth opened wide in one of his great bursts of laughter. "You kno-o-w?" he says. "I don't remember God's ever willing my mother to forget a single thing she willed herself to forgive!" (Yet when Aloise once asked, all big-eyed and fraudulent innocence, if Mother B would have shot people if *she* had been the Texas Sheriff, Father lost his good humor at once and answered shortly, "That will do, Aloise. My mother was a saint, and don't any of you ever forget it." Thus early do the children learn, as their own children and husbands and wives have since learned, that Buckleys tolerate disparagement of Buckleys only from Buckleys—and only from Buckleys within the same degree of consanguinity, at that.

—There was Uncle John, who was the oldest, and who died when he was sixteen* (and in such a way as to at least mitigate the callous and unromantic pacifism of the children's grandfather, for he died of pneumonia after he was waylaid and stabbed in the lung by a boy who believed he had been the victim of an unfair decision in a baseball match John had refereed);[1] and there was Tía (Aunt) Priscilla, and Papa, who was Willie then, and Uncle Claude and Tía Eleanor and Uncle Edmund, who was the baby. (It seems strange to the children, when they are very small, that the next-to-youngest should have the whitest hair, but by the time they are ten or so, it has become evident that Tía Eleanor's hair was a good forty years older than Tía Eleanor.) John and Priscilla and Claude and Eleanor and Edmund were all paragons of intelligence, wit, honor, diligence, piety, courage, CHARACTER (Papa's capitals), and any other virtue you could think of. They were all far superior to Papa, he says, and if Mama has not already explained that all the Buckleys were additionally gifted with the quality of modesty, the children might have pitied their poor, inferior Papa.

—Uncle Claude, who had a terrible temper when he was small, but when he got old, when he was 19, he lost the handball doubles championship of the University of Texas because he insisted on having Papa as his partner, so the children forgave him the fact that he once hit Papa on the

---

*Our uncle John's age at the time of his death is variously recounted as nineteen and twenty-one.

nose with a brick and broke it, which is why his nose is so big and curved. ("Big and crooked," says Papa. "Big and aristocratic," says Mama.) "Your father must be getting very vain in his old age if he's taken to inventing wild tales to explain the Buckley nose," says Tía Priscilla, whose nose is small and straight. "Your Aunt would rather face my terrible nose than your Uncle Claude's terrible temper," says Papa. Uncle Claude smiles and shakes his head and winks at the children, which is what Uncle Claude mostly does. The issue is, to this day, unresolved.

—When Papa was a little boy, he used to creep out of the house at four o'clock in the morning and run down to the town jail to share the prisoner's breakfast of doughnuts and *café con leche.*[2] The jailer allowed him this privilege because his father was the sheriff; the coffee, because it was served with milk, fortunately did not stunt his growth, though it will stunt the children's growth if they drink it before they are sixteen. (Once, when John asked Papa something about those early breakfasts, he said, *"café con leche* with milk in it." Papa laughed at him—very rudely, the children thought; after all, John's language was *French*—and, calling down to the lower dining-room, explained the joke to the little children, whose unduly prolonged and insufferably Spanishy giggles were ignored by their seniors, who sat in silence coldly hating Papa.[3] As was truly meet and just, John beat up Jane, Billy, and Patricia right after supper, but Papa, who was supposed to be strolling in the garden, unfairly walked into the nursery during the height of the fracas and sent John to bed with harsh language— which is why John got the .22 he's been promised only when he was 12, four years early.

—Papa's school had only one room and only one teacher. The teacher was a man and he had a red beard, but he was a very good teacher, nevertheless. When someone had dirty fingernails, he would say, "Are you in mourning?" When someone said "prespiration," he would say: "If you can't say *per*spiration, say 'sweat.'" When someone talked about the "kids," he would say: "In my school there are no young goats." And he would say: "In my school, however little you learn, you will learn to express correctly," so every morning they had a grammar drill on sentences like: "Each of the stories by the three men were amusing," or "While ill in the hospital, my house burned down." He would say: "In my school you will use words *accurately"* when he heard a big boy swear, and he would make the boy write three sentences on the board using the word "damn" or "God" or "hell" accurately. He would say "Gosh' and 'heck' and 'darn' are cowards' swear-words." Papa learned what he was taught, and he remembered and told the children. (Many years later, one of his daughters heard her father say quietly into a telephone: "Mr. X, as far as I am concerned, you can go straight to hell," and, smiling to herself, thought of the red-bearded teacher in the little Texas town. It was obvious that Father was expressing himself *correctly* and using his words *accurately*.)

—When Papa was still young, poor Grandfather died one night, after a stroke, surrounded by his family.[4] When he died, he didn't have enough money in the bank for Papa and the family to finish school, so for a while Papa became a schoolteacher himself. He had a little school on the Mexican border, where he taught all eight grades, in Spanish mostly, because all the children were Mexican. The school was a day and a night away from home, by train or horseback, so from fall to Christmas, Christmas to Easter, and Easter to summer, Papa boarded at a nearby ranch. Once, in January, when there was a long cold spell, he pulled back his covers at bedtime and found a rattlesnake coiled between his sheets. Unfortunately, Papa did not know about putting the pan of warm milk on the floor, like Kipling, so he called the rancher's wife (after all, it wasn't *his* house, or *his* bed, or *his* rattlesnake, the children would explain to each other later), and she swept the snake onto the floor with one end of her broom and killed it with the other. "And did she say: "Tsk, tsk, them pesky critters'?" one of the children, who were all in the age of conformity, would ask. "Of course," Papa would answer gravely. "Then why are you winking at Mama?"*

—It took over three years (half a lifetime, if you were Jimmy's age) for Papa to get to be 20 years old and by that time, as might be expected, he had accumulated vast hoards of money not even counting the money that Tía Priscilla gave him from what she earned translating Spanish and English in an Office, so at last Papa could go to the University. The children know *what* University: *the* University, that's what University, but even at that University, even though Papa was a schoolteacher, even though he was 20 years old, they made him take examinations to get in. When he

---

*Father never failed to shake his shoes out every morning before putting them on. This became his habit either from the wise shaking out of one's boots when camping in the West for fear a rattlesnake has crept in, seeking their warmth, or for fear, when it came to shoes, of spiders.

passed those, they made him take Freshman final exams *in Spanish!* Then they made him take the Sophomore finals and then the Junior ("Weren't you *tired,* Papa?" asks the sympathetic Priscilla) and finally the examinations that Seniors had to take before they graduated with a degree in Spanish. After all that, the University told Papa that he could be in the Freshman class, but had to take English and History with the Sophomore class and be an instructor in Spanish, which turned out all right, because every month the University paid him 28 dollars and 50 cents for instructing. ("Lucky *duck!*" the children murmur, wide-eyed and proud.)

These are the things Papa told the children about his bright college years. They were among the happiest in his life.

His first year was lonely, because he lived in a freshman dormitory, where the other boys were 17 and 18, and Papa was 20 and an Instructor.

After his freshman year, he lived in an off-campus house with students from all four classes, and he was happy.

He never saw a football or a baseball game away from the University, because he never had enough money to buy a train ticket, but he often saw home games.[5]

He ate at a restaurant in Austin where you could buy a meal of pea soup, steak, fried potatoes, bread and butter, apple pie, and coffee for 25 cents. ("Yum-*yum,*" Jimmy murmurs, late on the cue only because he is busy trying to find out how much asparagus hollandaise can be safely hidden beneath a lamb chop bone.)

He and Uncle Claude once convinced a freshman whose final report card was studded with A's that he had flunked out of college because E stood for "Excellent," D for "Doing Well," C for "Can Do Better," B for "Bad," and A for "Awful." "The thing is," the children point out to one another in the insomniac hour between summer bedtime and summer sleep, "Papa and Uncle Claude could say it, all right, but the thing *is,* how could they think that freshman really believed it?" The thing *was,* the children were to learn, that Papa, at least, most certainly did think the freshman believed it, for he never entertained the slightest doubt of the success of his practical jokes, which tended to be elaborate and transparent. "She pretended she'd known all along, but you should have seen her blush," he would say about one of his "victims," who had indeed known all along; or "He tried to laugh the whole thing off, but I could see by the look in his eyes . . ." "Don't tell *me* you didn't think that house was haunted! You were

The Buckleys, c. 1935. Front row: Patricia "Trish." Second row: Aloise "Allie," Aloïse Steiner with Baby Maureen, Reid, Priscilla "Pitts," Jane, Bill. Back row: John, WFB, Jim (Carol was yet to be born). Right: Carol Virginia Buckley, age 2; author of At the Still Point.

all as white as sheets," he would delightedly inform the children who pro-tested that they had instantly recognized the paternal "wo-oo-oo-oo's" coming from the cellar of the empty house next door. Then there was the yearly irritation of Christmas. *All* the children were firm believers in Santa Claus, Papa maintained, in the teeth of impassioned statements to the contrary; in spite of Jimmy's pointing out, Christmas after Christmas, that although Santa Claus experienced no difficulty in conversing in English with half the household, in Spanish with the other half, he always an-swered Mademoiselle's *"Joyeux Noël,* Sawhnta Close" with a courteously formal: "Thank you, Mademoiselle. Merry Christmas to you too." (In their young adulthood, the children decided that just as the dignity and reserve which Father kept between himself and all the world except for very young children demanded occasional release in the form of practi-cal jokes, so that same dignity and reserve demanded that these jokes be uniformly successful. In middle-aged adulthood, the children have not changed their minds.)

One year at the University, when Papa was worried about not having enough money, he heard of a hundred dollar prize that an insurance com-pany would give to whoever wrote the best composition about some kind of insurance, so he read about that kind of insurance and wrote the composition and won the prize. The next year he was worried again about not having enough money. But because he had won once, he wasn't allowed to try again, so one of his friends agreed to sign his name to Papa's essay for ten dollars, so he won the prize again, though this year it was about a different kind of insurance. The next year, though, he didn't write the composition, because he didn't think he could bear to learn any more about insurance.

In the summer vacations, Papa and Uncle Claude and Uncle Edmund—or was Uncle Edmund too young? was it Dr. Garnett?—went to Mexico and earned money and had adventures. One summer they traveled from village to village showing movies, which they were not very good at doing. However, the audience didn't mind much when the reels were in the wrong order, or when they got parts of some movies mixed up with parts of others, but they did mind very much when Papa couldn't seem to keep from showing the film upside down (*"C'est assez!"* Mademoiselle whispers sharply, as the children catch each other's eyes across the table, for it is well and disrespectfully known that, for Papa, locks do not respond to keys, nor corks to corkscrews, nor cars to starters), so after a while the boys decided that Papa could only take turns between being the usher and the ticket taker, but never the movie man. Papa said that was fair. Another time they sold soap that they made every night. It was wonderful soap; the boys used to ask for something very dirty to wash, and after they had washed it, it was all clean and bright again and the people in the villages were very pleased. By the middle of the summer they had sold so much soap that they didn't have anything left to make it with and they had loads of money so they decided they had might as well go home. The way home was through some of the same villages they had sold soap to, and at the very first one, all of the women came running out of their houses, screaming and scolding and calling the boys *"ladrones"*— ("Robbers," Jimmy translates squeakily, for Jimmy has only very recently been promoted from Nana and the nursery, and sometimes forgets that he is pretending not to know Spanish)—and the women held up the clothes they had washed. The clothes were still clean and bright but ("How can Papa and Mama and Mademoiselle *laugh?*" Aloise and John, who know the tragic last act, wonder) they were full of big ragged holes. So Papa and Uncle Claude and Uncle Edmund—or was it Dr. Garnett[6]—paid them back the money they had spent for the soap and gave them money for new clothes and "we got home with 16 cents between the three of us," Papa finishes, simply roaring with laughter.

"But they didn't *have* to buy the soap," argues Priscilla in the ensuing pause. (Priscilla is always tiresomely living up to the reputation she established at the age of three, when she answered Aloise's unflattering comments on a group of Japanese by sweetly lisping: "Maybe *they* think *we* has funny faces, *too!*"—or that's what Mama says she said.)

"No-o-o," Papa agrees, thoughtful and instantly intent, "nobody made them buy the soap. They bought the soap because they trusted three American boys who told them it was good soap." Papa glances round the table once, then begins to eat his lemon pie. The children look triumphantly, but not unsympathetically, at Priscilla. After all, you can't always guess right.*

And then . . . and then . . . but the stories of when Papa lived in Mexico, the days when he was a lawyer and when he was an oil man and when he was in revolutions and when he met Mama must wait, for the candles have flickered down and the sun has set. It is almost time for baths and prayers and bed.

Soon—too soon, it seems today—Papa has turned into Father, and the big children are sons and daughters whose eyes no longer widen as they listen. It is only the smaller children who still have Papa, and to them the stories are told.

NOTES

1. Differing from the other tradition of Uncle John's death: in a knife fight with a Mexican in a barroom brawl, the implication clearly being (a) that John Buckley was older than sixteen when he died, (b) that he had been drinking and—inseparably from that supposition—that he, like his two uncles before him, was an alcoholic.
2. He was actually running *up* to the jailhouse, if Walter Meeks was accurate when he pointed out to me the modest little house in San Diego, on a slope below city hall, that our grandparents and their children occupied.

---

* This story, in its entirety, including the rebuke, is remembered differently by me, but in minor details only.

3. Father made sport of a crass and boastful American who came to Mexico to do business but who put everybody off because of his boorish ways, telling this same story of him. "When I said to him that he might succeed in his plans a little better if he did Mexicans the courtesy of learning a little of their language, he answered me, 'Who says I can't speak Spanish? Why—waiter!—give some more *café con leche* . . . and be sure to put milk in it!" He laughed hugely, telling that story. It was this same buffoon who one night was at the casino playing at Rox Underwood's table. (I have never been sure whether this took place in Mexico City or Tampico.) The game was blackjack or draw poker, I forget. Rox Underwood, a Texan and a professional gambler and reputedly also a gunman, who was known for his icy demeanor, was, of course, the dealer. The uncouth American customarily drank too much, and this evening was no different. Unsurprisingly, he lost heavily. During one hand he accused Underwood of cheating him. ("He was such a fool," Father interjected at this point. "He hadn't the sense to know that to professional gamblers of Rox Underwood's caliber, a reputation for straight dealing was critical.") Rox laid his cards on the table and said to him in a soft, flat manner, "What did you call me?" "A cheater," the fellow retorted in a loud voice. "You dealt my card from under the deck." Everybody else at the table froze. But Rox Underwood continued speaking in the same level, unemotional tone, asking the man, "How much have you lost?" I forget the sum—well more than a thousand pesos at a time when the peso still packed weight. Underwood counted the chips representing that sum out of his pile and pushed them toward the American. "There's your money," he said. "Now, get out of here, and I don't want to see you again."

    Instead of thanking his stars, the American pushed himself back from the table, getting awkwardly to his feet and shouting in red-faced fury, "You don't tell me what to do. I'm coming back just as soon as I get my gun."

    Underwood paid no further attention to him, continuing the deal and the game. I am not sure it was not our father who spoke to the fellow on his way out of the casino to advise him to forget the incident—to go to his hotel, get a good night's sleep (sleep it off); if this was not Father, it was someone known to Father who tried to pacify the man. But he swept the well-meaning arm off his shoulder and stomped out into the street, swearing that he was coming back, pistol in hand.

    And he did so, bursting into the casino twenty or thirty minutes later and marching straight to Rox Underwood's table, saying to him, "All right, now you tell me not to come back, let's hear you say that again!"—waving his pistol in front of Rox Underwood's face. As Father told it, Rox Underwood never looked up. He placed his cards on the table and with a savage backward sweep of his right arm, knocked the gun out of the fellow's hand, saying, "Get the hell out before I kill you."

    That was the end of it; and that was also the end of the business career of this gentleman in Mexico, because he quit the country for good the next day. In my interview with Rox Underwood's widow in San Antonio in 1972, she confirmed the essence of the story. "My Rox was not a man to trifle with," she said.

4. Father was twenty, twenty-one, or twenty-two, depending on the exact date of Grand-

father's death; it is doubtful that he was surrounded by the family when the stroke afflicted him, because he was in Rockport at the time, on business.

5. Father explained to me in Bad Gastein, those last weeks of his life, that—to the contrary—he (and then later his brother Claude) did not have the ten cents' or fifteen cents' (whatever it was, very little for students) admittance fee, and though they were keenly interested in Texas's fortunes on the field, he and Claude and such of his friends as Walter Pope would walk around the ballpark, conversing, listening to the roars of the crowd to get some idea of how the game was going.

6. I interviewed Dr. Garnett in Austin, back in 1972. The tape exists. He was in his nineties, but spry and lively, his intelligence undimmed, living in his own condominium. There was a manservant. He offered me a strong bourbon and water, and had one himself. It was just noon.

    For some forty years, he was *the* American doctor in Mexico City, to whom everybody repaired, whether for a head cold, a broken arm, or cancer. He carried with him always (I was most impressed at age thirteen, when he showed me the implement) a razor-sharp machete that he used for chopping open the soles of peasants when they came to him with infections in their feet, because, he explained to me, their soles were three inches thick in callus and tougher than leather. And he confirmed the story I had been told about how he got to Mexico.

    He was operating on a patient in San Antonio when he heard what he described as an "unholy ruckus" in the surgical wing of the hospital. Annoyed, he sent a nurse to find out what was going on. She reported back that there were two unruly young men at the nurses' station demanding to see him, Dr. Garnett. "They call themselves the Buckley boys, and they say you must finish up in a hurry, because they've come to take you to Mexico."

    He smiled—he said . . . but grimly; he still had work to do on his patient. He and Claude and Will Buckley had become fast friends at (*the*) university, in Austin. He finished up and went out to the corridor; and there they were, grinning at him unrepentantly, he said, as the head nurse glared from her station. The first one who spoke was Father, who said, "Garnett, you are wasting your time here in San Antonio. The future for you is in Mexico. There isn't another American doctor there of any account. Claude and I want you to come with us tonight, on the train."

    Well, it took a little more convincing and a little more time than that for him to make the move; but Dr. Garnett never regretted it, telling me as he lifted his glass to his lips (taking a small but appreciative sip from it), "Reid, I have been grateful to your father and uncle ever since, all my life."

———— ⌘ ————

CHAPTER FOURTEEN

Sharon (II): Demosthenes, from *Speaking in Public*

THIS IS THE INTRODUCTION TO MY *SPEAKING IN PUBLIC: BUCKLEY'S Techniques for Winning Arguments and Getting Your Point Across*, published in 1988, an artful title by Harper & Row, unabashedly trading on my brother's reputation. I have compressed, using only those parts of it that I think give the taste of our upbringing in Great Elm.

The flavor of what it was to grow up in my family during the 1930s reflects our sire's determination to make us all (as Allie noted) "perfect," to which objective he spared no pains. Father was away all week in New York, of course, out of earshot of those pains; but Mother and Mademoiselle and our two Mexican nurses and the servants must all have been driven daffy by our untalented assaults on the human eardrum, and it is a wonder to me that they put up with it.

BUCKLEYS WERE NOT BORN WITH SILVER PEBBLES IN THEIR MOUTHS, courtesy of Demosthenes.

Toute au contraire. We were born with orthodontic jawbreakers cramming the space between . . . palate and tongue, which probably had the effect of improving our diction. If you could so much as enunciate Demosthenes so as to be understood whilst the roof of the mouth was plated with a hard rubber retainer, and whilst molars were clamped and cemented in silver jackets to which tough round little elastic bands were hooked, these stretched to attach to similar metalwork on canines, achingly vising the jaw together with the effect that lower and upper sections slowly accommodated into a correct bite, you were a blinking wonder of diction.

It really was tremendously difficult to use the tongue properly in enunciating some consonants and the *s*'s in combination with the *th*'s—as for example, *Demotheneeths*. [To this day, I cannot pronounce "The Thessalonians" without pausing between the indefinite article and the noun, by which time I lose track of what Saint Paul is talking about, who, though always profound, can be obscure.] My argumentative kid sister Maureen, until well into her freshman year at Smith College (where she excelled as a debater), was incapable of pronouncing the second *d* in *didn't* (*dint*, she would say) or the *d* at all in *shouldn't* (*shount* came explosively from her). These natural and prosthetically imposed impediments to clear speech were aggravated by our father's adventurous business career. Following his unreasonable expulsion from Mexico in [1921; he was merely attempting to stage a revolution], he roved the financial capitals of the world seeking financing. These included London and Paris, where he sojourned for long periods—which is why *color* or *labor* still look funny to us, because there ought to be a *u* in them someplace, why we all had to be taught that two negatives don't make a right, and why when a princess kisses me I turn into a frog.

I was born in Paris [and turned] three before we moved back to Sharon, Connecticut, and were once again installed in the huge pre-Revolutionary farmhouse called Great Elm. Ever seeking to civilize his wild brood, and sparing no cost in this reckless endeavor, our father set up a schoolroom under the supervision of a Miss Penelope Oyen and the British-strict Miss Constance Cann, whom [Miss Cann] we detested. We were taught literature and history, and just adequate mathematics, which instinctively none of us (except brother James) much took to because there is no arguing with 2 + 2 = 4, quite taking the zest out of life. We were a disputatious lot, with hot tempers that we lost in several languages several times a day. Listening perplexedly to little Maureen boil over one suppertime with my latest aggravated assault of infamous intent (I had desired to brain her with a croquet mallet, in which ambition I had been frustrated by my beastly older sisters, who took turns sitting on me out on the lawn while I raged and bawled and bit and kicked), Father remarked to his long-suffering consort, "Does it occur to you, Aloïse, that we have not been able to understand a thing our children say for several years now?"*

To tell the truth, he was hard of hearing. Nevertheless, we did jabber in a most awful and at times incomprehensible mash. The younger ones of us were brought up by Mexican nurses, though we were all under the general supervision of Mademoiselle Bouchex, who patiently drilled us in the subtle tonal difference between *accent grave* and *accent aigu*, while responding to our leaden Anglo-Saxon *oo*s with exasperated *eu*s. [Our sweet lithpings would sound out from the second floor against Trisha playing Beethoven's *Appassionata* in the downstairs music room, Janie pounding out Brahms on the concert grand in the adjacent Empire room, and maybe Bill treating us simultaneously to the Toccata and Fugue in D Minor (and sometimes F major or D flat) on the organ, whose crashing and groaning and piercing opening blasts resounded all through the immense patio with an amplifying effect that was not to be equaled until the advent of rock concerts, shivering the timbers of the old house and I do not doubt the eardrums of our mother and faithful servants.] We were afflicted with the curse of polyglot upbringing, unable to keep to one language when the choice expletive occurred to us in another. *"Mi papá,"* cried Jane in a tantrum one evening, *"que es el grande* idea? *Tu eres un grand* bully, *y este no es pas tu* business!"* [Which triumphant gibberish so delighted her father that he stored it in memory and regaled almost anyone he met with it, saying proudly, "She's the limit!"] We not only mixed up our languages, there was a foreign intonation when we spoke English, and our tongues could become quite tied in knots when we were excited, which you will have gathered was more often than not. Before one of us could chant "How Now Brown Cow," brought to Great Elm were a succession of what I suppose today would be called voice therapists, but in those days tended to be operatic divas *manqué* [of Scandinavian stock, five feet ten inches tall, and weighing two-hundred-plus pounds, with bosoms and diaphragms of frightening (to a child's eye) dimensions, who dressed in se-

---

*Shortly after (1938–39), he hauled younger progeny to England for a year. There were business reasons for his sojourn in France and England, of course, but I suspect principally because he imagined that English schooling would improve our diction, which resisted intelligibility almost as badly as Bill's handwriting resisted legibility.

vere black always and were endowed with] tremendous lungs and exalted temperaments, [and] who had us bawling, "Oh, Toby, Don't Roll in the Road," across the hall from and against Mdme. Bouchex's no less determined, *"Ne parlez pas avec la bouche pleine!"* (as we blew bubble gum through our *eus*), developing into a kind of linguistic reenactment of the Battle of Crécy.

Father [as I've mentioned] was home rarely during the week from the New York offices, but he could not stand this. . . . [T]hose of us still young enough to be pulled from formal institutions of learning in the cavalier fashion to which our sire was wont were packed off to England, there to be instructed in the King's English.[1]

. . . This was why brother Bill and I share the same quasi-British accent, with many of the same intonations and speech patterns. We were brought up paying attention to words, discovering new ones with the excitement of finding a silver dollar on the beach,[2] treasuring them, promiscuously employing them in letters and school papers to test out their possibilities. We learned the music of language first, then its sense. We all read omnivorously . . . and we were passionately opinionated. No opinion was by our reckoning worth the name that wasn't worth holding with all our hearts and souls, so that at every meal we argued ferociously about novels and poetry and the latest "flick" we had seen. They mattered desperately to us, and we could be reduced to tears if our siblings mocked a favorite character or put down a favorite author. Oh, yes, the younger ones of us sometimes fled from the table shedding tears of humiliation and rage when our pet ideas were lanced by the dreaded barbed wit of sister Allie or the no less wounding sarcasms of our brilliant eldest brother, John. It was a lesson for us all in cool, but I, for one, rarely kept mine, having yet to develop that sense of one's personal ridiculousness in the scheme of things that is the foundation of humor and the salvation of the ego.*

Within the bosom of the family, we were a quarrelsome bunch; outside, we closed ranks. We were mavericks and proud of it. In the largely Episcopalian and mainline Protestant, Anglo-Saxon Connecticut of the time, we were Catholics, Irish, and Southern. And new-rich Texan. In England, we were Irish Catholic Yanks, a cross of inferior breeds. In

---

*I've got my theology wrong here: personal ridiculousness in the scheme of *worldly* things, personally irreplaceable in God's "economy" of salvation.

France, we were Yankees Go Home.* In Mexico (where we spent 1941 and where I went to school), we were *Texan* gringos, the worst species. Wherever our parents took us, we were an embattled brood, defending religion, country, origins, and, in politics, our father's frontier Republicanism. We were not exactly outcasts, but wherever we found ourselves, we were different for certain, and we grew up ever watchful of the slight or insult, ready on the instant to fly to the defense of family and beliefs. By the time we went away to college, we were practiced and, for our age, pretty fair polemicists. It helped, of course, that our Catholic faith was the True Faith, our country the greatest and most virtuous country in the history of the world, our father a hero, and our mother a saint. We never wasted time doubting our convictions, because how could we be so stupid as that when they were in every jot and tittle absolutely and sempiternally correct?

NOTES

---

1. "Aloïse, we must leave for London, I, you, and the children." "London, Will?" "Yes." Alarmed . . . excited: "For how long?" "I think a year." "A year!" "Yes, a year." "But when?" "Next week . . . if you can manage it. I have staterooms reserved on the *Paris*." Mother did manage, as always, packing up the house, packing steamer trunks for the Mexican nurses, Mademoiselle, the six children, the brand-new infant child (Carol), giving our home tutors notice, providing for the servants and the caretaker (I believe it was still Mr. O'Keefe) and Ed Turpin and the black groom, who was not yet George Tucker . . . and never questioned our father . . . and I now think thrilled to be getting out of Sharon.

2. One minor example of the culture shock we were exposed to by being yanked from country to country was that, as well as having next to no central heating, and very few baths, which were huge and, when filled, with tepid water only, we learned to our dismay that the beaches of British resorts consisted of pebbles washed over by bone-chilling water, not proper beaches at all! Brighton was a poor excuse for anything other than a novel.

---

*Sister Priscilla tells me that we were actually welcomed in France during the 1930s . . . though my father told me that "Americans Go Home" signs appeared in Paris almost directly after the conclusion of WWI.

A major effect on us was that we were torn from childhood chums, which made it difficult for us to form attachments with other children our age, because we were in the expectation always that these relationships would be sundered. I can remember only two boys from my London days. One, a curly-headed snob who got on my case from the morning I arrived at the convent school ("Oh, rahhlly, is that the way you Yanks do things in . . . what is that place you come from, is it Connecticut?"). The other boy whom I recall was named, I believe, John, the son of a famous and ailing actor. John was sensitive and kind, and I formed a strong attachment to him. We loved the same books. He had a fabulous collection of British lead soldiers that made my mouth water. Twice I was invited to tea and to play with him in the big back garden of his (Kensington?) house, which was high-walled and gloomy, the presence of the dying father upstairs in his bedroom descending on and, as it seemed to me, inhabiting the shrubs and trees with foreboding. John laughed, but he rarely smiled. Once we had returned to the States, I was never to meet or hear from him again.

Such experiences caused us to treasure our siblings, who were our permanent society, and, later, to treasure also the friendships we formed in boarding school and college.

I must say more about a horrid (an adjective we learned in England but never used) little boy who was the son of a wealthy manufacturer. He had blond curly hair and pale blue eyes, I recall, and wore a supercilious expression whenever he glanced my way in class or in the corridors. For two or three weeks, he goaded me with schoolboy taunts, asking me whether the natives still scalped "colonists" where I came from, and, if so, how fortunate I was to have escaped their notice with all that horrid red hair on my head, or asking in a loud voice (to the snickering delight of his cronies but out of the reach of the ears of the nuns) whether we Yanks slept with our sisters, because no one else would have us. Then one morning, he attacked me at recess with a ruler from which he hadn't plucked the copper cutting edge.

Now, we boys, raised on the movies of Douglas Fairbanks Jr. (*The Prisoner of Zenda*) and Errol Flynn (I can't remember the title of a single one of his epics in the Caribbean, in which he generally opposed the evil Spanish viceroy, Basil Rathbone— was there ever such a villain?),* all fenced with our rulers during recess, but we pried the edge out of them first. This boy lacerated the backs of my fingers and hands and wrists, so I socked him. And I was happily beating the tar out of him when, to my outrage and mortification, sister Maureen, age five, spotting me in what she supposed was trouble, came flying across the cement courtyard, fists flailing as she hurled herself upon the boy, who did not know what to do—girls did not attack gentlemen, and gentlemen (not even he, the little snot-nosed bastard) did not hit girls—and who therefore fled screaming in consternation and, understandably, given the ferocity of

---

*I got to know him many years later, when he purchased the Witt house in Sharon—a delightful human being.

Maureenie's attack, terror. Gray-clad nuns swooped down on us like bats, and I, the new boy and presumed villain (his cronies all cried that I had viciously punched my antagonist), was reported and sent home in disgrace.*

Father happened to be home. I remember him reading the contents of the mother superior's note with utmost seriousness, asking me sternly to explain my conduct. Before I could get out two words, Maureen burst in, telling Father what a pig and a coward the other boy had been and the mean malicious tactics he had used. "He cut your hands with his ruler?" asked Father. I showed them to him—my wrists as well. The lacerations were still fresh. His face turned a deep red. Without another word, he took me by an arm (high up, just below the armpit) and marched me downstairs to the street, hailed a cab, and had us driven to the convent, where he very politely requested an interview with the mother superior. I recall little of that except Father's controlled anger as, in that deep bass voice, he said to the woman (to the effect), "Reid should not have socked that disgusting little boy, and he and I apologize for that; it won't happen again. But you tell his father that I am glad my son isn't a coward, and if his son ever chooses to pick a fight with Reid again, he is going to have the whey knocked out of him, with my approval." The exact words I don't remember, but I will never forget how my heart swelled with pride and gratitude and love. I knew that in my father I had a champion of unwavering loyalty.†

One last detail is graven in my memory. As we walked out of the convent, he looked down at me, smiling for the first time, winking, and saying, "Do you suppose you should take fencing lessons?"

---

*One darling (and quite beautiful) nun supported me—I can't remember her name, but I know she is in glory.

†Nothing disgusts me more than hearing a parent disparage his or her child in public. This is to me betrayal of an indissoluble loyalty.

CHAPTER FIFTEEN

———— ✧ ————

Sharon (III):
Childhood in Paradise

AFTER A BRIEF FEW MONTHS IN A RENTED HOUSE IN BRONXVILLE, WHICH either he found too expensive because of its proximity to New York City or he disliked because of its proximity to New York City, Father removed his family to Connecticut.

Longtime close associate George Montgomery writes in his flat, lawyerly style, "In the early 1920s, New York was already the unquestioned financial center of America and was rapidly becoming the world financial center.* But W.F.B. could not bear to live there any more than he had to. Already he had children (with seven more on the way). He acquired a house in Sharon, Connecticut, which was to become the unforgettable 'Great Elm' ... consisting of about thirty acres.† [It] was transformed under W.F.B.'s direction not merely into a showplace, but into a home for a large American family with almost all the advantages of indoor and outdoor family life." *(W.F.B.—An Appreciation).*

That took place in 1923, when he had purchased the old Sterling

---

*It is a bit of a shock to realize that New York's worldwide financial preeminence was new in my father's generation. To those of my generation, whenever could there have been doubt?
† Thirty-five acres, actually.

"Great Elm," Sharon, CT, c. 1945.
Front view, showing patio to the right.

house, as Great Elm was called after its builder (1756) and first owner.* How he discovered Sharon I am not sure. I know for a fact that old Dr. William Bradley Coley, the distinguished New York City cancer surgeon and researcher (grandfather of my lifelong friend "Peter" Bradley Coley), showed him the pre-Revolutionary farmhouse we named after the tremendous elm tree, fourth or fifth largest in the United States at the time, whose canopy covered an acre of the extensive lawns.[1]

Sharon was a long two-and-a-half-hour train ride from the city. The drive out to Sharon by motorcar could take as long as three hours in those days, but for the most part it was pleasant, rustic, and beautiful. These are

---

* The house was officially bought by A.S.B. from one Joseph Martin in 1930. That's what the records show in the Sharon Historical Society. But this sale, my brother Jim informs me, was a subterfuge for tax or personal financial reasons of which I am ignorant and which Jim can't recall. It was bought seven years earlier.

the foothills of the Berkshires, and the views that are sprung upon anyone can be spectacular. The surrounding valleys and hillsides of Sharon
were cultivated at the time mostly by dairy farmers who grew corn for
their black-and-white Holstein cows and sold their milk to buyers in New
York City, a market reached thanks to the Grand Central Railroad company, which maintained a tiny depot in a deep valley back across the line
into New York State—a settlement known as Sharon Union. There is iron
in these hills. Sharon boasted a foundry in Revolutionary War times and
manufactured rifles for the militia, which presumably fired when called
upon to do so, though the historical inference can be drawn that they may
have misfired, too, inasmuch as three of Sharon's patriots were captured
and exhibited in cages throughout England as "horrific Yankees."

To us children, Sharon was heaven on earth. It was a picture-postcard,
Norman Rockwell New England town with a year-round population of
just a little less than two thousand people.* Farming families—for example, the Carberrys and the Pitchers, nineteenth-century newcomers of
French descent (the Deveaux, Gilettes, Gobillots, and Shevillots)†—lived
in big two- and three-story houses with plenty of bedrooms for their numerous progeny, but most of the villagers resided in modest two-story
white clapboarded houses dating back, a lot of them, to the eighteenth
century. They were colonial architecture in concept, to which a few Victorian furbelows accreted in eaves and along roofs and porches. The lots are
narrow and long (eighty feet), extending on both sides of the green. Each
house has a screened back or side porch, a quarter-acre lawn, and flower
beds. In window boxes or on either side of the front doors bloomed, each
in its season, crocuses, jonquils, violets, blue and purple irises, tulips of
every hue, dahlias, petunias, pansies, and roses—big, luscious, red, plum-
colored roses, roses of Sharon (they are called, in botanical, not biblical,
reference), which lasted all summer long, it seemed. Lilac bushes (locally
pronounced "lilock") proliferate wherever one turns one's head and in late

---

*Population declined steadily from Revolutionary War times to the 1920s–1950s, to just
under two thousand, but it has swelled since by the influx of New Yorkers seeking to escape
themselves.
† *Gobilots* and *Chevylots,* in our tongue, whose dowager, however, speaking of the Chevillots,
we boys always addressed respectfully as *Madame* Chevylot. In the 1840s, when land was
being given away out West, many of Sharon's farmers sold everything they owned, their
places being taken by Huguenots from Canada.

The Great Elm, c. 1947.
"Great Elm" in background.

April scent the entire town with a delicacy that lingers long on the palate of memory.

Sharon is still famous for its wide central green, which runs a half-mile or so, the length of the town, fronting Main Street (there are only three or four other streets in the entire settlement).[2] From the sidewalk in front of the post office, one can gaze across an expanse of lawn,* ascending most of its length in a gentle slope to Upper Main Street, which runs parallel. At the south end of the green, there's the curious fieldstone Public Library, resembling a small fort, in the faux-medieval style of the fifty-two-foot-tall Town Clock, whose bronze bells tolled the hours for all to hear.

---

*The green is 125 feet wide at its widest, and more than 1½ miles long.

The clock was a gift to the town by the spinster Wheeler daughters, Laura and Emily, both now dead, in memory of their mother, Emily Ogden Butler Wheeler. It is Sharon's, became our, Big Ben, tolling erratically, however, because tall Sheriff Marvin Doty,* whose duty it was, frequently forgot to wind the mechanism, having had one too many at the Brown Cup, Sharon's sole watering hole.[3] At the tapering north end of the green—again, gazing with one's back to the post office—there is the gabled Bartram's Inn, the only hostelry in town.† Between the inn to the north and the library to the south, there are several dwellings in a row, each with its expanse of lush lawn, flower plots, picket fence, and gate.

But though Sharon's green is still parklike and singular, with handsome fifty- and sixty-year-old sugar maples dotting it,‡ back at the time of which I write, the entire expansive length—1.8 miles!—boasted a stupendous double row of American elms, some of them two-hundred, even three-hundred years old—huge gray trunks each measuring, at the base, several feet in diameter, soaring eighty and ninety feet to crowns that spilled over from their tops like, well, fountains—the unavoidable cliché when attempting to evoke the American elm, whose shape is so strikingly different from that of any other species of hardwood in the American forest.§ Unavoidable also is the platitude that walking the Sharon green in those days was like gazing up from the nave of an immense cathedral: the elms were indeed like gigantic Gothic columns, supporting the sky. Nothing like the Sharon green was to be seen in any other New England village when we children were growing up, and there will be nothing like that green or those elms ever again, not even if one assumes an eventual cure for Dutch elm disease.[4]

Getting back to early memories, there was the pink brick town hall with four imposing white columns, which housed the post office, and adjacent to that, Marcres's (pronounced "Marcus") drugstore, run by its crabbed old proprietor, Mr. Marcres, who was slovenly. The place had the

---

*Pronounced "Doady." An amiable fellow, he resembled a Western sheriff out of a movie, of which he was conscious, wearing his silver badge prominently on his shirt and carrying his pistol in a black gun belt loaded with cartridges.
† Now converted to apartments.
‡ Thanks in part to my sister Jane's initiative: as the elms succumbed, she replaced them with sugar maples.
§ The Southern pecan tree is, in shape, a poor imitation.

unshaven countenance of a homeless man.* It probably would not pass inspection by Sanitation today; one had to blow dust from the bottles of aspirin or rectangular Pepsodent toothpaste boxes or Johnson & Johnson Band-Aid tins that one tipped off the glass shelves, not to mention castor (yuck!) and cod-liver (double yuck!) oil, of which we children were dosed a spoonful once a week, on Monday mornings. Near the entrance was a large barrel bin, shaped like a hunched rabbit, into whose open maw, at two cents a shot, we cheerfully dipped our forearms up to the elbow, retrieving and devouring vanilla or gingersnap cookies without giving thought to what might be crawling about inside. Mr. Marcres was an amateur taxidermist, and in a big glass case (of which the Audubon Society must have severely disapproved) were chickadees, titmice, juncos, chipping and song sparrows, goldfinches, shrikes, redwinged blackbirds, a blue jay, yellowbellied sapsuckers, nuthatches, and hairy, downy, and other woodpeckers, including the gaudy gigantic pileated variety with its striking zigzag of black plumage and its red crest . . . fascinating me and other boys.† In the gloomy recesses of the store, toward the living quarters, reclined a surly dark brown police guard dog with black shoulders and a black muzzle, whose furious snarls and showings of white tusks cautioned customers not to attempt to pat its large head, Mr. Marcres warning them, "Don't cha tech that dog, I ain't responsible fer the consequences anybody is so foolish as teh tech it," an injunction I ignored all innocently.‡ I was five or six. I remember going straight to the animal and, I guess, astonishing it by resting my hand on the back of its head, grasping it, shaking it, and saying, "Oh, cut that out, you aren't fooling me."

I was (I suppose) lucky that the animal didn't sink its teeth into my hand or lunge with open jaws at my throat and face, but it tolerated—it was never submissive to—my fondling, its great tail thumping the floorboards every time I walked into the place thereafter; and though it kept up a low, menacing rumble in its chest, I paid no further attention to that. There was a second drugstore, at the far end of Main Street (by which I

---

*It was bought by a lovable man called Phil Reep in the early 1950s, spruced up, and converted into a favorite place to stop and exchange town news.
† The collection was burned in a fire, except for two specimens that are on display in the town hall.
‡ Having survived Bill's big setter Sultan—or "Ducky," who was in sister Aloise's phrase "unducky" except to Bill—we had kennelsful of other dogs on the place.

Family Class, 1940. Millbrook Horse Show (handwriting of Aloïse Steiner Buckley).
Left to right: "Vagabond," "Marie," "Faucet," "Golden Bantam."

indicate not a seven-minute walk distant), called Eggleston's (adjacent to Jenkin's Grocery Store), which was airy and filled with light from large street windows and spotlessly clean;[5] but we children preferred Marcres's, dingy and penumbral though it was, because Mr. Marcres sold the best and newest comic books and made the most delicious chocolate ice cream sodas ever. Mr. Eggleston, who wore gold-rimmed eyeglasses and somehow exuded a prissy manner (he was a nice man), had a soda fountain, too, and his malted milks were pretty good, but if you hankered after a chocolate ice cream soda, it was to Marcres's that you wanted to go.

The summers were hot, the falls crisp and golden with the autumnal explosion of scarlet sumac (always the first, along with poison ivy) and the succeeding reds and yellows and purples of beaches, hickories, and maples, all under skies so blue it was as though they had been scoured that morning with a steel brush, and the winters, oh, they were filled with snow then. It was paradise for us Buckley children, who were not packed off to schools in New York City like the children of other summer residents (*we* were year-*round* summer residents), whom we pitied. We were taken ice skating on the several ponds—Hatch's, Mudge's—within easy driving distance of Sharon. Even our parents skated every now and then, Mother *and* Father, awkwardly, uncertainly (you have to be born to ice, and they weren't), though I sometimes wondered how Mother was able to get along with skates, whose blades aren't high-heeled. We had snowball fights two or three times a day, which generally ended with my kid sister Maureen crying and me being roundly scolded by Nana (*"Eres bruto, pobrecilla!"*) or Mademoiselle (*"Vraiment, tu es tres méchantla, pauvre petite!"*), and made forts of snow, in which enterprise Maureen was an enthusiastic helper; and after we had poured water on them from pots and kettles, and it had frozen overnight in temperatures that regularly plummeted the moment the sun went down from the high twenties or low thirties into the single digits and not infrequently below zero, they were impregnable, lasting into the spring. Snow piled up in banks on the slate walk by the rear entrance (the one we children always used, because it admitted directly to the lawns and the swimming pool and the tennis court). Maureen and sometimes my friends Pete Coley and Jack Noyes and Dick Witt and "Dick" (his true name was Egbert, which he loathed, as who wouldn't?) Bogardus and his brother Sidney (Maureenie's age) and I bored caverns into the snow piles, using shovels and scoops, our mittens, and large cooking spoons, which we doubled at their necks, irreparably, to be scolded by the kitchen, poking air holes with broom handles, splashing the insides of the connecting tunnels also with water until they froze solid and glistened with ice like a fairy underworld . . . and these, too, endured the several thaws (when all the fields turned into a drear scape of colorless wheat straw and cornstalks, everything oozing mud)* well into March. On Friday evenings, Bill, Trisha (until they were shipped off to boarding school), Maureen, and I would sit on the bottom steps of the staircase leading down from the second floor to the long hall traversing the entire width of Great Elm, from back door to front door, anxiously, impatiently rubbing clear circles on the frosted panes of the tall window at the landing of the staircase to stare out across the ghostly snow-crusted expanse punctuated by the black trunks of the elms and maples and the one horse chestnut tree (beloved of

---

*Only E. E. Cummings could have found New England's springs mud-luscious and puddle-wonderful.

squirrels), directing our eyes to the bottom of the drive—expecting any minute—*any minute!*—to see the twin yellow beams of the headlamps of the car that had been sent to pick up Father at the Amenia station or maybe Pitts and Janie (who, by the time of which I speak, were attending Nightingale Bamford school in New York) or even Allie (at Smith College), [to] see those twin beams piercing the blackness of the night as the car—it was as though attached by the beams, being pulled along by them—rolled down Main Street from the clock tower and turned left into Great Elm's drive. (There weren't many automobiles, maybe one passing every fifteen or twenty minutes.)*

Oh, how exciting that was. Father never brought candy for us, we knew, because he disapproved of it, it was bad for children's teeth, but he did sometimes bring a present, and the moment the front door was pushed wide, he gathered us up into his arms as we leaped at him, hugging us, especially Maureen (which I resented), who was cute and small and had the roundest sky-blue eyes (just like his) and wore a mass of blond curls on her head.[6] Janie and Pitts and Allie *always* brought Milky Ways or Babe Ruths or jellybeans or orange and lemon and lime and cherry sugar-coated jellies shaped like sliced oranges and called I forget what, yum, they tasted so good, filling the mouth! (We fought for the blue-purple licorice jelly.) And sometimes sitting there side by side on the next-to-bottom step of the staircase, our impatience growing with the unendurably slow passing of the minutes (*"What time is it?" "Six-fifteen." "Why aren't they here?" "The train doesn't get in until five forty-five, and it's always late." "Well, if it's six-fifteen, why aren't they here?" "I don't know." "Why* don't *you know, you have a wristwatch, you always boast about it, what good is it if you don't know?" "I don't know, I don't know, shut up, will you?" "You shut up!" "I didn't begin asking stupid questions." "Who says they're stupid, and if they were, you didn't have to begin answering them, so there!"*)—waiting, bickering, picking at each other, Mother whistling her aimless silvery whistle upstairs from her bedroom suite (to which our nursery was directly attached), as anxious and impatient as we were, we knew, but being grown-up about it, exercising a self-control we could not *begin* to comprehend; and some magical Friday nights in late December or January, we stared and stared

---

* My sister Patricia remembers making bets on whether that car or the other would turn into Great Elm's drive, on which my guess is no one ever collected.

and stared out into the night through those frosted panes, rubbing at them with the butts of our palms and the insides of our wrists and with our elbows to keep them clear, catching sight all of a sudden of the mysterious aurora borealis, reddening and whitening and cartwheeling in the black skies, green and blue and gold and weird, and casting the reflections of their tints on the snow—spellbinding us, hushing us, putting us both in awe at the spectacle.

No sand or salt was tossed on roads in those days. They were plowed by huge old two-ton trucks with great blades bolted fast to their bumpers, but the fat flakes continued to fall, and to accumulate, and every now and then also, the tiny half-frozen, gale-driven, needle-sharp nuggets of white-out blizzards, which were driven almost horizontally to smash against windshields and fasten on and clog and weigh down the wipers, until they scarcely twitched, useless; and the back roads especially were caked with ice and slick, always dangerous days after the storm. One freezing-cold evening in late November—it may have been the Saturday of a Thanksgiving weekend—we all, several of us children, each with our Flexible Flyer sled (no sled was worth fussing with that wasn't a Flexible Flyer, and it had to be at least two seasons old, loosened up, the shiny yellow varnish worn off), were driven out to the base of Sharon Mountain, just where Jackson Hill Road spurs obliquely off Route 4; and there we found dozens of other boys and girls, including the Coleys and the Noyeses (Anne and Jack, my friends) and the Witts and the Bogarduses and sons and daughters of the Kennys and a lot of other people, Carberrys, Carleys, Petersons—catching rides with farmers who were coming from the railroad station in Sharon Union five miles away, driving wagons bearing dozens of tall, now-emptied forty-gallon galvanized-steel milk pails. Jackson Hill Road was still unpaved, hardpacked pebbly dirt, and it climbed two miles (becoming Fairchild Road) almost straight up, with two short level stretches at crossroads before it continued to Judge Peck's house and the Hinsdales', on East Street.* Near the bottom of this long slide was a

---

* The Peck house is gone. A mansion has taken its place. Beyond that (on East Street, whose nomination has vanished from new maps; it was an overgrown lane when we pushed through it on horseback) there is a peculiarly ungainly and ugly and even larger mansion painted hideous green and yellow. The Hinsdale place has been bought; its simple farmhouse lines have so far been respected; but in a hayfield below it, there has sprung up a not unhandsome conglomerate in faux-Provençal style that may be a condominium, it is so very large and

hair-raisingly sharp righthand bend,* banked up high with snow and ice from frequent plowing, frequent snows, frequent blizzards, which was the obstacle that we children had to negotiate to get to the finish line. Only the bravest sledders headed for that embankment, and only the smartest managed it without flying off the top. There were plenty of cracked skulls and some broken collarbones and maybe arms and legs, too, for all I know, but it was so exciting. We'd toss the clothesline reins of our sleds to the obliging dairy farmers, who hooked them to the rears or sides of their wagons; and up those frozen traces of the mountain their great horses would plod, nostrils and muzzles steaming, steam rising from their flanks, shod with nail-studded iron shoes that bit into the packed snow and ice, dragging us behind. Youngsters who had got to Sharon Mountain earlier came whizzing down by us as the team toiled, slowly but steadily pulling us along. At the very top, we would yell our thanks at the farmers—loosing the lines, running and slipping and throwing ourselves upon our sleds, *thunk*—and starting down.

From its topmost point at the Hinsdales', the narrow lane swooped in its descent across Jackson and Lucas and past Dr. Craig's house to the next crossroads, Jewett Hill Road (leading past the Witts' house to White Hollow) and Sharon Mountain Road and past the big old Deveaux house all the way to the bottom. How we flew! Our slick steel runners (we had filed off any hint of rust) dashed sparks from the ice or crunched sparkling across the occasional short stretch where gravel had come to the surface. We formed alliances as we went. The trick was to catch another sledder and tip his sled over or push him (or her) off it; and sometimes to pounce from one's own sled to the other person's sled and capture it that way. It was blackest night, with starshine only, oxygen slicing icily into our lungs, the crusted white shoulders of the road racing by us. We could scarcely make out anyone's features to recognize the person. We were most of us stuffed into one-piece woolen snow suits, buttoned or zipped up to the throat. We had heavy woolen mittens on our hands, and over our heads we had coarse woolen snow hats that pulled down low over the eyebrows and came up across the chin and mouth, where they were

---

long, or maybe a second summertime residence for John Edwards, that defender of the poor and weak. All of Sharon Mountain has been built upon these past forty years.
* There's now a house on that bend.

moistened with our exhalations and formed tiny icicles and burs of wool and ice.

When we approached the end of the ride, we were whizzing so fast it was scary. We jeered at kids who slowed themselves down by dragging the toes of their rubber galoshes behind them ("Chicken! Chicken!") as we zipped toward that terrible curve ahead of us. You had to meet it just right, *just* below the middle of the sharp rise of the embankment, and *just* at the correct angle, in order not to lose speed or fly off the top and go crashing into the woods. Oh, it was such a wonderful, exhilarating, triumphant feeling to have expertly calculated that bit of piloting, and to come *whooshing* off that embankment onto the hundred feet of straightaway and across the finish line, whooping and cheering and shouting, everybody else yelling and whooping and laughing for joy. And then we'd be off again, running after another dairy wagon lumbering toward us from Route 4, lofting our Flexible Flyers high over our heads as we tossed the clotheslines to the farmers and their hired hands, who laughed back at us, attaching them to the wagons. And this we continued to do until well after our bedtimes (nine o'clock sharp), pleading, "Just one more ride," until even we had to be satisfied that the last of the teams was already on its way up the mountain, and we had missed it, and no more were coming that night.

There was never, ever, more fun than these winter sled races in the snow and the ice and the smell of wet wool and of the tangy apple cider or steaming hot chocolate with cinnamon sticks in it that we were treated to afterward by anxious nannies and disapproving Mademoiselle and our relieved mother as we laughed and talked and talked and *talked* about our feats of derring-do, the fun we had had, the joy we had experienced. And it cost not a dime, not a red cent.

But this, of course, is one of many of the joys of New England country living that will never return (like leaf-burning parties), because there are no teams of great Percherons hauling milk wagons up from railroad stations any longer, and there are no roads even in the deepest of winter and in the most secluded of hills that haven't been scraped and cleared, sanded and salted down to the tar, and it may even be hard to find a Flexible Flyer, except maybe in an antique shop in Kent or Salisbury, because kids don't use sleds like they used to—not anymore.

NOTES

---

1. It fell to the Dutch elm disease in the late 1950s; the four sugar maples planted in the gaping hole it left are now half a century old, and large, and serve in my eyes only to remind me of the grandeur of the old elm, one of whose gigantic branches, sprouting off the main trunk about twelve feet from the roots, three feet or more broad and almost horizontal until it swept upward, I could lie upon in perfect security on my back, as though on a garden bench—gazing up at the sky through the elm's corona of bright green leaves, its canopy falling all about me and hiding me from view. It required seven adults holding hands to circle its base. In my mind, as a young man, I associated the Great Elm with my father—and when it was stricken, I remember looking anxiously at him, whose absence would leave a corresponding hole in my existence; who was felled by the first stroke at just about the same time that the Great Elm was diagnosed with the disease.

2. The green is continued a mile and more south of the village proper, from the Town Clock to the big curve west by the Gertrude Schly house, maybe a fifty-foot expanse of lawn on one side of the road, twenty feet or so on the other side, all meticulously mowed by the town.

3. One-hundred-twenty years old, capped with a conical red roof reminiscent of medieval tents, the clock is referred to always as a structure in "Gothic" style, with its granite blocks quarried nearby in Sharon, its red stones imported from Potsdam, New York. But it is properly called "Richardsonian Romanesque," I am informed by Liz Shapiro of the Sharon Historical Society, after a New York architect by the name of Charles Alonzo Rich, who is described as "renowned," would he had not. Guests of the old Sharon Inn, an old stagecoach stop situated on the opposite corner of the green from the clock, across the street, complained that the sonorous tolling (also described as a "dull donging") of the tower kept them awake nights. There followed a suit, which was pronounced against the town and its clock by a judge from Hartford who traveled to Sharon to spend the night in the inn, which he endured in wretched sleeplessness. The clock thenceforth was permitted to strike from seven A.M. to ten P.M., keeping quiet during the hours of rest.

4. The sugar maples will have to be replaced, and there will be resistance to that; they will be old and gorgeous themselves in the fall, and one would have to wait another century or so for the new elms to achieve the majesty of the original planting by the colonists. By that time, most or all of northwestern Connecticut will be paved over for the convenience of pale-faced weekend residents from New York, who have all built cunning rustic little $750,000 bungalows at the end of every once-great ruffed grouse covert.

5. Eggleston's became Walsh's drugstore in the 1950s. The drugstore and Jenkin's Grocery Store (best chocolate-covered peanut butter finger-length shortbread cookies ever, these in a clear glass jar) have been bought by newcomers, who have taken ad-

vantage of the solid construction of the two buildings, converting them into rather imposing (columned) or pretentious (columned) three-story dwellings with neo-Greek pediments, looking rather like façades on the set of a Hollywood antebellum Southern town, I can't quite pin down why.

6. Father rode the train at least twice a week. He had the liking of his generation for travel by rail, and his young manhood was spent often on Mexican trains, which is where he first encountered Pancho Villa and had other adventures. One of them was on a trip in the highly revolutionary state of Chihuahua or its neighbor, whose people following several years of fighting had become surly. He got aboard the only coach available and walked up and down to find a place on one of the bench seats. There was none. At one bench, however, by the window, sat a middle-aged Mexican who apparently did not like the gringo cut of Father's jib. Next to him on the seat was his suitcase. Father asked (in Spanish, of course), "Would you mind removing it, so that I can sit down?" The fellow glanced up at him in hostile fashion, turning his eyes back to the window, which was open. The train had begun to roll by this time, and they were out on the cactus and mesquite landscape of northern Mexico. Father asked the fellow a second time, speaking politely, "There is no other seat in the coach, would you mind putting your suitcase on the floor so that I may sit down?" The fellow grunted, *"No es mío,"* disclaiming ownership of the suitcase and turning his face back to the window. Father stood there a moment and then went to every other passenger in that crowded coach, asking, *"Esa maleta pertenece a Usted?"* ("Does that suitcase belong to you?") *"No, señor,"* these other passengers answered, neutrally but courteously.

Finally arriving back at the bench where the curmudgeon sat, he said, "Well, since this suitcase belongs to no one, I guess no one will miss it." Whereupon he lifted the suitcase from the bench, tossed it out the window, and sat down.

"Well," he would say to us, wiping at his eyes, which were streaming, with his handkerchief, "you should have seen the look on that man's face. But there was nothing a Mexican of honor could say, having denied ownership, and he just sat there glowering while several of the people on the coach laughed at him." "What happened then?" we asked, enthralled by this act of bravado (Father might well have been shot in those turbulent times). "Oh, he got off hurriedly at the next stop and I imagine boarded a northbound train to retrieve his bag." He laughed once more, turning to a more recent railroad experience.

On a Friday afternoon not many years before, when he was on the way home to Sharon from New York, he was trying to while away the hours by reading the *Journal American* when a five-year-old girl began running up and down the aisle shrieking at people, poking her fingers into their eyes, and, as she passed, slapping at Father's newspaper, yelling, "Ya, ya, ya!" She was watched in perfect equanimity by her mother and grandmother, who thought she was simply adorable. Father, in his sixties, put up with it two whole stops, all the way to Pawling; and then, the next time she came running up to him, he put his paper down suddenly, stooped close to her face, poked an index finger into her tummy, and shouted in his big bass voice, "Boo!" She went into near shock, he said . . . himself falling into paroxysms of laughter recalling how mother and grandmother now bestirred themselves to snatch the child up into their arms, crying, "Nasty old man, you can tell he's never had any children!"

CHAPTER SIXTEEN

———— ✦ ————

Sharon (IV): Family Values

WE BOYS GREW UP IN A FEMALE-DOMINATED SOCIETY, AS I INFER MY father did because of the clear intimations we got of the formidable personality of his mother and the striking personality of his elder sister, Tía Priscilla.

Mother was our all; but female domination descended directly from our oldest sister, Aloïse, who was smarter than anyone else and who, until she got to be thirteen or fourteen, was bigger and stronger than anyone else, and who was also more fun and imaginative and daring than anyone else. The saving item is that our sisters were all male chauvinist pigs.

Their contempt for girly girls was grim and total. Any thirteen- or fourteen-year-old coddled daughter of a pig-rich New York/Boston dynasty quite properly feared for her chin, or for her pretensions, under the withering scorn of my sisters. When she was twelve, Patricia could twist into a pretzel any nine-year-old boy, my age. Her horsewoman's hands and her scherzo-trained forearms were tempered steel. There was no macho-male dare that the Buckley girls wouldn't double-dare. (As they grew older, Mademoiselle was scoldingly anxious about this unbecoming tomboyishness in her charges. *Les jeunes filles bien élevées* did not participate in snowball fights in France, or wrestle males to the ground in France, or in France *"Non, nevairrre!"* stick their chins out and, hands clenched into fists by their sides, back boys their age against walls when they were displeased, saying, "Just try it, just you *try* socking my brother!")

But my sisters, like their mother, were deeply feminine, deferring to their brothers in matters that were properly within the male domain, such as slithering first (John or Jimmy or Billy) into the clay-slick stygian caves near Lakeville, or being first (Jimmy) in mounting one of the rodeo wild broncos Father imported from Lubbock (or was it Amarillo?) in a freight car (Will Buckley's children were *not* going to grow up into effete Easterners), or climbing to the very top of the sixty-foot copper beech on the south lawn (Billy and I), whose uppermost branches bent frighteningly beneath our weight, or cannonballing off the roof of the pump house twelve feet over skull-busting and bone-smashing paved flags into the pool (John, Jim, Bill, Reid). If we boys were ever in trouble, however, our sisters came instantly to our defense, which embarrassed John and, in London, once humiliated me (but for which I was grateful and very proud of my fireball of a sister, Maureen).

The solidarity that our parents fostered in their children was remarkable. God, family, country . . . and in that order. At a party, we would always be found gathered together and chatting animatedly, paying little attention to the friend whose birthday we had been invited to celebrate or to the other girls and boys. There was simply no one else in the world as interesting to us as we were to ourselves. Father disapproved of this clannishness, and let it be known; our handsome brother John, who was outgoing, was outraged. "Why do you attend a party unless you are nice to the person who invited you?" That riled us. "We are as nice and polite as can be. Who says we aren't?" He shot back, "Maybe you condescend to say hello and hand over a present, but five minutes later, you are all in a bunch talking loudly and laughing and paying no attention to anyone else. It's rude, and it's disgusting, and I don't want to be near you!" And he in fact cold-shouldered us, joining the party in another room.

And he was right. But simply no one was as wicked and funny as Allie, nobody as much fun as or sweeter than Pitts, no one nicer than Jim, no one as wickedly sarcastic and delightful (in her good moods!) as Janie, no one more interesting than Bill, and no one as darling and as fiercely loyal as Trish or Maureen. We were a corporate body. The thoughts, emotions, and experiences of Allie were mine, John's were mine, Pitts's were mine, Jim's were mine, Janie's were mine, Bill's were mine, Patricia's were mine. I felt always a proprietor's right to them. This did not, I believe, obtain going up the ladder; it was the youngest of us in cumulative proportion who profited from (or were branded by) our elders. In Maureenie and me, in our minds, flesh, and bones, reverberated our siblings . . . a oneness in being that Carol, born too young, and raised mostly in a solitary house (we older siblings were off to boarding school or college long before she had attained these rites of passage), did not fully participate in (profit from? see her *At the Still Point*). This oneness helps explain our irreparable sense of loss when Maureen died, because something of us, integrally of us, died with her. The charmed circle was rent. Each of us had had part of our being removed.

Pressing this topic further, I have always taken joy in the accomplishments and successes of my siblings, sorrowed at their reversals, as though they had happened to me. There has never been any jealousy between us, I believe not a smidgen. Jim's or Bill's successes are my successes, *our* successes. Their successes are wholly the product of their individual character and abilities, and the credit is theirs alone, yet they would not have been possible without the rest of us. Close-knit families with a small number of children share in this intimacy, each in different degree, depending upon the strength of the personalities of the father and mother, the principles they espoused, and the degree to which they passed those principles down. I have no idea, but I am guessing that the Kennedys are in this general respect like Buckleys. Bobby did not envy John, nor Teddy his elder brothers. The entire family rejoiced in the president, the attorney general, the senator, and grieved desperately at the brutal assassinations; and in these emotions, I have felt united to them in a special understanding.

Our peripatetic upbringing brought us close, but we also as a consequence missed the cultivation of friendships with coevals and the confident intimacy that comes from growing up uninterruptedly with people one's age. Despite nurses and governess, we spent a lot of time in close company with our parents, who were directly concerned with and involved in our maturation. If our parents ever baby-talked to us, that ceased by the time we were four or five. Within the limit of possible bounds (one did not speak with Reid, age six, as one spoke with Bill, age eleven, obviously), they treated us and conversed with us as adults, which had its negative effect on our relations with children our age. We were inhibited in communicating with them. The conversation proper and natural to children did not come easily to us, boring us. We were shy, socially awkward, every one of us,* and, despite, or because of, the cosmopolitan panache, timid. I do not doubt that this partially explains why so many of us lead what are to us compelling interior lives, propelling us to write, and are drawn to solitary pleasures, such as shooting and fishing, sailing and birdwatching; and why several of us (Jim and I especially) are sensitive to our natural surroundings and take such keen interest in the countryside.

We were different, and we felt that. We were what John indignantly accused us of being: a clan, a tribe. Besides, we were so often hauled away at critical passages of our youth to spend a year or two in foreign countries that we had a hard time remembering the names of everyone when we got back home. For me, at least, but I doubt not for several of my siblings (notably excepting Priscilla and Carol), that has become a life-long crippling social disability that I have never been able to cure. This may explain why, though in the realm of ideas we were *engagé*, passionate, and vociferous, we were politically little inclined. To the question of whether he had ever thought of running for office, Father answered with definitive simplicity that it had never occurred to him because he was certain that no one would vote for him. None of his progeny considered a career in politics† because, first of reasons, we are incapable of remembering people's names.‡ On the spot, we (Bill and I, Maureen, and, I believe, Pitts and Allie before her) can recall a ton of statistics and complex contrary arguments, but we cannot remember a name. It's as though we were born with a failure of nominative short-term memory measured in nanoseconds. This failing is not wholly attributable to self-absorption, though it may well appear to be the case, and this is partly true—we are to a degree self-centered, the dreams I dream and the thoughts I think (speaking for myself) were (and to lesser

---

* Except John and Pitts.

† Despite Father's adjurations to Bill (see his memoranda to his children), Bill ran for mayor of New York as Barry Goldwater ran for the presidency of the United States—to make a dialectical point, dead certain he would not be elected, and quite prepared to demand a recount or immediately resign if by some awful mischance he beat the incumbent; Jim was dragged into running for senator.

‡ There is another reason: none of us ever felt that our self-worth depended on public adulation. It was a private matter. One has the impression that political animals (the Kennedys, the Clintons, *mari et femme*) hunger for public acclaim, that their deepest beings depend on this for sustenance. It's as though they have no other measure by which to evaluate their existences, poor souls!

degree still are) of a thrilling personal character to which nothing on the social level could (or can) compare. But our failure to catch names is also partly accounted for by fascination with human contact, by absorption in the person with whom we are speaking.

This is tribal, too. We children knew one another intimately and shared unforgettable experiences keenly.* Exogenic contacts were, and are, of almost zoological interest to us. When I meet someone whom I find interesting, or for some reason attractive, I am immediately attentive to that new acquaintance's appearance, personality, character, and opinions. I am voracious about this. I concentrate on the person's attributes to the exclusion of anything else. The name flies by my head like a Frisbee in a high wind; it whistles into and through and out of my ears like a ghost, gone before it has registerd. When we meet again—maybe at the very next social gathering—I am still avid to learn more about my discovery, whose name (it stuns me to realize) I can't recall. "Hi, Reid!" "Oh, hi . . . how *are* you?" (I wince as I write, because I can hear the false tone of bonhomie in my mind all the time that I am floundering desperately to recall that nice/kind person's moniker.) This becomes over time acutely embarrassing; on the third or four or fifth meeting (which may take place weeks, months, even years apart), I know perfectly well who the person is, but to the greeting "Hello, Reid, how have you been?" I mumble an answer, burning with mortification that once more, for the life of me, I can remember almost every detail of the acquaintance, *but I cannot recall his or her name,* and it is now too late—rude, unpardonable—*to ask for it.*

There is no excuse for this gauche social ineptitude.† Few can imagine what relief I experience at a party when I am rescued by a third person who providentially turns to me, exclaiming, "Reid, what have you and

---

* Such as the two-day boat trip Allie, John, Jim, and Pitts took down the Wateree River circa 1940, during which they encountered more very large alligators than they would have wished; or our mule trek heading out of Patzcuaro circa 1943 to visit the still belching and fiery volcano of Paricutín, in Mexico, the last excursion we had with our brother Bill before he was inducted into the army.

† I'll not forget my wonderment upon being told that Jim Farley, the South Carolinian politician and one-time Postmaster General, kept ten thousand names in his head. This same marvel was attributed to Strom Thurmond, who at a party given by Esther and Jim Ferguson for him on his ninetieth birthday, said, "Why, of course I remember you, Reid Buckley—and your dear parents, Aloïse and Will." He had been a supper guest at Kamschatka several times during the 1940s, when I was a child . . . but that was forty years in the past!

Ouisa been speaking so animatedly about?" (Ouisa! Ouisa *Ancrum!* To spend a weekend with whom I drove all the way through a winter storm to Mount Holyoke College, I had such a crush on her! How could I have forgot?) My solution to the problem has been Draconian: I have simply quit attending large social gatherings of any kind (at which I am likely to encounter light or infrequent acquaintances) for fear of seeming rude. And I have in the meantime discovered that I cannot recall the names of warblers and other songbirds with which I have been intimately acquainted since childhood, which is the limit.

John was more like Mother, and this became evident to the rest of us in her tragic senility and in his last years: they were close akin temperamentally and could sit side by side for hours at the Noble Horizon rest home in Salisbury, scarcely speaking, his small, freckled, delicate hand in her pretty white hand, which his so much resembled. Mother relished the company of people, a very Southern grace, as did her eldest son and second daughter, our wonderful sister Priscilla. It did not astonish us children that within an hour or two of having met whomever, our mother could recount (in invariably amusing fashion) not only that person's entire life history but the history of his or her parents, siblings, in-laws, and children. She never forgot a detail of anyone's life, in which she was sincerely and delightedly interested, or that person's name, or the name of his grand-aunt and second cousin. That, as I say, was the South in her.

The rest of us took after our father. Father could be exuberantly social on festive occasions, and when engaged in social intercourse, we learned, as we grew older, he could be charming and on one level popular. He was a very private person, nevertheless, and that reserve lay just beneath the surface always. Few people called him Will Buckley as he grew older. He was only completely at ease in the company of his mother and siblings, cherished friends from the early days, or his wife and children. I believe he felt wholly secure only with them, from whom he had few secrets.* We children were only totally at ease in the same company. We enjoyed especially visits of our parents' respective families—darling Grandmother Marie Wassem Steiner, Mother's vivacious sisters Vivian and Inez and

---

* This describes his son Reid and Reid's case to the last dot. I am only completely at ease when surrounded by my family, including in-laws, and by the people I work with in my school, most of whom are of long acquaintance.

their doctor husbands Marion Lombard and Claude Perrier, and her brother Jimmy (everybody's favorite uncle, he was young enough to have been our father's son), who at the New Year's Eve balls would become happily soused and would bellow, "But when the Saints, *tatatatá*, but when the Saints, *tatatatá*, but when the Saintscomemarchinginnn," leading astonished guests in a conga line around the patio and up one circular wrought-iron staircase to the second-floor gallery and all the way around that to the corresponding wrought-iron staircase and down again to the ground floor, weaving past the orchestra and across the black-and-red-tiled floor all the way to the library, where the line wobbled and broke up and he went in search of a fresh bourbon. Father's quixotic spinster sisters Priscilla and Eleanor arrived always in the curtained Buick driven by Jack and towing their shining aluminum trailer, in which they traveled throughout the States, burdened with presents for every one of us and regaling us with their droll adventures.* His tall, slim, austere, yet affectionate brother Claude (and Uncle Claude's darling wife, Aunt Dora) and their children—dreamily beautiful Eleanor Anne (with whom I was smitten one Christmas when she presented me with a pair of ivory-handled six-shooters and a genuine black leather gun belt studded with large not-so-genuine sapphires and rubies and diamonds—Hopalong Cassidy, eat your heart out!) and her sister "Teats" (short for Doratita) and brothers Claude and Bobby; and the one-time scapegrace, handsome Uncle Edmund (and his stunning wife, Beryl), and their children "little" Beryl and Edmundito, Ross and Tony (handsome and beautiful all).

OUR PARENTS WERE FOR US CONSTANT WELLS OF HAPPY SURPRISE. WE could never be sure what would come from them. When they bought the old Sterling farmhouse in Sharon and decided that it would not satisfactorily accommodate their rapidly expanding brood of children, they consulted with architects and interior decorators, which was the custom, but they paid little attention to their recommendations when these conflicted

---

*Pitts recalled a story at lunch today (26-XII-07). The house on the corner of Lavaca was infested with mice. Tías Priscilla and Eleanor consulted on what was to be done. Arsenic, was the answer. So Tía Priscilla went down to the pharmacist to order a batch. The pharmacist, a young woman, wrapped the package and in handing it to her said, "Miss Priscilla, may I ask what you want the arsenic for?" "To kill my sister," Tía Priscilla replied.

with what they wanted to do. "They have no imagination, poor people," Mother often (superiorly) complained about them to us, with which judgment Father agreed entirely. "It never occurs to them," he pronounced at lunch or supper, "that just because something has always been done in a certain way, it can't be done differently." And we children could tell from his wide-eyed expression of amazement and the tone of his voice that he, like Mother, was truly sorry for them, and that they were planning some radical alteration. The two great wings that enclosed the open garden of the patio came first, then the swimming pool, and then the winter-proofed the patio so that we could keep orange and lemon trees glossily alive (the fruit was never edible) when outside the snow piled up and a freezing wind smarted our noses; next the dairy and the henhouse, the stables and the horses, the kennels and the setter dogs, the peach and plum and apple orchards, the tennis court. I don't recall the exact order of Father's indefatigable improvements, but how grateful we were for them!*

---

*A further—and last note—on our paternal aunts. Tías Priscilla and Eleanor were riding on a train back from New York City (or was it Mexico City?), destination Austin, which was scheduled to arrive at the inconvenient hour of 6:15 A.M. When night fell on the eve of their arrival, they set their alarm clock at 5:15 A.M. It awoke them smartly, and they dressed and packed their bags and waited, sitting on the lower bunk of the Pullman compartment. Tía Priscilla said, "Eleanor, would you raise the blind so we can see the sun come up?" Tía Eleanor thought that was a splendid idea, as Texas sunsets and sunrises can be spectacular; so she yanked the blind of the wide Pullman window to its top. It was pitch black outside: a solid, unremitting darkness. Not a hint of dawn. Tía Priscilla thought for a little while, and then asked her sister, "Eleanor, what does your wristwatch say?" "Why, 3:15," answered Tía Eleanor, with a start. "And the alarm clock?" "5:15." They had failed to adjust the alarm clock to Central time.

"So what did you do?" we children asked our aunts, who had dissolved in merriment at the memory. "Why, the sensible thing. We got undressed and went straight back to bed, sleeping another two hours."

—◦◊◦—

CHAPTER SEVENTEEN

Sharon (V): Scandal and Fun

GREAT ELM! HOW WE CHILDREN LOVED THE SPRAWLING VASTNESS OF that old house, from the third-floor aerie that became my quarters down to the midnight-blue carpet of the "dark" room that, in the beginning, no one lingered in—a central pivot, a passthrough, its walls hung with stiff gilt seventeenth- and eighteenth-century Mexican church icons, part of a large collection of religious furnishings that had been confided to Father's safekeeping during the revolutionary period from 1910 to 1921, because at that time, no Mexican trusted any other Mexican.* There was a large baroque altar against what was the wall of the (cheerful, light-filled) corner music room (now one of my sister Priscilla's parlors), above which, all of a sudden, from one day to the next, there glowed a celestial Botticelli of the Virgin that no one could go by without stopping to gaze at for a little while, it was so luminous.[1]

We entered the "dark" room from the central hall that still traverses Great Elm east-west. A large, rectangular chamber, it had no windows, hence its sepulchral aspect. It admitted east to the library, south to the Empire room, at the far end of which, above the fireplace, glowed a Rae-

---

*He kept most of the large pieces of furniture stored in the attics of the stables and the garage, attempting periodically to track and notify the original owners. I don't know what happened to it all.

burn portrait of a cherubic, rosy-cheeked boy child (another happy acqui-
sition, of the early 1950s).* The Empire room was the formal parlor of
Great Elm, twenty-one paces long by seven paces wide, occupying the
ground floor of the whole west wing of the house, at whose far end, under
the Raeburn, Father and Mother sat with their houseguests after supper,
sipping coffee and ice water served in small, deeply incised rock crystal
glasses that helped keep the water chill. This was delicious after a three-
course meal and two wines, white and red. Our parents at that time did
not offer any hard liquor after supper.

The furniture was heavy, of the Empire period, mahogany, with fruit-
wood or sandalwood marquetry. Along the faces of sideboards and on the
ormolu drawers of the several chests that were set against the walls were
gilt bronze appliqués in the neoclassical Napoleon III style. It had all been
acquired in Mexico, in which the Second Empire influence was an inheritance of the brief reign of Maximilian. Each piece viewed individually—
the benches, the sideboards, the enormous round table that occupied the
center rear of the room, for example—was an exquisite example of the
cabinetmaker's art, though we children did not favor them. To the plain
New England taste of summer residents, who were raised on sour apples,
they must have been an affront.† There was a set of six large, supremely
comfortable, glowing, Amazon basin rosewood chairs that we all loved,
with hand-chiseled backrests of marvelous artistry and wonderfully turned
arms (to accommodate the slack of the muscle of the forearms as one
grasps the rests). Father enjoyed telling us of a cunning old antiques dealer
in Mexico City who professed to have discovered this pair of rare chairs
by the greatest of good fortune. They had miraculously survived the plun-
dering and burning of a hacienda at the time of Benito Juárez fifty years
back. Its owners—French aristocrats, of course—were murdered (husband) and deported (wife and children). The fellow wanted a fancy price
for the pair, Father told us, grinning at the memory, but they were so
handsome and so unusual, he paid it.

---

*A protegé of Reynolds, Sir Henry Raeburn (1756–1823) became the most able portraitist
in Edinburgh before becoming London's most accomplished portraitist. Allie quipped,
"Look out, everyone: Father has entered into his Old Masters phase."
†Which brings up the subject of taste, which I touch on below, in the end notes.

Some six weeks later, the dealer came around to his law offices in the Zócalo, saying to him excitedly, "Señor Buckley,* *ha sido mi suerte fabuloso* [it has been my amazing luck] to locate another pair of those self-same chairs, and in splendid condition!" Father bought them, at a fancier price still. He was suspicious, of course; and one afternoon some weeks later, when happening on the vicinity of the antique dealer's place of business, he walked along the wall of the back courtyard and, lifting up on his toes, spied—as he suspected might be the case—two more chairs being meticulously carved, chiseled, and sanded by a pair of those gifted artisans who make all the world gasp in awe at the singular genius of the Mexican people. He said nothing to the dealer, but when the fellow came around two or three weeks later with yet another tale about his *suerte fabuloso* (which was assuredly a direct intervention by the Virgin of Guadalupe) in discovering a *third* pair of those *esplendidos y magníficos sillones,* Father readily acknowledged that they were splendid and magnificent, but—divulging that he had watched the fraud in the making and calling the dealer a *sinvergüenza*—flatly refused to pay more than a fair price for that third pair; which sum, along with his exposure, the dealer cheerfully accepted. (Señor Buclé was one smart gringo.)

We children were all happy that our father had shown the good sense not to be put off by the swindle, regretting only that his expulsion from Mexico prevented him from commissioning another pair or two.[†] To finish out the Empire room, around both walls hung pastels of the nine of us[2] and then a portrait of our baby sister Carol that none of her elder siblings admired as a likeness.[‡] The carpet in this room was of emerald-green wool and, like the "dark" room's blue carpet, deep-piled and luscious, wonderful to sprawl upon while reading a book (a favorite retreat was under

---

*I do not know how Father's surname was pronounced in Mexico, but in Spain I was addressed as Señor *Buclé,* as in "Boo-cleh."

†At the auction of the furnishings of Great Elm and Kamschatka, I bought two of these chairs, while my nephew Cameron Smith, sister Jane's eldest son, bought the other four. I don't know where he has his; I have mine in the little rose parlor of my school.

‡Julian Lamar had vanished from the scene by the time she was old enough to sit for a portrait. I seem to remember that this one was executed by an amateur, a friend. It did our little sister no justice: Carol was fairylike, she was so lovely and winsome as a very little girl, with the enormous blue eyes she inherited from her sire and a pair of darling dimples.

the grand piano, from the top of whose sounding board a museum-quality floral Mexican silk shawl dangled its tasseled ends, quite concealing one. I kept successfully hidden twice while Mother sat at the keyboard, playing her waltzes and Stephen Foster songs and Irish ditties from the 1880s and '90s, singing along with them in her high, thin, true, sweet voice, "But I'll be damned, if I'll be jammed" . . . "For it was Mary, Maaary, plain as any name can beee . . ." She never suspected I was there.)

We were many, but in addition to our upstairs bedrooms, there were retreats everywhere in Great Elm: the deep sofas of the library, where one could stretch out, immersed maybe in *Black Beauty* or *Kidnapped* or *Ivanhoe* or (weepily) *The Scarlet Letter* and *Beau Geste* (and also Wodehouse and Hemingway and Steinbeck); the upholstered armchairs, whose overstuffed arms were perfect for slinging one's legs over and reading; or the wide window casements of the playroom/schoolroom (now sister Jane's bedroom suite), on whose bench seats one could recline with one's back propped up against the projecting side of the central bookcase, catching the morning's bright eastern light . . . and reading; or the playroom's vast old couch where *two* of us could flop at one time, feet to feet, immersed in a novel or sometimes in poetry, which we loved, beginning with *When We Were Very Young* and *Now We Are Six* and Hilaire Belloc's nursery ballads ("There was a boy whose name was Jim/His friends were very fond of him"), proceeding from Shakespeare and Milton to Frost and Eliot, the major body of English poetry,* or simply dreaming of great and wonderful things and heroic feats and dozing while the Capehart played (and sometimes shattered) Bach, Beethoven, or Brahms, Kirsten Flagstad pouring forth the *Liebestod* from *Tristan und Isolde* or Helen Traubel her *Du Bist der Lenz* from *Die Walküre* or, as Brünnhilde, daughter of Wotan, giving titanic pagan battle to the Siegfried of Lauritz Melchior, while siblings in the other rooms (principally Jane and Bill and Trish) practiced and (not infrequently also, in their fashion) shattered Bach and Mozart, Schumann and Chopin. Maureenie had the habit of tossing her long blond pigtails over the backs of sofas and armchairs when she was absorbed in a book, and I used to exploit the opportunity to sneak up behind her as noiselessly

---

*My discovery at age seventeen of Gerard Manley Hopkins was one of the most exhilarating joys I ever experienced, enduring more than half a century now.

as one of James Fenimore Cooper's (mythical) Mohican Indians, giving a hard yank down of one or both of the shining braided tresses . . . and then running for my life.

Dare interrupt any of us when we were reading, whether an exalted member of the eldest four or a lowly member of the youngest, and an icy stare was sure to be sped your way. Reading was sacred in our upbringing, which has helped me to understand (though not to sympathize with) the absorption of my grandchildren in their little handheld video games, which may not have quite deprived them of the ability to discourse rationally, but which *has* deprived some of them of the inestimable pleasure of conversing with their grandfather.

A PROBLEM WITH MANY PRE-REVOLUTIONARY HOUSES IS LACK OF INTErior light.

New England's windows from colonial times and into the early twentieth century were small, high, and mean, the ceilings low, protecting against the cold. When Mother and Father erected the two major wings off the Sterling House's south wall* they insisted on nine-foot ceilings, and they opened tall southern windows along the exterior walls (through which lawn and garden showed) and along the interior walls (admitting the light of the patio). The patio itself is an immense atrium of light, fifty-two feet long, twenty-two feet wide—wider by a couple of feet than either the Empire or the playroom wings. The wall at the end is a white-painted wooden structure giving the effect of an immense single window. When the sun sets to the southwest in wintertime, light streams through this airy wall in quadruple shafts, like Jacob's ladder. The patio is a marvel.[†]

The adage that our parents repeated often was, "Never be afraid of color," to the distress of some of the New York City interior decorators, who were dismissed almost as fast as their counsel was hired. Our parents' joy in color is plainly an inheritance of Mexico. Father imported by rail

---

* The western wing containing the Empire room downstairs, the nursery and the bedroom suite upstairs; the eastern wing containing the playroom/schoolroom downstairs, guest rooms upstairs, with the patio in between.

† It was primarily built, I believe, by master carpenter and cabinetmaker John Carley, who thirty years later made exquisitely simple mantelpieces for my sister Aloise (in West Hartford) and me (in my house on Mudge Hill).

thousands of Mexican, Portuguese, and Spanish tiles in big wooden crates (the contents insulated from each other by straw), many of which are exquisite and would fetch a prohibitive price today. These they inserted everywhere that the predominating colonial interior design—primarily of wood trim, painted white—permitted. The romantic and revolutionary Mexican background was everywhere shouted in Great Elm. Almost all doorways were framed by tiles across their tops and down their sides. All the principal bathrooms were faced or accented with tiles, and at the patio's far southern terminus, just this side of the door, there is an Andalusian fountain with a narrow rectangular pool (into which I plopped a small-mouth bass one evening that by midmorning the next day had dispatched all the fat goldfish, which I detested). Everywhere one glances, the patio is a cheerful clashing of pigments that only the imaginations of Mexican workmen could have mingled.

Who were contracted and brought from Mexico, because Father did nothing halfway. These artisans spent the spring and summer months and an entire winter in Sharon applying their native genius to Great Elm's living spaces, assembling and grouting the tiles, applying the cheery decals in oranges and greens and yellows (the designs chosen by our parents; their hand was in everything) that decorated the immense scaffolding of beams, joists, and braces holding up the awesome glass roof of the patio, which, from time to time, were additionally decorated by white splashes gratis the canaries that I sprang out of their bamboo prisons on the second-story gallery. Mother enjoyed birdsong but disapproved of bird waste, and instructed me to lure the canaries back into their cages before they splotched the cushions of sofas and armchairs too evidently. Ella Boswell and Jeff Boykin, who washed off the evidence, reproving me also ("My, my, Mister Reid, you are *naughty!*"—Jeff grinning like a portly Joe Louis while Ella scolded, "Mmmm, mmm, um!"). But as the three of them privately enjoyed the bright yellow flashes of the liberated creatures darting from overhead horizontal beams to the ivy-encircled columns up to the second-story railing, perching there a moment, and then launching and zigzagging around the chains of wrought-iron chandeliers across the airy spaces between, neither Mother nor Ella nor Jeff admonished me too severely, and I in turn displayed the discretion of releasing the canaries only once or twice a year.

We have all thought and thought on the intellectual and decorative

audacity of our parents, and whence it came, and I've been impressed all
my life as a consequence with how culture and religion define us, and, cor-
respondingly, how precious both are to human development: a debased
hip-hop culture and an agnostic society (for being shorn of myth and ro-
mance) are barren.* In our parents' case, none of the Mexican daring
would have been possible had it not been for their upbringing; our father's,
proximate to the border, and immersed daily in the Spanish tongue; our
mother's, in New Orleans, redolent with the wrought-iron and other enduring vestiges of the city's Spanish and French origins. Both were inculcated in the rich and fecund Mexican culture (which, at least through the
1920s, was French as well as Spanish and Toltec), he through his business
career in Mexico, she through her vernal visits to her "uncle" Émile Berthier in Mexico City. Their Catholic religion also deeply affected the cultural mix. I cannot make sufficient point of this, and I will hit on it more
than once again. Without that Catholic faith, Mother and Father are
nothing, shadows. Without that embattled Catholic faith, we, their children, are nothing, disinherited. Shorn of that Catholic faith, our children
will amount to little more than matter in motion, of passing curiosity or
interest, human rubbish, bereft of transcendental significance. The faith
permeated and illuminated everything our parents touched, created,
thought, honored, and it is evident that they were conscious of being, in
New England, pilgrims in a Protestant land. There were crucifixes in every
room of Great Elm, of course, and Mother and Father salvaged from the
expulsion from Mexico beautiful sixteenth- and seventeenth-century
polychromed wooden *tallas,* as Spaniards call these brilliantly stuccoed
sculptures, in this case seven-inch and eight-inch figurines of the Virgin
and Saint Joseph and the curiously adult, for a newborn infant child, Jesus
on his back in his wooden crib, arms reaching upward, little dimpled
naked legs raised in the act of joyful kicking.† I cannot imagine Father or
Mother acquiring a Picasso, or a Braque, or even a Chagall, though maybe
a Sisley, a Renoir, an early Matisse . . . but a painter in the cubist or
abstract-expressionist schools, never; though I remember distinctly, when

---

* This has been the subject of my five novels.
† The Holy Family, which belonged to our mother and were on a table in her bedroom. She
and Father prayed before them every night. I believe Janie has them in her bedroom.

Aloïse Steiner Buckley,
1929.

I was eight or ten years old, and on one or two occasions later, Father raving about a Spanish painter called El Greco.

Today, El Greco may be the only Spanish painter's name that Americans are able to pronounce properly, but this was amazing in our father. When I visited him in Bad Gastein during the weeks before his death, he quizzed me closely on whether my wife, Betsy, and I had visited Toledo and seen the *Death of the Count of Orgaz** in the alcove of Santo Tomás church, and whether we had seen also that portrait of Saint Peter in his green cloak—had we ever seen anything like that in our lives?—and weren't El Greco's portraits of the twelve apostles an extraordinary work,

---

*I happen to be acquainted with his direct descendant, a charming and intellectually inclined Spaniard who summers in Comillas.

were they not *something?* This response in our father testified to the temperamental daring that set him apart from other people. He spoke rarely of art, raved never; which is why his fervent partiality for El Greco impressed me. This is more marvelous in him than it appears to us from the aesthetic configuration of our upbringing. El Greco is not strange to those of us born around 1920, 1930, and later. We were raised in an Impressionist and post-Impressionist rubric, which accepted iconoclasts, the flattening of dimensions, and cubist frolicking. That culture defines and limits us. I am, for example—speaking for myself and not for my siblings, though I suspect they would agree—unable either to understand or to enjoy, or for that matter approve of, minimalist, pop, hard edge, and "transgressive" art, which, to me, is abominable on all counts, from the aesthetic to the philosophical.* How, then, did our father come to love and admire El Greco way back in the 1930s, when almost no one outside Spain had heard of him, and when few art connoisseurs, Spanish or foreign (the exception was Berenson), valued him?

That prolific royal collector of the art of his time, Emperor Charles V of Spain—whose death in the monastery to which he had retired halfway up the *sierra* of Gredos was brought on by the pitch of emotions to which he was wrought from viewing a Titian canvas—*rejected* El Greco. One would suppose that his fanatically religious and ascetic son Philip† would have appreciated at least the tortured saints of El Greco's latter period, and one can tantalize oneself imagining how this discovery would have benefited the walls of El Escorial, but Philip did not like the Greek. Until well into the 1940s (and even as late as the 1950s), *Spaniards* did not all appreciate El Greco, *condescended* to El Greco (Spanish chauvinism? he was a Greek, after all), and not until the 1960s numbered him with Zurburán, Velázquez, and Goya in the pantheon of their art.‡

Then how come our down-to-earth father, on a visit to Toledo in, I am

---

* Hilton Kramer's acceptance of so much of it bewilders me.

† Who in Valladolid celebrated his nuptials by viewing an *auto da fé* and then a bullfight. I am unable to shake this horrific historical trivium out of my mind.

‡ I happen to have been offered (in 1963 or 1964), for purchase, Goya's *La Condesa de Chinchón*, a luminous masterpiece with which I fell in love, one of the five great Goya portraits, for the sum of 1 million pesetas, which was $16,667 at that time. I refused the offer (by a desperate Spanish nobleman) for several reasons unrelated to the sordid reality that I did not have $16,667 to spare at the time. See my pamphlet, *La Condesa de Chinchón*.

guessing, 1929, reacted so viscerally to the painter? It was an extraordinary leap in his imagination, beyond his upbringing though not inhospitable to it. The connection sprang, I hypothesize, from his Catholicism (Spaniards were in the main vibrantly Catholic at that time, yet did not on this account appreciate El Greco), from his profound though very private spirituality (again, Spaniards were until recently profoundly spiritual as a people, yet seemed, some of them—as I know—embarrassed by El Greco), and from his sense of Christian tragedy (once again, Spaniards until just the other day bore this ontological presentiment in their guts, yet did not all revere El Greco). I forget who first described the later portraits and the saints of the painter as human beings whose faces are the twisted flames of candles being consumed in their mysticism, but that's just about right. El Greco's portraits are metaphysical poetry, each a metaphor for the condition of man. There was this stratum in the character and in the deepest reaches of both our parents, their glad acceptance of ontology.

More: there was a peculiarly Catholic optimism in their hearts, quite alien to the gloomy bent of Calvinist New England. We Catholics know that existence in this world is a pilgrimage, but this does not prevent us from enjoying the journey and the portions of gladness on its way that are granted to us. That Catholics enjoy sin because they know it better than anyone is an ancient Protestant slur that contains this element of truth: Catholics, taught from childhood to examine the conscience, never, unless overcome by the hopelessness of vice, lose this habit of moral introspection, and are therefore deeply, acutely conscious of their personal sins and how very far they fall short of perfection, and this personal knowledge tends to breed compassion for others in the same fix, which is all human beings under creation, including certified saints until they breathe their last. Catholics do not less detest the sin for understanding and loving the sinner, which is a common Protestant moral error (loving the sinner, they are tolerant of the sin), reflected in Democratic politics and social doctrines. The reality of the human condition abided ever in our parents, and they grieved for their dead, but so also abided in them their certainty of the Resurrection. They were moreover as Christians *American Roman Catholics,* with the emphasis on that first word, *American,* at once practical and mystical and filled with happy optimism, like the majority of their countrymen in their time. How they pitied people who had lost or who had been denied faith. Faith is joyous, not Cotton Mather (or Philip II) gloomy. Faith pardons the suffering inherent in existence, consequent on the Fall. Faith makes the pilgrimage in this world bearable. Faith permits human beings to love this world, as Christ Jesus loved the world, cruel though nature may occasionally be and cruel though we human beings often are, making of this existence a living hell (Hitler, Stalin, Mao, Pol Pot, assorted African tyrants, Osama bin Laden). The Christian faith is the most democratic of all religions (the perfect spiritual complement to the rugged frontier experience, in our father's case) because it exalts all human beings in an equality that no other belief or system is able to justify, and makes of our existence, for each of us, a great drama whose triumphant end is eternal joy.

Protestants and pagans have, the first, imperfect, the second, no, understanding of this, poor folk. (This was how we children thought of our Protestant friends, as deprived, though lovable and in cases saintly human beings.) Protestant and pagan Americans are repulsed by ecclesiastical pomp. All that money spent on incense and gold thread that could have been distributed to the poor! They simply would not believe that at times the Vatican has been impoverished, as recently as 1922 church coffers containing net $19,000. Now, when Holy Mother Church pulls out all the stops, it can be baroque, magnificent, inspiring, but not to American Calvinists. They are afraid of color. They exist shivering through the winter of the human condition in cramped rooms with low ceilings and teeny windows that begrudge letting in a little joy. Protestant Americans associate Roman Catholic splendor with the alembicated narcissism of Oriental and Ottoman courts, with the hedonism and narcissism of Louis IV's Versailles, and hence with temporal absolutism, which is anathema to the New England temperament.* There is here a ball of worms of age-old misunderstanding and bias. Principally, non-Catholic Americans do not understand this: that it is the eschatological doctrines of the Catholic Church that alone justify the fundamental democratic doctrine of the dignity of the individual man.

This liberating and joyous Catholic faith our parents were blessed with by divine grace and their happy inheritance; they were invested with hope, which is trust in Christ's promises. Faith and hope combine in producing

---

* This misapprehension was exacerbated by Pius IX's nineteenth-century declaration of papal infallibility in matters of faith and morals (when the pope is speaking *ex cathedra*).

charity, whose definition is perfect love. What joy they were possessed of! The metaphysical destiny of human beings of the humblest estate is greater than that of a prince of this world. It is nothing less than to become the kings and queens of creation, to share in and with Christ dominion over creation.* To our parents, this was never in question. In addition, Mother and Father were drenched in the ebullient optimism of their native land, to whose people nothing was impossible here as well as in the hereafter, no dream too fantastical to admit being achieved. Not ever again in the history of humankind—not to the end of time—will our parents' combination of experiences be repeated. Never again will there be a generation so sublimely blessed as theirs was. Their nation had not known defeat, and this fact was a moral virtue.† They were born, both of them, in what to our generation is primeval darkness—in the age of the candle or oil lamp, before electricity, before running water, indoor plumbing, the refrigerator (which I still often absentmindedly refer to as the icebox, because that is what we had in the kitchen of Great Elm, a huge one), before the telephone, the radio, the automobile—in the era when a day's journey for ordinary people was measured by how far one could walk or, if lucky, by how fast a good horse could take one. Locomotive and steamship had been invented before Father and Mother were born, but in Father's youth, the nearest railhead to San Diego, Texas, was a hard horseback journey distant. He lived to see (though he did not like, preferring ocean liners) the age of commercial transatlantic aviation; Mother lived almost two decades after Americans walked on the moon, and she cavalierly crisscrossed the world in jet aircraft. It was the most radical and most marvelous century of discovery and technological progress in the history of mankind so far, and, the transistor chip notwithstanding, nothing in terms of human convenience and well-being will be the like. It was the age of American infallibility. How lucky they were, both of them, born to the simultaneous emergence of our country from its international status as an exotic experiment in a faraway and uncouth region of the globe to become economically and militarily the central power on earth. When our parents were still young, New York was overnight vying with London as the world's financial capital. What's more, they both lived to see (in the

---

* This is close to the Jewish view and is partly inherited from Jewish mysticism.
† See my novel *Saving DeSaussure Swamp: A Love Story.*

roaring twenties) their despised native American culture conquer the Western World, first by Louis Armstrong and Duke Ellington and Ella Fitzgerald in jazz, then by Jerome Kern and Cole Porter and Rogers and Hammerstein on Broadway, then by Cecil B. DeMille and Louis Mayer and the Warner Brothers and CapraandHustonandClarkGableandGary CooperandRosalindRussellandClaudetteColbert and the host of producers, directors, and actors that made the films of Hollywood great and (simultaneously) by Fitzgerald, Hemingway, Steinbeck, Dos Passos, and Faulkner, all gaining international recognition. The historical optimism and confidence of our parents' times on the profane level joined with the spiritual optimism and confidence that came to them from antiquity through their Catholicism. This was the spiritual dimension that created Great Elm and that was so mystifying to the frostbitten Protestant culture and upbringing of the New Englanders of that time, who were doomed to be disparaged a generation later and to sink into irrelevance as WASPs.

Not surprisingly, what our parents did with the old Sterling House in converting it into *our* Great Elm was the talk of Sharon and its summer residents. The whole Will and Aloïse Steiner Buckley ménage—their excessive (i.e., Catholic, i.e., low-class) number of rambunctious children, their exotic houseguests ranging from Mexican statesmen to revolutionary ex-governors resembling the Hollywood stereotype of Pancho Villa bandits with their brown skins and thick black mustachios, not to speak of Will Buckley's shocking contempt for Wall Street, for Wilson, for Roosevelt, for Wilkie, for the Cabots and the Lodges, for Walter Lippmann, for Ed Murrow, and for all the other respectable totems of those days, including the opinions of the editorial writers of the *New York Times*—blasted the conformity of that flossy little village, scandalizing it, earning its disapproval, though it was agog at what they saw and heard.

We children were aware and unaware of these (to us) strange reactions. We were different—that much, as I've said, we knew—and we were proud of it. We were ourselves agog at some of Father's acquaintances from the adventurous past, imparting verisimilitude to what we had partly absorbed as fable. Diminutive Cecilio Velasco with his close-trimmed mustache (and his stout wife and their many children) fascinated me, because I had heard Father refer to him as the bravest man he had ever known, and I remember studying him closely in my literal child's fashion in an effort to pry out the secret of his grit, as though it were a physical attribute he concealed somewhere on his person (out of modesty). He spoke a rapid, velvety Mexican Spanish, scarcely moving his lips and scarcely ever raising his voice, and we harkened to him attentively, impressed by how our father bent an untiring ear to the man who had been his accountant and close associate. They spoke about a politics and political figures that were already fading into obscurity and absolutely alien to our, his children's, ken. What Will Buckley saw in that little fellow who did not speak a word of English was mysterious to the summer-resident community. They must have been bemused also by the semiannual visits of the Warren Smiths of Caracas, Father's partner and Mother and Father's close friends. Frederica Smith was an Otis, of the San Francisco Otis elevator family, which was respectable enough, though she nevertheless provoked Father's alternating despair and mirth by proclaiming herself a Communist. "Why, Frederica," he exclaimed one evening at supper, "you have *five* fur coats in your closet, *five,* I counted them!—and you call yourself a Communist!"* (She was unfazed; she was one of the kindest and most loving of souls I have ever encountered.) Warren Smith was a South Carolinian by birth, son of a theater manager. He was portly when I first knew him and battled unsuccessfully life-long with his weight, trying diet after diet, ingesting massively of each (half a dozen whole carrots at lunch, for example), which quite defeated the purpose except in the case of the carrots tinting his white redhead's skin with a yellowish cast, causing him for a while to look as though he suffered from jaundice. He was an uncommonly handsome, fine-featured, silver-maned gentleman, who dressed in such fashion as to provoke Father's amazement (and Mother's amused affection), typically decked out in white buck shoes, lavender silk socks, a suit of aquamarine blue shantung with a double-breasted jacket sporting large mother-of-pearl buttons, a vivid blue silk handkerchief in the breast pocket, and a silver ruby-eyed elephant's head and trunk as a boutonniere,† a mauve silk dress shirt with a white detachable collar, Brazilian amethyst cufflinks, a purple four-in-hand of shot silk, and a diamond-and-black pearl stickpin that flashed at a distance of fifty paces. He used a gold-headed malacca

---

* He probably exaggerated: maybe there were two coats and a wrap.
† Nothing to do with the GOP, he had become a Venezuelan citizen; he just had a passion for elephants.

walking stick for his game leg and was altogether a sight not often to be met with in Sharon, Connecticut, or, for that matter, in New York, Paris, London, Madrid, Rome, Mexico City, and Caracas.

There were Father's motley intellectual friends and acquaintances, the Mexican poet and diplomat García Naranjo; the libertarian Albert Jay Nock, whose writings were to become formative for our brother Bill; and the Jew of Russian descent, Frank Chodorov, author and polemicist in the libertarian conservative school, who became one of my mentors and whom I loved dearly. My personal triumph was to bring the diminutive Cleanth Brooks and his wife, Tinkum, to visit Sharon for a weekend, he the coauthor (with Robert Penn Warren) of *Understanding Poetry*, the Bible of the New Criticism, which, as an aspiring poet, I read and read and read. Bill brought such as Jim and Marcia Burnham (he best known at the time for *The Managerial Revolution*), Frank and Elsie Meyer, John Chamberlain, Willmoore Kendall, Willi Schlamm, and other founding intellectuals of *National Review*, all of whom thought, spoke, and wrote heresy to respectable folk.

Almost as exotic to our neighbors were our close blood relations, who visited every year or so. Louisianian or Texan, they were utterly removed from the culture of New England and New York, their voices a melodious balm to the harsh Yankee intonations of Sharon's summer folk, who sounded always to my childish ears as though they were giving orders to march somewhere. The major difference between our parents and these people was Mother and Father's cultural cosmopolitanism and their New England/New York bourgeois provincialism. Our wealthy neighbors had all endured the Grand Tour at one time or another, which was how many of them thought of it, a necessary nod to culture, notwithstanding that Paris and London and Rome were striking for their backwardness and inconveniences. They would not have considered for one minute visiting Mexico, which was to them as strange a land and culture as Tibet. By contrast, my father had lived and worked for extended periods of time abroad, got to know the people, read their literature, cultivated their acquaintance, which is worlds different from touring foreign lands as a voyeur. My parents had seen and heard and read and experienced so much that was so very different from the Northeast of the United States that they had worlds to talk about, as did almost everyone who visited them. Father's brothers had themselves led exciting lives, or, as was the case of Uncle Edmund, the youngest of his clan, continued to lead an adventurously precarious existence as oilman and entrepreneur, departing from his base in Tampico and the seventy thousand-acre spread that he called Hacienda Santa Marta,* where he and his children hunted bobcat, puma, ocelot, and (rarely) jaguar with dogs, shot innumerable ducks, doves, and bobwhite (fifty coveys a day), lusted after by brother John (not to speak of lusting after our cousin Beryl, which he philosophically but regretfully acknowledged was forbidden).

Other than family, Great Elm's visitors ranged from international playboy brothers Reinaldo and Luis Felipe Herrera of Caracas; beautiful (I am using this descriptive too often, but I cannot help it, I am reporting) Chicha Freeman, also of Caracas, a touch sensuous for the taste of New England's matrons and too olive-skinned for New England's deep racism; tall, handsome, taciturn, one-legged George Montgomery, the WWI ace; beautiful (!) Helen Reid of the amygdaloid complexion (hey, she resembled Hedy Lamarr), daughter of Fergus Reid, and her *beau sabreur* of a husband, my stand-in godfather Jean de Lustrac, who spoke English like Charles Boyer, was a graduate of St. Cyr, and had fought and been decorated in WWI;† mysterious White Russian expatriates such as Mr. Chadinov and General Pleschkov (who, as a young man, had schooled the personal mounts of the ill-fated Czar Nicholas), as well as a wonderful and romantic White Russian concert pianist, a friend of Mr. Chadinov, whose name for some strange reason none of us is able to recall. [Bill finally came up with it, e-mailing me ecstatically: it was *Seversky*.] He had made his living playing before aristocratic music lovers in the chambers of pre-1917 Moscow and St. Petersburg palaces. He suffered from agoraphobia and was unable to perform in American concert halls. Tall, spare,

---

*He had originally purchased two hundred fifty thousand acres!

†He told me that of the graduates of his and the St. Cyr class ahead of him, just three officers survived WWI, which in part accounts for and extenuates the collapse of the French military in the face of the Nazi juggernaut. Jean Baron de Lustrac died April 1, 1973, in Norfolk, Virginia. He was Chef d'Escadron, Officier de la Legion d'Honeur, Croix de Guerre 1914–1918, Croix Militaire Beige, Membre du Comité de Cincinnati de France et Son Représentant au Comité Permanent aux États-Unis, Membre des Sons of the American Revolution.

white-haired, and aquiline of feature, Mr. Seversky spoke little at lunches, when I interacted with him, answering Mother's lively questions laconically. But when the dark mood possessed him—we never knew what triggered it—he would go into the music room and play Rachmaninoff, Rimsky-Korsakov, Tchaikovsky, Shostakovich, and Chopin, principally Chopin (he had been deemed most highly for his Chopin), on the small grand all day long, ignoring Ella when she brought in a little tray with a glass of fresh milk and a sandwich, which he never touched, though he sipped from the milk, ignoring Mother when later in the afternoon she brought in a fresh glass of milk and cookies, silently placing this beside the piano's bench on a little table, withdrawing and closing the door after her as he played on and on, all the afternoon—we children creeping in and listening to those cascades of glorious, passionate sound an hour, more, creeping silently out when we were surfeited—until at last he stopped, shutting the keyboard cover down and rising on unsteady limbs, walking stiffly, an old man, suddenly . . .

He would go directly to bed in one of the second-story guest rooms, without supper. Maureenie and I viewed him with awe; I was certain that he was destined to commit suicide, and maybe he did, because all at once, his visits ceased.

And there was also impossible Madame Spiradovich, who dressed as though her gowns had been designed by Cleopatra in the agues of a nilotic fever as reproduced by Cecil B. DeMille, in deepest sequinned black, surmounted, it seemed always, by a black-beaded turban (had she lost her hair?) from which an iridescent peacock's tailfeather sprang out at the forehead,* and whose proudest accomplishment was her having composed the song celebrating General Dolittle's raid over Tokyo, whose memorable refrain went, "Do, do, do it again, Dolittle."† When our par-

---

*Once when compelled by my father (I was ten years old) yet again to recite the "Charge of the Light Brigade" before his guests, in the patio, I sliced that peacock's tail sprouting from Madame Spiradovich's turban in half, with a swish of my toy sword—"Cossack and Russian there!"—to her fright and dismay, to my father's red-cheeked displeasure . . . but I gained my end at last, which was never to be asked to recite the poem again.

† She was an inveterate freeloader, poor thing, attending all of our many family weddings and insisting on being treated as a very special personage; that is, hand and foot. Elizabeth and Ella, Mother's black servants, were too well bred to say anything, but I know that they de-

ents' New England friends came for cocktails and suppers (eating crisp Southern fried chicken and unmushy rice and toasted buttermilk biscuits for the first time in their lives, and sipping uncomprehendingly from Father's cellar of choice burgundies and bordeaux—could one believe that this Texan had installed a *wine cellar* in the basement of the Sterling house with a capacity of several thousand bottles!) or for the Christmas Day eggnog and the New Year's Eve ball (Lester Lanin's orchestra), which these guests admitted were entertaining and became annual institutions, that New Orleans-bred Aloïse Buckley certainly was pretty and charming and knew how to put on a party and made everybody feel comfortable, and did anyone see her dance—why, her feet went so fast and she slapped her heels behind her so smartly doing the Charleston that her whole being twinkled with fun, it was indecent (fun being precariously close to indecent) . . . they could hardly wait to get back to their own blandly appointed houses that had been supervised by the most *de rigueur* New York interior decorators and tell what they had seen and heard, and how extraordinary (to put it kindly) everything about the Buckleys was.

Children will never again sled down almost two steep miles of ice-and-snow-crusted road, hitching their Flexible Flyers to milk wagons pulled by plow horses to get back up to the top of the hill. Nothing will ever replace or restore the elms of the Sharon Green. Nothing will ever replace or restore the Sterling Elm, our Great Elm. Nothing will ever restore or replace the America of the first years of her bursting upon history. Nothing will ever replace or restore our parents, Aloïse Steiner and Will Buckley, individually and bonded together one flesh, one body, one will, one devotion . . .

What a stew of sentimental rubbish. Of course, nothing will ever replace or restore what has been—the past, the individual human being with his or her genetic uniqueness and the uniqueness of his or her personal experience. I hear you. What you are spitting at me is the materialist's point of view: limited, finite, doomed . . . so very sad. The inheritance we have of our parents is

---

tested her. On the train ride back to New York from Camden (after the last of these weddings), Madame Spiradovich reached out a scaly hand toward Chicha Freeman, who went by the unpleasant old lady, saying, "Good evening, Madame Son-of-a-Beech," striding on down the aisle and endearing herself to me eternally.

not of that order, is spiritual, is Catholic, is continually renewable, is sacramental, has endured two millennia, and will be renewed, be restored, and endure into perpetuity, so long as there are individuals who within the uniqueness of their own genes and experience, and in the context of their respective ethos, respond to the same cry of the soul, which is, of course, the singular inheritance of our parents and of our country, irreplaceable and irrestorably lost to the degree only that we surrender to the philosophy of death proclaiming us nothing more than matter in motion, with no significance beyond our brief span on this earth, failing to exhibit as much soul.

NOTES

1. Father bought it at a Parke Bernet auction during the late 1940s. He frequented those auctions during the time when he and Mother were furnishing Kamschatka and when he was detained by business in New York over a weekend, averring that almost nobody attended Saturday mornings, and bargains could be had. There was doubt about the attribution. Some art connoisseurs said the painting was "of the school of Botticelli," not by the master himself. To us children, this was a pedantic quibble: the image of the Virgin shrieked of Botticelli. This may have been an impulsive purchase on Father's part. Certainly he told none of us children about it, though I won't forget his high and bashful excitement and his impatience at its being received at last and hung. We children agreed that this was one of Father's most inspired acquisitions. We loved that painting: and why we let it go out of the family in the sad auction that took place in 1982, when Great Elm was condominiumized and Kamschatka put on the block, is inexplicable to me.

2. By Julian Lamar. He was the most marvelous man. He had a studio in New York, greeting his clients in a blue painter's smock with a smudge pad, or something, held in his left hand. We were sat on a high stool. He would stare at us intently and then dart forward toward the canvas, like a fencing master, as though about to plunge a foil into it, rapidly smudging color on the canvas without ever removing his fiercely concentrated eyes from our faces, and then dart back to study us briefly before again thrusting at the canvas with his extended index finger, furiously slapping and brushing and smudging pastel tints all over it. Fifteen minutes during which we sat frozen yet astonished and delighted by the man, when he would announce, "Play time!" At which he would help lift us off the stool and conduct us to an adjoining room that was filled with every toy that a boy or girl child could imagine, from push trains to playhouses. Fifteen or twenty minutes there, and he would shout, "Painting time!" at which, with

his help, we would crawl back up onto the stools and pose for another fifteen minutes. We could see that he had been filling in the background while we played, and now, with fast, furious strokes and rubbings of the canvas, we saw emerge our very own faces and expressions that we knew were true to us, because we could feel them in the corners of our mouths and the squint of our eyes, they were so magically evoked. Two sittings, two or three hours each, and it was done.

He was a great success with the wealthy clients of his time (1930–40s), and then he disappeared for twenty years. Father suspected alcohol; my painter son Claude tells me that pastels are the most toxic medium imaginable (he will not touch them), and he would not be surprised to learn that Julian Lamar became deathly sick. All of a sudden, he turned up, in Camden, South Carolina, no less (how he found the town we do not know, it was not then well known). He painted a number of children there, and at Christmas of 1956, Father gave me a portrait of my sons Hunt (William Huntting, after his maternal grandfather), age five, and Jobie (named after me, Fergus Reid Jr.), age four. They are my happiest gifts from my father and hang in my little dining room with the portrait that Julian Lamar did of me at approximately the same age. The resemblance between father and sons is remarkable.* (Hunt was Father's first male grandchild to bear the Buckley name; Father was devoted to both boys, who were with us at Bad Gastein in the last, happy weeks of his life.)

---

*My grandson, Claude's son Aiden, now twelve, also resembles me closely as I am portrayed in the Lamar pastel.

—◦⌁◦—

CHAPTER EIGHTEEN

Sharon (VI):
Mais Pas Riche

SHARON WAS UNIQUELY BEAUTIFUL, A PARADISE FOR CHILDREN, AND, FOR our New Orleans born and bred mother, a prison that she endured uncomplainingly for fifteen years.

This is news to many, if not most, of my siblings.

She was young, just twenty-eight years old, and since Father departed every Sunday night on the train for New York and did not ordinarily get back until Friday evenings, she was lonely. In summer, there were the old-time residents, the Coleys, the Schlys, the Herricks, the Harold Hatches, the Robinsons, the Emories in West Woods, the Rhodeses, the Wrights. Several had interesting backgrounds, and they were on the whole nice folk. (Mother and we, her children, also, when we grew up, became devotedly attached to many of them.) But they were not her people. She was Southern, and the difference in her upbringing and general outlook, apart from religion, can't be adequately emphasized. We are indelibly imprinted by the ethos in which we are reared, which is, of course, influenced by climate. Snow and long winter nights have their effect on personality, chilling, numbing. Landscape also plays a part. I've noticed during the course of my lifetime that people who live in the midst of natural beauty tend to be dull by comparison: topography steals the stage. When last have you conducted a scintillating conversation with a Himalayan Sherpa? (When last have you conversed with a Sherpa from the Poconos or other lesser mountain range?) Or take the Swiss, who are on the whole innkeeping dull.* New Englanders, living in the midst of incomparable natural beauty, are similarly blighted, dull and often dour. Mother was by nature sunny (and thank God for which—for her). Let me summarize this in kindly fashion: filled with virtues though they may be, gay, spirited, and open New Englanders are not.

Mother was all those things. In the winters, there was nobody for her to talk to, other than us children, except often cranky Mademoiselle Bouchex, the Mexican nannies, who were almost always squabbling, and the help.† She was sociable, and loved to dance, but after the brilliant autumn, come Thanksgiving, the long, grim, dark winters set in, twilight descending at three-thirty in the afternoon and an often watery, pallid sun not arising until nearly eight o'clock—seventeen long hours. Mother conceded that snow was beautiful, and mentioned often how enchanting it could be to gaze out upon the lawns on moonlit evenings, the sparkle of it against the dark trunks of the great trees; but she had snow up to her delicate ankles five long dreary months, interspersed only by the wet and mud and bleakness of the periodic thaws, when the countryside reminded her of descriptions of wintertime on the moors in Hardy's novels, which are not cheery. And every other year or so, she was pregnant and bore the world another blessing, us. She loved us all devotedly, but she had no adult confident except, on rare visits from Caracas, Chicha Freeman, who was her age, and Helen Reid, who lived in Paris and New York and was also her age. The other occasional weekend guests were for the most part scandalously rich Mexicans and Venezuelans (the wives overburdened with furs and jewels). She did her spunky, ingenious best to keep up appearances, scrimping in her personal expenses where she was able, and in household accounts as well—becoming very good at the latter because she

---

*In a column dated January 9, 2007, brother Bill quotes (not approvingly) Henry James on the subject of the Swiss, who are accused of having "an insensibility to comeliness or purity of form—a partiality to the clumsy, coarse, and prosaic, which one might almost interpret as a calculated offset to their great treasures of natural beauty."

†Josefina González, "Nana," and Felipa Vilches, "Pupa," fought with each other the first year they came to Sharon, and during the thirty or forty ensuing years did not willingly address a word to each other. There were no Spanish-speaking people at the time in Sharon other than Mother, Father, and us children. Now, that's a feud!

had to be. Mother managed everything seamlessly, and to the outsider she seemed always to be living in the lap of luxury, or anyhow as she preferred. Sharon was nevertheless an exile for her.

Seventeen ever more desperate years. Mother's economic insecurity lasted from her twenty-eighth until her forty-fourth year (1923–1939), a long stretch, from mid-youth to early middle age; and this marked her in many ways. It may have contributed to her curious social insecurity, which my brother Jim noticed in the tapes I recorded of her at Kamschatka. She detested being condescended to in New York by Yankee dowagers. Her clothes were always pretty and became her, with their characteristic deep V necks and hemlines just below the knees of her lovely, slim legs, but I think not stylish, decidedly not expensive. (Hattie Carnegie and Saks Fifth Avenue or Bergdorf were the upper limit.)* In New Orleans and in Mexico, she had been a somebody. In New York and Sharon, she was that pretty, vivacious, but come-from-nowhere (that is, from Louisiana) girl with all those (excessive number of) children and almost always another on the way (she was, of course, Roman Catholic, one wasn't to forget that), married to that new-rich (as they supposed; would that he had been!) Texan oil tycoon of Irish extraction (the Irish were servants: terrible cooks, fabulous grooms, indifferent mechanics) who had been expelled from Mexico for starting a revolution—could one believe?—or for some such outlandish reason.

Mother surely resented this, for her husband as well as herself. Her Will Buckley was worth a hundred of them for all their airs and narrow Protestant provincialism to boot, and all their old Yankee money, much of which was probably accumulated by taking advantage of the South after the war,† if not in the slave trade. No hint of the hard times that she and our father were going through could in any way be *breathed* to them, or in any slightest fashion revealed. Father was fighting to maintain the grid of concessions he was in the painstaking process of acquiring in Venezuela—

---

*My sister Patricia objects here, maintaining that they were always stylish and very carefully chosen. Mother nevertheless was straitened in her ability to indulge her feminine love of finery.

†Preferential railroad tariffs. One forgets. The South was conquered. Until WWII, it cost more to ship manufactured goods on railroad lines from the South to the North than vice versa, thus helping to perpetuate Yankee economic hegemony.

concessions "spread all over the map" of the country, his partner George Montgomery wrote, but principally, critically, in the torrid jungles of eastern Venezuela. He depended on established oil companies and on wealthy risktakers to finance drilling on his ever more imaginative but also ever more desperate exploratory acquisitions; and in order to ensure a fair cut for Pantepec, he had to give the impression that he was personally well off, able to finance the whole venture himself if he cared to . . . and she would help him pull off that ludicrous charade.* Riverboat paddle steamers plied the Mississippi where Mother was reared. The ranch of the Diamond Five, King Ranch, Spindletop, and other Texan-sized bonanzas were in our father's blood. They were both gamblers born.[†]

Hence, partly, the large sprawling farmhouse and estate in Sharon, with its horses and tennis court and Olympic-size swimming pool and that truly incomprehensible patio whose fifty panes of high ceiling would surely one day be stove in by the snows (it has withstood sixty years of snow and ice, as well as sideswipes by hurricanes) . . . and also with its small herd of beef and milk cows, hogs, sheep, and chickens, apple and plum and peach orchards and the vegetable garden. These were not wholly whims or wholly reflecting Father's desire to have his children brought up in contact with natural realities. Among my earliest memories are the stench of decapitated chickens being lowered into a barrel of boiling water prior to their plucking, mixing with the sharp acid scent of the juices being crushed out of apples, the hayey, comfortable, flatulent oats scent of horses in the adjacent stables, and just beyond the stalls of the stable the acrid scents of cow urine and rich, loamy scents of liquid cow manure mixing steamily with that of the fresh warm milk being tugged from swollen teats and drilled into large tin pails (a stream of which was directed now and then at one or other of the setters sitting nobly alert behind the concrete trough, whose red tongues would wrap lusciously around their muzzles as

---

*I have myself been in cognate circumstances, though on a much less ambitious scale.

†Trisha also objects here, insisting that Mother was conservative and wished Father would settle for less in order to maintain their circumstances: which, if so, may have been the difference between being born poor (willing to risk because compelled to risk) and being born genteel, of the lower middle class (desirous of keeping what one had). I don't agree with my sister. They could not have maintained Great Elm, their present circumstances, had Father not continued to risk.

they licked the liquid up).* We even raised tiny, succulent *fraises de bois* (oh, yum, with sweet-sour *crème Chantilly!*) in the upper fields, rootlets of which Father had brought over from France.[1] My parents' guests may never have speculated to what degree we subsisted off these rustic trappings, but we slaughtered the steers and carved our beef from slabs hanging in the big walk-in freezer[2] at a lower level of the kitchen of Great Elm, cured our own hams, ate our own poultry, shucked our own corn, picked our own peas and carrots and tomatoes, pressed our own cider, drank our own milk, churned our own butter, soured our own cheese, and made our own ice cream not only from our very own peaches but also from frozen peaches (after WWII) that Father imported from Texas, none others suiting him.[†] Mother bought as little at the grocery store as possible, though there was always a surplus from Great Elm's produce to distribute to the truly poor (this was the Great Depression). I have vivid flashes of memory of visiting and bringing provisions to old Mr. Paul, of German stock, an invalid and recent widower. He had been our caretaker. His wife at one time cooked for our family, and he did yard work until he got too old. He was one of my mother's favorite persons. As a very little child, I sensed why, because kindliness emanated from him.

Mother's rare escapes to New York City during those very hard years were precious to her. Father's Mexican and Venezuelan friends, or his business partners (such as Joseph H. Himes), were lavish spenders, treating them to luncheons at such restaurants as Delmonico's. They went to "a show," as they always referred to the theater; they dined afterward at Sardi's and taxied to the Ritz or the Plaza for the dancing. Dancing was a wonderful event, hugely enjoyed by our ordinarily dignified and reserved sire, whose abilities were limited to a happy bouncing (his face spread in the silliest grin when he held a lady on a dance floor, hugely enjoying himself),[3] but especially by our mother, who was feather-light on her feet (as were her daughters, Jane and Maureen especially) and who well up into her sixties could dance a Charleston that wowed everyone watching,

---

*For a period during the war when help was scarce, sister Aloise heroically took on the burden of milking the cows, which required her to be on her feet at four-thirty A.M. Every now and then, I would join her and help in the milking, filled with admiration for my beautiful, gutsy eldest sister.

†Let me be clear about this: by "we" picking our own plums, etc., I mean the hired help did this, the groundskeepers and help attached to the dairy and stables.

even our sister Carol, forty-seven years younger than her mother and a nifty dancer herself. I learned in my late twenties (this was a rare, rare glimpse into the reality of which we children were mostly, blissfully, unaware) that one long winter she excused herself from these joyous escapes to New York, because, she told me more than thirty years after the event— half smiling, yet not desiring to make light of what she revealed to me, either (her lips trembled)—she did not possess a single black dress that had not been darned so often that it was unpresentable in the city. She chose not to confess this to our father (who, like his son my brother Bill, was absolutely unconscious of clothing and unaware of what anyone was wearing), pleading, I am guessing, the latest child in gestation. We children never knew about it. She wept in the quiet of her room.

I return, because I must, to the fauxbourdon of my parents' being that I mentioned earlier: principally, it was Mother's faith in her (and our) Lord, Jesus Christ, whom she loved ardently, and in only lesser degree her faith in Will Buckley, whom she believed in and loved only less ardently, that sustained her these great many years—they must have seemed endless to her—during which her youth was consumed and on any given Friday evening, after supper, when we children were gone to bed, in the privacy of the two-bedroom suite they had, she could not be sure that Father might not say to her, "Aloïse, Pantepec is bankrupt, and so am I. I can't continue. It's the Depression, nobody has any money, and those who have it won't risk it. I don't know what I will do, my beloved Aloïse, but we must sell this place, let Mademoiselle and maybe one of the Mexicans go, and move . . . I don't know where, maybe back to Austin, start over at . . . I just don't know what to tell you."

My sister Maureen and I had a glimpse into the precarious reality of our parents' existence at this time.

NOTES

———

1. Respecting which, what a con he pulled on Maureen and me. We told him we wanted to earn money. "All right," he said, "why don't you pick some of those strawberries?" "How much will you pay us?" at once asked Maureen, direct as usual. "Why, what would you say to fifty cents a pail?" "Fifty cents a pail!" we both exclaimed. A fortune.

So we hurried to the stable, purloined a couple of pails, and set off for the hillside. Three hot and sweaty hours later, hands and arms stained purple with mashed juice, and furious with our crafty father, we quit, both pails less than a third full. *Fraises de bois* are as tiny as they are delicious.

2. In which, as a five- or six-year-old, I was once inadvertently locked. I had trailed my older siblings in to view, as I recall, a pair of cock pheasants John had shot in the Hart swamp. I was peering, fascinated, at the beautiful birds when the others trooped out, the central light bulb in the ceiling was suddenly extinguished, and the heavy door was slammed shut and bolted. I recall the blackness, the silence, the feel of the frozen carcasses of beef that my hands flung out desperately to collide against, my cries, and the terrible cold that all at once descended on me. I knew almost from the start that it was useless to shout more, that they could not hear me through that massive door. When one of my sibling bethought him- or herself to ask rhetorically, "Where's Reid?" and another cried, "Oh, my God, he is in the freezer," and I was let out, maybe ten minutes later, half numbed with cold, I had never felt such affection or received so much attention (for such an extended number of *days*) from the people I loved most, and so the experience was worth every frightening minute of it!

3. Father heartily approved of dancing. This activity took him straight back to his youth in Austin. At weddings or balls or other festive family affairs, he irritated us children always by saying, "[John, Jimmy, Billy, Reid,] why aren't you on the floor? Why, when I was your age, you wouldn't have found me standing aside for a *minute!*" Dancing was one of the few social pleasures he and his generation regularly enjoyed. It cost nothing; if someone was paying for the pianist or the fiddler, one *danced!*

William Frank Buckley of Texas (IX): Indian Suit

MY FATHER WAS UNFAIR TO ME ONCE ONLY, WOUNDING ME MORE DEEPLY than he ever suspected.

This was in February or March of 1939, when, unbeknownst to Maureen and me, he was at the nadir of his fortunes. Nothing had turned out right for him. Every well he drilled was dry. There is nothing more useless nor so starkly testifying to vain hope than a eight-inch-diameter, three thousand-foot-deep hole in the ground.

Expenses kept compounding as his children grew. He had bought the ruin of Kamschatka, in Camden, South Carolina, and he had begun renovation. His credit was running out, not yet personally but in the pitiless aeries of financial assessment. Nine years before, he had proposed a deal to a French moneybags with the Italian name of Marcovici, who had accepted and who had written him a check for $2.5 million, which was to finance Pantepec's Venezuelan explorations. This was a tremendous stroke of good fortune for Father. I am able to guess only what that sum represents in current dollars, but $20 million is probably a low estimate. The next day, Tuesday, the great stock-market crash shivered half the Western world. Marcovici's wife came to the house my parents then rented in Paris, asking Father, in Mother's presence, whether he had cashed her husband's check. Father answered that no, as a matter of fact (that was probably his exact language), he had not. Madame Marcovici then said that if Father presented that check to the bank, her husband (and she and their children) were ruined. Father did the only thing that I believe he was capable of doing to be able to live with himself: he lifted that check out of his billfold and in her presence tore it up . . . and with it the funds he needed to keep Pantepec afloat.[1]

There had not been a bonanza since. Union Oil had drilled on nearly 1 million acres of Father's oil concessions, nothing; California Petroleum Company had drilled on another set of approximately 757,000 acres of Father's concessions, dry. A French banker had loaned Pantepec $1 million, which, though less than half the $2.5 million he had thought he had secured from Marcovici, was a coup in postcrash times, when the entire investment world was leery of speculation; but by the early 1930s, Pantepec had accumulated more than $2 million of debt, its stock was being traded for six cents a share, and nothing, nothing—dry hole after dry hole.[2]

It was meanwhile a sparkling Sunday afternoon, the temperature forty or fifty degrees, and we had driven out to visit the farm in White Hollow, about six miles north of Sharon. Father would take the train that evening to the city and be away the whole week long. We walked across the upper meadows of the hillside farm, our shoes crunching through the crust of melting snow to the sodden ground beneath, Mother braving the terrain in her high heels, as always, which she had encased in rubber booties. Maureenie and I ran ahead and shouted and gamboled. Our parents paid little attention to us. They were engaged in discussions the seriousness of which we sensed, the import of which we were ignorant of. A ruffed grouse, with the sound of a thunder clap and the suddenness of a bolt of lightning, burst out of a tall hemlock in which bittersweet vines still offered their browned fruit, whirring its wings so fast they were a blur as it soared into the blue sky, and then, with its banded tail widespread and guiding it like a rudder, glided the half-mile of the hillside down to the stream at its base, vanishing into a copse of red spruce. "Look, oh, look!" we shouted; but our parents barely responded to the heart-stopping event, smiling, nodding . . . continuing their conversation.

So it went when we visited the cow barn and inspected the new heifers, the huge, ferocious Guernsey bull in its separate pit, the hogs, and the pheasant runs. Maureenie and I exclaimed over this and that; our mother and father continued distracted. On the drive home, I said, "Let's sing!" I loved to sing. I had a high, clear voice, and sometimes on early spring mornings at Great Elm, I was so filled with the beauty of the grounds and the two-hundred-year-old elm trees everywhere that I glanced that song would burst out of my chest, and I would walk and run those acres of lawn, turning somersaults and singing a tuneless happiness at the top of my lungs all the way up to the swimming pool and beyond. "Oh," said our mother from the front seat, "yes, Reid, yes, Maureen, do sing. That would be lovely, Will, wouldn't it?" "Yes," our sire responded, less certainly, his mind elsewhere. Mother had a true, sweet voice. We sang Mexican ballads that Father ordinarily enjoyed listening to, even with his children massacring them. We did not know whether he was tone deaf or his shyness simply prevented him from joining us, but I never heard him sing a note. He endured our concert for several miles along the then-treacherous curves of the narrow White Hollow Road, when Mother and he returned to their conversation, of which Maureen and I understood nothing. I resented being left out of it. How did the subject of birthdays come up? We were approaching brother Jim's birthday, on the ninth of the month, and Mother's, on the eleventh. Since Father would be in town all week, not to get back until late the next Friday afternoon, did Mother suggest he buy a sweater or maybe even a new Peterson's guide to the birds for our ornithologist brother?

"I know what I want for *my* birthday!" I butted in. "I want an Indian suit with a bow and arrows and a knife and . . ."

To hear my father reach back with his deep voice and say, "Has it ever occurred to you, Reid, that you might earn the money to buy yourself an Indian suit?"

Earn the money? At what? I was not yet nine years old! The words cut me to shreds, silencing my heart, bringing tears to my eyes. "Will!" I heard from my mother in the sharpest rebuke that ever came forth from her mouth. "Oh, Will, how can you have said such a thing!"

I had been difficult to put up with the whole excursion, impetuous, talkative, overflowing with high spirits. She knew that I had been stricken mortally, turning at once to me from the front seat. "Pay no attention to your father, Reid, you'll have your Indian suit. It's just that he is concerned about business, which you are too young to understand—which *he* should have understood. Oh, shame on you, Will Buckley!"

Such words from our mother addressed to our father we children had never dreamed of hearing. Even Maureen was awed. ("See what you did!"

she whispered to me.) The rest of the ride passed in silence, every one of us miserable (except Maureenie, who was delighted that I had been rebuked). On getting out of the car at the front entrance of Great Elm, Father said to me, "I apologize, Reid." But he was still angry, I knew, and I felt rock-bottom awful.

As I've mentioned, his fortunes were at rock bottom that long late winter of 1939. Everything—his whole future, our future and welfare—was staked on a well in the jungles of eastern Venezuela that was due to be spudded in within the month. He had nobody in whom he could confide about this, except Mother, and she did not dare to confide in him her unhappiness, piling an additional burden on the many he bore silently and alone. They were an indissolubly bonded pair: they fought alone, having only each other. Maybe it was at this time that he was forced to borrow against Grandmother Steiner's life insurance. I've never been sure about that, but the desperateness of his circumstances must have been terrible. Our eldest brother John told of overhearing our parents in their hotel room in Paris one evening when they got back from some business supper (this would have been in 1938 or earlier), Father asking Mother, "Aloïse, how much money do you have in your pocketbook?" I forget her reply. Fifty, one hundred francs? "Well," he said to her, "that's all we have."* Maybe this recollection is faulty, an exaggeration, but it is an accurate indicator of his struggle, which persisted for years and years and years, and of which, saving these rare and imperfectly understood breaches, we children were kept oblivious.

The hurt of his snapped remark endured a long time. His words distanced me from him.

That next week, in the mail, I received an Indian suit that Sitting Bull would have envied.

---

*Warren Smith told me of walking with Father one morning in Paris following an expensive supper they had both hosted the previous evening for potential investors, none of whom stepped up to the plate. "Smith," he said to my godfather, "how much money do you have in the bank?" My godfather replied, "I am down to less than two hundred dollars. You?" Father nodded, he said, and then smiled, saying, "I guess that's just about how much Aloïse and I have left." The Smiths were compelled to return to Caracas; Father somehow hung on, continuing to seek financing.

NOTES

1. We heard versions of this story in our teens, never from Father; it is recorded in its essentials by Douglas Reed, the British journalist. The question pops up: What was William Buckley doing with a $2.5 million check in his pocket without depositing it at once? This money was vital to his company. The answer is that he was not in Paris when the great crash occurred; he was in Madrid. My godfather, Warren Smith, his close friend and partner, told me that he and his wife, Frederica, along with Mother and Father, watched the ticker tape in Madrid's Palace Hotel clicking out the collapse. "My God, Will, I am wiped out," Warren Smith exclaimed. He didn't mention what Father said in reply, but it might well have been a wry "I never had the money to put into the market in the first place." (He may have smiled, though he surely commiserated with my godfather—and I, possibly conceived that night—was born in the first year of the Great Depression, almost exactly nine months later.)

   I reconstruct events that took place on a Tuesday evening, European time, in October 1929. The check that burned in Father's wallet was, maybe (probably?), signed by Marcovici on a late afternoon meeting/bargaining session after banking hours, say Friday. Mother and Father took the night train to the Spanish border at Irún, thence changing trains to Madrid (different-gauge tracks), arriving Saturday maybe in time for lunch and meeting the Warren Smiths there, in the lounge of the Palace Hotel, where my godfather had reserved rooms because he, like Father, did everything in a grand manner. What the object of the weekend stay in Madrid might have been I do not know. But a check of that amount written against a French account could not be casually deposited in a Madrid bank; Father would have waited until he returned to Paris, maybe that Thursday following the crash. He would have arrived in the evening. This gave Madame Marcovici time to learn the terrible extent of her husband's ruin . . . and to decide to go to William Buckley (without her husband's knowledge, I suspect, though I do not know why).

   Something else seems to be missing from this story: I have not heard anywhere of a single expression of gratitude from either Marcovici or his wife, which is in such shocking contrast to the gratitude of the many humble people whom my parents helped. I am now seventy-six years old—God save the mark—and do not wonder at the partiality my parents felt for the poor.

2. Writes Mr. Montgomery: "During this period of agony, an incident indelibly painted for me the stalwartness of W.F.B. in the face of overwhelming odds and seemingly certain destruction. In the small office staff which W.F.B. maintained, there worked a boy of about twenty, who served in a variety of capacities, as messenger, telephone operator, receptionist, and general handyman. One morning while I was seated with W.F.B., the boy, Robert, came into the office and diffidently informed W.F.B. of his mother's illness and his need of a raise. Knowing the desperate financial straits of W.F.B.'s affairs, I silently commiserated with Robert on the futility of his request. To

my utter amazement, W.F.B. not only offered Robert's mother help with genuine sympathy and concern, which was predictable in him, but complied instantly with Robert's request, putting into immediate effect a raise higher even than what Robert had asked for." This instinctive splendidness is characteristic of our brother Bill.

One is reminded of the story Cecilio Velasco told about Father's imprudent generosity, when he lent a Mexican friend five thousand pesos he did not have, compelling him to take out a bank loan. Mr. Montgomery adds, "How many burdens of this sort W.F.B. voluntarily took on without visible evidence of concern, I do not know. I do know that without his advice and assistance during the speculative days which found me as feverishly enmeshed as any other little speculator, I would have been completely submerged myself. And that goes for a great many other people." There may have been no visible evidence of concern, but it was there, gnawing at him all the time. Which he permitted no one except Mother to know . . . whose courage was equal to his.

Aloïse Steiner of New Orleans and William Frank Buckley of Texas (II): Storm on the High Seas

———— ◌⁀◌ ————

THE YEARS 1938 AND 1939 WERE TURBULENT FOR OUR PARENTS, OSCIL-
lating sharply between dread and joy, the bodings of war endangering the
republic and, more personally, son John (eighteen), son Jimmy (sixteen),
son Billy (thirteen),[1] the trial of faith that Mother and Father were put to,
Mother's close scrape with death, the birth of their eleventh and last child,
the decision to take up a second residence in South Carolina (spelling the
end of Mother's exile), and the glorious vindication of Father's acumen,
foresight, courage, and gamble.

Mother conceived for the twelfth time* in February of 1938, and by
March, shortly before or after her forty-third birthday, knew that she was
once again pregnant. I have no idea of her medical history, or when her
pregnancy was pronounced a grave health risk, but I do know that longtime personal friend and family physician Dr. Max Touart—a delightful
man—counseled her that her condition was dangerous. One New York
City obstetrician, my sister Patricia remembers, suggested that she "lose"
her baby, whereupon she found another doctor.†

This personal crisis took place when Father was at his wits' ends trying

_____

*She had had one miscarriage after giving birth to Allie; Mary Ann, between me and Patri-
cia, died in the cradle a week after being born.
†Our sister Carol is very happy she did so. I used this choice in *Saving DeSaussure Swamp: A
Love Story*, and it was partly the ambivalence of the expectant mother, purely social, in that
novel that engendered the succeeding two novels, *Stump* and *Marbella*!

to keep Pantepec afloat. We children tend to forget this, or to take it for granted, because he never spoke of business to us at home, and he never complained. All options had seemingly run out. Well after well had come in dry. His reputation on the Street was at its nadir. Now his wife was in peril from an unexpected pregnancy. The stress was acute. We need to think back to before the era of the jet engine.* Father might be obliged to sail to Caracas to keep his eye on developments, which wasn't too bad, a two-day boat trip only, but in the ever urgent pursuit of financing, he had to be prepared also to travel to Paris and London. Once more, in those days, this wasn't a nine-hour flight; it was at best a five-day trip by ocean liner. But Mother seemed fine that summer, escorting her daughters Aloise and Priscilla to Austria.

Carol was born on November 12, in New York, a tiny but very pretty infant, and Mother survived, her and Father's faith rewarded. Then, some weeks after the birth, when no one was psychologically prepared for it and everything seemed fine, Mother came down with a fever. Maybe she began hemorrhaging, I do not know. Her condition was related to her pregnancy and the birth, whatever it was, and it worsened. Jane and Bill and Trisha were in England, the girls deposited in St. Mary's Sacred Heart convent school, Bill in Beaumont. Trish tells me that when they went to daily Mass, as required by their schools, Billy (I don't know how she knows this, I suppose Bill confided it to her—they were very close) kneeled on the hard rail of the pew from beginning to end of the sacrifice, as an offering for Mother.

What follows I remember dimly but strongly, though Patricia is adamant that it never happened, because—my dear sister says—"she [Mother] and Father would *never* have done *this*." But she wasn't there, she was in England. What I relate is imprinted in my memory.

Mother's condition had become alarming. We were taken to New York to bid her farewell. (The visit was not put in these terms.) I was just eight, but I recall sharply my wonderment at the solemnity of everyone. Nana and Pupa, dressed in their city black, were tearful, and I recall the shock of seeing my mother in bed, looking so very pale,† her voice, though soft and

---

*I am still in awe of the oceans. My children hop them as though they were ponds.

†I am absolutely certain that even though her visitors were her children, and despite the gravity of her condition, she had slashed her lips bright red, if not rouged her cheeks also.

loving, weak. That was an awful period, our entire world threatening to cave in, because whereas Father was our hero, Mother was everything else to us. Existence was inconceivable without her.

But she came through. I am certain that God rewarded our parents' faith and trust; and the happy event of little sister Carol's birth marked the turning point in their lives, for the rest of which, aside from Father's crippling stroke in 1954 and consequent death four years later in 1958, at a ripe age, they were blessed by God with an overflowing measure of earthly happiness. In their minds—and this filtered down to the least of us—there was no question that they owed everything to God, nor was there question in our minds that they had earned happiness through their moral virtue. Our God was a merciful and loving God, *who liked fun* and did not deny His children some measure of joy on this earth. Which made Him different from the God other Christians we knew worshiped.*

Janie, Bill, and Trisha did not get home until the monthlong (in England) Christmas holidays. After which—Mother fully recovered and Carol blooming at nearly three months old—Jane, Bill, Trish, Maureen, and I, with our tiny sister, under the supervision of both Nana and Pupa and also Mademoiselle, steamed with our parents to Cherbourg on the good ship *Paris*, and from there trained and boated to London.

Those of us who were aboard remember that sea voyage. A fearful storm—an unseasonable hurricane—struck us when we were three days out. How the *Paris* shook and shuddered! She was steel-clad but still carried wooden beams and bulwarks, which creaked loudly with every steep roll, at first lulling us to sleep. (I dreamed of swinging on a line from the topmost mast of a sleek corsair and sweeping Linda Darnel out of the evil grasp of Basil Rathbone and back to safety on my poop deck.) The storm came at us from the stern, portside. I remember peering out the portholes of our double cabin and seeing the gray seas outside rise like a mountain range (my stomach rising with them), twice the height of the ship, into whose frothing chasm we were plunging (my stomach ditto), and the sensation of the water passing under our keel and lifting the entire ship high before we again plummeted into the abyss while another fearful mass of

---

* That so many of the Episcopalian and Presbyterian children with whom we grew up in Sharon ceased practicing their nominal religions and ceased believing in Christ God did not greatly surprise us.

water, its numberless combers on the surface lashed by the wind and shredding foam, rose up to overtook us, breaking and crashing down upon us. The limited view I had out the porthole of our cabin was suddenly and terrifyingly wiped out under a wash of murky water as we rolled over to starboard and teetered, as it seemed, beyond hope of recovery. A sister ship of the *France*, the *Paris* was not a large vessel as ocean liners go, 233 meters long, 26 meters wide at the beam—I'd guess two-thirds the size of the *Normandie,* not half the *Queen Mary*, but she nevertheless displaced 34,569 gross tons, and the way she was wrenched about by the storm was impressive even to a boy, her screw raised screaming out of the water* as her bow plunged into the seas, everything on the topdecks that could not be secured swept overboard or smashed. We were confined to our cabins as the storm waxed hourly more severe. Heroic stewards managed to bring us soup and *les sandweech* for lunch, but there was no supper. Rosaries dribbled from everybody's hands. Mademoiselle was praying loudly and lachrymosely in French, Nana and Pupa rattling out Hail Marys in Spanish, Mother in English, and the rest of us in a mix of tongues. With every roll, Carol's crib rocketed from one side of the cabin to the other, and we had to secure it, wedging it against the open interior door connecting to Mother and Father's cabin and with ropes tying it to Maureenie's and my bunks at the other end.

This was the captain's first command, I was to learn. It might easily have been his last. Late on the second day of the storm, we were all called up on deck, men, women, and children, with our life jackets strapped about us, because the captain expected that we were going to capsize. Three times (he related to our parents after the storm) the *Paris* in fact heeled over beyond the point of no return, and three times a giant wave came smashing at her from the other side, righting and saving her. On the way topside, we ran, fell, crawled (scrambling on hands and knees), and walked on the bulkheads—I remember that distinctly, the wonder of it, we were walking on *the sides*, the *walls*—of the long corridors, first port, then starboard, then port again, and so forth. I read now that the "*Paris's* innards reflected much of the classical grandness of" the *France*, but there was little evidence remaining of this splendor toward the end. My sister Patricia takes issue with me, saying we were never allowed out of our cab-

---

*As I was told later. As must be obvious, I dug up her statistics for this account.

ins; it was too dangerous—that we only heard the crash of plates and were told of other damage by the steward. She was three years older, eleven, and presumably has a clearer memory than mine, but I saw what I saw.[2] Lurching along the corridor, I had a peek through a long rectangular window at one of the dining rooms, seeing the chairs all flung about and the round tables torn up from the floors, exposing their long screw bolts. It was somehow indecent and shocked me. I could not have imagined this image. And it would have been surprising for the captain to impound passengers in their cabins when he expected the ship to capsize—to drown trapped like rats. No; it was night, and curiously warm, and the hopelessness of the situation was evident even to me and Maureen, because there were two or three thousand of us passengers and crew, and it was clear that no way would the sailors be able to launch lifeboats, which were swinging wildly on their divots, nor, if they were launched, would we passengers be able to board them. The *Paris* was going to be swallowed by the ocean or tossed belly-up, and all of us were going to be flung into those monster waves and drowned.*

The crisis may have lasted two or three hours, after which we were permitted to return to our cabins, which, like the rest of the ship, were in shambles. The ordeal lasted eight or nine hours more,† the wind bit by bit slackening, the waves subsiding into deep green and purple, still angry, swells. I recall the groans of despair of my elder sisters Jane and Trisha, because the storm had accelerated the ship's passage, and we were now scheduled to arrive in Cherbourg at two or three in the morning instead of at noon. *Quel dommage!* ‡

IT WAS SOMETIME IN THIS PERIOD, 1938–1939, THAT MOTHER AND FATHER bought Kamschatka and began renovation of the rotting old hulk.

---

*I remember thinking how wonderful and courageous the French crew were, from common sailors to officers, who were solicitous and maintained miens of optimism and cheer throughout.

†I drew heavily on this experience for the hurricane and shipwreck scenes of my novel, *Eye of the Hurricane.*

‡The *Paris* was scuttled three years later in the port of Le Havre in order to block German transportation. I remember seeing the newsreel shots of her, on her side, and feeling sorrow, because she was a beautiful and doughty ship.

And it was springtime in 1939, in Camden, that Mother got the telegram. It spoke two words only: "ALOISE, OIL."

NOTES

1. All three would serve. John in the Army as a second and then a first lieutenant and in a very special way that will be explained. Jim as an ensign and then lieutenant junior grade in the Pacific, where he took part in many battles on his LST. Bill as a conscript right out of Millbrook School and then an officers' candidate in Fort Benning, who was among many of thousands of green troops in California expecting to be shipped to Japan for the terrible assault, in which an estimated 1 million American soldiers and 2 million Japanese would be killed, a fate American troops and millions of Japanese were spared by Harry Truman's decision to drop the A-bomb.

2. Are you able to imagine what redheaded adamancy is? White hot. My dearest and beloved sister Patricia scored the first four lines of the paragraph describing the aftermath of the storm with five diagonal strokes, writing in the margin a stormy "Just didn't happen." But it did, and largely as I re-create it, because there are too many details—the queasiness from gazing at the storm through the porthole, tying up Carol's crib, walking on the bulkheads, seeing the ravaged dining room, the fear and realization of impending death by drowning when we were on the topdeck—that could not have been invented, though their order of occurrence may have been different.

PART FIVE

Kamschatka, 1939– 1989: The Happy Years

—❦—

CHAPTER NINETEEN

Camden (I):
A Peculiar Town

*"Breakfasted at an indifferent house 22 miles from the town [Columbia]—
the first we came to. . . . The road from Columbia to Camden, excepting a
mile or two at each place, goes over the most miserable pine barren I ever
saw, being quite a white sand and very hilly.*

—From George Washington's Diary,
on his second-term presidential visit to Camden.

*"This is the kind of small, blueblooded southern town romantic Yankees
imagine, homesick Southerners pine for and Noel Coward might have been
amused by. . . . Along its broad, shady streets, in its rambling antebellum
mansions, wrapped in deep, pillared piazzas and pale wisteria, life in
Camden proceeds at the merrily eccentric tilt of a 250-year-old society
confident of what matters most: horses, dogs, good fellowship and good
manners . . . Camdenites don't put much stock in the pretentious or the
flash . . . There may be an unusual number of Mercedes–Benz station wagons bumping over the dirt roads here, but even they are usually discreetly
coated with a layer of dust."*

—From "Camden: A Class Menagerie," Lisa Anderson, *W,* 1983.

I HAVE BEEN ASKED, WHY DID YOUR PARENTS PICK THE FORLORN LITTLE city of Camden in the midst of nowhere, and in the nothing state of South Carolina, to retire to, when they had lived in New York and Mexico City and Caracas and Paris and London, not to speak of ritzy winter resorts in Switzerland, and now could have chosen any place else in the civilized world? What was the unique attraction of Camden?

I am at pains to answer that question . . . except, in my parents' defense, by offering the following.

MY PARENTS HAPPENED TO STRIKE CAMDEN AT ITS HUMAN ZENITH, when it was a happy place like few others, and when the tolerance and civility and physical good looks of the people were unmatched.

People of my generation all recall the DeLoach widows, with their snowy white hair, who drew gasps of admiration from everyone young and old for their straight backs and undiminishable beauty into their late eighties. As for tolerance and civility, Camden had welcomed Quakers and Jews back in the 1700s, had recently welcomed Catholic Lebanese settlers. A large Catholic family like ours was no strain on the cordiality of the natives.

The people of Camden were churchgoing, but their attitude toward religion might be described as an easy familiarity in contrast to the strict censoriousness of New England. There is a town on South Carolina's northerly coast, near Myrtle Beach, called DeBordieu, meaning "beside, or near to, God." It's pronounced "Debbydo," which would have driven New Englanders into paroxysms of antiblasphemous frenzy. I visited a bird-dog trainer near Scape Hore Swamp one winter, to purchase two pointer bitches from him. He explained the origin of the swamp's name. There was apparently a merry wench back in colonial times who gave the yeoman farmers in the area surcease from their hard lives; but she was one day arrested by the sheriff and tossed into the local brig, there to await trial and sentencing for her lewd behavior. Prostitution was a capital offense at the time, and it grieved this lady's clients to imagine her twisting from her pretty neck on a hempen rope. So one night, they broke into the jail, released her, and conducted her to safety and freedom through the thick wetlands, where the sheriff's bloodhounds would lose her scent. It was known as Escape Whore Swamp, in those plainer-speaking days.

When my parents arrived in Camden, the people were just beginning to enjoy a new prosperity. An acre of delta soil in 1859 fetched one hundred gold dollars; a slave was worth one thousand eight hundred dollars in gold. Following Appomattox (when black human beings were no longer capital assets) and the penitential years of Reconstruction, arable land did not again, until the 1940s, fetch in excess of fifty cents *paper money* an acre, which was when the pulpwood business began the resurgence of Southern agrarian fortunes. Camden had survived Reconstruction by grit, caste, and Spartan living and thanks to the winter resort business that was the salvation of so many mid-Atlantic towns of the era, Aiken, Pinehurst, and Southern Pines among them. Winter-weary Yankees rattled down South in railway carriages to enjoy pine-scented zephyrs; fox hunting; polo; steeplechase racing; dove, quail, and turkey shooting; the gorgeous efflorescence of the springtime azalea season; and Southern women, oh, indeed, Southern women, who were a revelation to folk of blue-nose stock. Camden developed a rurally oriented, country-squire way of life that was rich in satisfactions and redolent with self-satisfaction, once the hard, sharp, bitter memories of the "recent unpleasantness" had begun fading. Along with pulpwood, the migration beginning in the 1950s of Northern industry to Southern climes brought about the expanded opportunities and prosperity the "New South," which have been good for the Southern pocketbook but in many respects not so good for the Southern soul. The civil rights revolution laid Jim Crow low, and that awful period is now recalled by Southerners with embarrassment and even horror.*

The town—along with much of the rural South—has nevertheless remained in tone patrician; among its important characteristics are reverence for tradition, a prickly sense of honor, pride of family, disdain for riches, and a tolerance for—a glorying in—eccentricity. This must have particularly attracted my father, as it did me. Our family ties to Camden go back three score years plus, and for the past nearly forty years, I have called South Carolina my home. I have never (since childhood) felt at home elsewhere, except for my long sojourn in Spain, where I reveled in a people with the same high sense of honor, independence of spirit, wit, and attachment to lost causes, principal among which is themselves. Tradi-

---

* Alas, not all white Southerners have had a change of heart.

tions were quick in accreting in colonial and postcolonial Camden and were at once cherished. Equal in importance to upholding the honor of name and family were good manners and a good-humored disdain for life and property. The second people of quality held cheap, the first dear, and so risked it in deadly contests of honor.

Dueling was frequent. The story is told by Kirkland and Kennedy of a meeting on the field of honor between two "hotspurs," Colonel James P. Dickinson and Major John Smart, described as crack shots. According to Kirkland and Kennedy, "Two fires were exchanged and neither hit. [Major] Smart being the challenger was therefore asked according to code rules: 'Are you satisfied?' 'Disgusted,' he replied, which the authors note, was a response whose jocularity . . . ended hostility." (Smart later observed, "In practice I could hit a sapling the size of my wrist every fire, and Dickinson could too, but then the sapling was not armed.")

A major attraction for my parents, I am sure, was the South Carolinian's indifference to money compared with family. Back in the late 1940s, a pig-rich Yankee came to spend the winter months in Camden. He had a Cadillac driven by a black chauffeur. He bought himself a big house, fencing thoroughbreds, and a kennel full of setters and pointers. He bought himself three thousand acres of choice quail range down in the Manning area.

In those days, the old Camden breed of people—descendants of the Canteys and Kershaws and Whitakers—still defined the town's society. Poor they might be, but hospitable to a fault; and one December morn, this fellow was invited to stand for deer with the Boykin Hunt Club—which is a venerable institution and the font of dozens of wonderful yarns, many of them memorialized by architect Henry Boykin in two privately printed volumes. After the second drive on this particular day, a picnic lunch was held in a forest glade along the Wateree River. The Yankee went up to Stew Boykin and proudly extended to him a brand-new Weatherby rifle. "Well, Stew," he said loudly, "what do you think of this?"

Stew Boykin took the rifle in his hands. One-eyed, tall, spare, and distinguished, Stew* was a legendary shot. The Weatherby had been custom-built. It probably cost more than most well-to-do Camdenites earned in a

---

*As with his father before him, the first L.C. "Whit" Boykin, and his nephew, also L. C. "Whit" Boykin, and for that matter, most or all Boykins, it runs in the blood.

month. The trigger guard was elaborately scrolled and gilt, the trigger itself solid gold.

As Stew recounted the story, a dove was at that moment "loafing"
across the clearing. He brought the stock of the rifle to his shoulder, swung
the hooded bead of the muzzle past the dove, and fired. The dove fell
dead, decapitated.

"It's a nice gun," he observed, handing the rifle back to its stunned
owner. Stew later remarked, "I couldn't have repeated that shot in a thousand years"; but the effect of his casual display of the blood quite knocked
the stuffings out of this visitor, who within the year had sold his quail
plantation, his dogs, his horses, and that big house, and who was last seen
being driven to the Seaboard railroad station by his (grinning) black
chauffeur in the gleaming Cadillac, to board the Palmland Express back
North.

Such devastating indifference to wealth and amused attitude toward
ostentation, shared by black and white alike, is being replaced by Mam-
mon worship, alas. A portrait photograph that caught my attention in a
studio a few years ago explains the change best.

I had glanced at it on my way out; halfway to my car; I spun on my
heels and went back to study the picture. It was an arresting image, blown
up to two feet by three feet and placed on an easel near the entrance of the
shop. Its significance was quite wonderful. The subject was a honey-blond
forty-year-old bimbo of an unmistakably Southern belle type in full fox-
hunting regalia, her shimmering hair gathered in a net beneath a velvet
helmet, her effulgent bust and pinch-me waist accentuated by the snug fit
of her jacket.

There was more to it. Close under the muzzle, by the snaffle, she was
holding a silken-coated chestnut thoroughbred, whose head, neck, and
veined withers appeared in the picture. Protruding from the left of the
frame and just visible behind woman and horse was the silver hood of a
Rolls, and behind that a sweep of marble front steps and the soaring white
pillars of a brick mansion in antebellum style.

I inquired about the portrait. She was the wife of a doctor in Society
Hill. A Southern boy, he had done well for himself; and he had had his
wife's portrait taken surrounded by his other prized possessions, the sym-
bols of his self-worth.

The patterns of speech and vocabulary are being coarsened. One evening, I asked Whit Boykin, Stew Boykin's nephew and a great gentleman in his own right, as well as a legendary wing shot, about a certain person in the town. He said mildly, "That fellow was bred by a buzzard and hatched by the sun." The man had cheated him in a land swap. Whit did not call his enemy a f——— bastard or use some other vulgarity in the modern idiom. "What do you think of her?" I asked my Georgia-bred secretary and associate a year or so ago about a tough-looking lady who had been paraded into my school by a (then) member of my consulting faculty. Martha promptly replied, "She looks rode hard and put up wet to me." Which was both succinct and sufficient.

Since my parents' time, Southern society is becoming vulgarized and—worse—standardized.* Manners have decayed everywhere. When I grew up in Camden during the wartime 1940s, gas was strictly rationed. Dixie Boykin bought an elephant, ostensibly to plow his fields with, actually because it amused him to own an elephant. One evening in the 1950s, Mr. Leonard, Dixie's much-feared Yankee employer, climbed into bed with him and demanded a sip from the bottle of precious fifty-year-old Jack Daniel's that Dixie was pouring himself a nightcap out of. (Or so he recounted to my mother, who had observed at a hunt breakfast that he was looking poorly.) My father remarked dryly, "Mr. Leonard has been dead six months, Dixie." "That's just it," cried Dixie. "He was so cold and clammy, like a fish on ice! He kept saying, 'Give me a sip of that, Dixie, it's been a long time since I had a sip of that.'" "What did you do?" asked my mother, instantly concerned for Dixie's plight, never mind the improbability. "Why, Aloïse, I went down to the kitchen and got a soup bowl and poured the whole half-bottle of that precious, precious whiskey into it," he cried piteously. "And did that work?" "Oh, yes, there wasn't a drop left in the morning." "But why a soup bowl, Dixie?" inquired my mother, puzzled. "I mean," she said, "why not a glass?" "Oh, Aloïse," he replied, "don't you know? Ghosts don't drink. They laps."

---

*My pulmonologist told me when I first visited him a couple of years ago that he had met my brother Bill. "Really?" I said. "Where?" "At Princeton." "But you're Southern. What brought you to Princeton?" "That's what people ask my daddy. They say, 'Al, you sent your first son to Clemson, your second son to Carolina. Why did you send your third son to Princeton?' To which he replies, 'Well, I thought I'd like to have one son who says, "Oh, terrific" instead of "No shit." '"

⊷❧⊶

DIXIE BOYKIN WAS ALREADY CAMDEN'S LIVING LEGEND WHEN MY PAR-
ents arrived. A handsome, portly, meticulously dressed gentleman and
one-time rake, who always wore a tattersall vest, he was quite desperately
poor most of his mortal existence, a confirmed bachelor into his thirties,
whose house in town, which he shared with his bosom friend Matt Ferguson, acquired such a risqué reputation that it was given wide berth by matrons with maiden daughters. He unexpectedly married, and proceeded to
procreate one two three four five six seven eight children in about as many
years, which did not help his material circumstances. He bought Cool
Springs Plantation with it is anybody's guess what collateral; it had plenty
of room for his progeny, but with its thirty or so round white columns and
three floors, the first of which was reached by an ample gracious cascade
of a staircase with (count them!) thirty-three steps, as well as a ground-
floor English basement, not to speak of stables, it required keeping up.
My father had not yet got the idea of establishing a supper club that was
able to serve wine and spirits on Sundays,* but Dixie preceded him by
renting Cool Springs to affluent winter folk for grand suppers that he ca-
tered (he was a marvelous chef), and then by holding lavish Sunday night
buffets with huge haunches of roast beef and casseroles and other leftovers
from the Saturday night bash, to which he invited paying guests.

It was a wonderful arrangement that everybody enjoyed, including the
winter visitors who had paid Dixie the night before for the fare he was
now serving. Since Dixie was such an exuberant host, everybody drank
too much, including himself. One night, toward the end of the evening,
the poor fellow stepped into the downstairs rest room, flushed the toilet,
and then, upon straightening up, was struck by partial paralysis. He stood
there in a stoop, frozen with fear, sweat popping out all over his white
cheeks and incipient jowls. He could not straighten himself up fully. He
managed to turn around and open the rest-room door, which admitted
to the hall to one side of the staircase, and in his high-pitched voice
he shouted for help. "Whit! Stew! Baynard! Caleb! Ned! Buddy! Polk!

---

*By being a club, where everyone kept his own bottle in cubby holes (this was a sham), evad-
ing the blue laws prohibiting sale of alcohol on the Lord's Day.

McKee! Bill Wilson! Help! Ohhh, help me! I am dying!" People rushed to him, asking him what had happened. He blurted out that he could not straighten up, he was paralyzed, he was having a stroke, he was near death. Oh, help him!

Relations and friends engulfed him, porting his dear, rotund body down the back steps to a station wagon, into whose back bed they laid him tenderly, driving as fast as they were able to Dr. Andrew Whitaker's house. Dixie moaned and groaned all the way, "Jesus, Lord, I am dying! Jesus, Lord, help me!" They had to wake up tall, handsome Andrew (himself a close relation to almost everyone), who said to the men, "Bring him into my dispensary and lay him on the table . . . and the rest of you get out while I examine him."

"Oh, Andrew," whimpered Dixie, clutching his arm as he lay there on his side, in fetal position. "Am I going to die?"

"Calm down, Dixie. Now, collect yourself and tell me just what happened."

"Well, I was relieving myself in the downstairs bathroom, and when I finished, Andy, I couldn't straighten up! Is it a stroke, Andy? Am I paralyzed forever, Andy? Is it going to kill me?"

Andrew Whitaker was examining him the while. He stepped back, reaching for a very long pair of gleaming stainless-steel scissors, which he waved over Dixie, saying sternly, "Now, Dixie, I want you to shut your eyes and be a man!"

Dixie looked at those scissors and turned whiter yet. "Dear God, Andy, you ain't going to cut me with that pair of scissors as I lie here! Good God, Andy, you ain't . . ."

"Now, Dixie," said Andrew Whitaker in his sternest doctor's voice, "you do what I say, keep still, and shut those eyes tight, and do not open them until I tell you to!"

Which commands Dixie obeyed. He heard (as he related the incident), *snip, snip.* "Open your eyes, Dixie."

Which he did, to behold Andrew Whitaker extending the palm of one of his hands at him, in the middle of which rested a black button.

"What's that?" Dixie cried.

Andrew Whitaker had lost all medical authority, because he was now convulsed with laughter. "The button of your waistcoat, Dixie, damn you for waking me up in the middle of the night—that's what it is. You buttoned your vest to your fly, you old fool, *that's* why you couldn't straighten up!"

And that was it: in stooping over his little potbelly, he had by accident fastened the buttonhole of the fly to the last button of his waistcoat. "Well, I declare," said Dixie, popping off the examining table. "I'm cured!" he cried; and he went rushing out to his friends in the living room, shouting jubilantly, "Miracle! Andrew saved me. He saved me!"

Dixie was known for his elaborate pranks as well. During the great war, he and his companion in rakish doings, Matt Ferguson, let it be known that yes, they, even they, whose precincts were shunned by careful mothers with nubile daughters, had turned a new leaf: they were opening their house to refugees from Hitler's bombing of London. Bundles to and from Britain were all the rage at the time, and these victims of Nazi V2 rockets compelled the instant sympathy of all America. Camden was not going to take second place in that patriotic sentiment, and when town officials were apprised that Dixie and Matt had arranged for one dozen of these poor orphaned children to spend the war years with them, they decided that city hall would be at the railroad station to greet them upon their arrival, and that they would each be presented with a key to the city, a plaque carrying the distinctive seal of Camden, which prominently represented King Haigler, the Catawba chief who had saved the early settlement of a few hundred souls from massacre by the Cherokees, as well as a gift of ten dollars each in pocket money. The Garden Club and several churches planned an elaborate alfresco lunch in Memorial Park (it was April), and more speeches by respectable folk were scheduled.

The *Camden Chronicle* ran stories on all these plans, featuring interviews of Dixie and Matt, who had evidently reformed from being the town's bad (though well-liked) characters. Dixie blew mightily into a handkerchief as he explained in his high-pitched voice the many horrors that these girls had experienced, the screaming devastation of the rockets, the long fearful nights huddled in underground shelters, feeling the earth quake above them as the lights went off . . .

"These children are girls?" asked the reporter, interrupting.

"Oh, yes," answered Dixie, "poor, dear children."

"They are young girls, then, children?" Dixie and Matt's reputations as wild bachelors hovered in the question.

"Oh, yes, they are young," said Matt Ferguson, "but not too young, of course, to travel."

The appointed day dawned. All the town was athrob. Dixie and Matt announced that the orphans would be arriving on the noon train by way of Columbia. Camden might well have been New Orleans preparing to receive the visit of General Stephen D. Lee. A crowd of more than a hundred townfolk gathered at the station. City Hall dressed to the pins. The high school orchestra, which had been practicing British anthems for two weeks, played "Rule, Brittania!" Dixie Boykin arrived garbed resplendently in his Camden Hunt costume (he was a whip), with white breeches, black and tan boots, yellow vest, pink coat, and black silk top hat. I forget how Matt Ferguson was dressed. The train's whistle was at last heard. An excited susurrus rose from the crowd. The mayor glanced nervously at his welcoming notes. Dixie and Matt looked solemn but also excited. At last the locomotive hove into view around the bend, blaring its steam whistle and belching smoke from its stack. Everybody began cheering. The band struck up "God Save the King." The second car behind a Pullman sleeper was draped from end to end with a British Union Jack—the first to be seen in these precincts since Nathaniel Greene stood off Lord Rawdon in the Second Battle of Camden (1781), forcing Lord Cornwallis to evacuate. Everybody cheered again. The band played "The Minstrel Boy to the War Has Fled," and people became weepy. Dixie took off his top hat, placing it across his breast. The train puffed and huffed and jetted steam out its cocks as it stopped, with a sigh. A conductor swung out from the second passenger car, clanging a sturdy iron trestle down on the cement platform. Dixie reached up and took the fair hand of the first damsel, handing her down to the platform. Matt similarly took the hand of the next poor refugee . . . and soon all dozen of the girls were standing there, being greeted by the mayor and accepting in satisfyingly surprised fashion the keys to the city and the plaques and the cash gifts . . .

Everybody in the welcoming crowd on the station platform that noon hour meantime registered that these girls, every last one of them, were chewing gum. And that they were not pubescent female children but evidently mature young women. And that their lips were bright with paste, their cheeks red with rouge, their eyes dark with mascara. And that, besides all being buxom, their blouses were open to reveal the bounteousness of their endowment, and that their outfits, far from being dowdy and formless English woollen sacks, were tight-fitting and fashionable in a certain not quite respectable way. And that when the mayor asked solicitously of them, "Did you have a good voyage?" why, the first girl to descend to the platform asked back in an extraordinary imitation of a low-class cracker accent, "Ya mean from Columbia?" "No," stammered the mayor, "I mean from Liverpool?" "Where's that?" said another of the girls, smacking on her gum; and all the girls tittered and giggled, the mayor turned red of face, and everybody else looked about at the spectacle of Dixie Boykin and Matt Ferguson doubled over (as well as Dixie was able to manage that, given his rotundity) with laughter.

He and Matt had hired the imposters for the occasion, picking the toughest cookies they could find from the sales force at the Woolworth store and other emporiums in Columbia, promising them a good meal and ten dollars each. Camden being Camden, the banquet was held, the pretense was maintained, the girls ate mightily of fried chicken and rice, ice cream and cake, and enjoyed flirting with mayor, councilmen, and of course Dixie and Matt, society was offended, church ladies shunned the luncheon, the entire town rocked with laughter, and the girls were shipped back to Columbia later that afternoon, allowed to keep their ten dollars but not the plaques or the keys to the city.

I NEVER MET THE PERSON WHO DID NOT LOVE AND ENJOY DIXIE BOYKIN. Some few years later, the call resounded through the woods where Boykins and their kinsmen were hunting: "Mr. Dixie dead, Mr. Dixie dead!" It was a chill November morning. The lament bugled from driver to driver: "Mr. Dixie dead, Mr. Dixie dead!" Hunters quit their stands and gathered at a run. Polk Saunders shoved his Jeep into the clearing, braking sharply, jumping out, flushed with his sorrowful news.

He was at once besieged. "What happened to Dixie? How did he die?" Polk stammered under stress. "I dddddon't know," he said, the tears rolling down his cheeks. "He jjjust wwoke up dead!"

They are all dead: Stew, Dixie, Polk, Whit, Ned. Camden society has changed since my parents' time. After ten generations, there is no white male Whitaker left in Camden (Caleb, the last of them, moved to Palm Beach), nor is there a male Boykin (my generation of Boykins have all produced daughters) save one, who is in his forties now and unmarried, and with the demise of this generation, the name will die out among whites.* At my now advanced age, I mourn. Edwin Guy is dead, who owned vast stretches of swamp along the Wateree. Spare as a railbird, with sunken frontiersman's eyes under bushy brows, a high beak of a nose, and a prominent Adam's apple, he answered to everybody's imagination of Ichabod Crane and was dubbed Icky by man and boy. Like most of his friends, he was land poor, though his state was self-inflicted. He had inherited money from the Powe veneer company in Cheraw, where he was born and is buried, but he did love the swamps, purchasing as many acres of semiwilderness as he was able, and many more than prudence should have permitted. But inside the four walls of any parlor, he had a caged look, as though he were about to bound through an open window and escape into the wilderness. In fact, he did so regularly, hiding himself in cabins deep in his "Blue Lands," where for a week or ten days he would commune with nature and a case of Old Forester bourbon. His wife, the gracious and long-suffering Mary Tilden, would just as regularly hunt out those cabins and burn them to the ground. There were other sources of friction between them. Both were absentminded and dangerous drivers, and each accused the other of wrecking the one family automobile. (They were both quite right.) One Christmas morning in the 1950s, when the price of timberland soared in South Carolina and it was slowly registering in Icky's mind that in absentminded manner he had become a millionaire, he brought Mary Tilden to the window of their bedroom and said to her, "Look out there to the street, Mary Tilden. What do you see?"

She saw two brand-new Chevys, one red, one blue, otherwise identical.

"Which one do you want?" he asked her.

"The blue one. Oh, Icky, for me?"

"Yes, for you. I'll take the red one, you drive yours and I'll drive mine, and we won't argue about it any longer."

That afternoon, on their way back from different eggnog parties, they ran into each other.

But Icky is gathered to his fathers, too, and in the town he graced with his eccentricities for fifty years, he is no longer remembered, except by his stalwart son Jamie and a few of my passing generation. Nor is his kind

---

*McKee Boykin's four sons all now live in Charleston or elsewhere.

valued any longer. There is no Stew Boykin left to swing his rifle across the shoddy ostentation of the new-breed Southerner and shoot his vanity down, unless it is Tom Wolfe in his *A Man in Full*. My beloved friend and quail-hunting companion Robert M. Kennedy III (nephew of the coauthor of *Historic Camden*, great-grand-nephew of the Confederate general) is dead also, and the last of the male Kennedys to reside in Camden, his handsome and affable son Bobby having sold the family business and moved to Dewes Island. When big Bob was a young man, newly married and newly a father, and struggling with his cotton warehouse business (this was the Depression), a wealthy broker from New York, Weeks by name, came down to Camden to shoot with him. Mr. Weeks was an ardent bird hunter, and Bob Kennedy had a wondrous bitch setter who the first morning pointed eleven coveys and that afternoon another six. Mr. Weeks said to him, "I'll give you five hundred dollars for that dog." Astounded, Bob Kennedy said he would think it over during the night.

The next morning, they were hunting again, and Belle pointed nine coveys. Mr. Weeks said to Bob, "Have you thought over my offer?" Bob Kennedy replied in his long, slow, deep baritone, "Yes sir. All night long. Tossed and turned. Didn't sleep a . . . wink. Kept asking myself, 'If I had five hundred dollars, what would I do with it? What would I do with five . . . *hun*dred . . . dollars?'"

"Well?" asked Mr. Weeks impatiently. "What was your answer?"

Bob Kennedy said, "I'd buy myself a good bird dog."

And that deeply aristocratic, profoundly gentle, most noble view of the priorities has all but vanished. Unlamented by the vast majority of New Southerners who wish to acculturate with the idiom of Yankee tradesmen; who are ashamed of references to the Civil War, though not a few harbor in their sanitized souls the ghastly moral occlusion over which the war was so bravely and so shamefully fought; who count family for less, money for more; whose sense of honor is vitiated and attenuated; and whose values, as they lap from the soup bowl of this alien materialism, have been transmogrified. It is a pity.

CHAPTER TWENTY

———— ⌘ ————

Camden (II):
Coming Home

ACCORDING TO GEORGE MONTGOMERY, "1935 ... MARKED THE DIVIDING point in W.F.B.'s business career."

It was in this year that he "negotiated the all-important contract with Standard Oil," which I have described earlier, culminating in a partnership without precedent either in the oil business or on Wall Street. And it was in 1935 that Mother and Father were introduced to Camden by the Ben Belchers of Lakeville and by the Wilifred Wrights of Sharon, both of whom had winter homes in the town.

Father must have been feeling pretty good—even optimistic—after years and years of discouragement and defeat. The whole period from 1923 to 1935 had demanded extraordinary resources of character in him and unbounded faith, which was closely linked to his faith in God. He was quiet and unobtrusive about religion, and rarely, if ever, talked about God, but his religion, in defense of which he had risked and lost everything in Mexico, was the source of all his hope and determination. The deals with Union and California Oil, concluded in 1927 and 1928, respectively, had availed nothing, except to sink his reputation on the Street deeper. He was washed up, according to the financial community. He nevertheless managed during this period to eliminate $2 million in company debt. On two occasions when the company was slammed against it, in dire

William F. Buckley and William F. Buckley, Jr., 1950.
Taken in Vancouver on the day of Bill's marriage to Patricia Taylor.

need of heavy infusions of cash, Father saved Pantepec's stock from being watered by adroit maneuvering.*

We children talk about this amongst ourselves with, I think, insufficient projection on our part into the anguish that he must have been going through all these years, with the staggering burden not only of his ten children—three in college, the rest in boarding schools or being privately educated—and the lavish style of life to which he had accustomed them, but also now the burden of age. He was fifty-eight years old in 1939; the years must have begun to weigh on him that cumulative toll that is the tribute exacted of us by age, wearing him, no matter how disdainfully

*For more about this, see George Montgomery's contribution to *W.F.B.—An Appreciation.*

he dismissed them. His astuteness under stress and his imaginative initiatives were remarkable, however. If he was not their inventor, he was the man who most extensively exploited "farmout" agreements (under which the right to prospect on concessions was leased or sold by Pantepec to other parties) and "carried interest" agreements (under which the "working interest"—the big oil companies—financed geological investigations and the drilling of wells, and were paid back every penny of their exploratory expenditures before the "carried interest" received its share of the profits, if any). These two nimble, daring tactics made it possible for small, independent, impudent companies like Pantepec, without the enormous sums of money required for the testing of any given area, to leverage their concessions.

His "checkerboard" practice in acquiring properties also became famous in the oil industry, enabling the quick-moving independent company (big oil was by nature, or structure, slow) to pioneer the major plays: he would move early and decisively into a region or country (Venezuela, Canada, Australia, to name a few) where some interest had been tickled—promising geology, maybe a show of gas in a wildcat well—and proceed to acquire concessions so deftly positioned that any further showing of gas or oil was close, or adjacent, to his properties, enabling him to entice the giants.

Through and through, he was an entrepreneur. He was a Texan. Texas was boundless, like his ambition. When President Roosevelt ("that hypocrite!") asked the governors of the states to establish a fifty-mph speed limit for the duration, all dutifully complied, except for the governor of Texas—Coke R. Stevenson, at the time.* Furious, Roosevelt called him and delivered a tongue lashing over the telephone, to which Stevenson replied, "You just don't understand, Mr. President. No one can get anywhere in Texas at fifty miles an hour." Father thrived on challenges that would have paled the gray souls of today's typical MBA graduates. Our sister Aloise disparaged the generation of company officers succeeding Father as the "Depression Boys" for their indiginously gloomy pessimism about this or that play, predicting catastrophe; in which dissing she included her husband Ben, her brother John, and their close associates.

---

* The redoubtable Texan politician whom Lyndon Johnson squeaked by in 1947 for the Senate, partly thanks to my defunct grandfather's vote.

These young men—brilliant and inventive though they might be—had not been born poor, and were thus temperamentally incapacitated from sharing in what to all appearances was his imperturbable optimism.

But now, in 1939, with oil discovered at last and Pantepec stock soaring, Father was able to foresee a time when he might be able to slacken the reins—as much as this was possible for him to do. Mother plain hankered to be once more among her kind after years of exile in New England.* The Belchers and the Wrights pointed out Camden's convenience: the southbound Palmland Express departed Pennsylvania Station in New York City at ten P.M. and supposedly (it regularly lost steam and several hours in Hamlet, North Carolina) arrived at the pretty little Camden railroad station at half past noon the next day; the northbound Silver Meteor pulled into Camden from Miami anytime in the evenings between six-thirty and eight-thirty, but it arrived in New York City *sharp* at eight the next morning, permitting Father, as was his custom, to take a leisurely seven-block walk across town to his offices on 37th Street, two doors east of Park Avenue.

Camden's easy access impressed Father, and though he and Mother were charmed by the disarming people of the little winter resort town, I was surprised to learn from Mother that he at first considered buying a house in Charleston, on the Battery. I can't remember which—a big, white, sprawling clapboard mansion with a veranda—but he offered $25,000 for it and was irritably shocked when the owners responded with a counterdemand of $26,500. "Imagine, Aloïse, asking such a sum!"

I was freshly impressed by the value of $1,500 in Depression times. Father spurned the counter, and he and Mother purchased instead the rotting ruin on the hill known as Kamschatka.

Sixteen thousand dollars. It would cost them another $100,000 plus to restore house and grounds and to beautify them, but this was the best investment in happiness they ever made.

FOR MOTHER, IT WAS THE END OF EXILE AND A COMING HOME; FOR FATHER, it was a return also to a community whose values he largely shared. To us children, Camden was awful.

---

* They began visiting Camden during winters in 1935.

"Kamschatka," southwestern view

"Kamschatka," renovated 1940

"Kamschatka," c. 1940.
View of terraces leading to gate.

Aloïse Steiner Buckley, c. 1940.

We were introduced to Camden in the mid-1930s, our parents renting a series of great big houses until we at last moved into Kamschatka (1940), and we hated it! The land was ugly. It was flat. It was all sand, catbriars, chiggers, and poison ivy. And what were those pale, skimpy patches of green they called a *lawn?* No one in South Carolina had the remotest notion of what a *lawn* was. In Sharon we rolled and played on the lawns, we flopped on the lawns. Here, if you threw yourself down on what they *called* the lawn, you were bitten by ants, pricked by cactus, lanced by scorpions, stung by spiders, infested by fleas, or hooked by those incredibly sharp sandspurs that were everywhere. In Sharon, we lay on the grass on our stomachs and pressed our chins on the tops of the interlaced fingers of our hands, blades of grass tickling our throats, and dreamed . . . and dreamed . . . and sometimes fell asleep. Here in Camden, if we tried that, we'd be eaten alive.

But not all of us hated Camden. Allie found Ben Heath, a handsome pilot stationed at the nearby Sumter Air Force base, whose father was the editor of the *Camden Chronicle;* she would marry him in 1941, the first of the weddings celebrated in Kamschatka,* looking so very beautiful in her bridal gown as she swept down the magnificent pine staircase with her dark brown hair and celestial eyes.

She had to learn about housekeeping as a bride, having never done this for herself (she tossed out the first dozen eggs she cracked because there were no whites in them, honest), but she would become a terrific cook, and I loved visiting her at Shaw Field; she made me feel so important and grown-up. Allie *never* talked baby talk, either to her younger siblings or to her children. Ben was so wonderfully coordinated (he won the amateur junior golf championship of Michigan when he was sixteen) that he had been assigned to the training of pilots, would bring me blackened and twisted scraps of metal from what he assured me were fatal crashes, which I treasured with the morbid joy of all boys. John discovered quickly that the soft-spoken Camden girls were "comely," which was the gentlemanly word he used to describe them (in his collected fishing and gunning stories, *Manqué*), by which he intended to convey fair, alluring, and sexy as hell. The dove and especially the quail shooting overjoyed him, and he

---

*My daughter Lizzie's wedding was the last.

earned the reputation in a community of crack shots of being a superlative marksman. Whit Boykin, paragon of wing shooting (who was able to gun down five birds on a covey rise), told anyone who cared to listen that John Buckley was the fastest gun he had ever hunted.* Priscilla had golf, and golf was a prime pastime, Camden boasting a sweet eighteen-hole course under magnificent longleaf pines designed by Donald Ross and belonging to the huge old Kirkwood Hotel.† (She was so expert at the game that after she graduated from Smith, she would consider turning professional.) Jim was fascinated by the bird life on Kamschatka's grounds and in the deep, beautiful, riverine swamps. Jane, pretty, passionate, and most "comely" herself, was courted avidly by the tall, handsome, lean Camden swain of that time (before they went off to war) Kirby Tupper, a blond Adonis and a senior at the Citadel, son of "old" Kirby, the horse trainer; John Langford, also a student at the Citadel, son of the endearing, club-footed Esso dealer on the corner of Lyttleton and DeKalb streets; movie-handsome Caleb Whitaker, who lifted weights (and at eighty-four-plus still does), a Camden resident of pioneer stock, and the like. Bill was not, I think, crazy about Camden, but he enjoyed the drag hunts, and he was to place seventh in the good hands class of the last national horse show to be held at Madison Square Garden before war broke out (1941). For the oc-casion, he rode the most tractable and beautiful horse of our stable, Golden Bantam, a three-gaited standard-bred mare (Father's favorite carriage horse). Bill recalls that he competed against a youth called Edward Albee, and coming in one place behind him was a shy, darling, dark-haired, twelve-year-old brunette beauty by the name of Jackie Bouvier.[1]

Patricia, Maureenie, and I—ages eleven, eight, and five, respectively, when we moved into Kamschatka (Carol was still a baby)—detested Camden. It had its merits, of course. Eggleston and Mr. Marcres had never *dreamed* of a soda fountain bar like the one in Zemp's drugstore on DeKalb Street.‡ I mean the chrome spigots frothing with homemade root

---

*To "hunt" someone in South Carolina parlance is to take someone out hunting, in Whit Boykin's case at the time, as a paid guide.
†Defunct in 1954.
‡That was Dr. Sidney Zemp's pharmacy. The Zemps operated three drugstores in Camden. Dr. Robin Zemp and Dr. DePass had one down on Broad Street, which is where all the little old ladies congregated.

beer, sarsaparilla, cream soda, Dr. Pepper, and Coke, mixed, if you wanted, with a dab of vanilla or cherry syrup—it was *delicious!*—and served in large twelve-ounce glasses that were filled to the top with crushed ice (Yankee-land in those dear dead days had never *heard* of crushed ice) into which you plunged your straw and sucked and sucked and sucked and sucked, frothing bubbles in the bottom of the glass and not ever exhausting the flavor. The malted milks were something else again also. They were made right in front of you, fresh milk out of the dairy man's bottle and two scoops of rich Brewer's chocolate or vanilla ice cream, two heaping soup spoons of malt and chocolate syrup, and also a dab of vanilla for extra flavor if you cared for that (which I did), and *thick*, I mean so thick they were almost solid; you could have turned your glass right over quickly without spilling a drop on the counter and resisted stirring by those long, elegant iced-tea spoons, and so cold that they ached the throat if drunk too greedily. The Zemp soda fountain was something else again. Yankees didn't have a clue.

And like our siblings, except John,[2] we loved the riding. There was no place you could not go on horseback in Camden when I was a boy, the streets being paved only to Dusty Bend, just south of the railroad tracks that cross the town. Street signs everywhere requested,

MOTORISTS PLEASE DEFER TO EQUESTRIANS

and others admonished

EQUESTRIANS KINDLY KEEP YOUR MOUNTS OFF SIDEWALKS

which were of pure white beach sand and could be churned up by horses' hooves. All streets and lanes except downtown were surfaced in sand mixed with red clay. We would ride fifteen miles as far as Chesnut cemetery without once crossing pavement, picnicking on the flat slabs of the markers* We loved the drag hunts: as long as there was two-plus hours of hard galloping across rail and aiken fences in big, beautiful Peck Woods. And when I hit fifteen, I developed a passion for quail and duck hunting

---

*One of which (many years later) Maureen and I discovered was askew. I swung off my horse to peer in, and I made out the copper piping of a moonshiner.

also. Kind Icky Guy would pick me up at four-fifteen A.M. in the pitch black before dawn (he always made his appointments at the quarter-hour, then rued the fact that so many people misunderstood and were ready on the half-hour, either fifteen minutes too early or a mortal fifteen minutes too late) to stand with him and boon companions at English Pond, where we would wait for green-winged teals, wood ducks, "bullheads" (the ring-necked scaup, also called bluebills) and occasional "big" ducks (mallards, sometimes blacks, rarely pintails) to pitch in, Icky offering us afterward a choice of coffee with bourbon, tea with bourbon, consomme with bourbon, or plain bourbon, my father exclaiming irritably at lunch, "Aloïse, what is the matter with Reid? Doesn't he get enough sleep nights? I declare, his forehead is about to fall into the soup."

Though nearly thirty years my senior, Icky Guy became my first fast friend in Camden, changing my early, hostile perception of the town. Those morning hunts on his "Blue Lands" (for the color of the clay) across the river could be exciting. One drove miles over potted woods roads in the inky black until one came to a padlocked gate, which was opened by an obliging black man; and then maybe a mile deeper into the swamp, until one encountered a second padlocked gate, at which another obliging black man stood guard. The purpose of these obstructions was felonious. When a posse of federal game wardens found their way to the first gate, the sentinel would fumble clumsily with the lock, complaining of the numbing cold, exhausting several minutes and the patience of the feds before at last uncoupling the chain and swinging the gate wide for them to pass; they then encountered the second gate and were detained precious more minutes. For as soon as the posse had passed the first gate, the black man would boom in a rich basso that reverberated throughout the swamp, "Game warrrdens, game wardens acominggg!"—a call that was picked up and relayed by the black man at the second gate before the wardens reached it, "Game warrrdens, game wardens acominggg!" alerting the hunting party, who would hastily pick up their ducks and shells and gear and scatter deep into the woods; and by the time the posse had reached English, there was nothing but a few feathers floating on its black waters, along with bobbing (and telltale) hulls that had been ejected into the water and had floated too far from shore to be sunk.*

---

* These memories became the great swamp of my trilogy, *Canticle of the Thrush*.

Camden sported four social groupings among the gentry. There were the horse people, who wintered their racing thoroughbreds in the town, among whom were the trainers, such as Irish born and bred Jimmy Ryan, Kirby Tupper (senior), Burling Cocks, and the Englishman, Ivor Balding—lovable characters—as well as nationally known sportsmen such as Paul Mellon, Bill Woodward, and Mrs. Randolph Dupont Scott, along with assorted snobs and parvenus. There was also gruff, stern, handsome Harry Kirkover, expert amateur tennis player and all the field sports of his time, master of hounds, and into his old age a magical trainer of his many springer spaniels.[3] There were the winter visitors and residents, in the main Yankees and in the main affluent. These two sets intermingled and kept the town going during harsh post-Reconstruction years, some of them, like Woodward and Richard Lloyd from Philadelphia, becoming benefactors of the town. Then there were the issue of the founders, dating from the eighteenth and early nineteenth centuries (the inland South was late in settling), city folk and country folk, these the sons and daughters of plantation society. Most were kin and most of them impecunious. There was little money anywhere in Camden, speaking of the natives. In 1954, for example, the Charleston-style* Samuel Baruch mansion,† occupying the site where today an impressive Baptist Church stands,‡ went on the block before being torn down. There were no bidders. Decorated in high Victorian style, it held ornate French marble fireplaces and mantels. Out-of-towners bought these, though Camden native Charles "Bubba" DuBose did happily snatch up the handsome wainscoting of one of the parlors for his farmhouse off Route 291 beyond Mulberry Plantation and in what was then almost exclusively Boykin country. Boykins, Beards, Canteys, and Wootens were so numerous at the time that they were a challenge not only to keep straight but to count. The rebellious anarchical spirit of these people, when we Buckley children became acquainted with it, did strongly attract us. The people of Camden had inherited a native dislike for arbitrary authority, especially when exer-

---

*Shoulder to the street.
†A Confederate surgeon, father of Bernard Baruch, the Wall Street shark and infinitely distinguished "counselor to presidents," who was born in Camden.
‡Adjacent to my school.

cised by government, state or federal. Icky Guy, who was of a literary turn (rare for the town; two others only shared this incapacitating vice, Henry Savage* and Bob Kennedy),[†] and who had made his way as an editor for a Boston publishing house fifteen years before returning to South Carolina, feuded with wardens not because he was a hog who slaughtered game indiscriminately,[‡] but because he was cavalier (he would have said—hotly—*sensible* and *reasonable*) about laws governing the pursuit of migratory fowl. Once during Easter vacation, he turned to me at a cocktail party and whispered, "Four forty-five, I'll pick you up at Kamschatka . . . don't need waders, and don't tell anyone." I first sizzled with gratitude and excitement, I *dreamed* of shooting ducks, but then I bethought me, stammering, "But Mr. Guy, it's March. Is the season open in March?" To which he whispered agitatedly in reply, "The season is open when I say it is open, which is when the ducks get down from the North."

This became locally famous as Icky's dispensation. He justified it by pointing out that the seasons as ordained by ignorant bureaucrats in Washington made no sense for South Carolina. And about that he was right. No allowance was made for geography. Maryland and South Carolina were treated identically, which was idiotic: ducks and geese may migrate from Canada and other points to the Chesapeake Bay in November, but they do not reach the Carolinas until the waning moon of December, even later. Icky therefore shot ducks at his choosing.[§]

He was much more than a wildflower, besides; Icky Guy was a learned amateur naturalist, second only in knowledge to Henry Savage, and had a magnificent collection of eggs in trays of every (or almost every) bird that

---

*Naturalist, author, longtime mayor of Camden.

†My father once declared exasperatedly, "Boykins are all charming people, but I don't believe any of them has read a book since school," which was accurate.

‡Far from that: when it was April, and even he conceded the duck season was finished, he often invited me out to sit with him by English Pond before dawn to experience the thrill of hearing flights of ducks whirring overhead or, in the case of wood ducks, precipitously pitching into it, like zigzagging bolts of lightning.

§Icky feuded with state and federal game wardens over dove shooting as well. Once when he heard that the feds were hiring an airplane as a spotter to locate illegal fields, he hired a counter airplane to alert dove shooters and evacuate them if necessary. See sister Priscilla's rollicking account of dove shooting Camden-style in her memoir, *Living It Up at National Review.*

nested in the state. He permitted me to examine them, which I did reverently. His enthusiasm for South Carolina wildlife was right after my heart,
and in the close to fifty years of our acquaintance, it never dimmed. He
had (improvidently) bought all those thousands of acres along both banks
of the Wateree River and elsewhere as much to preserve the wilderness as
for the commercial value of the timber, which was not at the time obvious.
I was once with him on an expedition into a cypress swamp when he shin-
nied up a fifty-foot yellow pine to extract an egg from the clutch laid in its
high canopy by blue darters (cooper's hawks), which screamed furiously at
him and dove on his head like a pair of Japanese zeros, raking at his scalp
with their talons as they whooshed by; but, to my fervent admiration, he
was imperturbable, inching his way back down the trunk with the beautiful chocolate-splotched trophy held high in one hand, face radiant, shaggy
eyebrows and cheekbones streaming with blood from the gashes on his
scalp. Oh, Camden could be fun and exciting sometimes. But . . .

It rained. How it rained! You don't want to ride horses when it comes
down hard, unless you don't mind rubbing the insides of your calves raw
from the pinching of the wet stirrup straps, and don't care about placing
the burden on the black groom of soaping the tack the moment you get
back in (it gets stiff otherwise); you don't go jumping fences on horseback
when it rains unless you care little about breaking your neck. Now, you
can, if you wish, slog after quail behind a pair of sorry-looking dogs when
it rains, assuming you enjoy punitive futility (the scent is washed off the
light soil and pine straw; the birds, if you find any, stay so closely com-
pacted in irrigation ditches choked by honeysuckle that you have to step
on them to get them to take wing—or, if there is any wind to go with the
rain, they flush wild two gunshots away). Tramping about in soft yielding
corn or bean fields, with catbriars catching at your ankles and cockleburrs
getting in between your socks and your ankles and itching and burning
there, and several pounds of clay muck adhering to your bird boots until
you wonder whether with every step you are not dragging along all the
arable soil in the state, is not the most pleasurable experience, and . . . oh,
how it rained!

Throughout the 1940s. This is difficult to recall in our times of chronic
drought. I bought a sandhill farm in 1976, and it has been one dry planting season after another these past thirty years. But during the 1940s, it
rained! I read recently a marvelous account of the British and patriot cam-

paigns in the Carolinas in 1781–82, and I was struck by how often General Rawdon or Sumter or that cruel, brutal, but able counterguerrilla fighter Colonel Bannister Tarleton, or even our hero, Francis Marion, the Swamp Fox, were bogged down by rains that made of existing roads mud wallows—deluges that poured eight, ten, twelve days straight without letting up, rendering military operations impossible. So with our Christmas and Easter vacations.

We might arrive on the Eastern Seaboard's Palmland Express at two or three o'clock on a gloriously sunny afternoon with (for our New England-tempered constitutions) delightful temperatures in the sixties or even the low seventies, planning jubilantly to go riding or shooting the next morning, only to have cold rains set in overnight and persist unrelentingly almost all of the precious two weeks that we had. I remember pressing my nose and chin grimly against the chilled window panes of the pine room on the ground floor of Kamschatka, my back to the crackling log fire, the resinous scent of fatwood pungent in my nostrils, listening dully to the beat of the rain on the square brick flags just beyond the overhanging ledge of the piazza, wondering what had possessed Mother and Father to buy this big old hulk of a house which on top of everything else was haunted and in which my third-floor bedroom was a cubicle that oven-baked me every night (I couldn't sleep) because the main exhaust of the central heating ran up one of its walls. The girls all had their splendid double bedrooms, John and Jim and Bill slept in a cool and airy bedroom on the ground floor, but I—fourth son and eighth child—was relegated to the attic! I remember well during Lent crawling out of bed in the stygian darkness before six A.M. ("*Voy, Nana. Je viens, Mad'moiselle!* . . . I'm coming, for Pete's sake!") to be in time for Father Burke's punishing six-fifteen daily Mass (scheduled before dawn for the convenience of the Irish jockeys and steeplechase horse trainers, who, along with the Sheheens, made up the majority of the congregation in this Bible Belt town), to arrive at the pretty Spanish mission–style church on Lyttleton Street in a downpour and in the chill early spring darkness, and to leave the church half an hour later with dawn just glimmering on the eastern horizon but with the downpour continuing unabated. "What are you children planning to do today?" Mother would ask us brightly at breakfast, Father cocking an ear. "Nothing!" we youngest of us would answer rebelliously, staring out the tall windows of the octagonal breakfast-room wing across the brick terrace to the sunken east garden, rain sheeting down the glass panes, obliterating the sight of gorgeously blooming camellias and discouraging even mockingbirds from their canticles.

And the people! Oh, they were nice, friendly, well-meaning, but those syrupy, sweet, too sweet voices of the women like Karo on your pancakes—*aaarghyuk!*—you could call New England women just about anything, but you could not call them sweet; they'd split you down the middle. And the *time* it took these women to utter the *simplest* things or to accomplish the simplest task, like direct you to where the chewing gum was at Sheheen's grocery store, or handing you your change, or bagging your purchase, all the while asking how your dear "Momma" was or, worse yet, how your "folks" were, drove us wild, we who were used to the clipped, impersonal efficiency of Yankee women in voice, expression, manner. They were sincere, we at length concluded, astonished. They all knew our names and called us "Reid, honey," and "Maureen, darlin' " because, we reasoned defensively, we were the big family from the North that had just moved in; but to us they were a daze of blurry images and a puzzle and a source of acute embarrassment; between Christmas and Easter vacations, how in the world could we be expected to remember their names?*The deep, soft men's voices we agreed that we rather liked, but ask them directions to anywhere—say, to a picnic cabin on the river to which (as we grew up and were given permission to drive the station wagon) we had been invited for a barbecue—and in lieu of a straightforward set of instructions, you got "Just head on out of town three, maybe four miles on Route 261 past the Swift Creek First Baptist colored church until you come to Tombfield Road on your left. *Go on by that* (you don't want to get on Tombfield Road), go on by it to Cantey Lane, hang a right onto that, and then drive a little ways past a big bean field another maybe half a mile or so to where the road forks off by the big black gum, hang a left there, then another . . . oh, maybe another two or three hundred yards, no more than that, until you get to the top of the hill, hang a sharp right on the sandy lane just beyond the big post oak a mile or so over the branch, look for the clearing, can't miss it, you're there!"

---

*I have mentioned this mnemonic disability earlier.

SURE. WHAT WAS "MAYBE" THREE OR FOUR MILES OF BLACK MACADAM vanishing between pine woods when fog from the river rolled inland to obscure everything? How would you know you'd gone past the Swift Creek First Baptist colored church; you had driven by onetwothreefour churches, and they bore no signs white or black that you could make out, and they all looked much alike, squat steeples, cemetery plots, all those plastic flowers at the head of every grave pinned to the white satin ribbon on one of the wreaths in its center the celluloid facsimile of a telephone and the inscription, "Jesus Is Calling You," and how did anyone know that one had arrived at Tombfield Road in order to go past it to get to Cantey Lane when there wasn't a single sign, not one,* to indicate which of the several miserable spurs of sand you were passing left and right was Tombfield Road or Cantey Lane or neither, and what was a soybean field in December as distinguishable from a corn field in December or a cotton field in December or a browntop millet field in December, they'd all been harvested, for pity's sake, and half of them disked under, and what could anyone mean by hanging a left on the black gum tree—who can tell a black gum tree from a sweet gum tree in dead of night when it's begun to rain again besides—and what hill can anyone be talking about, there was no hill, there was maybe the slightest incline from dead flat if you were stretched out prone on the curb of the road watching cars cruise by—you might (could) have detected it, though it wouldn't have tilted the tea in a saucer or tipped the bubble of a carpenter's level. And a post oak? Oh, that's terrific! You distinguish a post oak in dead of night in the pouring rain in wintertime when there isn't a single leaf on the tree from a willow oak or a water oak or a chestnut oak or a white oak or a red oak, and a branch? What branch? There was no fork in the road that you can see! The only road before you is the one you are doing your best not to skid off on, thank-you-ma'aming over the plank bridge spanning a swollen creek and plunging deep into black woods, the haunt of Hecuba, as though the lane was being sucked out of existence, no branch in it anywhere . . . and no, you are not there, you have gone miles and miles, it seems to you, and you are not there you are not anywhere you are totally lost in a strange, hostile hoot-owl wilderness, not the glimmering of a light bulb nor the flickering of a barbecue fire nor a welcome clearing to be made out anywhere, no matter how hard you peer through the windshield with the wipers batting back and forth like bats flapping their

---

*In the 1980s, the state was bequeathed by the federal highway department a slug of money to spend on road signs, and they sprouted everywhere, overnight, magically.

wings, black tree trunks looming up on either side draped with smilax and grape and wisteria vines as thick as your thighs, the sandy lane has turned into a slick sheet of wet red clay as you yaw inexorably, unstoppably, irresistibly off its crown into the honeysuckle ditch running beside it that has flooded with all the rain and is probably slithering with cottonmouths and copperheads and maybe gators from the river, too, for all you know, and from which only a pair of strong, flatulent mules will extract you, if—clambering out of the car, slipping and sliding, losing your balance and being sucked knee-deep into the ditch, dragging yourself out of it, stumbling, soaked to the skin thigh-high, shoes squishing mud with every step—if ever you come upon the cabin of some kind Uncle Tom of a black man and persuade him on that foul night now past ten o'clock to abandon the bosom of his family and the blazing chimney to hitch up his mules and extricate you from your sea heap of troubles and help turn your car around and indicate that you are nowhere near Rembert or Hagood or Ellerbe's Mill or the Wateree River, for that matter. "No suh, you are not even in Kuhshaw County, you done described a great divagation, and you are somehow in Lee County . . . Camden? Why, bless yo' [idiot Yankee] soul, Camden is fifteen miles at least southwest of where you are standing, but don't you worry, suh, not to despair, suh, getting back to Camden is alligator turtle soup, suh! Just drive back up de lane where you came from across de branch might could be four or five miles, go on by a sixty-acre field planted to winter wheat, can't miss that, hang a left on a big hickory tree across the branch" . . .*

To run into the host of last night's barbecue the next day at a cocktail party and have him exclaim, stricken, "Why, where*evuh* did you and yo' sweet sister get to last night? We missed you!" with such candid friendliness and plainly such sincere regret at our unaccountable absence that I thought, despite myself, and said to my sister Maureen, "Aren't these simply the nicest people in the world?"

To which she replied with her customary fatuous superiority, "I wondered how long it would take you to figure that out."

---

*I guess I should explain that a "branch" in the South signifies a creek, though only to the initiated.

NOTES

1. The national horse show was a posh affair prewar. People in boxes and ringside seats dressed to the nines; on the last evening of the event, in ball gowns and tuxedos. When asked by an incautious master of ceremonies his opinion of horse shows, the famed (and greatly loved) steeplechase trainer Burling Cocks blurted memorably into the microphone, "Horse shows are where horses' asses go to watch horses' asses," a defining statement that rang across the loudspeaking systems and was greeted by hoots of laughter in the bleachers.

    I was greatly fond of Burling (pronounced "Burly") Cocks and his wife, Babs (Barbara), now both deceased, who gave our son Javier a job as a stableboy and then as an exercise rider when he was in his late teens, and who spoke always of him affectionately.

    Oh, and for the record, the only reason Bill's younger sister Patricia and his younger brother Reid did not also qualify to compete in the Garden at the national horse show, and surpass his achievement, is that such events were discontinued during hostilities.

2. John did not learn to ride until he was sent to Fort Riley; when he got out of the war, he sneered at the rest of us for our effete training in horsemanship, having been placed, as a recruit, with no previous introduction, on the bare back of a mean animal and made to hang on as the beast galloped over a number of rail fences. (This training took place in a chute.)

3. Harry Kirkover was short (five-foot-six or-seven), white-haired, and pugnacious, and he always wore the countenance of a self-centered grouch when I came to know him. But he was a lonely old man who lived in a large house on Lyttleton Street with a heavy growth of bamboo at one end of the front yard that he used for the training of his springers, which resided in a row of cement runs that he personally tended every day with the assistance of a black yard man. He had trained the dogs to cease barking at the sound of the little bell whose *tingalingling* he commanded from his bedroom or living room. When a visitor arrived, he would be taken directly to the kennels. Mr. Kirkover, in riding breeches and boots and a Harris tweed jacket, would open the gate of a run containing three or four of the dogs, and though they all sat expectantly, not one would come out until it was called by name. (The rush was then joyous; these were happy dogs on whom he expended all his bottled-up love.) He would permit them several wild racings around the grounds before he blew on a silver whistle he had about his neck. At once they responded to it, circling him, sitting, thrashing the gravel with their cropped tails, waiting for him to toss a small ball into the seemingly impenetrable cane. He would then say in a soft tone, "Jack" or "Belle" or "Bob" or "Lady," and the dog whose name he spoke burst from its sitting position, racing pellmell into the bamboo. Out it would emerge within seconds, ears flying and in triumph, slamming to a halt, sitting, and without a single additional command deposit-

ing the ball tenderly into his extended hand. I have never seen a happier or prouder human being than Mr. Kirkover at these moments. He congratulated the animal warmly, and then gave others their turn at a retrieve or two. After permitting them to play a little and fondling them as they leaped into his arms, lapping his chin and lips with their wet, red, eager tongues, he would set them down and say quietly, "Now, be good children and kennel." And one after another, docilely but with alacrity, they entered the run, which he closed behind them. Only then would he invite the visitor into his house.

From my fifteenth to my twentieth year, during vacations, Christmas, and Easter, I may have been his most faithful visitor. There was, I believe, a Mrs. Kirkover, but I have no remembrance of her. No children. I have never seen a house so filled with sporting treasures. On almost every wall he had glowing Rousseau oil portraits of his many champion setters, which he had bred and trained and run in field trials at the turn of and during the first three decades of the twentieth century. There was a richly painted oil of a stippled black-and-white male setter with black ears standing in a classic high-tailed point deep in broom straw (was its name "Peerless"?) who became champion of champions, show and field and who sired the "Eugene's Ghost" line of setters from which ours all sprang. Another very tall Rousseau of two of his setters, both lemon-and-white Llewellans (or was one of them a live-and-white pointer?), fascinated me. The pair were painted as though from the perspective of the skulking quarry, quail, pheasant, or partridge: they were frozen in a vibrant, dramatic, sudden stop, the foreleg of one of the dogs lifted, both heads straining forward from the shoulders. One gazed up at the flared nostrils and bulging eyeballs of the magnificent animals, who seemed to be trembling before one's eyes. It was to me riveting.

There were silver trophies everywhere one glanced: tennis, skeet, trap shooting, hockey, boxing (he was a lightweight champion as a young man), golf, polo, horse events of every kind. A gun cabinet gleamed with Purdys and Boss's and Greeners and other fine English side-by-side firearms. He was born well-to-do and of a vanishing generation in which it was respectable to follow the life of a professional amateur sportsman if one wished and had the means, and so long as one excelled. I don't think Harry Kirkover ever earned a dollar except accidentally. He led an absolutely selfish life, which may have accounted for the lack of children. He would sit in a favorite leather armchair in his library, from which, through a window, he could view Lyttleton Street running by, and he would talk into twilight, answering my innumerable questions in a low, gruff, yet kindly voice. He had known Babe Ruth and Jack Dempsey; he saw Man o' War get beaten by Upset, and Big Red's son and Triple Crown champion War Admiral whipped in the match race by Seabiscuit; he had played polo with Hitchcock against a crack Argentine squad, I forget which, there were several, and regularly shot quail at Jock Whitney's fabled plantation in Thomasville, Georgia. He knew Tilden and played several rounds of golf on the Master's course in Augusta with Byron Nelson. I breathed in his stories, which were always freshly remembered even when I asked him to repeat them. His memory for names and detail was phenomenal, and I sat two or three hours on an upholstered stool at his feet, spellbound. He was quite poor then, the collars and cuffs of his otherwise impeccable shirts were sometimes worn, but it was he who with Bill Woodward had designed the Carolina Cup course (did Woodward slip Harry Kirkover an honorarium for that?),* which is unique (in a natural bowl, so that the race could be followed entire by anyone standing anywhere along the rail or in the infield), for which his name and unmistakable physical appearance will be remembered always, allowing for the entropy of fame. Yes, Harry Kirkover's curmudgeonly Irish visage under a straw hat and his stocky, battlecock chest figure prominently among the photographs preserved in the National Steeplechase Museum. His memory—his personality—is otherwise extinct.†

---

* A sporting event that has always been of interest to me, partly because it was inaugurated in the year of my birth.

† His is one of the images that I used in creating both the fine, kindly, weak old Dr. deSaussure and his relentless enemy, Horace Forsthoefel, in the first novel (*Saving DeSaussure Swamp: A Love Story*) of my trilogy, *Canticle of the Thrush*.

Chapter Twenty-one

⌘

Camden (III): Happiness

For Mother, Camden was joy eternal.

Telephoning her was a special treat. "Is that *you*, Reid?" she would exclaim in her bell-like voice, as though nothing in this entire world could have delighted her more than receiving a call from her fourth son. "The weather? Oh, this is I think the most *beau*tiful spring ever!"

Every spring in Camden was the most beautiful spring ever for thirty-five straight years. Here Mother was a Southern woman among her kind. No one had higher credentials to being Southern—not even a native of Charleston—than someone born and brought up in New Orleans. In Camden, she did not have to explain herself. Since Pantepec had struck oil, the penny stock had become the darling of Wall Street speculators, who pushed its price up from pennies to as high as twenty-three dollars a share. All of Father's most extravagant dreams were, I think, fulfilled, that decade of the 1940s. He was a man of substance, and to a great many people then still living—in Mexico and the Southwest and in the oil business—a gallant and romantic figure, now justified, now truly rich.*

---

*In one report during the early 1950s, *Time* magazine attributed a fortune of $100 million to our father, which was enormous in those days, and a sum we, his children, were supposed to have inherited. The reference by *Time* was to the total worth of the stock of all Father's companies, a volatile measure that sank or soared according to the whims of speculators. In my laughable case—in Madrid, where gossip rules social life—it was supposed that I personally, alone, had inherited a major portion of that huge sum, a misconception that for business

That he was a Texan was no social disadvantage in Camden, either, nor that he had been brought up in straitened circumstances and had had to wrest his fortune by his own efforts. This made, as I've indicated, not a speck of difference. The most prominent residents of Camden, the Williamses of Mulberry Plantation, had a not a dissimilar history. There were substantial differences notwithstanding. The Williamses were a family of distinction going back six generations on this side of the water alone. Father was a third-generation American whose parents were immigrants from Canada. We are children of the old sod; our paternal descent is that of prosperous farmers, Anglo-Irish in origin and, way back, of Norman stock. Our family's escutcheon (the only Irishman who cannot boast a crest is my friend Wladislaw Pleszczinsky, possibly because he is Polish) portrays the heads of three bulls, which I suppose suggests bullheadedness; the motto is *Nec Temere, Nec Timide*, "Be Neither Foolhardy nor Timid," to which first injunction we have paid little attention in my family, while our callow disregard of the second does not chasten us sufficiently.

Though both Martha and "Big Dave" Williams boasted lineages, on her part going back through (Lee's lieutenant) General H. D. Hill to Revolutionary War hero "Billy" Hill (1741–1818) and on his part sprung from Kershaw and Chesnut bloodlines (the Chesnuts, like the Buckleys, came from Northern Ireland), and back to a David R. Williams (1776–1830), who had been governor of South Carolina, they, like everyone else post–Civil War, had fallen on hard times. Big Dave's father, Steven Miller Williams, had worked his way across the country to Oklahoma, where he and his two sons had made their fortune by, among other initiatives, laying pipe for the fledgling oil industry.*

The people of Camden had become well used to poverty since the world crashed down upon them and a way of life was scorched to the ground, trampled under forever. The "nicest" people in Camden were in fact still dirt poor, though indomitable. They gave one party a year, generally at Christmastide, and for this one celebration they stinted on neither food nor liquor. They were otherwise hanging on to houses that General

reasons I made no effort to correct. This was easy to get away with in Spain, because Spaniards, like the people of Camden, never directly talk of money. To put the matter into perspective, however, there were 85,000 stockholders, and my father never owned more than a small percentage of shares.

* Big Dave's father fought one of the last duels in South Carolina.

Sherman's bummers had chanced to omit burning, tall three-story structures in the midst of desolate acres of dried corn stalks or the withered rosebuds of cotton, selling the furnishings one by one—the sideboard, the dining-room table, the highboy, four-poster beds, and the porcelain and silver—to keep their land. (You could see in their parlors just where those fine pieces had once been placed, because they left, as though their shadows, pale patches against the walls.)

Poverty is humbling. Poverty breeds humility of spirit. And though poverty can be embittering, it also breeds generosity. In the 1940s, Camden was just commencing to shake off Sherman and the *revanchisme* of the North. Late into the '30s, such as Whit Boykin, with thousands of acres of land inherited from his father, Bolivar,* nevertheless hired himself out as a hunting guide; but some of them—Whit and uncles/cousins/ nephews Stew and Baynard and Burwell† and Ancrum and Sam and sundry other of the land-poor tribe of Boykins—were themselves emerging from close to one hundred years of relentless poverty as, all of a sudden, the new pulp-timber industry made their acres of blackjack oak and the yellow pines bordering swamps along the River Wateree producers of income. Barren land, the poorest, climbed dizzily in price in the decade between 1940 and 1950. I can't speculate what these people knew about Father's past and recent history, I suspect little (Father made no secret of his antecedence, though Mother was inclined to put on a few New Orleans airs), but the deLoaches, Louis and John, along with the Goodales and the David Williamses[1] and such, must have inferred he had had to fight his way up. The amiable folk in Camden rejoiced in Father's good fortune, admiring his success. He was still slim in 1935. Holding himself always with a straight back, he seemed taller than his five feet eleven inches, and he possessed those brilliant, round, sky-blue eyes of exceptional candor, whose gaze lingered in the memory. In his fifties and early sixties, Will Buckley was a handsome man, his cheeks fuller, softening his countenance. His smile was warm, and though all the formal photographs of that time show him compressing his wide, full lips in a stern expression,

---

* It was said of Bolivar deSaussure Boykin that he did not covet all the land in the world, just the land adjacent to his.
† Pronounced "Bur'l" commonly, "Burrel" by Yankees, "Burwell" by lawyers.

caused, I suspect, often by me,* among coevals he was affable and possessed an uncommon social energy. He displayed in these years the charm
that everyone without exception who knew Will Buckley in the Mexican
days remarked about him, and his company was sought after both by native Camdenites and winter visitors. It is notable that peculiarly in Camden, many of his new friends referred to him as Will, which had not often
been the case since Mexico. If Will Buckley was respected and popular,
however, Aloïse was loved.

I CAN'T STRESS SUFFICIENTLY THAT CAMDEN PEOPLE LIVED BY REV.
Martin Luther King's prescription—judging people not by their skin (read
money up North) but by their character—which was a prime element in
Mother and Father's contentment.

In their time, nobody gave a fig for William Buckley's oil-based wealth,
rumored to be stupendous. *How terrific,* was the attitude. So they purchased that old historic hulk that was falling to ruin on its hill and restored it gorgeously. *Fantastic!* So later on, in 1954, when that white
elephant and fire trap, the Kirkwood Hotel, with its two hundred fifty
rooms and servants' quarters and stables, went on the block, and William
Buckley bought the eighteen-hole golf course (though he did not play the
game himself) to keep it from being sold off to developers, incorporated it
into a club, giving the shares to townsfolk, how terrific and fantastic also!
And when he bought the property of what became the now quite famous
Springdale Hall supper club, and with the help of young Leonard Graham, and in close cooperation with, and with the support of, an enthusiastic David Williams (who sustained the club financially for many years

---

*One of these photographs, a family grouping in 1938, depicting him with his hat on and
positively glowering, and me sitting on the lap of Mother or Allie, I forget, complacently
victorious as I clutched to my jacket the large jar of hard candy that had been given to me by
Tías Priscilla and Eleanor and whose contents Father, upon viewing, ordered to be dumped
down the toilet, causing me to burst into tears and to refuse to pose for the picture, and causing Nana (*"Pobrecito hijo!"*) and Mademoiselle (*"Le pauvre petit!"*) and Mother ("It was your
own sisters who gave him the candies, how can you be so mean to the poor boy, Will, it's not
as if he is going to eat the whole jarful, or even half of them!") to scold my father indignantly,
who compressed his lips in ire but who did not dare oppose the united front of my defenders,
including Allie, and permitted me to keep the jar unplundered ... with which I posed.

after Father's death), converted the gracious old McKee Graham house into the social center that continues to serve Camden, super! I have lived in this small town now longer than anyone in my family except my mother, and I have detected no speck of resentment or envy or any other venal feeling; and if such sentiments do flicker in some folk, they show the courtesy of their breeding in not communicating a whiff of them to me or to my wife and children, to whom they have unfailingly extended the warmth of their friendship.[2]

Mother was so happy! And now that she was not bound to Sharon as though to a prison, she enjoyed the pleasant summers there and the tang, the chill, the crushed-hickory-nut-and-maple-leaves scent, and of course the color of the incomparable autumns. Father's success had made her at ease in Sharon. She lived there from early June until Thanksgiving, which are the best months. She then spent two weeks in New York, where she and Father had bought an apartment overlooking the East River* that Father used when he was in town. What can be more invigorating and beautiful than late November/early December, in New York City? Who has ever gazed out upon the myriad white Christmas-tree bulbs of Park Avenue as the boulevard unrolls like a dazzling scroll from the height of, say, 87th Street all the way down (miles and miles, it seems) to Grand Central Station, and not blow out of his lungs a gasp of wonderment?† In the second week of December, Mother moved down to Kamschatka, which her cadre of longtime household servants had cleaned and spruced up for her arrival. There she basked in the warmth and cordiality of Camden's entire population it seemed (before her final illness, she may have become personally acquainted with 70 percent of Camden's people, white and black,) through Christmas and Easter and into the magnolia season, late April, when the weather begins to turn sultry (Kamschatka had no central air-conditioning system), at which time she began the trek back north, spending the last two weeks of May in the city before again taking up residence in Great Elm. That was the happy pattern of her existence for the final forty years of her life, into old age.

---

*Now my sister Priscilla's apartment.
†The New Barbarians have been at work in New York City also, obscuring the grandeur of the façade of Grand Central Station by what was then the towering Pan-Am Building.

NOTES

1. He was a thorough gentleman, in my memory of David Williams, all six feet three
    inches and two hundred plus pounds of him. When my then-bride Betsy Howell and
    I were invited to Mulberry for a wood-duck shoot one Christmas Eve, Betsy, who was
    seven months pregnant with our first son, dropped a gorgeous drake woodie five or six
    yards in the water, too deep for her to attempt retrieving. She was greatly excited, it
    being the first duck she had ever downed. "I'll get it!" I said to her, but the bird flut-
    tered another ten yards out, neck drooping, mortally stricken. The water was a foot
    too deep for me in my hip boots to permit my reaching it. She was heartbreakingly
    disappointed.

    That was when Big Dave Williams came sloshing toward us in his waders. With
    his customary graciousness, he was asking guests whether they needed help picking
    up their bag. When he reached our stand, I pointed the drake out to him, which was
    just a few feet off to his right. "I'll get that duck for you, little lady," he called to Betsy,
    and he waded *sloshsloshsloshslosh* deeper into the pond, a mammoth hulk in the fading twi-
    light. Arriving at the bird, he bent massively forward to grasp it, his impressive *avoir-
    dupois* walloping the water . . . whereupon the duck gave a flip of one of its wings and
    skeetered another twenty feet toward the center of the pond. Mr. Williams (we *re-
    ferred* to him as Big Dave, but we children never addressed him as other than *Mr.*
    Williams) straightened up, breathing heavily—he was in his mid-sixties at the time—
    but calling to Betsy once more, "I'll get that fool bird, little lady, don't you worry!" he
    sloshed determinedly out for it, the water rising to above his waist. We shouted at him
    please not to worry about the duck. He would have none of that. "I'll get it for you,
    don't you fret," he kept calling over his shoulder. Though we could barely discern the
    sequence in the rapidly thickening twilight, once again, *just* as he stooped and reached
    with his free arm for the duck, his belly walloping the water and now scooping some
    of it in, we could see the duck spurt a few feet farther into the pond. "Drat!" he let out,
    or some other exclamation. Betsy and I shouted, "Please, Mr. Williams, it's okay,
    someone with a dog will come by . . ." He paid no attention. He was going to get that
    duck for the young mother-to-be or his name wasn't David Williams, master of Mul-
    berry Plantation. "I'll get it," he growled with grim resolve, breathing hoarsely as a
    third time he *sloshedsloshedsloshed* out to the bird . . . which a third time eluded him.

    The memory is both painful and funny. Every time he bent down to retrieve the
    bird, the front of his waders scooping up a pailful of freezing water, it would elude
    him. "Darn!" he would say. I can't remember, but it may have been on the seventh or
    eighth attempt before Big Dave at last captured the duck, emitting a loud triumphant
    grunt, and *sloshsloshslosshsloshslosh* waded all the way back to us, handing it to Betsy.
    What a gallant and kind man he was.

    If it is not evident, I have a special fondness for David and Martha Williams, the
    particular friends of my mother and father, and their children, Martha and her hus-

band John Daniels (RIP), David (RIP), Katie, and Joe. They are sensitive to tales about haunts associated with Mulberry Plantation, so I relate my experience briefly.

When we first arrived in Camden (1972), my second wife, Tasa, and I and her five children and two of my four children by Betsy and our infant boy Johnny (ten all told) rented and lived in a cottage on Mulberry Plantation known as Hannah's Cabin, to everybody in Camden's astonishment, because no one comprehended how we all fit in. This enchanting brick structure, slave-built of almost pink bricks, is essentially a horseshoe. The base is a large square living room, with fireplace. Then there are two wings. The first consists of two bedrooms, separated by a short corridor with closets lining one of its walls, the second wing comprises a very large room in which, in beds that we pushed together side-by-side and in double bunks, we stuffed five of our fast-growing boys.

Going back to the first wing, the bedroom immediately adjacent to the living room, with twin beds, was slept in by Tasa's daughter Patricia Olano and my daughter Elizabeth Hanna Buckley, who were approximately the same age. Tasa and I occupied the bedroom down the short corridor.

One night at the bleary-eyed hour of sometime after midnight and before dawn, I was awakened by three sharp, loud raps. "What's that?" asked Tasa. "Dunno, can't imagine." We'd been living in Hannah's Cabin a full year, with no disturbance. I got up, slapped on a bathrobe, and made my way down the corridor, neither switching on the electric lights nor using a flashlight. (Had I attempted to use a flashlight, I would have found—I knew—its barrel empty, the boys having filched the batteries for their own uses.) There was sufficient pale light filtering in to see.

Just as I began walking down this corridor, I saw the door of our daughters' bedroom open, and the slim figure of a girl fifteen or sixteen years old, wrapped tightly in a nightgown and peignoir, slip out, leaving the door, as I thought, ajar, and enter the living room. In my bemused state, I assumed that it was stepdaughter Patricia or daughter Lizzie, possibly awakened by the rapping, going to the kitchen for ice water. But upon reaching our daughters' bedroom, I found the door closed.

I opened it, peeked in, and there the two girls were, in their beds, fast asleep.

At almost the same instant, I was accosted by two or three of my sons: Santiago, Claude, Borja, I can't recall which. They were crowding a mini-hall to the left of the corridor I was in, which admitted to the large living room. They had been aroused out of sleep in their wing of Hannah's Cabin and had come through the living room to my corridor, asking me what was happening, who had made that rapping sound.

I asked them in turn, "Didn't you see the girl going into the hall just this instant?"

It all happened in a slice of time: my seeing the apparition (which I now surmise it must have been), my peeking into the bedroom of our daughters, and our boys crowding toward me to ask about the rapping. They had to have bumped into or crossed the girl I had seen. But they said, "What girl?" "The girl that just now went into the living room!" They had seen nothing. I felt no chilling in my veins, the hairs on my nape did not prickle. "Oh," I responded to them, "that's curious. I thought I saw a girl come out of your sisters' bedroom just now and enter the living room." They looked at me quiz-zically, one of them repeating that no, they had seen no one.

We agreed that since their mother and I and they had heard the rapping, whereas Patricia and Lizzie were sound asleep, the rapping must have occurred between the two wings, and most probably against the hard panels of the front—the living-room—door, it was so loud. I went to that door, which opened directly out into the little courtyard between the wings of the cottage. It was nighttime, starless, but not alto-gether dark, either just before dawn, or maybe there was a moon in the sky, not quite veiled by clouds. I detected nothing. The boys, peering behind me and on either side of me, with their sharp eyes, detected nothing.

I didn't know what to tell them. "Must have been a coon in the attic." But it was no raccoon, they knew as well as I. It was a sharp, unmistakable *rapraprap*, waking us all up. "Good night," I said to them, who were just half awake, drugged by the impera-tive of sleep that all healthy young boys enjoy.

When I got back to my bedroom, Tasa asked me at once, "What was it?" I told her what I had seen. "Well, who was it?" she asked after a pause, of the wraith. I told her I had not the slightest idea . . . and I climbed into bed and went at once to sleep myself.

Tasa and I spoke briefly about it in the morning. I did not mention a word of it to the children, for fear of making them uneasy when they were alone in the cottage, though I did ask the girls whether one of them had not got up to fetch a glass of ice water or for any other reason. No, they both replied, looking at me curiously. Martha Williams Daniels, my liege lady, as I have called her affectionately since renting the cottage, told me that old Hannah had been an emancipated house slave, wife of the Chesnuts' coachman, Richmond, well loved by her family two generations back, but she knew of no "hant" answering to my description.

And there the incident rests. We never had another visitation, apparition, or dis-turbance, and lived happily in Hannah's Cabin several months more, as guests of Hannah, until the big cottage at Kamschatka became available to us.

2. In the event it is not abundantly evident, Camden, its fields, its woods, its swamps, and its people, are the backdrop for my novel, *Saving deSaussure Swamp: A Love Story* in the *Canticle of a Thrush* trilogy.

———— ✧ ————

CHAPTER TWENTY-TWO

Camden (IV):
Rev. Edmund Burke, Christmas
at Kamschatka, and an Excerpt
from Carol Virginia Buckley's
memoir, *At the Still Point*

AT MIDNIGHT MASS, EVERY CHRISTMAS, WHEN THE TIME CAME FOR THE homily, Father Edmund Burke would raise both his arms, throw back his head, his cheekbones rosy and glistening in the candlelight, and shout in a New York–born Bronx brogue that resounded throughout our little chapel, "This day the whole world explodes with joy. All over the world, joy bursts the hearts of the children of God, because this blessed day is our Savior born!"

And we his parishioners—I his acolyte—felt our hearts explode with that joy, no matter the lateness of the hour. His voice trembled with the exultation of happiness he was feeling, his whole being rocked and aflame with it. He beamed at us in the congregation, God love us every one, and we beamed back, our hearts lifted, loving him who brought us the word of God.

John Edmund Burke was born in New York City on November 8,

1899. His father was a native of New York; his mother hailed from Washington, D.C. He had one sister. He attended St. Lawrence Academy as a boy, received his secondary education from Mount Vernon High School in New York, and attended St. Benedict's College,* from which he received his degree "about" (his word) 1928. He can't have entered St. Mary's seminary directly after college, given what we know independently about his life, but he was ordained on May 26, 1934, at the Baltimore Cathedral by Archbishop Curley. He was appointed that next month to St. Patrick's, in Charleston,† and on September 30, 1938, was destined to Camden. To the question of whether he had built any churches, schools, or rectories, he answered, "No." Had he left a will? "No." He possessed nothing.

That's all we know about him. There is no other record left by him or filed about him, either in the parish or the diocese. I had to make inquiry of the archives of the Diocese of Charleston to glean this much, along with a copy of a photograph of him as a handsome young man with tight curly hair, a high forehead, and a pensive gaze. Oh, yes, somebody has written across the top of the form that he died on November 8, 1952, which would have made him just fifty-three years old, to the day.‡ There is no obituary in diocesan files. That bare record is all that exists about one of the most fervent and delightful servants of our Lord Jesus Christ to have walked this earth. His memory is dead in the offices of Our Lady of Perpetual Help, the church of which he was pastor for fourteen years. His memory is next to dead in the bishopric. It lingers only in the fading recollections of people my age and a little younger (my sister Carol, for example), yet . . .

He was the most devout man I ever knew. The Mass in those days was still in Latin, and when I brought him the wine to bless, or the water into which he dipped his fingers, I thrilled to the absolute abstraction of his gaze and demeanor as he murmured in barely audible tones the sacred rite in the language that nearly two thousand years of Christianity had made

---

*I don't know where, can't read his handwriting—this information comes from a form he filled out for the Diocese of Charleston.
† South Carolina was at the time—and still is—missionary country for Catholics.
‡ I am guessing the cause of death to be stomach cancer.

sacred. He had his back turned to the congregation almost all the Mass long; nothing was permitted to distract from his worship, in which, through him, we joined. He was there with us celebrating the sacrifice, and he was not there at all; his mind and spirit were with God. He had long, narrow, immaculately cared-for hands and long, beautiful fingers, and that was lucky, because he had made his living before becoming a priest thumping the piano in vaudeville and also tickling the ivories to a barrel-roll beat during the intermissions of silent flicks; and before that, he had been a sailor (he was known to his classmates in the seminary as "Sailor" Burke—I got that much from one elderly parishioner).

He was full of fun, and fun loved him. He enjoyed a good supper, and the ceiling of his nautically appointed private study was (scandalously) stippled with corks from the bottles of champagne of the best parties he had attended, several of them at Kamschatka. Father took to him at once (he was very much a man's man), as did Mother (he was very much a woman's ideal priest) and the rest of us young children (to whom he was by turns severe, kind, affectionate, and most often *fun*). He loved us "wee ones" (as he referred to us) especially, squinching up his eyes, peering at us down his long Irish nose from his six-foot-plus height and asking us in that Bronx-tinted Irish, "What have you been up to today of any interest to the Lord, hey?" When he laughed, he burbled with laughter. His cheeks filled with laughter like two balloons, and he pursed his lips the while as he struggled to keep his mouth closed. His face and mind were ruptured by laughter, which was a physical convulsion within him that he seemed unable to contain. He happily entered into conspiracies with us children, played our games of the imagination with us. I confided to him that I was the Bat, to be distinguished from Batman, though equally feared by the Joker and other malefactors. He nodded his head complacently. "How many villains did you bring to justice this past week?" I would give him a number. "Don't you think it should have been more? After all, you are the Bat, and Gotham City won't long survive until you rid it of its wrong-doers." This was our private virtual reality, and our private joke, because we both knew that in the realm of adult reality it was nonsense, yet in the much more vivid and truer world of boyhood it was fact. "Father, this is Reid. I wanted to ask you . . ." "What does the Bat wish to ask of a grateful citizen of Gotham City?" He gave me a slim little prayer book that I have treasured these past sixty-five years, which is now so worn and fragile that I use it only during the passion on Good Fridays, when I take it out and read the seven Penitential Psalms (* of man's loneliness in this universe and of his ultimate salvation, the most beautiful poems ever written.), and glance at the inscription, "To my dear friend, 'The Bat,'" and below that, in the flowing script of his era, "Rev. J. E. Burke, Camden, SC, Feb 2 42."[†]

We slipped in and out of the make-believe, depending. When I had sin on my soul, which was frequently (are younger sisters not made to have their pigtails yanked, and is it unnatural for a boy to wish to be the immediate violent cause of his younger sister's demise?), and wanted to confess, or simply wished for his counsel, he fell at once serious, and listened with absolute attention in his study or in the confessional, asking me sharp questions that would not permit of me any false attitude, sanctimoniousness, self-pity, dodge, extenuation, telling me just exactly where I had done wrong, and why it was wrong, and by waiting a whole month to get this off my soul how stupidly I had risked condemnation because I had betrayed Jesus God's love for me, I had smacked Him right in the face with it. Those chill predawn mornings before the six-fifteen daily Mass, he would enter the sacristy jovially and ask us acolytes how we were and how our families fared, and make a few wisecracks, and then, suddenly, as he turned to the enameled basin in the corner and soaped and washed his hands, drying them on a little towel, and began donning his robes, the small talk and the kidding were done, he had become all at once solemn, his high forehead corrugated in concentration, the skin between his eyebrows furrowed, he was not with us at all, he was praying. He never said, "All right, we're ready, let's go into the church," or anything at all. He simply nodded curtly at us (there were almost always two of us boys on Sundays, often just me at daily Mass), and we would precede him into the church, entering to the left of the altar. From the moment of the Introit, his solemnity and total devotion increased with each movement in the order of the Mass. When he blessed the wine, and again when we altar boys offered the salver of water into which he moistened his white-pink

---

*Boy, could those Jews write!
†That little prayer book had been inscribed to him, "God bless you—Father Fred Maynard, St. Charles College, Gatonsville, Md." The apostolic succession at work. The little book is leather-bound, printed in Czechoslovakia. Its title is *A Manual of Catholic Devotions*, Mangan Company, Providence-Chicago-New York, 1925.

sinewy fingers, drying them meticulously on the little cloth we presented
to him, he did not once glance at us, he was looking at nothing on this
earth, he was immersed in the mystery in which he was taking part. And
when, just before Communion, he uttered in his low, virile, thrilling voice,
"Ecce Agnes Dei, qui tollit peccati mundi," "Behold the lamb of God, behold
Him Who takest away the sins of the world," extending the host held
above the chalice of Christ's blood toward the congregation, his cheeks
mottled pink, we were seeing Him.

The forty days of Lent under Father Burke was the most moving experience I have ever been exposed to. Ash Wednesday was arresting (especially to children, the notion that we were dust, and to dust—dust!—we
would return), but there lingered in the corners of his lips the mirth that
was natural to him. Often during the early weeks of Lent, he accepted
suppers at Kamschatka, but then came Passion Week, when all the statues
in the church and even the Stations of the Cross were robed in purple.*
When those familiar figures and images were hidden from sight, it seemed
as though a preternatural silence had fallen on the chapel. There was no
visual conversation. There was the terrible trepidation that God was preparing to abandon His kingdom. The interior course settings of Father
Burke—his bearings—deepened at the same time, and as they accumulated, the toll of the forty days on him became visible, he was fasting, his
self-mortifications intensified, the blush of the bon vivant had drained
from his cheekbones. Tall and spare, he had evidently lost many pounds.
The weekly Stations of the Cross were an experience none of us forgot.
He entered the church briskly, recited a short invocation at the foot of the
altar (he had a lithe way of kneeling, bending the knee toward the object
of veneration and falling forward on it), and without further ado began
the rounds of the images depicting Jesus in that terrible last journey. By
the time he reached Station XII, where Jesus dies on the cross, we were
shaken. He paused long by the pew at this station, genuflecting slowly
("We adore Thee O Christ, and we praise Thee . . . "), rising slowly ("because through Thy holy Cross, Thou hast redeemed the world"), contem-

---

* This was done by Miss Brown with the help of her friend and living companion, Miss
Virginia Wallace, two spinsters who lived across Lyttleton Street from the church (and one
house up), whom I came to know well.

plating the Christ hanging outward by His hands from the crossbeam in the awful abandonment of death.

Holy Week was a terrible time. At the Maundy Thursday Mass, with its long Passion gospel, Father Burke seemed wasted, waxen, worn close to exhaustion. During the Stations of the Cross on Good Friday, which began sharp at noon, the first hour of the Passion, and which lasted almost forty-five minutes, he paused after the second and third falls of Christ ("I love Thee, O my Jesus, with my whole heart. I repent of having offended Thee. Never permit me to offend Thee again. Grant that I may love Thee always; and then do with me what Thou wilt")* for lengthy intervals, to recompose and recollect himself. He left the church immediately after the final invocation. At three-thirty P.M., he returned to it. The solemnity was at its highest, but the pent suffering seeped now as though in a long breath out of him: *"Consummatis est."* The ordeal was over, the Passion done.

I do not remember seeing him on Holy Saturday. On Easter morning, he was a changed man. His appearance was still drawn, his wrists were knobby from the weight he had lost, but his smile was back, and his homily was a paean of happiness. The glorious Resurrection had taken place, that triumph over Satan and mortality, and the world was able to revolve another long, sinful year before the time came once again to repent, to do penance, and to commemorate the cosmologically stunning event in comparison to which, for Christians, the Big Bang is a mere *poof*!†

I have known only two people who so totally absorbed themselves in prayer as Father Burke was able to, by which I mean intimate and direct communication with the ineffable. They were John Paul II and my mother. When in 1987 the still vigorous pope visited South Carolina and spoke at the Williams Bryce football stadium, tens of thousands of people filling the grandstands, he smiled at the crowd as he strode in, and laughed at something that was called out to him, calling back, and then—all of a sudden—walked directly to an improvised shrine that showed an image of Our Lady, flung himself to his knees before it, and was immediately ab-

---

*He used the text according to Saint Alphonsus Liguori.

†No greater happiness at the Resurrection have I encountered, though it has been amplified by Anglican Bishop N. T. Wright's scholarly examination of the event in his profound recent book.

sorbed in devotion while all the vast crowd around him fell as close to silence as this is possible for thousands of people packed together, remaining on his knees . . . was it five, ten, fifteen minutes? It was a very long time, during which he was oblivious to what was going on about him, before he reverently crossed himself and rose to face the celebrants with open arms and a glad broad smile in which love and merriment shone. In a similar way, Mother would kneel—in her bedroom, or in the pew she liked to use at church—her lips sibilating her prayers, her eyes glassy, absorption in her worship total. She was so beautiful at those times, an image of devotion into very old age. This is one of the imperishable images of her that all her children will carry to their graves.

A second remarkable characteristic of these three (remarkable) people, Mother, the late pope, and Father Burke, is that they all three loved fun, had a high sense of glee, and exuded the happiness that they drew upon for whatever awaited them. They derived that happiness from their inner spiritual peace. From them I learned that faith *is* happiness, for which reason I pity, lament, sorrow for, and yearn somehow to help those who are bereft of faith, and despise such as the late Francis Crick, who made intellectual sport of the pious and who gloried like a wicked British schoolboy in his disdain for their superstition. The superiority of our arrogant materialists—of the "New Atheists," Dawkin, Hitchens, et al.—not noticeable in the urn that contains, or will contain, their ashes, to which, of course, along with their brains, in which their ability to reason is consumed, their pride is at the end reduced.

WHEREVER WE WERE, CHRISTMAS WAS BOTH HOLY AND FUN.

Father rarely gave costly gifts, but as consciousness of advancing age began to weigh on him, it seemed that he looked for excuses to manifest his love and affection in a manner that did not embarrass him and that he felt would not embarrass the recipient. One unforgettable Christmas, in Camden, when I was fifteen, he presented several of us with .20-gauge Winchester Model 21 shotguns, skeet grade. I was beside myself with joy. They were the finest side-by-sides manufactured in our country since the Parker company had ceased fabricating its fowling pieces. The stock of mine was of exceptionally configured walnut, and I treasured the weapon for years and years.* On another Christmas he gave all his sons and his then only son-in-law and such close junior executives as Dean Reasoner quite gaudy garnet and gold cufflinks and studs, from Sulka, which were handsome, and which I wore for forty or fifty years, until I ceased going to dances and fancy suppers. I can't recall another such personal gift from my father, though he was generous to the point of folly if any of us was pinched or in need. The point I want to make is that we children looked forward ordinarily not so much to the presents as to the immersion in family unity and the joy we derived from it. We sang carols, and while we still celebrated the holidays in Sharon, we sallied out on cold Christmas Eves as a family unit—Allie, Pitts, Jim, Jane, Bill, Patricia, and down to Maureen and me—to bring joy, as we assumed, to our neighbors, and death, as it turned out, to one of them.

The Colgate mansion a half-mile down the Amenia Road was a vast marble and stucco Italianate villa, or palace, or—we children privately thought—mausoleum, which a certain Mrs. Colgate, who had lived many years of her life in Tuscany, had had built for her, and in whose hugeness she lived totally alone, except for servants. I forget why she had no family. But this particular Christmas (which, I surmise, was the last we spent in Sharon), Allie and Pitts and Jim and Jane debated whether we ought to risk caroling her. We had never done so; no one in Sharon, native or summer resident, had any contact with her at all; she was rumored to be grim and disagreeable and a little scary. Would she set dogs on us? Allie made the decision, we went, and we sang our repertoire at the foot of the entrance portals, the palace looming above us on that cold, clear night in ghostly manner, with gargoyles glinting from between the fourth-story eaves, staring down in our direction . . . giving us all the shivers. No notice was taken of our caroling through "Joy to the World." "Hark the Herald Angels" sang, or bawled, with nil effect. We were Nooëling, Nooëling for all our might, wondering whether this hadn't been an awful mistake, when we discerned the glimmering of a candle from deep inside the house approach one of the windows on the second floor, and a heavy velvet curtain

---

*I shot with it all over the world, for quail, grouse, redleg partridges, doves, and snipe, finally relinquishing it to my second son and namesake, from whom, alas, it was stolen in Camden by one of the employees of the then-plumbers.

being drawn partly back. Revealed was a very old woman with her long gray-white hair hanging unbound down her back, wearing a gray or white or light blue sleeping gown and peignoir of some sort. She stood there with the candle dimly illuminating heavily lined features, staring down at us with a countenance absolutely devoid of expression. We labored into our "Silent Night," at the end of which she drew the drapery or the curtain shut, and the candle receded from our view.

That was it. The next morning Mrs. Colgate was found dead in her bed. Whether we had eased or brought some minimum solace to, or inconvenienced, or, awful thought, contributed to her passing, we never knew but speculated openly about. (Our brother John, who did not participate in our caroling, favored the hypothesis that we had hastened Mrs. Colgate's demise, for which opinion he was roundly booed.) I don't truly recall whether that was the last night that our voices rent the Christmas Eves of Connecticut, but we never attempted to carry on the custom in Camden. Besides, we were at war.

The decorations of Kamschatka for Christmas were nevertheless elaborate. Mother planned them all, and, until she grew too old, helped put them up. On the front doors of the basement and the second-floor piazza entrances were pungent, sweet-smelling wreaths of cedar, pine, and holly with its bright red berries. The smooth polished banister and the numberless rails of the entire glorious central pine staircase, falling in wide expansive steps, like lapping waves, from the third floor all the way down to the second floor, were wrapped in garlands of pine, sprigs of holly, and, on the curved newel posts at the bottom, swags of bright red satin ribbons. Above the frame of every major doorway was a garland of pine from the midst of which mistletoe dangled. Smilax punctuated with the giant cones of the longleaf pine decorated fireplace mantelpieces. The whole interior of Kamschatka, all three floors, smelled of fresh-cut, resinous pine branches.

In her memoir, *At the Still Point* (Simon & Schuster), our sister Carol remembers Christmas in Kamschatka differently from the rest of us—and from the viewpoint of a little girl:

It is Christmas, maybe 1945 or 1946,* and I am allowed to stay up almost to midnight Mass. I have had an extra-long nap. I sleep in a front

---

*Sister Carol is therefore seven or eight years old.

bedroom on the roomy third floor.* I have a white wallpaper with roses twining up and down. I have a rose rug, too, and white-painted furniture. Pupa is trying to braid my hair, but it is quite slippery and not thick enough. The silky bows keep falling off.

Downstairs I can hear my mother running up and down the stairs, her heels tap-tapping, her voice calling out, "Oh, Elizabeth . . . Ella!" My mother's calling voice has a lilt to it. The house is bustling and for two days there has been the smell of baking and of furniture oil that Jeff rubs up and down the banisters, polishing the pine glossy-smooth. The first floor is full of pots of ugly red flowers—I am insulted to be reminded not to eat them!

In the downstairs dining room, the mahogany table—the big one, not the one I sit at—has been extended its full length. The walls are covered with a creamy magnolia-print paper, gilt mirrors, and an oil portrait of a soulful young Andrew Jackson, turning his face to the left so that his dueling scar doesn't show.† On the table is a silver epergne filled with fruit and nuts nestled in little clusters on the magnolia leaves. There are silver bowls‡ of after-dinner mints and bonbons. Ella has set the table three or four times. She is a perfectionist. She asks me please to go play somewhere else§—she can't concentrate while I am there. She floats red camellias in a pair of Lalique bowls.

Jeff is also too busy to play, vacuuming up a storm—loud, so people can hear that he is working; Jeff does work hard, except when he has a sleepy smile on his face and his breath smells funny. Sally, in the kitchen, who is usually nice to me, tells me plainly to "git." She won't even give me a bite of corn bread stuffing or a nibble of pumpkin pie crust. Sweat streams down her face, and the kitchen smells of that, and cinnamon.

Maureen won't play with me because Patricia is home from Vassar.¶ Patricia is her favorite sister. Maureen is my favorite sister, though I

---

*It wasn't "roomy" for her adorable elder brother by eight years, who was consigned to a cramped ell next to Mademoiselle's full-sized bedroom, which, as I have explained in another context, was stifling hot.

†Jackson received the scar from the saber of a redcoat officer in Camden for refusing to shine the redcoat's boots. He was sixteen or seventeen.

‡Two are in my possession.

§ Ella and Elizabeth and the other servants addressed Carol as "Little Miss."

¶Maureen is twelve or thirteen, Trisha eighteen or nineteen.

think this Christmas maybe I'll make Jane my favorite.* Jane has a long brown page-boy, wears red lipstick, and has boyfriends. She is beautiful and very rebellious. She goes to Smith College and smokes! Behind Father's back, of course. My father's back, of course. My father says smoking is cheap and bad for your health—what does he know! Reid, who sometimes plays with me, is awful.† He always is when "the boys" are home. He always wants to be with them, impressing them. They aren't impressed, but they seem to like him all right. John does a lot of talking, and so does Billy.‡ They talk talk that you can't get into, batting sentences back and forth, clipped and fast like a Ping-Pong ball. Jimmy is quiet and laughs at their jokes.§ Pitts hangs out with the boys.¶

She goes shooting with John, walking through the crisp woods, waiting for the dogs to freeze in point. Sometimes, if I promise to be very quiet, I am allowed to go and watch. When the dogs point, rigid and trembling with excitement, I hold my breath. There will be a tremendous flutter as the covey breaks, and then the pow-pow-pow of shotguns, and the smoky smell of spent powder. The dogs on command—"Fetch it! Fetch it!" they're ordered—race to retrieve the quarry, then return to John and Priscilla and delicately drop the birds at their feet, not a feather misplaced, not a tooth mark to be found. They wag their tails for a job well done, and I am allowed to pat them thank you. We bring home the quail and have it for Sunday brunch: roast quail, bacon, grits, and broiled tomatoes. Pitts plays golf too.

My other sisters just ride horses, but mostly Jane and Patricia "rest" in their bedroom upstairs, reading and smoking. Sometimes I'm allowed in, sometimes, of course, it's grown-up time, the time they don't want me to hear the things they say. They're right, because sometimes I tell Mademoiselle or Pupa, and of course I always tell Maureen. Always.

Mostly, I feel very, very excited, because of Santa Claus. He almost

* Either twenty-one or twenty-two years old.
† Either sixteen or seventeen.
‡ Respectively, either twenty-six or twenty-seven, twenty-one or twenty-two.
§ Either twenty-four or twenty-five.
¶ Either twenty-five or twenty-six.

comes just for me, I'm the only one who gets a stocking, though the stocking is always a disappointment. It has things like oranges in it, and walnuts! I wish it had gum. My sister Patricia has shining red hair and a temper to match and likes to break rules: she always gives me gum, and anything else I want! I like it that they are all home. I hate it that they are all home. Lots of the time I'm "in the way."*

Our Mexican nurses, Nana and Pupa, are planning a *"posada"* for after dinner and before midnight Mass. I wonder how many other people in South Carolina parade around after Christmas Eve dinner, chanting lugubriously in Spanish that there is no room at the inn? We march in a dolorous line, singing off-key,† and Nana, who is always self-important, plays Joseph, knocking at the inn doors and getting turned away. When Mary and Joseph finally find a room in the stable, the *posada* is over. We are blindfolded and given brooms to try to knock down and break the *piñata*. I, of course, always fail, though everyone is rooting for me, and piggy Reid finally steps in and knocks it down.

Oh, goodness, the things Reid does! Once he walked around all summer in Sharon, saying the Mass in Latin in every single Great Elm room—and there must have been thirty at least if you count the servants' quarters. He wanted to "purify" the house! My father says he danced and sang in England once, in front of a whole crowd of people waiting to see the king. That was the same king that Billy wrote to, asking that he repay Britain's war debt to the United States. Reid was the first member of the Millbrook football team to rub black grease under his eyes to shade them from the glare.‡ Just like the pros. Unfortunately he left quite a lot of grease on his hands and kept fumbling the ball.§ He also rode horses recklessly and often fell off.¶ "There goes

---

* As Carol explains in the balance of the book, she was the afterthought, so very many critical years (five) than the next-youngest sibling, Maureen. All the others were in their (naturally selfish) teens and even older, in their twenties. She dwells often on my saintly tolerance of her.

† Humph. Not everyone.

‡ If that ever happened, he was about thirty years ahead of his time . . . which is just about right.

§ Alas, so.

¶ He never "fell off." He was thrown off. The difference is absolute.

Buckley back for [more] blood," cried a bystander at the Goshen [Connecticut] Horse Show. Reid positively floated on that one for the rest of the summer.*

But right now, Reid has stolen the limelight at the wrong time. I am meant to break the *piñata*, not attention-grabbing Reid. I am the baby—the *piñata* is for me! He looks puzzled and hurt when no one applauds him. I don't care! The *piñata* has just more oranges and walnuts. I know it is Nana who has filled it (and probably my stocking too!) Nana is Felipa's† enemy. They have lived and worked side by side for over twenty years, but they don't speak.‡ Nana is mean, and makes up to Mother all the time in a phony way that even I can recognize. And Mother falls for it!

My mother even falls for Father's jokes! Sometimes I think she's dim-witted—and sometimes I think she pretends. To please him. My mother works hard at pleasing everyone and it makes her tired. My father, however, looks pleased just to see me; his eyes light up when I enter the room. He knows that I'm brave and good even though he never says so—to say is to spoil and a "spoiled brat" is the worst thing you can be in my family.

Father won't be smiling at me for very long. He will become a cripple from strokes. He will sit in a wheelchair, and sometimes for no apparent reason tears will roll down his cheeks. But tonight I don't know that, tonight after the *posada*, the colored carolers will come from the First Zion Baptist Church, Jeff's church.

We hear them first outside on the drive, great deep baritones and lush contraltos: "Go Tell It on the Mountain." Mother acts surprised and runs to the door to invite them in. Then it's "Little David, Play on Your Harp," "Nobody Knows the Troubles I've Seen," and then "Silent Night" and "Joy to the World!" Mother always asks for one of the spirituals a second time. If they choose to sing "Sometimes I Feel Like a Motherless Child," tears come to her eyes. Me too—songs about mothers make me very sad. The carolers are invited to the kitchen for

---

* The tale is much more elaborate and exciting, but I forbear: it all had to do with a beautiful girl from Mamaroneck.
† Pupa's enemy.
‡ Though they were the only Spanish-speaking people other than the family in one hundred miles.

eggnog and fruitcake. Their eggnog is on the kitchen table in a very nice glass bowl. Ours is in the dining room in a great silver bowl that sweats from the icy cream inside. There is a discreet envelope by the toaster made out to First Zion. Everyone says "Merry Christmas!" and the carolers leave by the back door. Some of them haven't smiled from beginning to end; others make little bows, tipping their heads, and smile constantly. No one, black or white, seems embarrassed by this charade. It seems quite natural and spontaneous; it all seems a part of Christmas cheer.

When the carolers leave, I am taken to bed. The mysteries of midnight Mass and the scents of candlewax and evergreens and the sound of voices soaring in the black night are not yet for me. No stirring Father Burke sermon. They said he came from vaudeville and I believe it. What an Irishman he is! What a charmer, though I resent him because he always pinches my dimples and says he is going to fill them with plaster of Paris. When I make my first confession at age seven, he gives me absolution and a penance of three Hail Marys . . . and a can of plaster of Paris.

I cry. I don't want to go to bed. I want to be with them, *los grandes*. Always—just want to be one of them. And it never happens. Pupa takes me upstairs and I cry and kick and scream, and John, who is a sucker for distressed little children, comes up and tells me a story about the Lone Ranger. He is another of my heroes. And then—this is very typical of my brother John—he ends the story by saying that the Lone Ranger has to wear a mask because he is sooo ugly, and cross-eyed, too! This makes me feel terrible all over again, but I do not dare to cry with John. Only Pupa can see me cry, and Maureen.

The next morning is mine—but there is almost no one around to enjoy it with. For they are sleepy and still in bed. Only my tired parents hover about, and Priscilla, I think, and Maureen, and of course the nurses. And every Christmas I get pretty much the same thing: dolls and books. I like dolls, but year after year after year I ask Santa for the Bones Brothers Ranch from the F. A. O. Schwarz catalogue. I am in the middle of a horse phase, and sometimes I do not speak, I only neigh and snort. I trot and canter everywhere and ask people to address me as Gallant Bess. Sometimes I am Missy; sometimes Black Beauty.

Santa Claus will never bring the Bones Brothers Ranch. Finally, when I am twelve, Priscilla, who is also my godmother, and Bill, who is my godfather, buy it for me. Of course I am too old for it by then—I am already beginning to collect photos of Montgomery Clift. But I appreciate what they have done; I know what they mean.

I take my dolls and books upstairs and put them carefully on my bed. I am very happy. I never think to go downstairs again. I will have my Christmas lunch early in the breakfast room with Pupa. I play for the rest of the morning in my room with my dolls. I look through the books quickly, flip through the pictures. I give the dolls names—that is the hardest part. Some names don't suit, and I have to start it all over again. Then I must introduce them to my other dolls, and soon I am making up stories about them. I instruct the new dolls about how to behave and tell them their roles. Otherwise, they won't fit in and can't be part of my stories. I hear the laughter downstairs and the talk, so much talk, but really it is better up here alone. It is cozier, and it is all my own. And that is how I'm learning to be—more comfortable alone than with the family downstairs.

CHRISTMAS IN CAMDEN HAD ITS PERILS.

Father, like most Texans I know, loved smoked turkey, which I, like most people I know, love less. But off the back terrace of Kamschatka, near Cottage 1,* he had caused to be erected (from elaborate blueprints) an outdoor brick barbecue which was cunningly shaped in the chimney area so that fumes from hickory, sage, and mesquite (imported, sent to him from Austin by his adoring sisters) were exhausted, after having passed through the meat; and on the glowing embers of which he himself (in later years, Jeff Boykin under his careful watch and direction) tenderly deposited a mammoth turkey (also imported from Texas; no inferior provenance would do, unless it was his brother Edmund's spread along the Santa Clara River near Tampico), which was covered and permit-

---

*Built to house our sister Allie, her husband Ben, and their rapidly proliferating brood. There were ultimately three other (smaller) cottages for overflowing children and their spouses, as well as Father's spacious and beautiful Georgian office at the end of the west garden—a nice matinal walk for him between assorted camellias and (in season) beds of pink, purple, blush-red, and white azaleas.

ted to bake for twenty-four hours. Oh, the anticipation. "You are going to taste *real* Texas smoked turkey," he remarked to us, his mouth set in such fashion as to indicate that had we never in our impoverished gustatory imaginations dreamed of a viand to compare. Those of us children whom he was able to collar for the grand uncovering* waited with expectant breath as the top of the baking tureen was plucked off. Typically of him in this moment of triumph (or disaster), Father hung back, expectant, yet worrying that he might have put the kitchen staff to a lot of trouble for nothing. The center of any stage, even that of his own carpentry, he was too shy to occupy. And to tell the truth, when the turkey came out well, it was pretty good. Father—on those occasions proud, expansive, jubilant—carved the first slices himself, and they simply crumbled away from the edge of the blade like lace pastry. But *mama mía!* when the turkey turned out after twenty-four hours not fully baked, or baked to a diminished blackened corpse subsiding from the high scaffolding of the breast bone, how clouds gathered on his forehead! He would turn away and walk to his office or to his bedroom suite, not to be seen again until supper.

John, bursting in from quail shooting: "What a morning. Nine coveys! We picked up twenty-three birds. Would I be boasting if I allowed that my superior skill accounted for seventeen of them?"

"You would be," said Allie.

"You generally do," said Jane.

"He's just telling the truth," said Priscilla loyally, and also from considerable experience of shooting with her elder brother.

"You stick up for your brother," said Mother, instantly loyal herself. "John, do get out of those wet trousers and boots, you are tracking mud into the hall and wetting the carpets. Lunch is in ten minutes."

"Mother, give your peerless nimrod son a kiss . . . say, where's Father?"

"He's upstairs in his room," answered Mother, a touch defensively.

"The turkey?" asked John.

"The turkey," we all as a Greek chorus answered.

But Father got over it before Christmas. That blessed morning after midnight Mass we slept late, getting up about nine or nine-thirty. Now that we were all older and were not receiving bicycles and such, the Christ-

---

*In their wisdom, my elder siblings discovered excuses to be absent.

mas tree was situated on the righthand corner of the little pine room, and presents spread out from its skirts in a tumble. We gathered there for the grand opening, during which Jeff and Ella served us small mugs of egg-nog out of the great bowl of milky Mexican silver (there is no silver like it) that Father had had cast and incised for him by the old Sanborn's drug-store in the Zócalo.* Father Burke had been invited, and though weary from the midnight Mass and the follow-up ten A.M. Mass, he appeared in grand good humor, bowing to and kissing Mother on the cheeks, chor-tling, exchanging greetings with Father. We were always shooed by Mother into the dining room. ("The poor servants can't begin their Christmas until we get through lunch. You mustn't delay, children.") The table setting was the grandest that Mother's store of exquisite china of-fered, and there were tall-stemmed glasses for water and champagne (and maybe Mother's favorite Chateau d'Yquem), girt 'round about their crowns with carved gold leaf. Turkey (common Butterball, more often than not, as I've indicated) and corn-bread stuffing and gravy and cranberry jelly and rice and lima beans and stewed onions and crisp thin biscuits were served. Everybody talked too much, and half a dozen conversations were carried on simultaneously, which, as you have read, irritated our baby sis-ter Carol in her bedroom on the third floor, and which Father detested, calling it a barbarian American custom. He liked everyone to harken po-litely to whoever was speaking.† It may have been at this Christmas lun-cheon or at a supper the week following that one of Father's most elaborate (and successful) practical jokes had its inception.

FATHER BURKE TOLD ABOUT THE INHERITANCE THAT OUR LADY OF Perpetual Help Church was expecting to receive from the estate of old Mrs. O'D——, a devout lady, who had passed away that October in her home in Old Chatham, New York. He was looking forward to the bequest with elation. It wasn't money he was hoping for, you understand. Mrs. O'D—— was a lady who had traveled extensively, and who had promised

---

*I now own it . . . and every Christmas morning serve my children and sister Priscilla egg-nog from it.

†There was a second reason for this preference, which I now understand and sympathize with: for a person partly deaf, as he was, simultaneous chatter can be bedlam.

him something special for the garden. The church had been built in simple Spanish mission style. It was lovely, with its rounded asymmetrical steeple. Off to one side, connecting with the rectory, was an open patio with a fountain in the center and pretty decorative tiles in Spanish design. Mrs. O'D—— had mentioned to him a certain jar that she had acquired in Oaxaca or maybe it was Puebla, Mexico, which she declared would look beautiful in this garden. " 'Or,' the dear woman said to me," he explained enthusiastically, mimicking her voice, " 'it is such a handsome precious jar, Faitherrr, that y'might be wanting to place it at the entrance of the church.' Aloïse, Will, I can't wait!"

Three or four weeks later, there was a call from Father Burke. Mother and Father were alone, except for Carol; the rest of us had gone back to school or college or work. Mother spoke with him. Oh, how downcast he was. "It came this afternoon, Aloïse, that bequest from Mrs. O'D——!"

"How wonderful, Father. You must be excited."

His voice was mournful, however. "I was, Aloïse, until the delivery men unwrapped it."

"What's that, Aloïse?" Father.

She cupped the receiver with one hand. "The jar arrived, Will, he's just telling me about it!"

Father Burke continued. "It's huge, Aloïse, it must be four feet tall, weigh three hundred pounds. It's shaped like a pear, and it's done in an awful pink terra-cotta glaze . . ."

Mother was simultaneously transcribing for Father. "He says it's very large and ugly, a great big pink terra-cotta thing . . ."

"He can sell it," said Father.

"I can't sell it, Aloïse, tell Will," said Father Burke, overhearing. "Who would buy it? It's a monster. It took two men to deliver it from the truck. And anyway, it would be ungrateful . . ."

They invited him over for supper.

"We Irish are a remarkable people in many respects," Father Burke began without preliminaries.

"In most respects," agreed Father.

"In most respects," said Father Burke emphatically.

"Including reprehensible respects," added Father with a glint in his eye, quite probably thinking of Irish drunkenness, Irish string beans, and Irish politics, as in Tammany Hall in New York or Chicago.

"I am getting to that. The life of a parish priest isn't simple. When a parishioner makes a gift in his will, it can't be rejected, which is discourteous, and it can't be sold, which is disrespectful to the dead."

"So you're stuck with this jar," said Mother, displaying her practical Swiss-German ancestry by getting to the point.

"That's the dreadful right of the matter, Aloïse, I am . . . stuck with it, and . . ."

"What has this got to do with the Irish," put in Father, "apart from Mrs. O'D—— being of Irish extraction? I must say, I despise the professional Irish in this country. Saint Patrick's Day parades have always struck me as an embarrassing ostentation."

"When you drive into a new town, Will, how do you locate the Catholic church?"

"By asking which is the ugliest church in town, and usually of dark brick."

"Exactly. And why?"

"Because an Irish parish built it under an Irish-American priest," he added pointedly.

"Which brings us to the problem of the Irish," Mother said, perhaps a mite too quickly. But both men nodded.

"The Irish are blessed with a million sterling qualities, Aloïse," said Father Burke, "but they can't cook—could I have some more of that veal?—and they have terrible taste in other matters."

"So what are you going to do with that great big ugly jar?" asked Father, who was also deeply practical, despite his visionary dimensions, which is why he married Mother and was devoted to her.

"I don't know," replied Father Burke in a truly pitiable tone. It offended his uncommonly fine aesthetic sense, to have that great big awful pink terra-cotta jar defacing the view of the church from Lyttleton Street. He shook his head. "Right up front there, at the door, where she desired it to be, poor darlin' soul, which wish I can't deny her, could you?"

Which was when the idea was kindled in Father's agile mind.

Three or four weeks later, he again asked Father Burke for supper. This was a genial affair. It was the Tuckers and the Robinsons, fellow parishioners and winter residents, and among them was the brilliant, saturnine Vladimir Chadinov, the White Russian expatriate, who was spending a weekend with us.* Ordinarily our priest would not have been included, because this was a Saturday night, and there was an evening Mass at six o'clock, but Father himself got on the telephone and urged Father Burke to come. He would enjoy Chadinov, who was a most cultivated gentleman. "Besides," he added mysteriously, "I have something to show you."

The conversation was general until dessert had been served, when Mr. Chadinov was asked by Mother, "Before the Reds took over, you were a curator at the Hermitage, in St. Petersburg, weren't you?"

At which Mr. Robinson asked, "Florida?"

To which the startled White Russian demurred. No, he had not been. "Of course not, Aloïse!" Father said to her across the table. "I declare, you seem sometimes incapable of getting anything straight. Chadinov is an expert in Egyptian art, not the French Impressionists."

"Actually," said Chadinov in his habitually modest fashion, "it is pre-Columbian art for which I am well . . . known, as one might put it."

"Pre-who?" asked rail-thin Mr. Tucker.

"Before Columbus," said plump Mrs. Tucker hastily.

"In Mexico? What could they have been possibly making art about?" asked her sister, plump and jolly Mrs. Robinson.

"There's no museum by that name in St. Petersburg, Florida," stated Mr. Robinson, who had been worrying the question.

Which ended that elevated conversation until coffee, served across the hall from the dining room, in the pine room, when Mr. Chadinov said to my father, "Will, when are you going to let me see that piece you purchased at the Parke Bernet auction last week? You were high on it. Has it arrived?"

"Yes, it has," admitted Father, seemingly as though uncomfortable. "This very afternoon, in fact." And he eyed Jeff Boykin—who was entering with the tray of glasses filled with icewater—in subtly meaningful fashion, which meant that Father probably opened his eyes very wide and raised his eyebrows very high, to which, in response, Jeff smile broadly, winking owlishly.

---

*Actually, I have no idea which visiting guest Father corralled for his deception; it may have been Mr. Himes, his partner in several ventures, but Mr. Chadinov, with his thick accent, would have been a good choice.

Anybody who had happened to witness this interchange between master and butler would have been perplexed.

"Well, when am I going to see it?" insisted Mr. Chadinov.

"I am afraid you'll tell me I was taken in for a sucker—a rube from Texas. The auctioneer claimed it was very fine, one of a kind. But they are paid to say that kind of thing . . ."

"Oh, show it to him, Will," said Mother. "Do!" To the other guests, now intrigued, and to Father Burke, "He has it right out the front door. He has been dying to show it to you all evening." And she jumped to her feet, stepping lightly down from the pine room to the polished square bricks of the hall and leading everyone to the front door.

This, I should remark, was the first-floor door we children and our parents used; the formal entrance was by the second floor, which is how the guests had all entered Kamschatka.

And which is why they had not seen the enormous terra-cotta jar that stood to one side of the door on the ground floor. Everyone gaped. Father Burke's mouth was open, and his eyes practically bugged out of their sockets. Mr. Chadinov went quickly to it, examining it closely. He straightened up, saying in as excited a tone of voice as he was capable, "Will, you were lucky. There are so many counterfeits on the market. This is indeed what the Parke Bernet auctioneer claimed it is: a magnificent pre-Columbian terra-cotta jar dating, I would guess, from 400 or 600 A.D., and from that distinctive pink glazing, which only the early Mayans achieved, I would guess probably dug up in the ruins of Palenque. I am struck dumb by its beauty, Will, but you must also keep in mind that it is priceless. There may not be another one like it on earth."

All the while he spoke, Father Burke was gaping at the jar, and he was now all but dancing on his toes. At Mr. Chadinov's last words, he shouted, "I've got one! I've got its exact twin. The same pink glazing. At the church! Oh, oh, oh, I must run!" And he rushed into the night, jumping into his car and swinging down the long circular driveway to Kirkwood Lane . . .

It was nearly nine o'clock. The other guests soon departed—leaving Mother and Father and Mr. Chadinov convulsed in laughter. No, Father hadn't had a replica made, nor had he found its mate at Parke Bernet or anywhere else. After dark, when the Saturday evening Mass was over and as Mother and Father's guests were sitting down to supper, Father had sent our chauffeur, Leslie Carlos, and Williams the groom to heist Father

Burke's awful great big pink jar from the church's entrance and bring it to Kamschatka. Pretty soon, as my parents expected, there was a call from Father Burke.

Face wreathed in grins, Jeff handed the receiver to Father. "Will Buckley," said the priest without ado, "your penance is one hundred Our Fathers. Now, may I speak to Aloïse?" Father passed the receiver mutely to Mother. "Aloïse," said he, "for your shameful part in this foul deception, which lit the evil flame of cupidity in your confessor's soul, you are sentenced to one hundred Hail Marys." And with a great gust of laughter, he hung up.

This was the most successful—it may have been the *only* successful—practical joke my parents pulled off.

Orare pro anima sua.

PART SIX

The
Death of W.F.B.
and After

FATHER'S FINAL STROKE STRUCK HIM DOWN THREE-QUARTERS OF THE way across the Atlantic, aboard ship, on his way back to New York after what was supposed to have been a restorative summer in Bavaria followed by a week in Paris revisiting and bidding final adieu (this was unexpressed) to old friends.

Just one week later he died—in New York, October 5, 1958.

I asked my surviving siblings to give me a brief account of their state of mind at Father's death. Carol e-mailed me memorably, "Remember feeling somewhat numb. Remember we all worried about how Jim would take the news as Ann [his wife] was to tell him on his arrival from the Philippines . . . But mostly I remember our wonderful sister Aloise, who decided that the waiting room with Mother and at least seven or eight Buckleys needed some brightening up. Off she went to Woolworth's and bought gobs of paper autumn leaf garlands, pumpkins, and bright apples to festoon the room. She brought a Scrabble game, Monopoly, and Sorry. And when the German neurosurgeon pompously announced that no one had ever died on his operating table, she answered, in her acerbic Allie way, 'How soon after do they die?' Mother burst into a flood of tears."

The Buckley tribal response to grief was expressed by Allie absolutely on pitch. We seek to expiate it in action. Whenever any of us hits a reef, siblings congregate with as many plans of therapeutic action as there are siblings, almost all of them amiss, absurd, impractical, or if none of these, hyperbolic. Never mind. This past month, July '07, when Carol had every one of her sensible suggestions about what to do about brother Bill in his agonizing brush with death ignored or rejected, wired me that she had fallen back on the old AA advice, Let go, Let God.

But one must do something. One must not sit and mope or weep or slough into despond, mention not despair, which is unbecoming, smacks of self-pity, and exhibits lack of character. Besides, it does no good. As a tribe, we can't sit still for grief. Why? Dumb question . . . sitting still hurts too much. So we seek to expunge it, decorating our parlors with autumn leaf garlands, pumpkins, and bright red apples.

Priscilla adds in another e-mail that when a nurse "came down the hall and ordered us to be quieter (this was at Lenox Hill Hospital), Allie replied, 'I hate Lenox Hill. I don't even like the child that was born here.' "*

As it turned out, sister-in-law Ann was not compelled to break that news to Jimmy. He e-mailed me, "I was in the Philippines on business when [Father] died. I had received a cable from . . . John a day or two earlier advising me that he was seriously ill. The man at the other end of the 'phone asked me to sit down. He then said that I had just received a cable advising me that Father had died, and he offered me his sympathy. The news was an emotional blow, though hardly unexpected." An emotional blow. The restraint in Jimmy's account comes straight down the paternal line from grandfather to father to son. He has had resort to this inner strength since his beloved wife Ann was paralyzed last May in a car accident.

Of all my siblings, Bill was probably most intensely stricken by the blow. He had become closer to Father than any of us, thanks to his name-making book on Yale† and the founding of the outrageous *National Review*, which—with razor-edged wit and humor that drove the nabobs wild—tweaked, punctured, or lampooned the (principally at the time) northeastern liberal Establishment's intellectual airs and conceits—and which may have been the family enterprise Father took most joy from. He

---

*Pitts adds in a parenthesis: "Which she [Allie] didn't mean, that child being her adored Pam."

† *God and Man at Yale,* 1954 Regnery: which is still readable, and remarkably, sadly, germane.

and Bill found plenty to talk about for hours at a time, and I believe it is safe to assume that he confided in Bill his perturbations about other children, Allie because of the insouciant independence of her spirit, which trembled almost always on rebellion against God and man whether in New Haven or Hartford, Janie ditto, who could be a tinderbox, but chiefly (I suspect, as you will understand) me.

Bill wrote me hurriedly,

I got the news from Mother over the telephone late on October 3rd. She said that Father had suffered from what was clearly another stroke and had been taken to the ship's hospital. She hoped I could manage to get on board the boat (I think it was the *Isle de France*) to expedite Father's getting out and into an ambulance.

I established that the Customs Service maintained a tiny little detachment at dockside in the East River whose purposes were to look after extraordinary problems. The challenge was to get them to permit me to board the Coast Guard cutter along with Customs officials in order to help Mother.

The general, and apparently flat, rule was: No foreign bodies permitted. I called several people I thought might be influential (this was about 8 A.M.) [4 October] and had no luck. I don't remember what it was that caused me to phone Ralph de Toledano,* but I did, and in fifteen minutes he had a friend of his in Congress phone the right person—and I was admitted minutes before the cutter went out. We reached the ship about ten minutes away, east of the Statue of Liberty, and I made my way to Mother's cabin. She was very desolate and it meant a great deal to have a member of the family there.†

I went then to the ship's hospital and was admitted to where Father lay. But he was unconscious. In fifteen minutes we were on shore, where an ambulance and a car were waiting. Father died late that night, though perhaps it was the next morning . . .

---

* The conservative writer and literary critic.
† Note Bill's instinctive humility and tact.

. . . Bill's ambivalence about the time/day of Father's death expressing his emotional commotion.

FOR ME AND I AM CERTAIN FOR THE REST OF MY SIBLINGS, THE SHOCK OF Father's death has not been mitigated by time.

I may have been peculiarly susceptible to it for several reasons: the first because I was living away from my family, in Spain—three thousand miles from Sharon, from Camden, from the States, leading a life that was radically independent of that of my siblings, whom I did not have close by me for support; second because the news was divulged to me so brutally. It came in a sheaf of five or six telegrams that were delivered after the haphazard fashion of Spain in those days (in particular the Andalusian fishing village* in which I was living with my small family), the freshest of these cables days late. I can't remember them all. The first I opened said FATHER TAKEN SERIOUSLY ILL ON THE OCEAN. The second, FATHER BETTER. The third, WILL YOU BE ABLE TO MAKE THE FUNERAL. The fourth, FATHER DEAD.

A third reason was the fresh memory, piercing me to the heart, of his weeping face as he stared at me and Betsy while the Cherbourg-bound train pulled slowly and smoothly out of its berth in the Paris *gare,* gazing fixedly and with such open love at me, his youngest son, as the tears poured down his cheeks. I walked rapidly along the ramp, keeping company with the sight of his dissolving face, walking faster and faster as the train gathered speed and at last pulled inexorably away, swallowing up the sight of him in a tunnel.

That had been just seven-eight-ten days ago . . . I remember thinking as I held the cables numbly in my hand. Clearly had he had the premonition of his hastening death those two weeks we spent with him in Bad Gastein, when he told me stories about his childhood that none of us had heard; when he said to me in the hotel room one afternoon as he was lying back on the bed, preparing to take his afternoon nap, that it was time for him to go, that he was wearing Mother down to the bone. Betsy and I had returned to Marbella, depositing our sons Hunt and Jobie with their

---

*As Marbella, now a notorious resort for the riche and the louche, then was principally. See my novel, *Marbella!,* 2006 P.E.N Press.

nurse/governess, Annie Rooney, and then flown straight back to Paris to be with him and Mother their last few days in the city that had been so rich for them in hopes and setbacks and adventure . . .

In Paris, he had permitted himself such pride in my little satirical piece for *National Review*,* placing his open right hand flat against the small of my back and impelling me toward distinguished longtime (and probably bewildered) French acquaintances, saying in his deep, resonant voice, "This is my son Reid. He has just written the most wonderful piece for the magazine. Here, you must read it!"—stuffing copies into their hands. "Oh, it's rich, it is rich!" He was shameless.

I have written earlier in these pages that I walked up into the sierra with my Chesapeake Retriever "Bones" in an attempt to reconcile myself to my grief, staring out across the southwestern Mediterranean until night fell. Less than two years earlier he had done me his last critical service, changing my life entirely.

THIS IS DIFFICULT FOR ME TO RELATE, AND PAINFUL. IT IS HIGHLY PERsonal. Like all my family, I cringe from anything that might be termed "confessional." But this book is about the effect that my parents had on us as children, and what I record now is therefore not to be avoided. (The reader may skip to the next chapter.)

I had telephoned him from Sharon. It was after Thanksgiving of 1956. He and Mother were installed in Camden for the winter and spring. Would it be all right for me and Betsy to visit them that next week? Why, of course. Was there anything the matter? No, I answered hesitantly . . . "I just want to have a talk with you about something."

I wasn't yet twenty-seven years old, but I had fathered three children. I had been separated from the Air Force four years back. In the interim, I had written an unpublishable novel, then a second. I was getting book reviews published in (at the time) no-name conservative journals—*Faith and Freedom, The Freeman, Modern Age, National Review*—for which the standard fee was $15, or was it $25? Very occasionally, I published an article, for the handsome honorarium of $80 or $100. I worked three days

---

* Called "A Fable," which along with the sequels is unreadable today. Who remembers Wayne Morse?

a week in Irvington-on-the-Hudson as an editorial assistant to Frank Chodorov, then editor of *The Freeman*. Living expenses were modest in those days. But I was getting nowhere.

Frank Chodorov said to me one afternoon, "Reid, there is no question that you can write; you just don't seem to have found what to write about." That became for me a bitter half compliment, like being called handy with a six-gun when the Wild West has shut down. It was, I concluded, irresponsible of me to keep pursuing dreams of glory with a beautiful (and I feared restless) young wife and growing children.

I talked this over with Betsy. She was kind and understanding and loving, but when she asked me, "What are you going to do?" I replied, "Speak to Father, get his advice . . . maybe go to work for the companies."

She did not take this notice badly, though she said, "Are you sure you want to do that?"

"I don't think there's a choice, do you?"

I felt creep into my spirit—then or later—the self-righteous sanctimony of the martyr. I WAS DOING THE RIGHT THING. How noble of me.

A week after my call, Father—typically—had his personal secretary and assistant, Miss Hembdt, send me Pullman reservations on the Palmland Express round-trip NYC/Camden/NYC. The journey was solemn but relieved by my sense of heroic resolve. One mustn't knock self-satisfaction. Every son and daughter of Eve has the right to enjoy the cheapest emotional charge in human experience at least once in his life. I have known people who seem to be perpetually self-satisfied, and entirely complacent in their satisfaction, which engages my awe.*

The night of our arrival it was plain that Mother had been advised by Father that I wanted to have a serious discussion with him, because she ordered my favorite curried shrimp and rice with my favorite dessert (chocolate soufflé) and chatted brightly of a great many matters none of which I was able to follow but that made us all laugh. It was over coffee and ice water that Father at last broached the question. "Reid, when do you want to see me tomorrow?"

I felt my stomach hollow out. This was now irreversibly to be the radical change in my way of life, which I dreaded but had to confront. "In the morning?"

---

* Al Gore, John Kerry, and John Edwards seem to thrive on it.

"That's fine. Say at ten? I have some business to get done before that."
"At ten."

"Good . . . Aloïse, I am feeling a little tired . . . where is that man, that impossible Swede, that . . . ? "

Mother supplied the name of nurse/attendant/masseur/therapist quickly. (Father couldn't abide the poor man: " 'Why, Mr. Bu-u-u-*ck*ley,' " he'd say, mimicking the unctuous voice of the devoted little fellow, " 'How *well* you are doing!' " Upon which fell his curmudgeonly harrumph: "As though learning to walk is a great achievement for a man who is seventy-six years old!").

"Well, call him. It's grand seeing you both, Betsy, Reid, I wish you children would come down more often." We kissed his bristly cheek. The Swede entered the pine room, helping Father heave out of his chair and into an upright position, then helping him walk slowly—with such difficulty!—to the wheelchair in the hall, in which he was rolled to an out-side elevator that ascended to the second floor porch, opening at the door of his and mother's bedroom suite. Mother followed his every movement with her eyes; then, face averted, harkened to the sound of his progress and the Uriah Heap–ish cajoling ("How *well* we are doing this evening, Mr. B.!") to the elevator, and then to the sound of the elevator rising and stopping.

There were tears in her eyes when she faced us. "He is failing, Reid," she said. "Day by day. He tries to hide if from me, but I know. Oh, how I pray to the Lord to grant him just one more Christmas—just one more, dear Jesus!"

She was to be granted two Christmases more. We bid her goodnight shortly after, going to the downstairs bedroom that had become mine since the war (occasionally shared with my brother John).

Next morning at 10:00 A.M. sharp I presented myself in Father's hand-some offices at the end of the west garden. A few sesanquas were in bloom, nothing else. Caroline Richardson, his Camden secretary pro tem, daughter of Mother's great friend Alice Marie, bid me a bright good morning as she shut herself behind the door of her little office, leaving me alone with Father.

His domain was a big, pine-panelled rectangular chamber, with taste-ful crystal sconces and stock nineteenth-century English engravings of fox hunting, for which (the engravings) I knew he cared little. He sat at the south end of the room, behind a leather-surfaced desk in Sheraton style that would become mine. He smiled at my greeting, though his mien was guardedly grave. He must have had a good guess about the topic I was to bring up. We siblings all lived under the delusion that our private financial affairs were just that, an understanding in strictest confidence between the Connecticut Bank & Trust Company and ourselves. But this was totally to underestimate our sire. When for tax reasons he divided the vast majority of his personal fortune ten ways, making his children inheritors before his demise, this did not in the least signify that he deprived himself of the right of calling Mr. Fenniman or kind Al Barton on the telephone to determine whether we (younger ones, at least) (and Allie) were being spendthrift.

He bid me pull up a chair across the desk from him. I was feeling quite noble, I remember, as I sat down. I, the sometimes maverick son, who lost my temper regularly as a boy, who, unlike my siblings (excepting Allie and John, the rest were tiresome in their dogged brilliance as students) refused to apply myself to my studies when I was first condemned to boarding school, who had entered into unrelenting warfare with Ed Pulling, my headmaster, who had made a scene when Josefina González, my Nana, was retired back to Mexico after thirty years of devoted service and cranky moods, who had insisted upon getting married much too young and before I had given evidence that I could support myself (not to speak of a wife and children) . . . was being sensible at last, responsible, mature. I ended my tale of woe by saying, "I could teach, though I suppose I'd need to get an MA in English for that. I don't know what else I could do, unless there'd be a place somewhere in the companies for me."

Nothing could have astonished me more than my father's reaction. He had said nothing, but his strong jaw had tightened during my recital—I noticed that. Now that I was through, he pressed his thick right hand down flat on the surface of the desk, pushing himself to his feet with the help of the other hand, which clasped the arm of his swivel chair—leaning forward over the desk, toward me.

It took tremendous effort. He was livid. His blue eyes flashed. His lips were clamped shut. "Young man," he said to me, "whatever gave you the idea that anyone could be a success doing what he didn't want to do in the first place. I never knew a man who was successful doing what he did not want to do."

And he let himself back down in his armchair, breathing heavily. He was trembling with ire. At his words, my sense of nobility had evaporated. My cheeks flushed hot with mortification. He went on, "I must say it wouldn't make me very proud if my son were a teacher. And what could you do for the companies, tell me that? Do you have a degree in geology? Do you know the least thing about the oil business?" I was now trembling, in shock and bewilderment. I had thought he would applaud my sensible decision to seek some other way of making a living. I was astonished by his dismissal of the teaching profession, he who had been a teacher himself, who held the entire intellectual class in such respect. (I have not yet been able to ponder this out—there is a reference missing here to his past experience.) He went on, delivering the sternest lecture I had had from him ever, scathing in his contempt for the falseness of my piety and for my lack of grit (when I had thought I was being brave and manly). He used no such cutting words as "cowardice," mind, but I understood full well what he was telling me. I was miserable because I knew from the first few words he spoke that he was dead-on. It was like a veil being swept aside, scales lifted from my eyes—revealing to me my true character, which was, I now perceived, contemptibly weak. I did not possess the courage of my gift, assuming I had any. Years later, my first editor at Doubleday, the unforgettable Maggie Cousins, was to let me have it also, telling me that she was indifferent to whether I made money on my first novel, because I was a writer, and writers write, and it makes no difference what else they must do in order to permit themselves to write. Her wisdom was different in tenor from my father's, yet struck at the same vein: I was feeling sorry for myself, a wretched moral cowardice that I have endeavored never again to succumb to.

Father calmed down eventually. The outburst had taken a great deal out of him, and I think he was physically as well as emotionally spent from it. His advice to me was that I go back to Sharon and keep trying to learn the craft, and not to worry about making ends meet for the time being, he would give instructions to the bank to cover any overdrafts out of his personal funds.

That luncheon and that evening at supper he was kindness itself and his affectionate most. He never alluded to our talk, though I knew he must have related the gist of it to Mother from the special hug she gave me and her whispered, "Pray hard, honey, I will." Betsy and I trained back to New York and drove to Sharon the next day. I had of course given her a brief account of the meeting, expressing my shock at Father's wholly un-expected response, but not confessing to her how on the mark my father was and how mightily I had deserved his scorn. The two years I had spent in the Air Force had seasoned me in many respects, but I had not come to terms with myself. (The rebellious spirit resists chastening always.) I dis-covered later that month that Father had made a transfer of $5,000 to my account, enough to keep me going for months. This was typical of him: he would tell us what was right—that supreme obligation as a parent he never shirked—but he would support his children always.* I discovered later that my brother Bill, who had been apprised of the matter by Father, had covertly slipped $3,000 into my bank account from his personal funds, in mute testimony of his faith and support, which has been lifelong.

Bill helped in other ways, persuading my brilliant English teacher in Millbrook School, John McGiffert, who had first inflated my literary as-pirations, to help edit my third attempt at a novel, this one a Gothic hor-ror, which was fun in parts.† I tentatively explored humor, and I learned from Jack McGiffert as much as I was able, but it was insufficient: Jack was himself, though a critic of the first rank, a failed poet and writer, his dangerously sultry wife had run out on him, and a personal bitterness now colored his criticisms. I made the next major decision, which was, I reflect now, subconsciously in emulation of my father. I was to pack up my past, seek adventure in another land, and make my fortune.

In January of 1958, Betsy and I moved to Spain with our three chil-dren. There were several contributing reasons for this radical change of venue—for leaving Sharon and the Northeast of the United States be-hind, for distancing myself from my family—chief among them that liv-ing in Spain cost reputedly a fraction what it did in the States. I was to learn that living in the most remote village at the farthest reaches of civili-zation was nevertheless, with dear Betsy as my spouse, to live at 10 or 25 percent more than the sum of my income and earnings, no matter what

---

*An amusing sequel to our talk was my suggestion, for reasons, of economy, that Betsy and I let go our part-time cleaning woman and occasional cook. Father was horrified (this was the 1950s). Good gracious, no decent household could get along without a cleaning woman or a cook!

† In it I first began testing the mock-heroic voice that is indispensable to *Servants and Their Masters* and to *Marbella!*

they amounted to. I fell in love with Spain extravagantly, and along with Betsy threw myself heart and soul into every aspect of its rich culture, from partying all night to caping young fighting bulls in *tientas*. I made fast friends whose affection has endured nearly half a century. Betsy founded an actors studio that brought up many of the stars of Spanish theatre and entertainment, including militant Communists, one of whom I became very fond.* I rock climbed in the Guadarrama, shot redleg partridges all over the country, tried vainly to learn to dance Flamenco, caped heifers and young bulls in *tientas*, intruded upon Generalísimo Franco's sacred Friday afternoon meeting with his ministers in the Pardo Palace, dissuaded, as I thought, close friend Luis Figueroa[1] from assassinating the Generalísimo,[2] backed my borrowed stallion into Brigitte Bardot as she was doing a publicity shot in Seville, hunted and finally bagged an elusive *urogallo* (the giant grouse, or capercaillie), in the mountains of Asturias, and dealt with bandits, none of them as colorful as Pancho Villa, all of them American. I enjoyed every minute of it.

Nevertheless, the fifteen years that ensued were a personal struggle on the economic front. I used social contacts I had acquired to secure a concession for the companies in Spain's Rio de Oro, a strip of Moroccan desert in which there is no river and, as it turned out, there is no gold either, yellow or black. I worked at all sorts of jobs, from wholesaling bric-a-brac, wickerware, furniture, wrought iron lamps and sconces, ceramics, knitware, prêt-à-porter, and haute couture to American retail markets,† to peddling soft ice cream on the street corners of Madrid, to investing in and helping to run a travel agency whose single virtue was that it smuggled dissident Cubans out of Castro's Gulag and thence to the States,‡ to real estate—at which last, happily, with the backing of my godfather, Warren Smith, I turned a small fortune. For a period of seven or eight years I also wrote movie scripts, learning from that experience (let others call it hack work) the art of writing fiction at last, though only one film, a thriller, was produced.§ I became a good friend of Ava Gardner and rewrote her

---

* Ana Belén, she sang like an angel.
† See my pamphlet, *Good Taste Doesn't Sell, Bad Taste Sells Loads*.
‡ It was called Cafranga, S.A.
§ *Summertime Killer,* quite awful, in which the best actor was my Chevelle station wagon, which in a climactic scene toward the end—to my indignation—was plunged over a precipice into the sea!

part in the *Greatest Story Ever Told* because she couldn't get her tar-heel tongue around Christopher Wren's superb dialogue. Along the way I trudged out more book reviews and articles and had my first novel accepted, which was published by Doubleday in 1967.* That led to lecturing and debating on the American circuit, which would ultimately prepare me for founding my school. My career was never facile, my literary commercial success negligible, and I was almost always stressed to make ends meet, which (I often mused), like right angles in Third World construction, merely said howdy to each other in passing. *But I was doing what I had wanted always to do and what I believe the good Lord intended for me to do.* I was writing. I would write buried in a Colorado avalanche or ten thousand fathoms under the sea. I would write whether there was an audience for my output or none.† I owe my perseverance to one great man, my father.

Who stiffened me. Who had faith in me. Who gave me the grit when most I needed it. Who, in the last two years of his mortal illness, summoned the will and the courage, and somehow the energy, to do this great service to his youngest son. And who was now gone.

NOTES

1. Figueroa, known for most of his life as the Conde de Quintanilla, became the Count of Romanones, descendant of the great liberal Romanones of the nineteenth century, whose spectacular wife was Ailene Griffith, OSS spy, professional beauty, horsewoman, historian, and novelist (*The Spy Wore Red*), who well up into her sixties casually wore bikinis that most women in their twenties wouldn't have dared expose themselves in. She became a special friend of Betsy and arranged for her to become *Harper's Bazaar* consultant in Spain.
2. Luis Quintanilla called me one Thursday evening from his house on Castellón de la Plana to ask me in his precise, British-tinged accent whether I would like to drive next afternoon to his ranch in the west of Spain, near Trujillo, to shoot the great bastard.

    I was appalled. "You can't think of doing that, Luis, you mustn't!"

---

* *Eye of the Hurricane.*
† I no longer care. I have become indifferent to anyone's opinion. Writing is a personal thing with me, my demon, or *duende,* as Spaniards would put it.

"What are you talking about?"

There was a party going on in his house, I could hear Flamenco music and lots of chatter. I said to him in great earnestness, "Luis, you simply can't do that. Think of Ailene. Think of your three sons!"

"Whatever are you talking about? I am inviting you to Pascualete to shoot the great bastard."

"I know, I know, but you have got to get that out of your mind."

I could hear him mutter, "Sta loco." (I was thinking, "No, Luis, you are the crazy one.") I then heard him muffle the receiver with one hand while he called for the closest of my male friends in Spain at the time, Teddy Vicuña, saying to him in Spanish, "I don't know what's the matter with Reid, will you speak to him?"

"H'lo, h'lo?" I heard Teddy bark into the telephone in his peremptory fashion and in his clipped and very British accent.

"You've got to stop Luis," I said instantly.

"From what?"

"He has asked me to go with him to Pascualete tomorrow to shoot the great bastard."

There was a pause . . . followed by a gale of laughter. "Luis wasn't speaking of Franco, Reid! He has invited you and Betsy and Inés and me to shoot the great *bastard, el abutardo!*"

Which was different. I got a double on those magnificent, turkey-like migratory birds from Africa, which I have regretted shooting ever since, though it beat tyrannicide.

CHAPTER TWENTY-THREE

———— ❧ ————

Memoranda from
W.F.B. to His Children

THE FOLLOWING IS TAKEN FROM "II. MEMORANDUM," *W.F.B.—An Appreciation,* written and collected by Aloise but I suspect under the gentle prodding and with the aid of Priscilla. (I omit the funny memo on my sideburns, which is quoted in the 1970 *Life* article. I cut one long insertion.) What should be noted is the immediacy of communications by mail back in the 1940s and 1950s. Delivery from New York City to Sharon, Connecticut, was twice a day. A letter posted in New York in the morning normally hit the mailboxes in Sharon by the next morning. Only the telegram was faster. These memoranda were thus often like extended conversations . . . or like the last (corrective) word in a conversation that had begun in the Empire room after lunch, when Father had expressed the desire for a "talk" with one, or several, or all of his children.

Another thing to observe is that he, like all his children (I don't think a one of us escapes this character trait), either from a deep shyness of character coupled with a dread of hurting any loved person or from sometimes insurmountable moral cowardice, was able to put in writing admonitory thoughts that he was unable to iterate face-to-face.

❧

THERE WAS NOTHING COMPLICATED ABOUT FATHER'S THEORY OF CHILD rearing: he brought up his sons and daughters with the quite simple objective that they became absolutely perfect.* To this end, his children were, at one time or another, given professional instruction in: apologetics, art, ballroom dancing, banjo, birdwatching, building boats in bottles, calligraphy, canoeing, carpentry, cooking, driving trotting horses, French, folk dancing, golf, guitar (Hawaiian and Spanish), harmony, herb gardening, horsemanship, history of architecture, ice skating, mandolin, marimba, music appreciation, organ, painting, piano, playing popular music, rumba, sailing, singing, skiing, Spanish, speech, stenography, swimming, tap dancing, tennis, typing, and woodcarving.

[Not to mention instruction in natural history through rearing and caring for a variety of wild animals, from red and gray foxes to racoons, skunks, possums, badgers, porcupines, woodchucks, chipmunks, ferrets, rabbits, flying squirrels, star-nosed moles, and a variety of white and vari-colored mice and rats whose principal function in this ecology was to feed the several snakes we kept, green, black, king, water, hog-nose, and garter, nonpoisonous all, but including boas and pythons of respectable length and girth that did not overjoy Mother to see slithering under the sleeve of Jim's blazer at supper. In a word, we had a regular zoo in the open woods across from the swimming pool, kept in pens of various sizes and in enclosed wooden structures which we (my elder siblings) built and maintained one (dreadful?) summer under the tyrannical guidance of Frank Trevor (RIP), the naturalist professor from Millbrook School, who was one part genius, one part fanatic, one part left-wing ideologue, and ten additional parts bad temper. Only Jim and I were ecstatic.]

[Resuming Allie's account] . . . from a random culling of the old filing cabinets (until lately stored in the unused part of the chicken coop at Great Elm) it appears that there was very little in the human personality, or in the personalities of Aloise etc., which he considered unworthy of his attention.

Protruding teeth and romances; poor diction and sophomore marks at college; quarreling, careers and the choice of a fraternity, were all subjects to which he gave time and thought; about which letters and memoran-

* Too few of us requited his ambition.

da—often from a hotel in Caracas, a sleeping car in Spain, an apartment in Paris or a rented room in London, arrived in due course in college letter box or on the Great Elm breakfast table.

The more ephemeral fields of perfectibility he took over himself and (since from their adolescence on, he and his children were on terms of affectionate inarticulateness) conducted by means of letters and memoranda, usually signed "Father." Every memorandum was, as a matter of principle, directed to all "the children," so as to conceal from those for whose benefit it was intended the fact that it was they upon whom Father's *ojo* was *puesto*. In March 1956, for instance, sixteen-year-old Carol received at boarding school a letter informing her that:

> Your mother and I feel very strongly that your children should have at least two injections of the new polo vaccine by June 1 at the latest. This is a matter of such importance that I am sure you realize that any procrastination on your part may result in the death or a life of total paralysis for one or several of your children.
>
> I am informed that these injections are relatively painless and can be given to children as young as two months of age.*

Carol, realizing that Father would have considered it indelicate to the point of rudeness to address these instructions *only* to those of his grandchildren's parents whom he knew to be procrastinators, was only momentarily startled. In the interests of common courtesy, the memo was, as usual, headed "To the Buckley Children" and followed by "cc: Aloise, John, Priscilla, Jimmy, Jane, Billy, Patricia, Reid, Maureen, Carol."

Often, however, he addressed his children as a unit, as members of a family which he hoped and planned should become and remain a family or a clan in a very concrete sense. Thus, in 1949,† he wrote his children:

> I have just read *Prairie Avenue*, by Arthur Meeker, an impressive novel about wealthy families in Chicago during the golden period of 1885 to 1918. These people were pure materialists, without morals or religion, although uniformly contributing members of churches.

---

*Father was seventy-five years old when this memorandum was dictated by him and gravely stricken by the infirmity (a series of strokes) that was to kill him two years thence.
† He was sixty-eight.

Notwithstanding their conviction that they were establishing families that would last forever, these had disintegrated entirely by 1918. The following are the appropriate forewords to the three books and the epilogue of the novel:

Book I "The sunny street that holds the gifted few . . ." *Old Chicago Saying*

Book II "This is the rejoicing city that dwelt carelessly, and said in her heart, I am, and there is none beside me." *(Zephaniah 2:15)*

Book III "Their inward thought is, that their houses shall continue forever, and their dwelling places to all generations. . . . Nevertheless . . . man that is in honour, and understandeth not, is like the beasts that perish." *(Psalm 48)*

Epilogue "For he remembered that they were but flesh; a wind that passeth away, and cometh not again." *(Psalm 79)*

> Affectionately,
> Father

This seemed unduly critical in view of the fact that Father had just circulated another Memorandum to the Children:

> As you probably know, Americans are famous for being the poorest conversationalists in the world. Education and cultivation of the mind do not seem to improve us. We can't stay on a subject and we are constitutionally incapable of listening. As a people we are always thinking of something we are going to tell the "bore" as soon as he stops talking. A political conversation is never a "give and take," but leads to a monologue usually by the least interesting and least informed person present.
>
> I am enclosing an article from December's *Reader's Digest,* which you should all read again and again. It is the best thing I have ever seen written on this subject.

> Father

None of his children was quite sure to which it was *really* addressed. Needless to say, the end generation made it a point to be intelligently mute, or mutely intelligent for a good two weeks.

On one occasion, Father, who considered smoking a sin just this side of adultery, or dirty talk, was irritated to the point of addressing only the guilty. In one of the very few memoranda addressed not to "The Children" but to individuals called Aloise, John, Jane, Billy, Patricia, and Reid, he offers the passing comment that:

> Knowing of your catholic interests in literature, I am quoting from a life of Columbus which recently appeared. Rodrigo, one of Columbus' associates, landed in San Salvador, and made the following quaint statement:
>
>> "They pressed lighted tobacco upon us,
>> and Luis de Torres and I, being
>> Andalusians and nothing daunted,
>> inhaled the smoke and straightway
>> were seized into a spasm of coughing
>> and into a dizziness that
>> lightened our heads and mellowed
>> our humors and then to vomiting.
>> Surely this weed was a drug and
>> all the natives used it and
>> perchance that accounted for their
>> debility, for, indeed they were a
>> fragile people; seemingly not ill
>> and yet never robust."
>
> Father[1]

This preoccupation with the collective character of his children did not, however, deter Father from coming down to earth, if earth needed to be come down to. "My dear John," he wrote just before John's fourteenth birthday:

> On Sunday you told me that you would see Mr. Tuttle [of Millbrook School for Boys] Monday and would write me that day the

name of a book on saddle horses. You did not do this Monday, Tuesday, or Wednesday.

My getting a letter from you about this matter is not of great importance, but it is very important that you do what you promised to do. I have noticed invariably that those of my friends who keep their slightest promises are successful and those who don't keep their small promises are not successful.*

This is a very slovenly habit to get into and one which promises to be a lifelong habit with you and Aloise if you don't correct it right away. After this, when I ask you to do anything I wish you would think it over seriously and if you decide it is too much trouble tell me then that you won't do it.† I quite understand that your training in doing things has been very deficient, but you and Aloise are now old enough to do some thinking for yourself and develop your own character.

> Affectionately,
> Father

cc. to Miss Aloise Buckley

Again, to Jim, age sixteen:

Mr. James Buckley
Millbrook School
Millbrook, New York

My dear Jimmy:

I am returning to you your check for $10.00, and am sending you an additional check for $24.00. The $34.00 is a return of money you

---

*He kept handy, in his billfold jacket pocket, a thin notebook on which it was his custom to jot down whatever it was he promised us, his children. I remember that vividly. One of his favorite related adages was "If you want something done, give it to a busy man to do."
†It is an amazing measure of his character and of his occasional unreality to believe (1) that any of his children would have the audacity to tell him to his face that he was not going to do this or that, (2) that his direct instruction to speak thus to him would be taken by any of us seriously.

paid me to reimburse me the purchase of the binoculars, which I am giving you as a present. Your Mother and I remarked Sunday afternoon [I am guessing on one of their long walks through the thirty-five acres of Great Elm] that we were very pleased at the seriousness with which you take your debts. She said you had paid her everything you owed her.

With lots of love,

Affectionately,
Father

On another occasion, Father wrote the headmistress of the Ethel Walker School:

I have intended for some time to write or speak to you about Maureen's speech. She does not speak distinctly and has a tendency, in beginning a sentence, to utter any number of words simultaneously. Anything that the school may do to improve this condition would be greatly appreciated by us. I have always had a feeling that there was some physical obstruction that caused this, but doctors say there is not. She is one of two or three children in our family who have no wisdom teeth—perhaps this has something to do with it. I hope you will pardon my adding to your many problems.[2]

He did not circulate, beyond the eldest five of the family, his description of the night when, in Mother's absence, Father and eight-year-old Maureen were roommates:

After Maureen and I had played two games of Parchesi and I had read her one story and she had read me one story, I mentioned the fact that it was almost two hours past her bedtime. Your sister asked me pointedly where her Mother and I habitually undressed for bed. I replied that your Mother usually undressed in the bathroom while I read the evening paper, and when your Mother had come to bed, I took my turn in the bathroom. I added that, in view of her superior sex, Maureen would be given priority in the bathroom.

Your maidenly sister gave vent to an enormous sigh and said: "Well, I'm glad to know our *main* problem is solved!"

I hope you all appreciate the ladylike delicacy of your sister's instincts.

Father's own delicacy was manifest far less directly than his young daughter's. [Sister Aloise goes on to tell the story of Father's concern about my sideburns, which I recounted for *Life*.]

Not long after this, however, Father, repenting his rebuke, sent out to the Phoenix Bank in Hartford, a

Memorandum for Mr. Fenniman:

It seems to be the consensus of opinion that Reid should be getting an allowance of $100.00 a month beginning in June, and that out of this he should be able to accumulate enough money to buy clothes and books and so on at the beginning of college; and that therefore his room and board bills should be paid, and that in addition he should get $100.00 a month.

One or two of the children were so presumptuous as to suggest that Reid be given a lecture on the value of money and on the difficulty of acquiring it, which I will not pass on to Reid.

W. F. Buckley

WFB:cpr
CC: Miss Mildred Hembdt
Mr. Fergus Reid Buckley

For Father's atonements were as roundabout as his remonstrances.

Reid's small pomposities, when he was growing up, were a source of continuing joy and exasperation to Father, and at times his correspondence with or concerning Reid almost doubled the volume of mail at the Sharon Post Office. In 1939, for instance, when Reid was nine years old, Father wrote from New York:

My dear Reid:

I have just submitted your music to a music house here and have
sold it for $1.00. I will give you the dollar when I get out to Sharon.

They fully agreed with you and me that your music was a masterpiece.

Affectionately,
Father*

When Reid was fifteen, he received a routine letter from a firm of certified
public accountants, asking him to confirm his balance at the bank. Reid
answered:

Dear Sirs:

In reply to your inquiries concerning my account at the Sharon
National Bank, I have at the present date the above mentioned
————. I drew a check for the amount of ———— in late January: it
was made out to Miss Celia Reilly. The recent bank statement sent to
me by your firm confused the issue as you see by crediting my account
for ————. I delayed answer till the matter was cleared up. I received
word from C. R. that she had as yet not cashed my check a few days
hence.

I would appreciate it if you informed me what your business
is with me: purely a question of curiosity concerning why any
person deems it necessary to become acquainted with my personal
account.

Yours truly,
F. Reid Buckley†

---

*I remember being so overjoyed by Father's letter that I ran up and down and across the
acres of lawn of Great Elm, singing for all my might; and then hurried to the huge old
Capehart record player in the playroom, putting on records of Beethoven's piano sonatas,
listening with fierce, fellow-professional keenness.
†Not four years later, he was to read of J. Alfred Prufrock, and from then on never willingly
signed his name F. Reid.

Impressed with the manly dignity of his reply, Reid sent a copy to Father, adding that, "I do not intend in the future to tell anything about my pecuniary affairs to any company that feels it would like a bird's eye view of me financially." The episode filled Father with such fearful joy that he circulated one hundred copies of the correspondence to his relatives and friends.*

HERE FOLLOWS AN ARTICLE THAT FATHER CONTRIBUTED TO OUR FAMILY newsletter, *The Grelmschatka,* "three years and two sons after it occurred," in atonement for his inability to deliver a toast at my wedding to Betsy Howell (he was too shy, even among family and close friends). It's very funny in parts, and to me emotionally wrenching in all parts, but it is, I think, a distraction from the memoranda, and I therefore cut to the following.

IT IS WORTHY TO NOTE THAT HERE FATHER'S FLOW OF ENTERTAINING anecdotes about his son ended at Reid's tenth year, though entertaining incidents had continued for some years longer. The absurdities of adolescence were far less amusing to him than those of children,[3] and what amusement they did provoke in him was apt to be tinged with exasperation. Carol's easily outraged dignity, at the age of thirteen, gave rise to the practical joke which can be read between the lines of the following "Memorandum to the Children."

Ex Catawba

Editor of Grelmschatka:

It is with great humiliation that I find it necessary to report an incident in our otherwise pleasant tour this summer of Spain and Portugal. When we got to the beautiful hotel at Busaco, Portugal, I

---

* Reid has fought the battle for privacy ever since, refusing to provide his Social Security card to vendors, claiming, correctly, that in the 1935 debates of the Congress on the SS bill, it was declared that the SS card was *never* to be used as an identity card; a valiant though losing battle that was finally closed in 1975 or 1976, when the Congress specifically authorized use of the card for business transactions. (The fascist scoundrels.)

stopped to register while your Mother and the two girls [Maureen, twenty-one, Carol, sixteen] took the elevator. Unfortunately, and in the presence of two bell boys, Maureen had a recurrence of the hiccups, a malady from which she suffered on occasion to the great embarrassment of Carol. When the three ladies arrived in their room, Carol's face was red and she expressed the thought that it might be well to leave before night or at least have our meals served in our rooms, as she feared that news of this occurrence would spread over the hotel like wildfire. To our amazement, immediately after dinner we received the following communication (in Portuguese, of course) from the manager, which I am sure you will all understand and which I am glad not to have to translate into English, as it might fall into alien hands.

"*El Senhor Gerente presenta sus cumplimentos al distinguido Senhor Buckely y su distinguida familia y espela que gozaran de heste humilde hotel.*

"*Al mesmo tempoy perdone Uste nostro atrevimentose sente obligatto a le participar que en heste establecimento esta estrictamente prohibidope le Capitulo 34, Articulo 10, Regla 203Ao hicope. Me despos de consulta con nostros socios, estamos intermente dispostos a le servir sus comidas en su habitazio.*

"*Ahora, perdone Uste pelo me atrevo a la confianza, inspirado en los francos semblantes de Vd. y de su distinguida Senhora, de sugerir un remedio eficaz para esta desagradable enfermadady es, nala menos, se abstener de comer tan vorazmente, reforzado per cuantiosas dosis de carbonato de soso.*

"*Me, si Uste se ofende con hesta bien intencionada insinuacion (que espelo no sea el caso), Vd. podra largarse de este hotel, e irse con Dios, junta con su Senhora (siempre distinguida) y su afligida hija y su hermanita quien, siento insinuarle, esta demasiada disposta a la coqueteria, calidad menos desgradable per supuosto, pero si mas reprensible que el hicopo verificando su despedida, per suposto, despos de pagar su cuenta (incluyendo esta noche por ser ahola despos de la cinco).*

q.s.m.b.
Father*

---

*Father was seventy-three at this time.

Sometimes Father got into what can only be described as a rut, on a given subject. One of the longest was the car rut—probably because cars and Father always disliked each other intensely—and the car rut consisted of at least twelve memoranda dealing with their effect on character, on physique, on intelligence; their stupidity, brutality, malice and wilful disobedience, etc. Only a few of these can be found, but the series seems to have been started with the following letter to "My dear Jane":

> We were having a general conversation last night and Priscilla said
> that you had recently found out that you were charged with your car.*
> I suppose I didn't take the precaution to tell Mr. Fenniman that this
> was a graduation present from your mother and me. Would you drop
> me a note about this and confirm this sad news and tell me just what
> the price of the car was. I will send a check within the next week or
> two to the bank to reimburse your account. After this, when you get
> hardup, you should always write me about it; I may not be able to
> help you but I can give you a lot of sympathy.
>
> Lots of love,
>
>   Affectionately,
>   Father

[Jane was one of his favorite daughters and children. Even at a very early age, when she was in her teens, he knew there was a special integrity about her. But what he lets peek here, Circa 1945, humorously, is the terror and the desperation that he had endured for so many years until the miraculous discovery of

---

* This needs a little explaining. Father was determined not to permit a rapacious Uncle Sam from reaching into and making off with the fortune he had worked so hard and risked so much in the making; and so, on the advice of lawyers and bankers, he dispossessed himself officially of almost everything he had, giving it to Mother, his ten children, other members of his family, and a long list of associates, old friends, servants, and other worthy beneficiaries. In actuality, what he dispossessed himself of to pass down to his children he made free with when and how he wished, or thought either desirable or meet. He simply told his bankers (Bill Fenniman and his junior partner, wonderful Al Barton at the time), "I am short of cash. Now, why don't you take X amount out of the accounts of the children and place this in my checking account." And it was thus done. Or he might say, "Reid needs a little money now, I don't think Patricia or Billy or Aloise would miss a few hundred dollars from their accounts transferred to his." And it was done.

oil in 1939, just six or seven years before he penned this letter to his daughter; of which anguish for him and Mother we, his children, were either entirely un- aware (from Bill on down to Carol) or only vaguely understanding (from Jim one step down to Jane), or if in partial or full knowledge (from Aloise on down to Priscilla), youthfully insensitive to. I now wonder . . . had he ever longed for one of his children to ask him what it had been like to bear his burdens? I think none of us would have dared to assume this intimacy. Which may shock readers of the twenty-first century, who have progressed from the times when parents established clear lines of demarcation between themselves and their children, and what was appropriate to each.]

Perhaps it was the memory of Jane's firm rejection of (a) a hunter (a horse that hunts), (b) a pearl necklace, (c) an ermine jacket in lieu of the car Father promised her in a moment of aberration, that reopened the smoldering feud. At any rate, the memos of the following two years were devoted almost exclusively to cars.

For instance:

I think there is entirely too much driving of cars by our children. It is not unusual for two or three cars to come into New York in a day. In the first place, the best and most sensible way of getting to New York is by train; that is how over 90% of the people of Sharon move from one place to the other. The cars are extremely expensive and their operation is expensive, and they are dangerous as well. I am sure that there is a very large mileage registered on the car of every member of the family.

Outside of John and Priscilla, none of you has earned enough money to buy a car, and I think you should be very careful in your use of one.

Some of you have gotten into the practice of arriving swankily in a car and turning it over to Mr. Cronin to park, asking him to put up the dollar for parking charges. Anyone who hasn't a spare dollar, or having one fails to carry it in his pocket, should not be driving a car into New York.[4]

I have thought of this matter a number of times, and I am sure your Mother has.

W. F. Buckley

Another memo, from Camden this time:

Now that most of you have your own cars, and the so-called (by the children) "family cars" which suffered greatly during the War for many and varied reasons have been replaced with new ones, I hope you will all try not to age them too much during the coming Holidays.

First of all, if those of you who are nicotine addicts should be overcome by your craving while you are driving, please use the ashtrays. While I agree with Mayor McCorkle that everything possible should be done to keep Camden clean, I also would like to keep the inside of the cars clean, so please do not throw papers and trash on the floor. Regarding the City of Camden, I feel that you are all old enough to make your own decisions.

Second, Ben Heath* tells me the station wagon should never be left out overnight. So if you use it in the evening, be sure it is put in the garage, no matter how exhausted you may think you feel when you come home. Moreover, be careful when you do put it away, because station wagons have become too wide to enter normal garages.

Third, if you are unfortunate enough to scratch or dent a fender, report it to the main office. We carry expensive insurance policies to cover all damage over $50,000; any damage under that figure will be paid for by the responsible party.

I hope that none of you younger children will take the preceding sentence as a suggestion that you have only major accidents.

Affectionately,
Father

The following communication, circulated the summer after the war, was a mere recapitulation of several others.

---

* Sister Aloise's handsome Air Force captain (and then major) husband, son of the then owners of the *Camden Chronicle*—after the war conscripted (along with brother John) into the companies by Father. (Ben Heath is now married to the lovely Maria Elena; see my pamphlet, *Good Taste Doesn't Sell, Bad Taste Sells Loads*.)

Memorandum to the Buckley Children

I have been much concerned of late with the apparent inability of
any of you, at any time to go anywhere on foot, although I am sure
your Mother would have informed me if any of you had been born
without the walking capacity of a normal human being.

A few of the older children, notably Priscilla, walk a few hundred
yards behind a golf ball, but all the others "exercise" exclusively by
sitting on a horse or a sailboat.*

Concurrently, I have noticed that the roads around Sharon are
crowded with Buckley cars at all hours of the day and night, and it
has been years since any of you has been able to get as far as the Town
Clock, much less the Post Office without a car, or if under 16, a car
and a chauffeur.

All the cars are left out every night in all kinds of weather, un-
doubtedly because of the dangerous fatigue involved in walking from
the garage to the house.

I think that each of you should consider a course of therapy
designed to prevent atrophy of the leg muscles if only for aesthetic
reasons, or you might even go to the extreme of attempting to regain
the art of walking, by easy stages of course. The cars might then be
reserved for errands covering distances of over 50 yards or so.

Affectionately,
Father

And a resigned protest to Bill's future father-in-law:

Memorandum to Austin C. Taylor

I have tried for many years to interest my children in conventional
sports, but I have not been very successful. Billie is easily the worst in
this regard, having no interest in tennis, golf, or other activities which
satisfy the great majority of the nation. If you expect to entertain him,

---

*Not fair: all of us swam hard hours a day, and most of us played tennis—ferociously.

you will find it necessary to furnish him with 1) a horse, 2) a yacht, or 3) a private airplane.

Aloise joins me in affectionate regards to you and Babe.

Will

The Buckley children were at all times kept *au courant* with the life and times of their brother Bill, sometimes unkindly referred to as "The Young Mahster," by means of memoranda of which the following, dated May 25, 1941, is typical.

Memorandum to Aloise et al.

You will all, no doubt, be glad to know that Billy has again achieved his high B average, and is subsequently back on the Millbrook School Honor Roll. The reason for this academic improvement is the fact that he has terminated all connections with the Silo and the Mill (and vice-versa),* has completely ostracized the piano, and has let Pantepec† and the foreign situation go to the dogs.

It may come as a surprise, therefore, to some of them, that one of Father's "ruts" was critical of Bill, and lasted from the time Bill learned to write, at the age of six, till he learned to type at the age of eighteen.

February 16, 1940

My Dear Billy:

I think more strongly than ever that you should take hold of your handwriting situation and work on the new system along the lines that I had discussed with Miss Reilly.‡ You will never be able to take

---

* Respectively, the student newspaper and literary magazine.
† Father's oil company.
‡ Our pretty Irish governess, who came back with us from London in 1938. She was blessed with a lovely Dublin accent, a rollicking sense of humor, and the rosiest of cheeks, and became my special friend, whom I adored.

your present handwriting and do anything with it, in my opinion. It is not very intelligent to go through life with a handwriting that other people cannot understand. Aloise has done that and has almost incapacitated herself for writing. I am sure that you will get down to work with Miss Reilly and correct this situation.

Affectionately,
Father

Again:

October 10, 1940

Mr. Edward Pulling
Millbrook School
Millbrook, New York

Dear Mr. Pulling:

My wife sent me a letter from Billy today which reminds me of his very illegible handwriting. He uses the backhand, very awkwardly, and it seems to me it will cause him a lot of inconvenience and annoyance in the future as well as retarding his speed in writing. I realize that such things as handwriting should have been taken care of long before a boy gets to Millbrook, but nevertheless I wonder if there is anything you could have done for Billy in this connection.

And a year later:

My dear Billy:

Your mother and I were delighted to receive your midterm reports and to learn through Miss Reilly that you were back on the "A and B" list again. You should be very proud of your work, in which you have shown great character and determination.

The only stumbling block seems to be your handwriting, which continues to be illegible. I do think that you should buckle down now and correct this. I am sure you will be able to do this with a little application.

> With lots of love,
> Affectionately,
> Father

Bill's handwriting is still illegible, but he types very well indeed.[5]

[REGRETFULLY, I EXCISE SEVERAL OF THE CONCLUDING PASSAGES OF Allie's tribute to our father. They are luminous with love and pride for his son Bill and all his children. She ends as follows.]

But the old filing cabinets are also crammed with testimony to the fact that Father's children were far more to him than a source of mingled amusement, exasperation, pleasure, and disapproval. He loved them with a watchful and anxious protectiveness which, moreover, was not in the slightest *laissez-faire*. Not that his children didn't make their own mistakes, but only after the long exchange of formal memoranda (in the Buckley family, the equivalent of a tooth-and-nail battle) which invariably ended one memo short of the ungentlemanly ultimatum which might have led to the discourteous refusal. Thus ended, for instance, the correspondence with the college senior who planned to go into editorial work, a correspondence which began:

Dear Maureen:

Your Mother and I have thought for a long time that you are intellectually and temperamentally suited for a law career, which you would find you would enjoy very much.

I am sure that Jimmy would have no trouble getting you into Yale Law School and as a matter of fact I don't think he would allow you to go anywhere else.

You should write to the Dean of the Law School as soon as . . .

Another exchange, this time with the middle-aged mother of seven children:

Dear Aloise:

> Your Mother and I both think that it would be far more sensible for you and your family to live in Sharon than in Hartford. The Bingham house is now on the market and I am sure it can be bought very reasonably.
>
> Mr. Cole[6] can take you through the house either this Saturday or next. Be sure to let him know which is . . .

. . . If Father noted in later years that Maureen still gobbled her words, that Bill's handwriting was totally unreadable and Aloise never seemed to emerge from a cocoon of cigarette smoke; that, in fact, the barrage of memoranda he had shot at his children had remained to a large extent unheeded, this was no reason to desist. And so, from his hotel in Bad Gastein two weeks before his death came an admonitory note to a thirty-six-year-old daughter.

My dear Priscilla,

> Since you and Carol plan to spend several weeks in Mexico I think you should know that young ladies of good families do not go unescorted in Mexico City. This is a custom I think you girls should respect . . .

Affectionately,
Father

Which work by the daughter who most resembled him was signed, A.B.H.

NOTES

1. Father used to say of me that inasmuch as I had a lighted cigarette pincered between the fingers of one outstretched hand seemingly always, it was as though I was being pulled along through existence by the smoke. Of those to whom this memorandum

was addressed: Aloise smoked excessively, but she died at age forty-eight, of a massive thrombosis—too soon for cancer or emphysema to surface; John smoked a lot, but he died of quite another addiction, alcoholism, at age sixty-four; Jane (eighty-one), another heavy smoker, has been dying cruelly of emphysema (as well as other maladies) for the past several years* Bill (eighty), who quit cigarettes forty-five years ago but took up an after-supper cigar, suffered badly from emphysema and a variety of other ailments; Trisha (seventy-nine), who smoked little and now not at all, is a recovered alcoholic who suffers from no other maladies to which mortal woman is prone through the simple expedient of hieing herself rarely to a doctor and then paying no attention to what he has told her and doing not a thing that he has instructed her to do; and I (seventy-seven), though I quit smoking thirty years ago, have been afflicted by emphysema these past several years. Our father was prescient. His grandchildren are in the main as stupid as his children were.

2. Maureenie, my kid sister and playmate (she was three years younger than I), was the first of us to go: of a stroke (the fell paternal genetical inheritance), at age thirty-one, leaving five children, one an infant. She developed in college into a witty conversationalist and expert debater, and after graduating (and spending a few years as an indispensable aid to Father Keller's "Christophers") became a marvelously efficient (and terrifically funny) editor at *National Review*. (See the book we put together on her posthumously.) I rediscovered this sister after my marriage to Betsy Howell and hers to Gerald A. O'Reilly (which I avidly fomented, kicking Maureen and Gerry off the hay wagon on secluded White Hollow Road; I was satisfied to note that by the time they caught up, they were holding hands). Her death forty-two years ago shook her siblings more profoundly than any event in our immediate family since.

3. Adolescence to our father was not a prolongation of childhood with greater freedom and means of enjoyment, but the deadly serious commencement of preparation for life. Character formation begins at that time. "Will reminded me that, in his own youth, he had had to work his way through college and help support a family besides." From "The Squire: A Reminiscence," by onetime novelist Van Zandt Wheeler, *W.F.B.—An Appreciation*.

4. At the time of this entry from *W.F.B.—An Appreciation* was written, Bill had published a paltry two books. The count now, forty-eight years later, is fifty-three books . . . and counting. How the thoughts he conceives in his head have been transfigured from their illegible impression on paper into the lucid sovereignty of print is, of course, one of the abiding mysteries. He is the only person I know who has managed to transfer illegible handwriting to illegible e-mail. This is a typical sample: "Itwimld be wpmdergil if ypiand Tasa could busotya in Sta,gotd pbyour qst bavj grpm Dgarpm Tgyrsfay sbd s[wbd yjwmught."

Translation: "It would be wonderful if you and Tasa could visit us in Stamford on your way back from Sharon Thursday and spend the night."

---

*See the Post Datum for an update on our sister Jane.

Only one person alive is able to translate his handwriting, Frances Bronson, his secretary for the past thirty years or so;* no one, other than maybe his guardian angel, can translate his e-mails unless one is clever enough to move the position of one's hands over a keyboard one letter to the right or to the left of the intended key, and sometimes not consistently.

The handwriting business is curious. Aloise, Bill, and I have (or had) atrocious handwriting. I gave up cursive long ago. I print, but often what I have printed hurriedly is illegible to me ten minutes after I have written it—which can be a problem at my school, where I jot down quick scrawls on each student as he or she speaks. (These often have to be translated to me by such longtime associates as dear Karen Kalutz, else I will find myself saying of one speaker that he is too harried [hurried] in his delivery, of another that she is fidgeting [fudging] the point. In one calamitous instance, I—rapidly scanning my notes—blurted out to a straightlaced and humorless female human resources director of a large corporation, "You are both too sensual [read *sensitive*] and fetching [read far*fetch*ed] to make your case authentically [read *auth*oritative*ly*], because you are nevertheless unbecoming [read *un*forth*coming*].")

Maybe Father would have been advised to subject Bill and me and others of us to shock treatment. In 1966 or '67, Julian Huxley underwent electroshock therapy for his (frequent) bouts of depression, and lo and behold, for the first time in his life, his handwriting became legible.† But drawing conclusions from positive findings in such an experiment would presume that Allie and Bill and I are (were) depressed when writing illegibly, whereas, in my case, I am only depressed when being compelled to write so that other people, including myself, can actually understand what I am, or was, thinking at the time, which, for its inadequacy, is too often depressing enough. Our siblings are happily blessed with clear handwriting, and our brother John with an elite-font calligraphic style. (Maybe his handwriting was a Swiss merchant's inheritance, though Mother's handwriting was large and flowing, and as generous as her heart.) Since our education, though eclectic, was so similar, the fault must be a genetic impairment, maybe a slothful tolerance of disorder, which is why our sire's strenuous efforts to cure our condition never took. In the case of brother Bill, I have been thankful always that never during his several ocean crossings on several sailing vessels was he capsized and stranded on a desert isle; because, had that been the case, and had he floated an emptied bottle of (good) wine to advertise his predicament and location, no one would have been able to read what he was communicating, and he would be there still, climbing the palm trees for coconuts.

5. A local (Lakeville-based) real estate agent and insurance broker with whom we all had very pleasant relations for several years. Frank was a peach of a guy. On a visit by me to

---

* And now also his close assistant Linda Bridges.

† *Of Moths and Men: The Untold Story of Science and the Peppered Moth,* by Judith Hooper, an absolutely delightful history of the Darwinian movement, New York: W. W. Norton & Company, 2002, p. 186.

Sharon in the summer or fall of 1963 (from Madrid, where I was living), Frank told me that my sister Maureen, with four children and a hardworking husband, should take out some life insurance. "How much do you recommend, Frank?" I asked innocently. "Well," he said, "given how many and how little the children are, I would suggest five hundred thousand dollars." That sounded like a staggering sum to me; but I talked to Maureen about it just before I left for Spain. She was at the time radiantly happy, healthy, in love, and beautiful, and three or four months into the gestation of her fifth child. She got around to speaking with Frank in April or May of 1964, and she settled on three hundred thousand dollars. Not three months after she actually signed the policy, she had her stroke and died. It is a tribute to Frank Cole's graciousness that when we met thereafter, he treated me with unaltered friendliness and affection.

CHAPTER TWENTY-FOUR

—————— ⌀ ——————

The Ten Siblings, 1958–1980

FATHER DID NOT LIVE TO REVEL IN THE HEIGHT OF HIS CHILDREN'S fame* and influence. That began seven years after his death, with Bill's mayoralty campaign in New York City (1965), peaked with Jim's election to the Senate (1970), and continued (with diminishing panache) through the Reagan administrators (1980–1988).

It all centered around Bill, his books, his magazine, his column, his articles, his debates, his television program, his charm. Bill was—is—a phenomenon.† He had more energy and was more productive than anyone on the scene, conservative or liberal. He also had more courage, a virtue little commented upon. The only figure of those times who came close to him in fame and notoriety was Norman Mailer. Bill was the center of New York, Washington, and also national attention. It was exciting to be a Bill Buckley conservative in those days. Bill made merry and merciless sport of the tired old fuddy-duddy Rockefeller Republicans, as they were called, not to speak of the tired, dull, oh so correct (and oh so boring) liberals of the time, who were represented by the Kennedy clan on the recklessly happy side, by Gore Vidal on the louche side, by the likes of Walters

———————————————

* The word "fame" dissatisfies me. I associate "fame" with battlefield heroes, Hollywood stars, heavyweight boxing champions, and souls who have never questioned the present tense of the verb *to be*. Fame has to be nationwide, and I don't believe we Buckleys ever were that. That fame is fleeting is, in our case, certainly so, because only Bill's name continues to resonate, and among ever fewer Americans.

† Bill died as this book was going to press, age 82.

Lippmann and Cronkite on the oh so desperately dreary pundit side, but who were epitomized intellectually by John Kenneth Galbraith and Arthur Schlesinger Jr. For young people growing to maturity in those days, Bill Buckley was the action. Frank Chodorov's Society of Individualists (libertarians) and the Young Americans for Freedom crowd* joined in what became an exciting movement whose galvanizing political defeat was the Goldwater/Kennedy campaign and whose political apotheosis was the Ronald Reagan presidency. Our special joy in the election of Ronald Reagan was not that we suspected he would be a great president (that never entered our minds) but that we conservatives discerned that he was not the buffoon that he was painted to be by the nabobs and solons of liberal-left-dom, who were compelled to eat kitsch.

To be a young conservative after Bill Buckley was fun. It was outrageous. He was feared by ideological opponents, not only for his merciless reasoning, which regularly skewered them in public debate, exposing their pompousness,† but also for his wit and good humor. If one wished for a fresh, original, catchy, irreverent, and sometimes also intellectually boggling comment on just about anything political in those days, one went to Bill Buckley. *Time* and the *New York Times* quoted him regularly. His Pentagon Papers caper (1971) was perhaps the pith of this insouciance. Daniel Ellsberg had been anointed a moral hero of the left by committing treason, by turning over to the *New York Times* top-secret documents. After consultation with Pitts and his closest friends and editors, Bill let it be known that *National Review* had its own hoard of top-secret State and Defense papers, which it proceeded to publish (after a weekend of all-night stands with sister and brother, Jim Burnham, Frank Meyer, and Bill Rusher, and I forget who else feverishly composing a sheaf of absolutely false documents that were so faithful to the style and personality of the ostensible authors that when, for example, Dean Rusk was shown what he had purportedly written, he responded, to the effect, "Well, I can't say for a fact that I didn't write that, I might have written it"). The faux Pentagon Papers had Dean Rusk and assorted generals and admirals and other

---

*YAF was formally founded—consecrated?—in Sharon, at Great Elm. There's a great big stone on the south lawn proclaiming the organization's libertarian-conservative principles.
† Asked by his producer why Bobby Kennedy refused to appear on *The Firing Line,* Bill said "Why does baloney resist the grinder?"

Last wedding at "Kamschatka." Piazza (left to right): William Hunting Buckley;
wife, Casilda Aguirre de Carcon; groom, Cornelius J. Riley; bride, Elizabeth Hanna Buckley;
Katherine Joseph Buckley; James Buckley Heath; Fergus Reid Buckley, Jr.
Terrace (left to right): Jennifer Smith, Christopher Taylor Buckley, Liza Smith,
Cameron Buckley Smith, Jessica Calhoun.

worthies uttering positions that were diametrically opposed to what they
were reported as thinking by the Ellsberg papers, causing a furor in liberal
circles. Bill let them stew two full weeks in their ideological anguish before letting on, at which—oh, dear—how they foamed all over their editorial pages and columns with indignation. Pitts summed the caper up for
me: "What [we] proved was that if you were relatively well informed and
knowledgeable you could create a credible set of Pentagon Papers without
having to abet the burglary of secret government documents, as the *Times*

and the *Washington Post* had done when they collaborated with Daniel Ellsberg in his theft."

The caper proved much more, principally, how stuffy and self-righteous the liberal camp was at the time. It was a caper that only Bill could have conceived and that only Bill had the chutzpah to pull off. I can't imagine anything remotely comparable taking place today and being enjoyed on both sides of the political divide, we have become as an intellectual establishment so imaginatively impoverished.

The rest of the family enjoyed the ride and contributed to it in our several ways. Allie, the eldest, ensconced in West Hartford and producing one child after another, was maybe the most talented literarily (we her siblings thought so), but it required goading by Bill and heroic persistence by Pitts to get her to write. She hated doing so. It was torture for her. After a piece in *The Ladies' Home Journal* ("Baby in the Bathroom"), she was beseeched by popular magazines for articles, trade publishers for books, but she ignored them. Under the pressure of her siblings, she did produce a Christmas story every year for several years, published in *National Review*, and her posthumous collection, *Will Mrs. Major Go to Hell?* is a delight that may likely be read when the rest of us and our works are ashes. Married to Ben Heath, who joined the family oil companies after World War II, she was locally feared, liked, hated, and enjoyed by the citizens of Hartford. Senator Prescott Bush became her devoted friend.

John was almost totally absorbed by his risky gas and oil exploration business, which he inherited from our father. He was handsome, urbane, and social and drank too much. He married blond, beautiful Ann Harding (of the Pullman car family) from Omaha, who also drank too much. They had a tempestuous marriage that suited them just fine until her tragic early death, wholly unexpected, from which my brother never recovered. In the flossy Salisbury-Lakeville-Sharon area, his periodic jousts in the *Lakeville Journal*, principally with such as Judson Phillips (alias Hugh Pentecost, the detective novel writer), provided good entertainment. Both men were witty. John was in addition sarcastic and pugnacious. He enjoyed the certitude of being right and on the winning side in his curmudgeonly views, which was then largely the case.

After Bill and Jimmy, Priscilla is the most public member of our family, having worked independently as a journalist (United Press) in New York and Paris and then for thirty-some years as *National Review*'s doughty and never-failingly sunny managing editor and editorial writer, retiring in 1985. Without the balm of her personality, her common sense, and her immense moral authority, it is doubtful that the gaggle of intellectuals gathered in the editorial offices of the magazine could have been kept together.*

Jim remained quietly as John's principal partner† in the family businesses; but I think we all sensed that he was restless. He was the unobtrusive member our family, never intruding his opinions, seldom voicing them, but cherishing and cultivating them in mind and spirit as he took advantage of the opportunities afforded by the highly competitive search for oil and gas in Venezuela, Ecuador, Canada, Australia, Israel, Spain, and elsewhere to pursue his main interests, which were ornithology and the Arctic and Antarctic and their fauna. He was gentle, rearing his family of one daughter (a successful freelance writer) and five sons with his extraordinary wife, Ann Cooley, in the rural bliss that was then Sharon (to which he escaped from New York City on weekends). Not until he was dragooned into managing Bill's campaign in the 1965 mayoralty race against John Lindsay, leading to his being drafted into running for senator, did our shy yet profoundly principled brother become a public figure. His most famous action as a senator was his pre-Watergate public denunciation of Richard Nixon. The flamboyant Daniel "Pat" Moynihan‡ defeated Jim for a second term, as was to be expected. Jim took a post briefly with the State Department, went on to preside over Radio Free Europe, and for the last nearly thirty years of his public life was a crackerjack judge on the U.S. Court of Appeals for the District of Columbia Circuit, thus exercising his wise and moderate influence on the three major wings of our government, legislative, executive, and judicial.

Our sister Jane married handsome Bill Smith, an ex-Navy commander of Ohio farming stock, and lived in Calgary for several years, where her husband worked for the family companies while she gained a reputation for outlandishness. *Faute de mieux,* the Smiths had a house in one of those godawful Levittown-type developments that had sprung up like prairie-

---

* To name just a few, James Burnham, Frank Meyer, Willi Schlamm, John Chamberlain, Hugh Kenner, Geoffrey Hart, Ralph de Toledano, etc.

† Along with Ben Heath and a lawyer called Dean Reasoner. Their *eminence grise* was George Montgomery, the Coudert Brothers partner and one-legged WWI ace.

‡ I became quite friendly with him, and fond of him, which is neither here nor there.

dog villages on the Calgary range, large bay windows gaping at each other across narrow streets and sidewalks. Neighbors became accustomed to seeing that crazy Mrs. Smith sitting in a children's playpen, reading, her evening bourbon and a pack of cigarettes on a round table beside her, a tall lamp shedding a pool of light over her book, whose pages she turned immutably as her two-year-old twins screamed and hollered and rampaged all around her. Bill Smith became an independent operator, struck it rich in oil leases, and retired to Sharon in the mid-1950s as a country squire, raising sheep on a large estate. Jane, sharp of mind and tart of tongue, was the one of us who *refused to write*. (One sole article, on quitting smoking.) But apart from bringing up six strapping children, she was active in *National Review*, culling and answering letters (pungently, when it came to the bores) and I think also, for a brief period, attempting to make sense of that sink of everyone's despond, the screwed-up circulation department, whose incorrectible vagaries she bequeathed to our sister Maureen.

We skip Bill. My elder sister Trish, who at the time of which I am writing—the immediate decades after Father's death—was a hot-tempered Catholic conservative of flaming redheaded beauty, adored Bill, deeply loved (and nurtured) me, and suffered through twenty years of a personal cross while producing ten children by her brilliant, by turns wise and erratic, Catholic convert husband, Brent Bozell of Omaha.* Brent was Bill's best friend at Yale. He wrote a seminal article for *National Review* (on the philosophical antagonism between virtue and liberty) that has yet to be bridged by the conservative movement (torn between Burkians and libertarians). His growing devotion to Catholic causes ultimately caused him to split away from *National Review* and found, with Patricia, the militant pre-Vatican Council II *Triumph* magazine, for which I occasionally wrote.

Trish and Brent, to my huge happiness, moved to Spain during the 1960s, setting up at El Escorial, from which they edited *Triumph* and Brent at last got out his book on the Supreme Court, *The Warren Revolution*. It was tortuous in gestation. A few years back, he had dashed off the hugely successful *The Conscience of a Conservative*, which propelled Goldwater into the national limelight. Before that, he had collaborated with Bill on *McCarthy and His Enemies* (Bill's second polemical book after *God*

---

*His conversion to Catholicism was the result of a successful conspiracy between Trish and Bill.

and Man at Yale), which was moderately successful; but long years then passed, surprising and disappointing many people, before he produced the Warren Court book.

Brent was a raw-boned Midwesterner of shining intelligence and a probing philosophical mind. He was my sponsor for the Fence Club at Yale and my mentor for critical years after, coaching me to victories in the Buck and Ten Eyck oratorical competitions. Whenever anyone had a problem, Brent was there, with a loving kindness that was saintly. Which was his ambition: to be a saint. He wished to serve God with all his might and heart and soul. Brent was charismatic in the literal sense of the word, filled with (or touched by) the grace of God. He moved human beings who met him powerfully; he could move crowds with the molten passion of his oratory, as he did at Madison Square Garden in 1964, at a rally for Goldwater, when fifteen thousand people rose cheering to their feet. (I met a young man many years after the event who told me that he had never forgotten it.) But Satan coveted Brent, afflicting him with a tragic infirmity. None of us had the least suspicion that he suffered from what was then called manic depression, now labeled bipolar disorder. The disease crippled Brent's literary output because (I surmise) it incapacitated him for the prolonged intellectual stamina of writing a closely reasoned, book-length polemical treatise. He wrote slowly, agonizingly, in creative spasms followed by dry months, at which times he was prone to manic activity. He was possessed by the haste and urgency, I believe, of his apocalyptical vision.*

An exhilarating thing for us all in those days was the sense that we were making headway, that we were making a difference. My special venue from the mid-1960s into the late '70s was colleges and universities. No more than the flower children did I trust anyone older than thirty. I learned a lot, principally that without patience and humor, nothing is ever to be gained, and that there is no corner on virtue, none on goodness, and that whatever their ideological affiliations, most young people thirsted for decency and justice. My job was to demonstrate that the conservative way of thinking satisfied those desires better than socialism or Marxism, Maoism or the Weathermen. Oh, I ran into hostile crowds. There was a fellow in

---

*Anybody who has read the passages on the priest in my *Servants and Their Masters* and the three novels of my *Canticle of the Thrush* will know what I am talking about.

the university at Missoula who came down the center aisle of the auditorium glaring at me, sat in the front row, glared once more hard at me, then opened a very large newspaper, spreading it wide across his face and holding it there from the moment I began to speak until I had finished. The moderator announced that there'd be a five-minute break after which I'd answer questions. In those days, I smoked. I got off the stage, and as I walked by this fellow, I placed a cigarette in my mouth, took out my trusty Zippo lighter, stooped, and lit his newspaper from the bottom into two flaming pyres, which got his attention.

There were sons of bitches out there, of course. Several times I had to be escorted to the stage by campus cops, obscene and profane insults were hurled at me often, and I was on occasion physically threatened. At one college, again in the far West (Oregon?), a huge banner was stretched across the stage, proclaiming, "FASCIST PIG." (Guess which of the two words was misspelled.)* But more often than not, patience and humor won out. I became popular. At the annual Bucknell revolutionary Colloquy conference, run by the students and bitterly left, I was the only speaker (I believe) ever to be invited back.

I suppose I should say something about my speaking school. It is wonderful, as Bill, God bless him, loyally proclaims to anyone within earshot, knowing little about it. I put modesty aside in the service of truth: our Executive Seminar in Communications Skills is far and away the best program of its sort in the United States, or elsewhere. It teaches clarity of thought, clarity of style, and clarity of expression better than any other institution of learning in this country, or elsewhere.† Putting on no more than fourteen seminars a season, each limited to twelve students, we have graduated more than 2,600 executives and professionals in the past twenty-one years. Practically everyone who submits himself to the Executive Seminar (it is not for the faint-hearted) is on his or her way up, and we have had mere millionaires go on to become billionaires. Filthy lucre is

---

*Uh-huh, "FACIST PIG"!

†Which includes Yale, my alma mater. The dean of Yale College has just this fall announced a crash program in critical thinking, good writing, and the ability to express oneself well—which is an admission of neglect by Yale over the past half-century of the talents that distinguish the civilized human being from apes. As the good dean writes, "The ability to write well, to say what you think clearly and cogently, and to argue persuasively are hallmarks of all educated people."

not our primary concern, though it's nice. We do take pride in helping our students get ahead in their career fields. In witness we have had the scholarly chairman of a department of engineering of a major American university who is—oh, dear—facing thirty years in a federal penitentiary on a charge of embezzlement, last I heard. But then there was that brilliant young fellow who, when yet in his teens, as a budding chemist, worked with the research group that discovered not one but *two* new elements in the chemical table, their leader being awarded the Nobel Prize. At twenty-three, bored with chemistry, he switched to finance, attaching himself to a well-known California investment house, and once again proved his intellectual prowess by multiplying the value of his clients' portfolios 850 percent in just two and a half years, and this during the dot-com stock-market collapse. He is a wonder. Alas, last I heard, he was on the lam, something to do with a minor.

The overwhelming majority of our graduates are neither so spectacular nor so subject to human failings. We have letters from students thanking us for changing their lives. In those words. That file must now contain dozens and dozens of such letters. It is our reward. We make a difference. And we are doing so for folk all over the world now, Europe, South America, Asia, and the Orient all the way to Outer Mongolia,* and in every conceivable career field, including all of the major industries, high-tech and industrial, entrepreneurs of every sorts, and such varied clients as actors, stand-up comedians, politicians, the conductor of a well-known municipal symphony orchestra, the only black rear admiral in the U.S. Navy (a superlative speaker), ex-NKVD agents, the Soviet pilot who defected by flying his MIG to Japan, and one maniac who came to the seminar toting a loaded pistol.† Two springtimes ago we had a professional bounty hunter who has survived three shootouts with the bad guys, and whose primary business now is teaching police departments across the land how to deal with violent fugitives. (He is the sweetest guy!) Two months ago we had the chief inspector of the Federal Bureau of . . . never mind, an inquisitory federal agency, much feared in certain quarters. He is a tall,

---

*A gentleman from Cadbury-Schweppes, born and raised into adulthood without light, heat, or running water, a linguist, a botanist, and holder of four U.S. patents.
† I did not realize I could be quite so disarming.

good-looking, utterly humorless fellow in his mid-forties. At the seminar, if anyone around him grinned or chuckled, he turned a cold eye on the miscreant. For two days, I did my best to awaken this fellow's sense of humor, or humanity, but he was the coldest of cold fishes. On the third day of the seminar, before the final and culminating exercise (the nature of which we do not reveal), we offer our clients a flute of good, dry American champagne. I handed this gentleman a special glass, filled with a colorless liquor. He drained it down at my request. I noted a slight tinge of color on his gray bureaucratic cheeks. "Did you like that?" I asked him. "Yes, it was fine," he said, scrupulously courteous as always. "Do you know what you just drank?" "N-n-no," he replied, a mite apprehensively. "That was moonshine," I informed him, "white lightning, corn liquor, hootch, straight from the still—the best in the state of South Carolina."

I am combative, as are my siblings. The sense we had of gaining ground in the battle of ideas made our lives joyous. Maureen was the center of our exuberance all during this early period (1958–1964) of influence; until, in her kitchen, she dropped dead, leaving five children, one an infant, a stunned husband, and a shocked and irrecoverably grieving family. Gerald A. O'Reilly, her husband, descends from a large tribe of Irish New Yorkers, and for his sense of fun at once had become our very favorite male in-law. He is a sports addict (in his mid-eighties now, he still plays tennis), partial to watching track, baseball, and basketball, in this peculiarity being unlike all of us except me. At *National Review,* Maureen astounded colleagues by her unflappable temperament and her talent for mollifying irate subscribers, who became attached to the magazine primarily because they fell in love with Mrs. O'Reilly.

And then there was Carol, twenty years younger than Allie, eight years younger than me, and five years younger than the one of us she most loved, Maureen, whose death dealt a near-mortal blow to her faith. She was living on a plantation in the remote southeastern piney woods of Virginia, isolated from the rest of her family and at this time coming to understand that she could not continue. She went through rough personal trials, but several years after her divorce, she married the intrepid commodities trader and (now well-known) art collector, Raymond Learsy—a union that sadly also ruptured but that during the high water of Buckley political prominence found our Carol as a dazzlingly pretty New York City hostess with an immense apartment at Park and 75th, at which I regularly parked on breaks from the lecture schedule. Living with Ray was no bed of roses, but to Carol's siblings he was dapper, funny, generous, and kind, and all of us took to him in part, I suspect, because in his radically perilous business, requiring steel nerves and a gambler's serenity of spirit, he reminded us of our father.

Our family goals in those days were simple. The first was to elect Barry Goldwater president, in which end we failed disastrously. The second was to prevent this nation from being defeated by the Soviet Union, the third to elect Ronald Reagan president, and the fourth—I think, looking back half a century, the major goal—to save America from the deathly dullness of the Northeastern establishment's stuff-shirted and intellectually dry-rotted good ole chap liberalism, in which we succeeded . . . for a time.

Our time.

CHAPTER TWENTY-FIVE

———— ∞ ————

Aloïse Steiner Buckley
of New Orleans (V): Grief

I ASKED MY SISTER PRISCILLA TO GIVE ME AN ACCOUNT OF MOTHER'S
state of mind during the months following our father's death. This is it.

Mother went into a deep, un-Mother-like funk.

That lightness of spirit that underpinned everything she did was
devastatingly missing, I think probably because for the last six or seven
years of their married life, Mother had been not only wife and mother
but also, perforce, head nurse in what was now suddenly a convales-
cent home. Oh, she would laugh, and we would have fun together, but
the old spark was missing.

It was not until the following July, when Aunt Inez came up from
New Orleans to spend the first of what would be fifteen or sixteen
summers in Sharon with Mother, that Mother was jolted out of her
depression. It was wonderful, loving, kind, understanding "Pinky" (as
we called Aunt Inez) who did it. Pinky suggested all sorts of things to
entertain Mother, and each idea had been rejected. "I just can't, dear,"
Mother would say. "I really don't feel up to it." Or variations of the
same theme. That finally touched off the red-haired explosiveness that
Pinky usually kept safely banked.

"You just stop it right now, Alla," she said. "You are wallowing in your grief, and I'm ashamed of you."

We stood around appalled, as was Pinky. But that had done it. "No, I'm not ..." Mother started, and then ... then she giggled at her younger sister. "How dare you," she said, laughing in the old familiar way, and hugged her. And for the balance of that summer, at least in Pinky's presence, the unnatural lugubriousness that had so worried us was held more or less in check.

But we were still worried. Allie and Trish and Jane and I discussed the situation at length and came up with a master plan that we hoped would put some distance between those final years when Father was an invalid and the new life without Will that would last another twenty-seven years.

We planned a major trip, the three of us—Trish, Allie, and me—with Mother to places (most of which) she had never visited with Father. We would start in Rome, where there would be a papal audience, and then visit Egypt, Jordan, Israel, and Greece. It took quite a lot of persuading—each of us telling Mother that the other two were *simply dying* to see Egypt, and particularly the Holy Land, where friends of Jim and Ben's would give us a guided tour of the Israeli side of the border. But that, of course, their husbands, Ben and Brent, would be reluctant to let them go for an entire month unless it was to help Mother, whom both Ben and Brent adored. (Bill Smith had vetoed Jane's participation.)

And so, in January 1960, four of us flew out of New York for Rome, Mother first class, and three of us in tourist. It is hard to tell who enjoyed the trip most, Mother or her girls, but when she returned she was restored to her jolly old self with many a new story to tell, most of them on us.

Mother was sixty-three when Father died. She soon regained the health and vigor that characterized her lifelong, but the physical toll of caring for her husband in his last years marked her, one of the most sorrowing consequences being the distancing that her youngest child and daughter, Carol, suffered, which Carol chronicles so unsparingly and tenderly in her book, *At the Still Point.*

As Pitts writes, Mother lived another twenty-seven years, but only seventeen of these were fulfilling to her. Her collapse in 1975 at Hannah's Cabin, following her unsuccessful cataract operation, was almost certainly a stroke, though it was never medically diagnosed (see chapter twenty-eight). Her mind wandered thereafter and became increasingly unhinged from reality. Tasa and I gave her a seventy-fifth birthday party at the picnic cabin and pond on Mulberry, to which we invited just about everybody in Camden. She was still up to that, and had a good time. We snapped a photograph of her in an old lady's country bonnet that we had placed on her head, holding her youngest grandson, Tasa's and my Johnny, who was just a little more than a year old. We have a photograph of her taken a generation earlier with her first male grandchild, Jimmy Heath, and not only are the similarities between the two tots touching, but what is remarkable is how lightly thirty long years of grief and vicissitudes had marked her dear face. But she could no longer read—she, who had been such an avid reader—and this, apart from being a terrible cross for her, deprived her of intellectual stimulation, though almost to the end, she derived great joy from human contacts.

My wife, Tasa, and I were very close to her from 1972 to 1980, until she was removed from her beloved Camden, placed in an apartment in New York (a disposition that was intended with all charity and sense but that I think was mistaken), and then finally removed to Noble Horizons in Salisbury, Connecticut.

While she was still in Kamschatka and well (1972–1975), I taped her memories, a copy of which I sent to my brother Jim. One year, *Harper's Bazaar* featured her along with Rose Kennedy as one of the one hundred most eminent women in the country, in the category of mother and grandmother.[1] When Father died, she had thirty-one grandchildren. The number was to swell to fifty. I had the first male grandson bearing the Buckley name, my son Hunt, and the last, my son Johnny. But I had added to her circle of love five stepchildren, four of whom she came to know well and cherish, and who called her Mimi, as did all the other grandchildren. She was once named South Carolina Mother of the Year, and this honor pleased her almost as much as the recognition she received from the Republican Party when, after a formal luncheon, she was pinned with a diamond, ruby, and sapphire gold brooch representing the flag, which she wore every single day thereafter. In Sharon, she continued to be our capable mother who ran the sprawling household with magical grace and efficiency. In Camden, she was a queen, courted by everyone in town (everybody knew her), by such political institutions as Strom Thurmond, and by newspapers in Columbia and Charleston and Charlotte, which ran feature stories on Kamschatka, and in which she was generally photographed halfway up or against the backdrop of that magnificent central staircase, looking diminutive and a bit dazzled and distracted. Her social calendar was full always. She received long visits from her siblings (Uncle Jimmy Steiner and his wife, Alice, as well as Aunts Vivian and Inez), from Frederica and Warren Smith, from Chicha Freeman, and from Helen (Reid) and her husband, Jean de Lustrac, who, as he aged, became ever more dapper, ever more the picture of the *beau sabreur*. She gave two or three suppers a week and went out two or three times a week. She was at the beck and call always of her children, nevertheless. She endured with unshakable faith the terrible blows of the deaths of Maureen, at age thirty-one, her ninth child and fifth daughter, and then five years later of Allie, at age forty-eight, her firstborn child.* Age whitened and thinned her hair. (She blued it unmercifully at the hairdresser.) Notwithstanding, not until close to the very end, she never walked up stairs, as you and I do: she tripped lightly up them. She was as light on her feet as a feather, which made her a wonderful dancing partner.

She traveled widely; with her daughters Priscilla, Jane, and Patricia. She came three times to Spain for long visits. Trish and Brent and their brood of eight or nine redheads were living in El Escorial, I and my four children in Madrid. She did everything, saw everything, marveled at everything, and charmed every last person to whom we introduced her, including doormen, waiters, and cab drivers. I always swelled with pride thinking of my mother. What irritates Pitts and me a lot, though we understand it, is that most of the grandchildren remember her as a kind and darling but dotty old lady. They came to maturity when Mother was slipping into her dotage, post-1975, and their memories of the extraordinary woman our mother was are skewed. The stories are innumerable, many of them related in the posthumous volume the grandchildren (principally John's daughter Aloïse, the poet) put out on her. One tale that is not in that book I cherish.

---

* The death in 1986 of her youngest sister, Inez, or "Pinky," three years before Mother died, was an incalculable loss to her.

After Father's death, Mother took trips often with Martha and David Williams, and then, upon their deaths, with Ruth and Stanley Burke (he a devout Catholic) of Millbrook, New York, who had moved to Camden in the winters. Ruth Burke was a witty observer, sharp and fun to be with. She told me once about encountering Mother after a lunch at the Springdale Hall club, as she was being helped out of the building by her nurse. Ruth guessed from the vague, alarmed glance that Mother sped her way that she no longer recognized her, though she was tormented by the knowledge that she did know this woman; and so Ruth said charitably to Mother, "Aloïse, I'm Ruth—Ruth Burke." To which Mother replied, "But of course you are! How are you, dear Ruth? And how is dear, dear Stan?" To which Ruth Burke replied gently, "Aloïse, Stan died three years ago." "Oh, oh . . . of course!" exclaimed Mother, who then leaned close to Ruth's ear and whispered to her, "And they tell me that his widow is not, you know," gesturing at her brow, "all there!"

In this pantomine of Mother's senile failing, I, of course, and most of my siblings recognize ourselves in our as yet nonsenile yet cursed inability to remember anyone's name. (I cannot recite all the names of my Heath or Bozell nephews and nieces consecutively.) But the alienation of Mother's failing mind infected her spirits also during the final years of her residence in Kamschatka and Great Elm. Age is a most terrible treason. Traits of character that had never been evident in her prime, which she had overcome or had never harbored, all of a sudden surfaced. She could be petty, peevish, spoiled. She had visions of grandeur, some of them acutely embarrassing. We her children all this while became increasingly uncertain whether we were "getting through," whether she was understanding us. We concealed from her the condominiumizing of Great Elm. One winter season and part of a second, we lodged her in a cottage belonging to Springdale Hall, telling her that Kamschatka's heating plant had failed and was being repaired. Since I was in Camden full-time, it fell upon me to keep up this deceit, which I detested. I am not certain she believed any of us; I can't be certain she did not know the truth—that she was no longer capable of running that great house; that her servants of thirty and forty years were one by one retired or dying or dead*—and

---

*Elizabeth and her husband, Leslie Carlos, Sally and Lucille, dear Jeff Boykin, but not Ella Boswell Whitaker, who is 103 years old as I write!

unconsciously was complicit in our elaborate circumlocutions, choosing to believe them though she knew full well deepest down that they were rubbish. (Tasa, who is astute in these matters as in many others, is of the opinion that Mother distinguished the reality from our deceptions all along, but out of her love for us sought not to let on.) And then we sold Kamschatka . . . but Mother was by that time so far gone that it is possible, had she known, she may not have cared. We live too long.

NOTES

1. The difference between the values of the Kennedys and the Buckleys was nothing more pronounced than the *Harper's Bazaar* award. Mrs. Kennedy is photographed in a white satin Givenchy ball gown, dripping in diamonds, and she is posed in front of a baronial fireplace. The *Harper's Bazaar* people caught up with Mother when she was out shopping in New York. She was photographed in the vestibule of brother Bill's town house, dressed in one of her simple frocks with the characteristic deep V-neck.

    Mrs. Kennedy is quoted as saying, "My greatest accomplishment has been bringing up our children, with my husband, to make full use of their talents and resources for a notable purpose: benefiting the community, not themselves." Mrs. Kennedy may have spoken these words, but PR folk wrote them.

    Our mother said simply, "My greatest accomplishment is not having one single child who is a failure."

    For the Kennedys, everything is (or was) a political event. For our mother, everything was heartfelt.

    Mother coincided with Mrs. Kennedy at several retreats and spoke always warmly of her.

CHAPTER TWENTY-SIX

Aloïse Steiner Buckley of New Orleans (VI) and John William Buckley, RIP

ON THE WAY TO HER DEATH, AS I'VE NOTED, MOTHER SUFFERED THE loss of her husband, which shattered her, but out of which despond she was pulled by sharp, firm words from her sister Inez and the active therapy plotted by her daughters. This trauma was followed by the deaths of two daughters, Maureen and Aloïse.

It was pondering these events as I questioned her about her life that one day after lunch, in the basement-floor pine parlor of Kamschatka, she said to me, "Reid, beg the Lord that you never lose a child. Not even the death of your wonderful father broke my heart more." She was destined to suffer this terrible bereavement one last time with the death of her beloved eldest son, John, at age sixty-four.*

She was a very old woman then, seventy-nine, and ailing, her mind becoming more and more addled, confined to the Noble Horizons (dear God, what a name for a geriatrics institution—hath no one the least understanding of Mercutio?) detention center (one waits to die) in Salisbury, Connecticut, where John had periodically visited in her and his final years.

---

*Wretchedly, in a hotel room in Canada.

Janie and Priscilla and Jim and his darling wife, Ann,* all of whom lived close by in Sharon at least part of the time, would visit and find Mother and John sitting amiably together on a couch, not speaking but holding hands. She roused herself once more for her eldest son's funeral. He chose to be buried in Lakeville, beside his wife, Ann Harding, who had died a score years before. He had meticulously prescribed what he wanted at his funeral . . .

Which I remember ineradicably. It was the fourth or fifth of December 1984, several days after his death on the first of the month, and bitter cold. Frozen shards of snow lay on the tombstones and on the sunken beds of browned lawn in front of them, as in saucers. Three crows cawed from a ragged old oak tree. We all watched the black limousine drawing up to where John and Ann's gravesite could be seen by the occupant, who did not emerge. Mother was in that limousine. She had herself arranged to be driven out to the cemetery, summoning resources for the occasion that none of us suspected she retained.

John was proud of his service to the country as a lieutenant in the first cavalry at Fort Riley, subsequently in the OSS in France. The sorriest bunch of American Legion veterans I have ever beheld drew up beside the grave, paunchy, disheveled, rifles slung across their shoulders at varying angles. The legionnaire in command gave his squad the order to come to attention. Taps was sounded, which aches always in the tear ducts. The three crows cawed an accompaniment. The corporal or sergeant gave the order to fire the last salute to my brother from his comrades and countrymen. *Pffffssst, cracrcrackcrack!* went the rifles, half of them misfiring, the others firing out of synchrony. The order was given to reload and fire again. The crows jeered, *Cacacaaa,* from the top branches of the old oak. *Pffffssst, cracrcrackcrack!* went the rifles. A third time the order was given, and a third time those legionnaires fired their ragged salute, *Pffffssst, cracrcrackcrack!* while the crows cawed and cawed and cawed in mockery.

John would have laughed his head off, though with that touch of ironic despair over the poltergeist that hounded him even to the grave. The sub-

---

*Whose final trial of faith took place early in May 2006, when she fell asleep at the wheel driving back to Sharon from Lakeville, just past the Hotchkiss School, crashed through two telephone poles, and, in breaking her neck, severed the spinal cord, leaving her paralyzed from the neck down.

John William Buckley on "Pickles,"
Springdale Race Course, c. 1946.

freezing wintry scape, the huddled mourners, the disreputable honor guard, the derisive black birds he used to pick off one by one at two hundred yards with his .222 Manlicher with the huge scope—it was a scene from Gogol or Dostoyevsky, which, richly cultured as he was, he would have instantly recognized and made a crack about. Mother in the limousine wept alone. All of us—friends George and Jodie Stone, Paul Terni, Dean Reasoner, R. Hunter Barrett from Fort Worth, not many others; brother-in-law Ben Heath, siblings Priscilla, Jim and Ann, Jane, Bill and Pat, Trish (Brent was too ill to attend, as I remember), Gerry O'Reilly (Maureen's widower) and his wife, Seton, Carol, and John's three orphaned children, Lee, Aloïse, and Johnny, and Tasa and I—stood there at attention and felt the ache of bereavement, too, though we were nevertheless convulsed with laughter. This is the desperate destiny of being a Buckley: we are undone by humor, even at the graveyard. Nobody came to John's deathbed to shout, "Oil! Oil! We've found oil!" as, in his cups, he used to predict would be the case, laughing wryly at his fate. John had not found a lot of oil in his business career, but he had discovered an awful lot of what became critically important to his surviving children and many of his siblings, and that was natural gas, off the royalties from which we would be prospering for years. No, he could not have imagined what a ridiculous spectacle his funeral would be.

He had the hands of a *pistolero*.

He was a crack shot with rifle, pistol, crossbow, sling, dart, bean shooter, and, of course, shotgun. Twice I witnessed him bag a triple on the cunning and erratic ruffed grouse of our hunting grounds in northwestern Connecticut, the bird that I was snapping my muzzles on exploding in a fuss of feathers just as I was swinging past and pulling the trigger, two others thumping to the ground before I could collect my wits.

John always smiled and shrugged his shoulders after such a feat, as if to say, "*Mon cher ami,* what can you have expected?"

Of the boys, Jim and Bill have the good hands, long-fingered, sinewy. Mine are broad, with the thickish fingers of a farmer. They are my father's hands. Not John's. His were small, narrow, freckled, and very white, with short, delicate bones, like our mother's. The sight of Mother and John, sitting side by side in Noble Horizons, their hands clasped, fingers intertwined, is engraved in the memory of his siblings.

Who as a young man shunned us at parties, embarrassed by our tribal cohesion. When he came back from the war, I shared the downstairs bedroom at Kamschatka with him. (I had been released from the ovenlike cubicle on the third floor.) I was fifteen or sixteen, he ten years and a ton of experiences older than me. He suffered from terrible nightmares, striking him after midnight. He would roll back and forth in his bed, and sit up suddenly, cursing and shouting and mumbling unintelligibly in his gutter-perfect French, only an occasional word of which I caught (*merde, cochin*), and then fall back on one or the other side of the mattress. It was frightening to be jerked out of one's sleep in that fashion. He had once been a sleepwalker, I knew, and I feared sometimes that he might mistake me for some enemy and attack me with a knife or one of the many guns leaning against the closet in the vestibule. But in the mornings, he had no memory at all of what had tormented him. When I questioned him, he had nothing to tell me.

He had not set eyes on me in five years, and glanced at me quizzically now and then (how had I grown up to be taller than he, and who had given me the nerve [Mother] to have appropriated several of his J. Press tweed jackets?). He was the elder brother by a decade, and he clearly established that hierarchy in his relations with me, though he could be occasionally indulgent, as when teaching me about the negative lead necessary to knock down a grouse that rocketed out of high cover behind one, or how to pick out a single bird when a covey of quail exploded under one's feet. If I happened (rarely!) to drop a grouse instants before the charge from his .20-gauge over-and-under slammed into it, he'd mutter sardonically, "Nice shot, Reid," but with a look that let me know who was the alpha hunter on the field and that conveyed he did not intend to let it happen again. Pitts, John, and I hunted together often, either at Camden, for quail, on the three thousand acres Father had leased in Lee County, or in Sharon, for grouse, on the mountain or at the farm in White Hollow. He was good to hunt with. He had bird sense, he knew what he was doing, right up into his late forties he never seemed to tire, and he never shirked thrashing his way through the most tangled briars and thickest alders. When luck had favored him during the day, he'd say to us, "You go ahead and take that single, Pitts," or to me, "Reid, the woodcock went into that clump of sumac . . . I'll flush it out for you." Which was generous, though of course his expectation was (a) that Pitts would miss the quail and he would bag it with one of his lightning-fast snap shots, and (b) that the woodcock in the sumac would tower up to his right, not my way, presenting him with a dream target. But not until his wife, Ann, died suddenly seventeen years later, and I flew in from Spain to be with him, did the distance between us dissolve.

He was built with unusual upper body strength, and wrestled his freshman year at Yale. (That strength and aptitude descended from his paternal grandfather, John, the sheriff.) His biceps at that time were so developed that they prevented him, when he bent his arms, from touching his shoulders with the fingertips of his hands. To impress us younger males, he would lie flat on his back, on the soft blue carpet of the "dark" room. I or one of my teenage friends would place our feet (we had kicked off our shoes) in his outflung hands, which were stretched out behind him, and he would lift us straight into the air, maintaining us suspended there several seconds.

I have described Jean de Lustrac as a *beau sabreur;* my brother John was another. He was funny, blessed with terrific wit, which, as in the case of

Allie, when he was in a rotten mood, could master him and be cruel. Most of the time it was simply hilarious.

One extraordinary weekend he brought to Great Elm the most gorgeous redhead my avid eyes had ever rested upon; which they did, at length, when she was reclining on the hot slates at the edge of the pool, warming and drying herself in the sun, heedless of my eighteen-year-old fascination. I had never seen a two-piece bathing suit, wow! Only Betty Grable wore those. (When my sister Janie—a smoldering brunette— defiantly donned one, it caused a minor crisis with our parents.)

John had dated many girls, and they liked him, that was evident. He was the life of almost any party. He had come back from the war in perfect physical condition, an exceptionally handsome man, compact at five feet eight inches, with the small, perfect features of our mother and browning hair whose copper-red tints he had inherited from Henry Wassem, our maternal great-grandfather. That he brought this girl home to be intro- duced to Mother and Father and the rest of us indicated a major emo- tional commitment. This bird was for wedding, not just bedding . . . not that Mother and Father for a single moment would have admitted to themselves low carnal designs in their eldest son, which most of my sis- ters, if pressed for the truth, lying, wouldn't have, either. My siblings were scrupulously, even exaggeratedly, polite to her, as was our wont with strangers (tossing many of them into confusion). She came from Warren- ton, Virginia. She was open and friendly and passed muster (I was besot- ted: she actually listened to my answers when she asked me a social question, treating me as an adult, which John never yet had.) John an- nounced at supper Saturday night that the coming weekend, he was going down to Warrenton to visit with her family. Mother and Father—we all— exchanged glances. Oh, this was serious indeed, and we were all excited; and when we had gathered that Sunday afternoon on the back flags to bid John and his girlfriend adieu as they drove off, Allie snapped at the rest of us, "Okay, what do you think of her?"

As I have indicated, the consensus was favorable. I can't recall why, but for some reason, I was in New York that next Saturday morning, and in the Catawba offices, doing I don't recall what, when one of the telephones happened to ring, which I picked up.

My eldest brother. "What are you doing there?" he asked, surprised.

I shot back, equally surprised, "Aren't you supposed to be in Warrenton?"

"I was," he said, a touch surly.

I paused before asking him the next question. "What happened?"

He said what he had to say crisply, but I could tell he had been impatient to talk to someone about it. "Reid, I got there Thursday late afternoon, her parents were somewhere else. She had friends over for supper, and they talked about horses. This foal was by that stud and out of the other mare. That was *all* they talked about, this colt being out of that mare by the other stud. *They talked about nothing else,* Reid, at supper, after supper, until they went home."

He continued. "Next day, yesterday, Friday, it was the same thing. Her parents arrived, and we all went out for lunch. All anyone talked about was horses, that filly showed leg, that colt had plenty of bottom, this, that, and the other foal was by this stud, out of that mare. They seemed to have nothing else to talk about. We went to a cocktail party, and it was the same thing: horse talk. They are crazy about horses in Warrenton. They are obsessed by horses in Warrenton. At supper it was horses. By this stud, out of that mare. I couldn't take any more of it, Reid, you understand that—not a word about a movie, a novel, Harry Truman, Eisenhower, the Katyn Forest massacre, Joe Stalin—nothing but horses!"

"What did you do?" I asked him sympathetically, but also fearfully.

"When everybody went to bed, I got up, packed my bag, and called a taxi. It was past midnight. Haven't slept a wink. Had myself driven to the train station. I hopped a night train to Philadelphia, another to Washington. That's where I am now, waiting for the train to New York."

I considered what he had said a moment. "You left without saying a word to her or her parents—nothing?" I was aghast. I couldn't believe that he had just walked out.

There was a pained paused. "I sent a telegram from Philadelphia."

"What did you say?"

"By God Out of Virginia."

And that was that.

John eventually married Ann Harding of Omaha, and theirs was a fast though often stormy union, which ended one summer morning when Ann was making breakfast at their house by Lakeville Lake and suddenly realized that their six-year-old son Johnny was not to be seen. With, I guess, a mother's instinct, she went dashing out of the kitchen and down to the dock. There he was, in the water, up to his waist, laughing happily at her. She ran to the water to pick her son up when she fell, right there on the beach. A fellow who was painting the boat house saw this and ran to pull her out of the water, but she was already dead.

She was just thirty-seven. We never told John, but we had an autopsy performed.* Ann was constantly battling weight gain, and she had been on a "starvation" diet, as it was called. The doctors said that if she had eaten as little as a hardboiled egg that morning, instead of breakfasting on black coffee and cigarettes, there would have been enough protein injected into her system to have permitted her to survive the seizure and this particular crisis; but they added that she would have died anyhow within six or seven months; one of her cardiac arteries was, unbeknownst to anyone, almost closed by placque. (This was several years before anyone had heard of cholesterol.)

John never got over the shock or ceased grieving her. We had come to know each other truly from that afternoon after Ann's death, when, after flying in from Spain overnight, I reached his house in Lakeville. I walked into his living room, which was crowded with family and others, spotted him, went directly to him, opened my arms, and hugged him hard against my chest. We remained in this embrace for several minutes as he wept on my shoulder and I felt tears spurt to my eyes. He had visited me in Spain twice, on business occasions. I had divorced and remarried, and he was entranced by my second wife, Tasa, who was thirty-seven when we first visited Sharon, and blond, and closely resembled Grace Kelly, and in whom he found a resemblance to Ann. He loved Tasa, and Tasa instantly loved him.

Alcohol killed John. Mother, who was deep in her dotage by the time his addiction became critical, sensed the loneliness and unhappiness of her son. John often took her to the Interlaken Inn for lunch, just below the Hotchkiss School. Whenever I happened to be in town, I would join them. The drill was that we would endeavor at the beginning of the lunch

---

* This was the kind of high-handed decision that we siblings were prone to about one another and acted upon, expressing our sense of proprietary interest in one another, and therefore our unquestioned right.

to strike up conversation with Mother, which could be a strenuous effort on our part, and on her part too wearying for her befuddled mind to maintain. She drifted off into her private world while we brothers jabbered with each other. John asked me at one of these luncheons why I was eating no meat and spreading no butter on my roll. I unloaded the story of the multitude of food allergies that had afflicted me; Mother suddenly intruded, asking sharply (the note of irony unmistakable), "Reid, is it your allergies that are preventing you from having your hair cut?"

Tasa and I visited John regularly when we traveled up to Sharon from Camden. We would meet him and the Paul Ternis at some inn for supper, which he insisted on paying for, and then follow him back to his house on the lake to watch him down scotch after scotch, asking us whether *we* wanted another drink. Upon our demurral, he would say brightly, "Well, would you believe it? I do!" And fetch himself yet a third or a fourth scotch, stumbling to the bar and back. How I wish I had had the courage to tell him he had had enough. I was, I suppose, inhibited still by my status as a younger brother on these dreary evenings, but I don't excuse myself, though I have no idea what I could have done about him.

Telling an alcoholic that he has to stop drinking is an exercise in futility. John's memory, which had been telegraphic and a wonder to his siblings, survived the drinking until close to the very end. Incredibly. Once when the subject of cameras came up, and I showed him my new Canon, of which I was enamored, he opened a fair-sized Mexican chest in which there may have been thirty or forty 35mm cameras, pulling each of them out and explaining the function, virtues, and limitations of every one. He was technically drunk while he put on this performance. He was this way about anything to do with firearms and ballistics, speaking of these subjects with inerrant total recall. He could quote Virgil in Latin and long passages from Shakespeare. He could dazzle anyone by, as just one example, scribbling on the paper napkin of an outdoor café in Madrid, "Never trust a Greek bearing gifts"—in Greek, which I don't know how to reproduce here—sliding it toward me, warning me, as he smiled at the brash fast-talker across the table (a Greek-American) who was trying to sell me a bill of goods. And he remained, for years and years, despite the odds, the same way about the oil business, absolutely in command of the relevant data.

By act of the board, nevertheless, John was ousted as president of Canada Southern and subsequently from his posts in the other companies, which was inevitable and necessary for the protection of the stockholders. John was no longer the brilliant, creative entrepreneur with a knack for negotiations. By eleven in the morning, he was out of commission. Hurt, desperate, betrayed by, as he viewed it, his most intimate associates, he became a recluse, holing himself up in his house among his trophies of American and African big game, his cases of expensive shotguns, his racks of fine trout rods, his sterling silver plates and other trophies from the Philadelphia Pigeon Club and the Campfire Club in New York, his lithographs and oil paintings of woodcocks, ducks, and, principally, ruffed grouse, king of game birds—holed up with his memories and his bottles of scotch.

But this is not the way I choose to remember my brother. I prefer to recall him as he was freshly back from the war, gallant and filled with optimism and confidence, riding our big bay horse Pickles in the Camden Hunt. It was two or three years after he had returned from France that he at last told me about his nightmares.

He had done his job in preparation for D-Day. I am not certain whether he had been infiltrated into France, with his perfect command of the language, and then exfiltrated, or whether he had been assigned more prosaically to intelligence. I know that it had to do with the Resistance and preparations for the invasion.

It was the Battle of the Bulge, Christmas time. Top sergeants and lieutenants of both grades had been slaughtered on the beach and subsequently in the terrible orchards, and now, at Bastogne, the Germans had counterattacked. There was urgent need on the front for more junior officers. MPs were sent to round up staff personnel in the pubs (and doubtless in the fleshpots) of London, and all of a sudden, these found themselves boarding two of those hastily assembled (one each month) "victory" troop ships bound for France. John was among them.

There were three thousand high-grade uncommissioned and low-grade commissioned officers jammed into both ships. Halfway across the channel, a U-boat torpedoed the lead ship, which exploded and went down, leaving hundreds, more, as many as two thousand young men in the ice-cold water, waving their arms in almost certain expectation of rescue. But the order was given for the second troop ship, on which John was aboard, to plow right over them—not to stop, not to try to take the survivors aboard, but to steam ahead and leave them in the wake shouting, yelling, flailing their arms for attention ever more desperately, until one by one, suddenly, the realization came upon them what was happening, and they understood that they were being doomed to freeze and drown, that their comrades were churning the black waters away from them; because had that second ship stopped, it would have been a fat target for another torpedo, and the need at the front was critical.

A day or so later, John and three other first lieutenants were racing to Paris to get their assignments to the front. The cold was bitter, the most frigid winter temperatures in years, and thanks to one of the most colossal logistical foul-ups in military history, American soldiers clad in summer uniforms were freezing solid in their foxholes. John and his buddies in that jeep were not only cold, but consumed by what he described as "a powerful thirst." They came upon a farmhouse, at which they stopped, John hopping out to knock politely on the door.

It opened a crack, a crusty Normand farmer in his late fifties or early sixties blocking the entrance. *"Que voulez vous ici!"* the man snapped.

John asked him unctuously whether he might have a bottle of calvados, the Normand brandy.

"What money do you have?"

"English pounds"—they had landed with nothing else.

"What good are English pounds to me!" said the farmer, shutting the door.

John knocked again. He knocked twice, then, hard, three times.

This time a furious man yanked the door open, cheeks mottled with ire. *"Je vous est dis*—I told you, English pounds are of no use to me . . ."

John interrupted him. "We can pay with cigarettes." Cigarettes were more desirable than gold in those days. "Luckys, Chesters, Camels, whatever you want."

The choleric farmer shouted, *"Je ne fume pas!"* ("I do not smoke!") And he slammed the door . . .

But this time on the hardened toe of John's combat boot, who had placed his right foot in the jamb. Swirling in his mind suddenly, he told me, was the image of all those boys in the black waters of the Channel, waving and crying for help.

He yanked the cumbersome Army-issue .45 automatic out of its holster, placing the barrel of it flat against the farmer's brow, saying in a cold voice, *"De ce moment, Monsieur, vous etês un fumeur."* ("From this moment, Mister, you are a smoker.")

He would smile at the memory when relating this story, but then fall silent, his mouth bitter and his expression infinitely sad.* The death of Mother's second child and first boy came at the very end of her career; she survived her beloved son by a scant three months.

---

*I have my sister Priscilla to thank for corrections in the tale I remembered.

CHAPTER TWENTY-SEVEN

—— ✻ ——

Aloïse Steiner Buckley
of New Orleans (VII):
1895–1985, RIP

I WASN'T IN SHARON OR NEW YORK WHEN MOTHER DIED, TRISHA WAS. I have asked her to describe those last days.

Brent and I drove from Washington to Sharon the afternoon of March 9, Jim's birthday (Mother's would be two days later, March 11), in response to a call from Jane—Mother was gravely ill.

We went straight to Carol's house on the Great Elm grounds, as arranged (Carol was in Mexico with her two girls, frantically trying to get home), arriving at the [Sharon] hospital late that afternoon. What seemed like a small crowd milled around in Mother's room, none of whom I recall except for Pitts and Jane, all urging Mother to eat her supper. She was in her own world, and wouldn't, or couldn't, until Jane moved in, in Jane's way, and gently spooned some of Mother's favorite chocolate pudding into her mouth. There was no sense at all of urgency. Brent and I went off to a restaurant (Jim, Ann, Priscilla, and Jane were having a subdued birthday supper for Jimmy at Great Elm—we didn't want to intrude), after which Brent suggested we stop by and say good night to Mother.

Walking down the hall, from far off, we could hear the terrible

Aloïse Buckley at 53 with her first grandson,   *Aloïse Buckley at 75 with her last grandson,*
James Buckley Heath, c. 1948   *John Alois Buckley*

breathing, rasping, startling coming from that small frame. It was suddenly quite clear. And so I stayed, asking Brent to bring me some coffee and a book. Somewhere along the line, the local priest dropped by and administered the last rites. An hour or so later, Ann, Pitts, and Jane arrived (Jim was in emotional knots and couldn't),* and Ann offered to lead us in a rosary. She asked me which mysteries I preferred, and I said the Joyful, but meant the Glorious Mysteries. It's the sort of thing you remember. They left, and I settled in for the night, sipping coffee I couldn't taste, and turning pages I hadn't read.

Sometime in the very early morning, a woman doctor dropped by. The hospital had been quiet except for Mother's terrible breathing, which went on and on† The doctor felt Mother's doll-like abdomen, which was badly distended, and shook her head. She looked at the chart and said softly to the nurse, "I know it's a little early, but there's no reason for her to suffer," and pulled out a hypodermic. I lay back

---

* There was a very special bond between Mother and Jim.
† Mother had been diagnosed with congestive heart failure.

again in my chair by Mother's bedside, by this time too tired even to pretend to read, and I suppose I began to drowse.

I sat up abruptly. Something had startled me. It was Mother. The rasping had stopped; the room was quiet. The breathing was soft and gentle. I leaned over her bed, knowing even before the nurse said, "Yes, in a little while." Then the breathing faltered, stopped, and I thought, insistently, "No, no, please, Mother, breathe breathe breathe." And it would begin again. And then, as insistently, "Let go, Mother, it's okay, let go, go to God." And this litany repeated a few times before the final gentle exhalation. The nurse closed her eyes, opened the window, and went out to call the doctor. I held Mother some more in my arms, for some reason dabbed perfume on her,* and fussed around a bit as daylight filtered into the room. When the nurse returned, I went out into the hall and called Brent, and then Jane. "Mother's gone." Brent brought me home, but I couldn't sleep. Mother was dead.

Later that afternoon, Pitts, Jim, Jane, and I played a few games of paddle tennis, more badly than usual. And we laughed in our delight in one another. Everything would be all right.

---

* Trish is her mother's daughter.

CHAPTER TWENTY-EIGHT

———— ✺ ————

Aloïse Steiner Buckley
of New Orleans (VIII):
Norman Mailer, To Lose a Shoe

I WROTE THIS FOR THE BOOK (*REMINISCENCES OF ALOÏSE STEINER Buckley 1895–1985,* collected and edited by Aloise Harding Buckley) that was assembled largely by the grandchildren upon their grandmother's (our mother's) death. It is a tender—and sometimes hilarious—recollection of her.

I. *Wherein the Steiner Sisters Take on Norman Mailer*

At a time of acute personal distress, Norman Mailer wrote me one of the most sensitive, compassionate, and inspiriting letters that I have ever received. The literary conceit here is that the reminiscence is addressed to the third generation, Mother's grandchildren.

That was in the winter of 1971.

The letter was an unexpected moral boost from a writer whose art I deeply admired; and it was all the more affecting, as well as surprising, because I had met him once only, and then for the briefest interval. A month later, in February or March, I flew into New York from Madrid to begin the second of my two annual lecture junkets, which generally had me six to eight weeks on the road. I had written Mr. Mailer telling him that I would be in town, and he had telephoned suggesting that we get together for lunch.

It was on me, I insisted. I picked a favorite restaurant whose name I don't recall—just off Madison Avenue, on 63rd or 64th Street (I think).

That morning of the luncheon date, while I was frantically tacking together talks in one of those cramped fourth-floor cells in Catawba's headquarters at 103 East 37th Street,[1] among discarded ledgers, fly-spotted maps of remote territories dotted red and blue with pins of popped petroliferous dreams, dingbats, boomerangs, slings and arrows, old seas of troubles in musty kit bags with their smelly litters, and secretaries who had been sent up a decade before to search out a lease that was not to be found, but who were still rummaging in the paper avalanches that spilled from Ross Jordan's office,* though both the lease and they had long been forgot, Ben Heath†—Uncle Ben, as I always affectionately called him—gave me the marvelous news that Mother was at 60 Sutton Place South, on a short visit from Camden, I don't recall why. At once I telephoned her.

"Darling!" she belled into the receiver, "Is this really you, Reid? Oh, honey, how wonderful! When can I see you?"[2]

"Hi, Maw! That's not going to be easy, I'm afraid. I leave tonight for Chicago, and then on to Califano . . . sorry, I've been halfway through Health, Education and Welfare, on my way to OSHA, where they make those rubber galoshes, by gosh, I am on to him too, but I mean California.‡ I don't get back until late April."

"Oh, no! Oh, that can't be! Darling, darling Reid, I must see you."

"Well, what about lunch?"

"That would be marvelous! Oh, yes. But I forgot to tell you, your Aunt Inez is here with me, up from New Orleans."

Mother had mentioned my next-favorite person in this world, whom I hadn't seen in three or four years. "Wonderful!" cried I. "Bring her along!"

"Darling, can you afford it? Won't it be too dreadfully expensive? I'm

---

* Ross Jordan was the (very lovable) office manager. His untidiness was legendary.
† My sister Aloise's widower.
‡ The reference here is to then-Secretary of HEW (Health, Education and Welfare) Joseph Califano, who used to boast that the budget of his bureaucracy exceeded the budget of California.

sure it will! I hate to think of you children spending your money on me. I know how hard you work . . ."

I convinced her without too much ado, telling her which restaurant to meet at, and at what time . . . and only then, as I replaced the receiver on its cradle, realizing the enormity of what I had done.

I had invited my sweet, darling mother and her even sweeter, darling sister to an intimate lunch with brawling, left-radical, and for all I knew foul-mouthed and probably blasphemous Norman Mailer! What had possessed me?

And how would *he* react to the surprise, someone with whom I was in fact so lightly acquainted, despite the chance coincidence that my writer's block and failing marriage had struck a sympathetic chord in a veteran sufferer from both afflictions? What possible interests in common had the Brooklyn-born literary prodigy and brat with New Orleans-born, gently raised, pure-as-drinking-water Mother and her even purer little sister?

Not all of you grandchildren who knew Mimi* well may have had the same pleasure of your great-aunt Inez, "Pinky," as she was called by her siblings, the youngest of the three Steiner girls. Aunt Inez was redheaded and astigmatic, and tended to fall asleep in the midst of conversations, for which she was profoundly apologetic, pleading a touch of narcolepsy, though I noticed that there were some conversations during which she more often nodded off than others. She was even more petite than Mimi, and (if this is possible) even more saintly, even gentler and kinder, and worlds more innocent. In Uncle Bill's obituary you've read about Aunt Vivian's angelic innocence. Well, Aunt Inez was cut from the same bolt of cloth. I remember being told by Cousin Claire Lombard (who regularly alluded to the Steiner sisters as "the three graces") that when my *Eye of the Hurricane* came out, Aunt Vivian and Aunt Inez at once flung themselves to their knees and implored the good Lord in these terms: "Dear Heavenly Father, if our beloved nephew's novel should cause even one soul to sin in deed or thought, please let it not sell." Within a week, Doubleday's fancy Fifth Avenue offices began to pile up with unsold copies of my book, bless their souls.†

---

* Their pet name for their grandmother.
† Doubleday's offices are no longer on Fifth Avenue and no longer so fancy. Claire Baily Lombard (RIP) was the beloved wife of my beloved cousin Robert Lombard, son of my aunt

I telephoned Aunt Pat,* who, as you all know, is clever and sophisticated, and who I hoped would hit on some brilliant strategy for extricating me from my plight. "Do you know what I have done? I've gone and invited Mother and Aunt Inez for lunch, along with Norman Mailer."

"You must be out of your mind!"

"I think I am. Definitely, I am out of my mind. The observation, however, is uninteresting."

"But have you gone mad? Dear Reid, do you realize what could happen?"

"My imagination has been running rampant for the past half-hour," I said wretchedly. "I have a high, a very rich and potent, imagination. Pat, dear Pat, how do I get out of this?"

"You don't. There is no way. Some people are simply born bereft of the most elementary savoir faire and will put their foot in it. I am afraid you are one of them. When will you ever learn to shejule your shoshal affairs shensibly?"†

"Won't you please come help me see this through?"

"Are you quite daft after all? I have a fashion show to put on this afternoon for the Little Sisters of the Poor, for which I have rented all of Oscar's‡ production for the next season. No, you must see this through yourself, like a man."

I telephoned Aunt Carol, who is, as you surely know, exceedingly clever and almost as sophisticated as Aunt Pat, and who, I hoped, would hit upon some dazzling ploy for picking me from my pickle. "Do you know what I have gone and done? I've invited Mother and Aunt Inez for lunch, together with Norman Mailer."

"You must be out of your mind!"

"I should have warned you that Pat said that first, so it's not original."

"She's so right."

Vivian—two of my closest friends. I have written about them in *Credo: Reflections of the Republic 2000–2004.*

* RIP, April 15, 2007.

† Pat is Canadian born, and has trouble with her *sch*'s, pronouncing them in the slushy Welsh, or Sean Connery, fashion. Her major problem during her bridal days was locating the Canadian fleet, of which she was imperiously proud, which got lost at sea.

‡ De la Renta, the then supremely trendy fashion designer.

"But it doesn't help," I said wretchedly. "Carol, dearest kid sister Carol, how do I get out of this?"

"You don't. There is no way. Some people are simply born to put their feet in it. Do you remember the song, 'Up in Harlem, at a table for two, there we were, the four of us, baby, me, your big feet, and you?' "

"I am laughing until my sides ache . . . Carol, you must come to lunch. Will you? Please?"

"I wouldn't miss it for anything."

I was first at the restaurant, then Carol, who slipped into the bench seat beside me, saying, "I have been getting horrible vibes about this"; and then Aunt Inez and Mother, to whom I now announced that Norman Mailer would be joining us.

"You mean the famous writer?" asked Aunt Inez—a little vaguely. She had definitely heard of him, she had most certainly not read any of his works, or they wouldn't have been selling, either.

"Of course, Inez," said Mimi, who loved to play the sophisticate to her sibling. "How nice, dear. What do you suppose we can talk about?"

That had been considerably on my mind; but soon in walked Norman Mailer himself, his tangled hair not so intimidatingly wild as I had feared it might be, conservatively togged out in a dark suit and tie. I stood up, waved to him; smiling bravely through his interrogatory glance as he registered first the two septuagenarian ladies at the table, and then (*dear* Carol), appreciatively, the dimpled and soignée beauty beside them; stepping briskly forward to shake my hand and mumble, "Sorry I'm late."

"Norman," I said in a rush, "I want you to meet my Aunt Inez, my mother, and my sister Carol."

I had no idea what to expect, but he bowed gallantly over the hands of the two elderly women, grinned politely at Carol, and sat down.

Mother said, "Mr. Mailer, Reid has told us so much about you, I can't express how anxious we have been to meet you."

Norman gave me a sidelong glance. Just what had I regaled my aunt and mother with? But the innocence of Mother's question was transparent, and with a courteous smile he acknowledged her compliment and began to talk to her and Aunt Inez about books, about the theater, about films. He charmed them, and they charmed him. Had he been to Mardi Gras? Antoine's? Had he never had the coffee and beignets at the Café du Monde? Somehow the yellow fever got into the conversation, and Aunt

Inez, who had confined herself to appreciative murmurs up until now, told about how, when her dear husband, Uncle Claude Perrier, was a ten-year-old boy living in the Vieux Carré, his older brother and boon companion died of the fever, and they washed him and wrapped him tightly in his shroud, and set him out in the bricked courtyard on a kind of platform upon poles, much as, curiously, the Indians used to do with their dead, until the men came in the great wagon piled with other dead to take him away; and then, impelled along by the dynamics of the recollection, how her darling late husband and his brother used to have to wait for the brightly painted . . .

She stopped, suddenly.

"Brightly painted what, Inez?" prompted Mimi.

"Brightly painted I can't say what, Alla."

"What do you mean, you can't say what, Inez? You left us hanging, Mr. Mailer wants to know, *I* would like to . . ."

"Call me Norman, please!"

"And you must call me Aloïse!"

"Please, Mrs. Perrier, won't you . . . ? "

"Oh, my name is Inez!"

"Thank you. But won't you please . . . ? "

"Of course she will!"

"I *can't*, Alla!"

"*Why* can't you, Inez? That's ridiculous. Brightly painted what? It can't be *that* bad."

"Sanitation wagon!" burst out her furiously blushing sister.

"Oh," said Norman Mailer.

"Well, maybe not for lunch," said Mother, in one of those private sequiturs that used to drive Father crazy. "What about the wagon?"

"It was painted bright red and green," said Aunt Inez, feeling trapped in the story, "with fine yellow stenciling on the sides, and all the brass was polished, the harness on the horses was freshly oiled, the round little chimes on the broad straps were shiny bright—everything was just as clean and spic and span as could be, for obvious reasons . . . I really can't go on, Alla, I can't!" she said desperately.

"Well, why ever did you start?"

"It sort of popped out of my mouth before I knew it!"

"*I* know that story," I now put in. "Uncle Claude told it the last time I saw him—at the supper party you gave me, Aunt Inez, when you suggested that I roll my index fingers up under my nose one hundred and fifty times twice a day, like a drum, or a window blind, pushing up with them as I did so."

"I declare, Reid, I never told you to do any such thing!"

"Oh, yes, you did. You took me aside after supper and said to me, 'Honey, at a certain time in life, everything starts to droop a little.' And then you told me what to do about my hook nose."

"Why, that's pure invention. Aloïse, don't believe him. I said no such thing!"

"What about that wagon?" asked Norman Mailer.

"Oh," I cried, "Uncle Claude loved it because it had great big silver barrels that the men used to roll down the brick path to the . . ."

"Hush, Reid! Don't let him, Aloïse!"

" . . . to the bottom of the garden, where they took shovels and emptied . . ."

"Reid, dear!"

"But that wasn't what Uncle Claude most loved about it," I went on, propelled by the recollection. "The uniforms of the sanitation people were wonderful, especially the man who drove the team, who stayed up on the box—the boss—scarlet and green with gold epaulets. He wore shiny black boots, too. Uncle Claude and his brother and the other little boys in the neighborhood used to run ahead of the wagon and shout . . . what was it they shouted?"

"I don't . . . think I remember," said Aunt Inez in a hollow and just audible voice, miserable because I had obliged her to tell a fib, because she did so remember.

"Oh, go on, of course you do," said Mimi, nudging her with an elbow. "Go on, Inez, tell, for heaven's sake!"

"Well, they ran ahead of the wagon shouting—they were so impressed by the uniform, you see, they had never seen anything quite so splendid, they imagined he was a very high personage indeed, and so they ran ahead shouting, *"Viens le* . . ." Her voice dropped to the merest whisper.

"Viens le what!" cried Mother, wholly exasperated.

"Le President de la Merde!" And she dissolved in blushes, while everyone roared, and the tears came to Mother's lovely green eyes, and she gasped, "I don't believe it, Inez, I never heard that, it is awful . . ."

"It is *dreadful*, Alla, you never should have insisted that I . . ."

"It's wonderful!" cried Norman Mailer, in a kind of ecstasy, because this was first-rate material indeed; and he broke into reminiscences about his upbringing in an urban Jewish neighborhood, which was a world totally strange and removed to the sisters Steiner, as much as old New Orleans and its French ways had been to him.

To tell you the truth, I don't recall what precise stories were exchanged that afternoon, but Carol and I were quite left out of the conversation. As the meal went on, Norman Mailer waxed more and more gallant and courtly, Aunt Inez and Mother more and more ingratiating. "You don't mean it!" Mother would exclaim. "Why, you are simply fascinating, Mr. Mailer," Aunt Inez gushed, with a shining sincerity. "Call me Norman!" "Oh, yes, I keep forgetting!"

Not often had Norman Mailer had such an audience; maybe never had he met two such *feminine* women, in whom goodness was so transparent. He felt, I think, as strangers so often did when encountering the almost irresistible charm of Mimi and her sisters, that he could confide anything at all to these two ladies, and at one point he explained—this I do vividly remember—how trying on the temper it was to make a movie; whereupon Aunt Inez chirped in her lovely New Orleans accent, "But Mistuh Mailer, I can't imagine you ever losing your temper!" Carol and I nearly choked, he having not ten days gone by punched one of his cameramen over some disagreement or other. He gazed at Aunt Inez in wonderment and joy and allowed as how he had been known on certain very trying occasions to blow a very little gasket; and continued telling his tales, fascinating them, being fascinated by them.

When lunch was over, Mother and Aunt Inez elected to walk to 60 Sutton Place South, which was just seven or eight blocks away. Norman Mailer insisted on accompanying them. Oh, they wouldn't hear of it! But neither would he, two gentle women like themselves treading the dangerous East Side pavement unescorted! (Shades of Rhett Butler!) And grasping them both firmly by the elbow, he ushered them jauntily down the street, calling over his shoulder to Carol and me to wait for him.

"Do you believe this?" Carol asked of me.

"Not hardly."

"You don't suppose this is the real Norman Mailer?" she said, her firm grasp of the realities shaken. "A decorous, clean-speaking Norman Mailer the world has never been permitted to view, one that only two little old ladies like Mother and Aunt Inez could have brought out!"

He was still smiling, but glistening with perspiration, when he got back, because it was unseasonably warm that late winter afternoon, and his fifteen-minute return walk was uphill part of the way—shouting at us immediately upon coming within earshot, "You conservatives always have a fucking ace in the hole, don't you!"

This morning, on my first day back at the desk after six weeks in Spain, I picked up the two-day-old notice in the *New York Times* that Fanny Mailer, Norman's mother, age eighty-seven, had passed away. May she rest in peace. And may she and Mimi, and Aunt Inez, meet.*

2. *And Mimi Drops a Shoe*

Your great-aunt Inez died this past December 9 [1984], just three months before Mother.

How she loved the little vacations she had in later life with her big sister. They regularly attended noontime Mass at St. Patrick's, in the course of which they also invariably went to Confession. Now, except for the grace conferred by the sacrament, this was about as redundant a religious exercise for them both as can be imagined, because between them they had probably not committed a sin worth splitting in twenty years. Nevertheless, they regularly bored priests with their imagined lapses, and on this particular morning, Mother, entering the booth first, emerged looking a good deal paler than her bright applications of rouge should have permitted. But she knelt back down at the pew and bowed her head with that instant reverent plunge into devotion that we, her children, will never forget. Aunt Inez took her turn in the booth, and shortly she re-emerged, also looking shell-shocked as she knelt beside Mother.

After a few sibilant minutes had gone by, Maw lifted her head and whispered, "Pinky, uh, did the priest by any chance give you a rather long penance?"

"Why, Alla," said Aunt Inez, turning a hot pink, "he gave me *six thousand* Hail Marys!"

---

* That was my last meeting with Norman Mailer, whom I have since always wished well. His recent death has shaken me deeply. God bless him, a genuine writer, half a genius.

Mother said, "He gave me ten thousand Our Fathers!"

"Alla, he didn't!"

"Yes, he did. I don't think that can be right, do you?"

"*I* don't think so, Alla . . . but what can we do?"

"We can go to the sacristy, Inez, and find some other priest, and tell him what has happened—that's what we can do!"

Half dragging her reluctant little sister, who felt it was impious in any way to challenge an anointed servant of the Lord, Mother marched up the great aisle. They intercepted a white-haired Irish priest behind the main altar and related their story. He gazed at them in amazement, saying, "Must be some mistake." He thereupon sent ushers to investigate, and they discovered a drunk in the confessional—a happy Irish bum—having a high old time.

In the fall of 1974, Mother and Aunt Inez went to Europe for what was Aunt Inez's last visit to the Continent.

A year earlier, in February 1973, Mother had a double cataract operation performed by the great Dr. Ramón Castroviejo, but though the surgery was technically successful, she never fully regained her eyesight.[3] She was deprived of the voracious reading that irrigated her mind, and something about the physical stress of the experience had deeply affected her spirit. She returned to her beloved Kamschatka not well, curiously silent, forgetful. Tasa and I and our nine children were living in the old slave cottage at Mulberry Plantation, and one night, along with the Henry Boykins,* we had Mother over for supper. We gave her a scotch and water. She drank it down rather quickly, but absently. She seemed vague, troubled. We sat down almost at once for supper, Mother worrying us greatly, because she was groggy now, as though she had too much to drink. Suddenly her cheeks turned a congested purple, she slumped, and her forehead dropped down on the table. We rushed to her, lifted her up, carried her to a couch in the living room, revived her, gave her water. Hunt† drove her home. He said she was frail—he half carried her to her room—but that she protested that she was all right.

I believe now that Mother had the first of several strokes that were to assail her and successively debilitate her in the eleven years remaining.

---

*He is the architect, son of Stew Boykin.

†My eldest son.

Anyhow, we, her children, could not explain the sudden onslaught of senescence after that eye operation, and it was with some trepidation that sisters Priscilla and Jane saw Aunt Inez and Mother off on their European jaunt. But it was a huge success. Paris revived Mother with a rush of happy memories. When they got to Madrid, Tasa's parents, Rosario and Guillermo, met them and squired them everywhere—to Toledo and Segovia and Ávila.[4] Guillermo tells a lovely story about the visit to that walled city, whose stones still resonate to the mystical presence of its great saints.

"You know," he says, "how your mother had that habit of lifting an index finger to her lips and crying, 'Oh, no!' when she was impressed with anything? Why, wherever we visited, when the guide said something of interest, that finger would go to her lips and she would let out a little, 'Oh, no!' [which Guillermo does not know that in English was almost always followed by "You don't tell me!"]. In Ávila, the guide related how when Saint Teresa was a young girl, she prayed to be permitted to suffer martyrdom. 'Oh, no!' cried your mother from our position near the back of the crowd. At another time the guide told us that Saint Teresa had built many convents and hospitals. 'Oh, no!' cried your mother. Finally, at a third place, a church, the guide said, 'And what you see in the glass case is the finger of Saint Teresa, perfectly preserved.' 'Oh, no!' went your mother. The guide turned scarlet [se enrojeció], shouting in Spanish, 'I don't know what is the matter with that lady in the rear, there, but everything I have been telling you is true!"

On occasion, Maw accused me of the slightest tendency to exaggerate. This is, of course, preposterous. She was a romantic to the core, and a poet who would not sacrifice the glorious what-with-a-little-inspiration might-have-been to the cloddish, plebeian, in fact, but I, irrigate the dull sod of our existences with a sprinkle or two of fancy? Never! There is one story, the last I will tell, vigorously denied by Mother, to which not the slightest embellishment has been added. There is no need.

In 1962, Mother came to Madrid to visit Patricia and Brent [Bozell]—who were living at the Escorial—and me. Often, we lunched at the Castellana Hilton, a deluxe, pretentious hotel that I very much disliked but that was conveniently across from my office, which was a modest palace* on the [then] gracious Avenida de la Castellana.

---

*Owned by a gentleman called Samprún.

As you know, Maw had a habit while eating of tucking her slim right leg under her, sitting on its ankle. When we were through, and I was about to summon the maître d'hotel for the check, she stopped me, saying, "Honey, I've lost my shoe—isn't that silly?" "No problem," said I cheerily, lifting the tablecloth to peer under it in the area of her feet, but seeing nothing. I went around the back of her chair, again lifting the tablecloth. "Do you see it?" "No." I now got down under the snowy linen, but still I did not locate her shoe. This eccentric behavior, however, attracted the attention of the stately maître, who stalked over to us. He had one of those long, gloomy Spanish faces with bags under the eyes like alligator skin into which pitchers full of cynicism and *longueur* have been poured, a long, doleful nose dropping down its center. Mother confessed, blushing. "My son is looking for my shoe." I surfaced at just about this time. "It's not there," I said, getting to my feet. "It's got to be there, I know, but I can't find it." "Madame has lost her shoe?" queried the maître with an incredulous look. "No problem." He snapped his fingers in the air. Instantly, a squadron of waiters converged on our little round table. *"La señora ha perdido su zapato,"* he announced in sonorous tones, attracting the attention of all nearby diners, who peered curiously in our direction. Mother, I saw, was mortified, but the waiters dived under the tablecloth, searching on hands and knees along the thick carpet under the fall of the linen. To no avail. "She must have kicked it across the room," I heard one of them mutter. "Maybe she never had it in the first place," said another. The maître stretched his dignity sufficiently to lift the hem of the heavy silk curtain that protected our corner table from the harsh sun of the patio ... that luxurious moiré fall uncovered nothing. "Reid," cried Mother in a hoarse whisper, "tell them to go away." "But how can I, Mother? We can't leave until we find your other shoe." "I don't care," she said fiercely, flushing as brick-red as ever I remember her flushing, her eyes filling as if with tears, a kind of desperate hilarity in her throat. *"Tell them to go!"* "But Mother ..." "I ... am sitting on it."

Maw, as you know, wore corsets. Her foot had gone numb from her sitting on it during the meal, and so had her fanny, and only when she began fidgeting in her embarrassment did she feel the spike-heeled shoe.

I called off the mystified maître and his lackeys, liberally tipping everyone, helping Mother limp out of the dining room, which she refused ever again to visit.

Whenever I recalled that luncheon of the lost shoe, Mother would cry, "Why, Reid, you *know* that's not true! You know there's not a word of truth in it!"—in the meantime pealing with laughter, because she knew very well that it was the unvarnished truth, every word of it, and though she was still mortified by the episode long years afterward, she had the grace always, always, of laughing heartily at herself.

That lovely, bell-like laughter. How merry her soul!

NOTES

1. It was a lovely old building.
2. Our mother's unmistakable bell-like, burbling, warm, enthusiastic, welcoming telephone greeting thrilled the caller, because she made it seem, always, as though your call was the most wonderful event to have befallen her on that day and maybe even that whole month. It was giving, loving, and unforgettable. This quality has been inherited by sister Jane and is evident in one of my daughters-in-law, Rosemary Joseph, wife of our son Borja de Olano, who makes it seem always as though nothing in this world could make her so happy as to hear your voice.
3. The expatriate (living in New York City) Spanish eye surgeon who protested all his life that it was his father, in the hills of Santander, not he, who discovered and practiced cataract surgery. He married Nancy Smith, daughter of the *parvenu* Wall Street shark and terror, Ben Smith. My sister Patricia bested Nancy in horsemanship when they were young ladies.
4. Guillermo Yllera was my Tasa's stepfather; the soul of amiability and kindness, he was killed in the early 1980s by poor medical attention following an operation on one of his legs (he had been a professional soccer player for Atlético de Madrid team in his youth). Rosario, Tasa's mother, twice widowed, died December 7, 2006, in a nursing home in Madrid. She was ninety-seven years old. (Tasa's father, Enrique Leguina, died gallantly in Spain's terrible Civil War, leading his battalion across the Ebro River in a cavalry charge.)

POST DATUM

Mother was buried three days after her death in Camden's Quaker cemetery, next to Father.*

In the garden of my brother Bill's house in Peacock Point, Stamford, Connecticut, stands a cross, a sculpture in stone. He tells me he has left instructions to embed his ashes in its lateral beam and have the cross shipped to Camden, to be erected on our family plot.† Tasa and I intend to have a portion of our ashes placed in that plot, close to our parents', and I have already had the tablets chiseled, awaiting only the terminal dates.

We are just about there. I don't think any of us will be pulling back on the steering wheel and shouting "Whoa!" Of the surviving tribe, Pitts is an amazingly hale eighty-six and, despite two replaced hips and the replacement of a knee, went skiing last January for two weeks in Switzerland, as is her custom, which she sees no reason to change. She has produced two charming recollections,‡ and she is likely to continue hearty

---

*Mademoiselle Bouche, as well as Ben Heath's parents, are buried there. Part of the ashes of my son Javier Olano were scattered in this plot, and I have placed cenotaphs to the memory of the two sisters and one brother who are buried elsewhere . . . I have ordered Janie's.

†His wife, Patricia Aldyn Austin Taylor Buckley, died April 15, 2007, two A.M., as I finished editing this.

‡The charming recollections are entitled *A String of Pearls* and *Living It Up with National Review*, which may be the single ugliest title in the history of publishing for what is otherwise a great fun book.

and hale into her nineties, playing golf and skiing and shooting released quail and extending her loving counsel to all her nieces and nephews, who seek her out especially. She once told me, speaking of the emotional travails one of the third generation, as we dub our nieces and nephews, was suffering: "I never knew a problem that an eight-hour-a-day job didn't solve."

Jim is also amazingly hale at eighty-four, and fully devoted to caring for his wife, Ann, who was paralyzed by a car wreck this past May, which terrible destiny she has accepted with the grace, goodness, and faith that have characterized her always. In fall of 2006, Jim published his second book, an interestingly structured rumination on his career, which has been out of the ordinary.* One reviewer summed up our modest brother's quietly adventurous life by remarking that his "travels took [him] to some of the most remote parts of the world, including a dozen trips to the Arctic and the Antarctic." He quotes Jim: "I have helped capture musk ox calves on Ellesmere Island and Greenland, spent time with an Eskimo whaling party off Point Hope, Alaska, hobnobbed with Antarctic penguins and elephant seals, observed walrus in Siberia's Chukula Sea [little could be kula, no?] and Canada's Foxe Basin, watched migrating caribou in Alaska's Brooks Range, and fallen in love with polar bears.'"† He neglected to tell this reporter of the time he was fast asleep in a rudimentary tent in the Arctic Circle, when a cuddly thousand-pound polar bear inserted its black nose and half its face under the flap, sniffing curiously. To polar bears in the wastes of the Arctic, human beings are an exotic meal. Neither Jim nor his companion had thought to bring along a rifle or any other kind of weapon, and so, *faute de mieux,* Jim punched the bear as hard as he could on the nose, which caused the beast to draw its head back sharply and go howling off into the wilderness.

For the past five or six years, we have been expecting Jane, who is nearing her eighty-third birthday, to die any day now, an accommodation that she has stubbornly declined to grant. This is quite in character for her. Temperamentally, she was born a contrarian. She has not written a book, which is shocking, but also in character. Whom should she wish to please by adding to the already bulging bibliography of her siblings or by shuf-

---

* *Gleanings From an Unplanned Life.*
† From Martin Morse Webster's review in *Crisis,* 2007.

fling off this mortal coil or, in her case, the plastic tubes of the oxygen tank? In May 2006, the doctors told her children to plan for her burial. They congregated mournfully in Great Elm, but my sister, instead of giving up the ghost, was released from the hospital in better shape than she had entered it, plainly to spite us all. There is a nasty streak in Janie's character; she will oblige no one other than herself, because she is too busy caring for her children and family and deepening her faith to expend her energies frivolously. Taking one of my forearms three years ago, pressing it hard, Janie said to me, "Reid, nobody knows how deep my faith is." She has defied the unbelievable concatenation of mortal illnesses with which she has been afflicted, from emphysema to cancer to heart failure— mentioning *just a few*—with a spirit, or obstinacy, that has been native to her since, I think, she realized she was the apple of her Papa's eye, that *tres grand* bully. Five years ago, fed up with the calamity of her health, she held her own wake, to which two hundred fifty friends and relatives were invited. In its macabre fashion, it was a grand party, everybody had a good time, but it was also the last plucky gesture we can expect of the sibling who, apart from the comfort of her incomparable brood and devoted sister Priscilla, has perhaps been accorded the least personal happiness of us all in this life, yet who has grown maybe more than any of us in the profundity of her trust in Christ.[1]

Bill is eighty-two and suffering also from emphysema, not to mention diabetes, sleep apnea, and assorted other dread or progressive and potentially terminal diseases, though he manages somehow to churn out his column twice a week . . . in which he continues, it seems to me, always to ask the interesting questions. Their wit and literary grace as essays, given the medium, continue to amaze. I would rather read my brother Bill on almost anything than almost anyone else on almost anything. The originality of mind with which he was blessed at birth will, I think, never desert him. When the time comes for doctors to inform him that he is going to die, he will reply that the sentence is only interesting to the degree that it is not asymptomatic.

He has otherwise retired from his killing schedule of activities—from editing *National Review*, cruising across oceans in his sailboats, flying planes the failings of whose navigational systems tend to crash-land him in open fields belonging to girls' boarding schools (Ethel Walker), diving to the bottom of the ocean to view the wreckage of the *Titanic*, playing the harpsichord in public concerts, sparring with the legion of ideological foes who inevitably, despite themselves, become his personal friends, lecturing and debating across the land, accepting honorary degrees, and his remarkable television program, *The Firing Line* (the longest-running show under one host in the history of the medium), which he wrapped up four years ago. He is now reduced to writing and publishing no more than two books a year, one fiction, the other prose.*

Patricia turns eighty in a few days and is waiting joyfully, though a mite impatiently (in the opinion of her children and siblings), to be taken into the arms of Christ Jesus and to reunion with her beloved husband, Brent. We all disapprove of her eating habits, which are to eat nothing for breakfast, little for lunch, and less for supper.† The contrary Buckley blood runs strong in her character also. Like Aunt Beryl before her, she has turned night into day, so that the best time to contact her is at four or five A.M. She continues to have to be dragged to doctors for checkups and continues to pay no attention to their recommendations, not to mention driving between Washington and New York at velocities that would bring terror to the hearts of NASCAR contestants. She counts illness as a moral failing, which, of course, metaphysically speaking, is correct. (Disease has its origin in Original Sin.) Meantime she has raised in her ten children what is probably the most closely united brood of us all, and continues editing books and articles and scholarly journals with a professional authority that boggles my mind. I don't think she will be getting up at meetings anymore to slap obscenely sacrilegious rad-fem heretics' faces, even though she is still disposed, at the drop of an epithet, to defend the sanctity of the Virgin Mary and the divinity of Jesus before the gates of hell, a metaphor for which is contemporary American culture.

I am seventy-seven this year, escaped a stroke five years ago with light consequences, and do battle against emphysema, which has now, blast it, prevented me from cutting, bucking, and splitting my own firewood with my ancient Pioneer bow saw. With this book I have finished my *oeuvre*.

Carol, the afterthought, our baby sister, will turn sixty-nine in October; she was diagnosed three months ago as having diabetes, but she is

---

* The shocking sudden death of his wife, Pat (April 15, 2007), has devastated him with, I think, an incurable grief.

† She protests that she eats two pieces of toast spread with peanut butter every morning.

otherwise in battle-cock health. I don't believe she will write another book (which is a pity; she is loaded with talent and blessed with human sympathy), unless it be an outraged rebuttal to many or most of the interpretations I draw in these pages.

In sum, we are done. Within the next five years almost certainly (it is reasonable to suppose) the majority of us surviving children of Aloïse Steiner and Will Buckley will be dead,* with maybe Priscilla, then ninety, and Carol, then seventy-four, surviving, Pitts probably contemplating joining an expedition to schuss down the Himalayas, Carol taking revenge on her brother Reid for being so obnoxious by encompassing him, despite herself, in the love ever brimming from her heart (against which her rapier mind does uneven battle). It is reasonable to ask, what has all the sound and fury signified?

On the ideological level, we inherited an anachronism that we have tried lifelong to defend and perpetuate. Vain endeavor. Our parents were the product of a nation that has vanished, and we, their children, have manned the ramparts in defense of that ghost. From this standpoint, our existences have been futile, our works folly.

Father was the son and grandson of immigrant pioneers, and the town he grew up in was part of the last frontier. The values of the ethos he breathed are no longer cherished. The republic that he and Mother revered exists no longer. Bill declared that the business of *National Review* would be to stand athwart history and shout stop, but this *beau geste*, though noble, has been ultimately to no avail.

The long philosophical, ideological, and political battles fought by Bill principally (in the intellectual and journalistic realms), by Jimmy second (in the political realm), by Pitts third (editorially), by Trish fourth (as a journalist and activist, though the battles she and her husband, Brent, waged were centered in ontology), and by the rest of us idiosyncratically, in our own ways, are water over the dam. The new conservative movement Bill ushered in, the "new politics" that Jim triumphantly proclaimed back in 1970, in the euphoria of the night he was elected to the Senate, culminated on the foreign-policy front triumphantly with the tearing down of the Berlin Wall in 1989 and the collapse of the Soviet Union two years

---

*Bill gave us a bad scare just five weeks ago. The diagnosis of irreversible kidney failure proved incorrect, but his recovery is incomplete.

later. *National Review*, the Society of Individualists, Young Americans for Freedom, and all the multitude of Bill's derivative activities helped materially to bring about that happy, glorious event.

In this certainly our heritage and labors amounted to something of which we can be proud. We defeated a great eschatological heresy. We helped liberate eastern Europe from Soviet tyranny and the entire world from the totalitarian menace of communism and the threat of nuclear holocaust, a colossal achievement . . . though our universe is now threatened with a hundred-year war of civilizations, in the waging of which we may wonder whether our country retains the philosophical integrity and the moral stamina to win . . . which I have written sorrowfully about (see *Saving deSaussure Swamp*, the novel, and the prose work *Credo: Refections on the Republic 2002–2004*).

On the domestic front, our tide crested 1980–1984 with the first Reagan administration . . . since when just about everything we have espoused as a family has been defeated in the political arena. The American people would like government to be efficient (hence the successful bid to reform federal welfare in 1995), but they want more and more government to address more and more of the vicissitudes of existence, hence the rejection of any proposal since to limit government. This year all three major Democratic hopefuls are running on domestic platforms that will imperil the financial stability of the United States, not even attempt to reform Social Security, and commit us to socialized medicine despite the evidence in England and Canada of its bureaucratic horrors, and on the foreign-policy front will cut and run in Iraq, seek to appease Syria and Iran and the rest of militant Islam, and desert Israel.* This is the prospect, barring unforeseen, though always possible, intervention from On High. The conservative hopefuls in Republican ranks will not win their party's nomination for 2008, and the rank and file of the party seek only accommodation with the Democratic left.

In short, the American people have rejected the founding, the America of our parents. What the American people now desire to see wither away is the republic, not the state, to the end that we may become another France or Germany, with stagnant economies and bloated government, or,

---

*Jews are now openly terrified of an imminent second Holocaust (see *A Race against Death*, by Peter Bergson, New York: New Press, 2007), and they have reason to fear.

in our pagan hedonism, an England. Narcissism rules the waves. The character of the people has become bureaucratic and slavish. The character of American society is gross beyond the wildest imagining of even a decade ago. (See my pamphlet *The Future of American Culture.*) The term *conservative* now signifies next to nothing, and the Republican Party has reverted to being the party of incremental statism, as it was during the 1950s. Reagan proposed abolishing the then-new (Carter presidency) federal agencies of energy and education. Those bold planks in the GOP platform have been quietly pushed into the attic. Two Republican presidents later, the achievement on the domestic front of which George Bush II boasts most proudly (next to tax cuts) is his No Child Left Behind act, which depends on the very federal bureau that Reagan at one time sought to eradicate. The notion of small government as a desirable political goal has gone up in smoke (see my 2006 broadside, *An Essay on American Stupidity*).

In its political projection, therefore, this book, this reminiscence, is quaint. The people of the United States have decided, I think, now irreversibly, that they wish for a comprehensive welfare state at the cost of the philosophy of the founding of the republic, which envisioned a self-reliant citizenry and strictly limited government. By edict of the Supreme Court, moreover, infanticide in the womb has been proclaimed a Constitutional right of the American woman. The inversion of values about which I rant in *USA Today* prevails. That violence and soft porn are tolerated on television in prime time, while prayer in the schools, by judicial fiat, continues to be banned, is the conventional yet absolutely breathtaking paradigm.

The ever-lowering common denominator of our people chases the lowest common denominator of vicarious vice. Not only have we lost the battle to preserve the founding, but the critical mass of our society (the intelligentsia) has turned against the Christianity that gave birth to our civilization and saturated the American political epiphany, without which as basic a concept as equality before the law can in no way be rationalized or even defended. (See my *Credo*; also see *From Dawn to Decadence: 500 Years of Western Cultural Life,* by Jacques Barzun).* In the concluding novel, *Marbella!* of my trilogy *(The Canticle of the Thrush),* I mock that decadence, following its philosophical and political logic to its

---

*HarperCollins, 2000.

vicious conclusion. The apocalyptical character of my pessimism is rejected by most of my siblings, though I think out of a patriotic nostalgia obscuring reason. We do not like to entertain the possibility that this beloved land has become unlovable, its people vile and servile, its governing institutions corrupt, its Congress cowardly, and its vision materialistic, solipsistic, and on almost all counts contemptible.

So that's that. On the personal front, however, the heritage we received of our parents has been priceless and permanent. We have led happy, exciting, and productive lives. We loved and did our best to honor our parents. We love one another. Our children are a joy to us. And for the rest, we trust in Christ and Christ's promises. How lucky we have been!

10 July 2005, Casa Santa, Comillas
1 April 2007, Peor Es Nada Sandhill Farm, Camden

NOTES

———

1.   Shortly after I wrote these words, Janie was terribly nauseated at supper one evening, and next morning, unable to breathe, she was rushed to the hospital, where she was diagnosed with pneumonia. This happened May 25, 2007, at the commencement of the Memorial Day weekend. She was at once placed on a ventilator in critical care, and the watch began. Jane has been on oxygen day and night more than a year now. Her lungs are almost entirely rotted out.

She got steadily worse, in and out of coma, oblivious to her surroundings. This was at last the end, the doctors said (as they had eleven months ago). Her six children once again gathered in Great Elm. After several days of on-and-off treatment in a ventilator, the corporate decision was reached by them (sister Priscilla concurring) to take her off it and permit her to breathe her last on her own, if what was left of her lungs permitted. Jane was in horror of choking to death, and this terrible end was mercifully averted by an oxygen tube and light doses of morphine. She was able to communicate thanks to a merciful drug that brought her out of coma at intervals. She wanted to die at home, not in the hospital. Sunday, June 3, 2007, issued at 11:59 A.M., arrived this heartbreaking e-mail from Pitts:

Jeffy [Janie's daughter] called from the hospital to say that Jane would like to see me. (She had indicated that she didn't want to see Jim or me, presumably because she didn't want us to see the tubes down her throat and nose.) I went over. She was awake, and I held her hand. She indicated she wanted to write. I put a pen in her hand, and over the next twenty minutes she wrote three notes. "Good to see you." "I'll miss you." And "It's time." "Yes," I said, "Jane, it's time. You've suffered enough." I asked if she would like to see Jim, and she nodded yes.

This described events on Friday, May 30, when she was strong enough to come home to Great Elm. It was expected that she would give up the ghost shortly. The funeral was scheduled for the impending Saturday. Friends and mourners were coming all the way from France, and it would be a shame, I thought, were Janie to miss it. But she failed to die over the weekend. Her blood pressure climbed that Monday evening, day before yesterday, but as I scribble she continues her labored breathing and in moments of clarity communicated to Priscilla partly by sign language and with assents of her head.

This morning, Tuesday, June 5, she was doing better, reported her children. Then, between noon and six o'clock, none of them answered the telephone. I called repeatedly. They were all evidently at the hospital. It was indeed time.

This evening, at 6:45, Pitts telephoned me—collapsing with laughter. "Reid, Janie just called her children. She wants them to fix her a whiskey sour. They didn't know what they should do, so they called the doctor. He said, 'Well, why not?'" If dearest Janie does die this evening, or tomorrow, what a class act . . . to the very end!

PD. She enjoyed an hour and a half of cocktails in her bedroom with her sister Priscilla and two of her daughters. She had a light supper. The next morning, Friday, June 8, the medical indices declined severely. She slipped into unconsciousness. Her eldest daughter, Kimberly Niles, e-mailed the family that the end was imminent. At around half past three this afternoon, Janie drew a deep breath . . . and joined the family awaiting her at last. RIP, 1924–2007.

INDEX

NOTE: AJB refers to Aloïse Josephine Buckley. WFB refers to William Frank Buckley Sr.